The Law of War and Peace

HUGO GROTIUS

THE LAW OF WAR AND PEACE

[De Jure Belli ac Pacis]

A NEW TRANSLATION BY LOUISE R. LOOMIS

WITH AN INTRODUCTION BY P. E. CORBETT

Published for the Classics Club by

WALTER J. BLACK · NEW YORK

Contents

BOOK THREE

Translator's Note

MY attention was first called to the need of a new English version of Grotius' great work by the shortcomings of the only version available for the use of undergraduate students in a course which I was then giving at Wells College in the History of European Thought. This was an abridged reprint of a much older translation by A. C. Campbell, published about 1901 for the Universal Classics Library, now out of print. The more I had to do with this edition the more I resented its faults—the ill-judged omission of the important Prolegomena, or author's preface, as well as of numerous later passages, and even whole chapters which were necessary links in Grotius' argument, the pretentious style and slipshod, inaccurate rendering of the text, in spots absolutely misleading. A pamphlet containing fifty-five pages of extracts from Grotius' book, translated by W. S. M. Knight, was published in 1922 by the Grotius Society as Number 3 in a series of Texts for Students of International Relations, and re-issued by the London Peace Book Company in 1939. But although a good piece of work as far as it went, it was much too brief to give the reader any idea of the magnitude and scope of Grotius' performance.

In 1925, indeed, the Carnegie Endowment for International Peace brought out in two large volumes, as one item in its series of Classics of International Law, a Latin text of the *De Jure Belli ac Pacis*, together with an unabridged and careful translation by Francis W. Kelsey and several collaborators. For the serious student of law this edition provided all that was required, although the close, literal style of translating made the reading of the English version needlessly heavy and tedious. However, this edition too has for some years been out of print, although even if it were not, there would still be room for another planned for the younger student and general reader.

For the Classics Club then I have prepared a fresh translation from the original Latin, as edited by P. C. Molhuysen and published at Leyden in 1919, a year when certainly the world needed to summon back the spirit of the humane Dutchman to talk of law and justice between nations. I have compared my interpretation with that of the Carnegie edition at many points and been glad to find the two agreeing substantially in most instances.

To bring the book within the compass of a Classics Club volume there had to be abridgment. I have saved space by omitting the headings of the numbered sections within the chapters, and also the voluminous footnotes, which consist chiefly of further material illustrative of topics discussed in the text. The brief notes assembled at the end of this volume are mainly references to the sources of the quotations included in the text or else to subjects treated elsewhere within the book itself. These references I have taken for the most part either from Grotius or from his earlier editors.

It was necessary also to cut the text considerably, as the groups of dots scattered through the pages will show. What has been left out is, first, a plethora of quotations from the authorities, ancient, medieval, and modern, whom Grotius cited, whenever possible, to support his argument. The quotations still retained may suggest the immense range and variety of his studies in literature, history, and jurisprudence. As a special aid to readers a simple glossary of the authors cited in this volume appears at the back.

In addition, I have cut a number of short and long discussions of topics which would seem to be of minor interest to most readers of today, such as, for example, applications of rules of inheritance to cases of feudal relationship, or refutations of legal theories and arguments now quite obscure or obsolete. But wherever as much as two consecutive sections of a chapter have been omitted, I have inserted a bracketed note, giving the subject of the deleted passage.

A few Latin words of basic importance in a law book I have ventured to translate in a way I thought would convey most clearly to a modern reader what they seem to have meant to Grotius when he used them. *Jus*, of course, is any kind of written or unwritten law or obligation regarded as binding, or any recognized right. *Justus*, therefore, may be translated either as just or merely as lawful, that is, sanctioned by a law which may or may not be morally just or humane. Grotius contrasts what he calls *justitia externa*, or just dealing according to an external or purely conventional code of law or custom, with *justitia interna*, a justice which is internal or morally righteous, not a matter of appearance only. *Aequus*, equal, is his adjective for equitable and fair; *rectus*, straight, for morally upright and honorable, not crooked. *Lex* means law in the sense usually of positive law, statute or ordinance, although in the two phrases given below it has the more general sense of *jus*. *Licet* denotes whatever is permissible or legitimate by either law or custom or moral standards. The adjective *municipalis* Grotius, like his contemporaries, employs to distinguish the domestic laws and rules peculiar to each state from the supranational bodies of law or convention which he calls *jus* or *lex naturae*, law of nature, and *jus* or *lex gentium*, law between states, or international law. To the ordinary reader of today, however, municipal law is the law of a city, not of a state. I have accordingly used the term civil law to indicate law governing the internal life of the separate states.

In several passages I have been saved from inaccuracy in the rendering of technical legal phrases through the great kindness of Professor P. E. Corbett of Yale University, an expert in Roman Law and the author of the Introduction to this volume. He read my text in galley proof and made a number of invaluable criticisms and suggestions. I am indebted also to Miss Faith Maris, editor of the Classics Club, for her untiring help and patience in preparing a troublesome piece of work for the press.

                                                        LOUISE ROPES LOOMIS

Introduction

THIS is a new translation of one of the world's most famous books, *De Jure Belli ac Pacis* (Law of War and Peace), written by the Dutchman, Huig van Groot, and first published in 1625. In the tradition of the time the author's name was latinized as Hugo Grotius, and he is so known wherever men study the history of human thought.

Grotius was born at Delft in 1583, in the midst of the struggle for the liberation of the Netherlands from the political and religious domination of Spain. His family was socially eminent, well established in the practice of law, prominent in civic office, and intimately associated with the new University of Leyden. The boy, whose home was a meeting place for scholars, scientists, and philosophers, proved a formidable prodigy. He wrote creditable Latin verse at nine, edited learned texts at fifteen, and reveled with apparently equal satisfaction in the literary, philosophic, legal, and theological works of Greece, Rome, and the Church.

Yet the youth was no recluse. He had only completed, with great distinction, a three-year arts course in the University of Leyden, of which his father was a curator, when, at fifteen, he was taken to France in the suite of a diplomatic mission. That was in 1598, the year in which Henry IV, having won Paris by turning Catholic, issued the tolerant Edict of Nantes. The mission failed in its purpose of winning more effective French support against Spain; but it gave Grotius the opportunity of making acquaintances that were highly important in his later life. He spent a year in

France, living in court circles, learning French, and apparently reading some law.

Eight months after his return to Holland, Grotius was admitted to the bar at The Hague. His first years of practice were of the usual desultory and inconspicuous sort. He was torn between the solid promise of a legal career and the allurements of literature. In 1603, when he was only twenty, his reputation as scholar and writer, coupled with the influence of his family, won him appointment as official historian of the United Provinces, with the special mandate of recording their long battle for freedom. It might have seemed that the die had been cast in favor of letters. But Grotius was too energetic and ambitious a character to content himself with historical writing. Amid all his distinguished activities as historian, poet, and theologian, he kept a place in the legal profession. In 1604 he became engaged in a case for the Dutch East India Company, and this seems to have launched him on the work which, amid all his multifarious occupations, was in the end to bring him most fame.

Having to defend the capture of a richly laden Portuguese vessel by one of the Company's ships in the Straits of Malacca, Grotius found it necessary to explore and expound the rights of nations and their shipping on the seas, and to define the lawful occasions and the lawful limits of violence. This led him to the heart of a question to which the writers of Greece and Rome had paid some attention and which, since the advent of Christianity, with its doctrines of peace and brotherhood, had been actively debated by the Church Fathers. This was the ancient and harrowing question whether war could ever be just, and if so, what causes justified it.

The immediate result was a written commentary on *The Law of Prize* (*De Jure Praedae*), which remained unpublished until late in the nineteenth century. But *The Law of Prize* not only furnished from its twelfth chapter the text of a famous tract published in 1609, *Free Sea* (*Mare Liberum*), but contains in early and concise form much of the plan and substance of *The Law of War and*

Peace (*De Jure Belli ac Pacis*). The fact that the idea and the design had been in the scholar's mind for twenty years, being elaborated and matured by accumulating scholarship and experience, goes some way to explain the magnitude of the later work and the speed with which it was finally made ready for the press.

The period of twenty-one years between *De Jure Praedae* and *De Jure Belli ac Pacis* was one of intense literary and political activity for Grotius. To it also belong his marriage and the birth of his six children. In 1608, being then advocate-general of the Fisc of Holland and Zeeland as well as historian of the United Provinces, he married Marie Reigersberg, daughter of an eminent family in Zeeland. The essay on *Free Sea* (*Mare Liberum*), in which he stated the case against national appropriation of wide areas of ocean, was published in 1609. That was the date of the twelve-year truce with Spain, marking the effective triumph of the Dutch cause. In 1610 appeared his study on *The Antiquity of the Batavian Republic*, which set forth the history and government of Holland as the leading sovereign state in the federation of the United Provinces, and justified the revolt against Philip II. This may be regarded as a brief precursor of his *Annals of the Low Countries*, which was only to be published after his death. Three years later he was made Pensionary of Rotterdam, that is to say secretary and legal adviser of the city's Council and its representative in the Provincial States (Assembly) of Holland. In the same year he was sent to London to assist in negotiating a settlement of commercial and maritime issues between the English and Dutch East India Companies. There he argued with great skill but little success the legality of the Dutch attempt to establish a monopoly in the East Indian trade and of their forcible expulsion of English merchants, taking a line as advocate directly contrary to the principles he had so eloquently formulated in *Mare Liberum*.

It was during this visit that Grotius evoked the panegyric by Casaubon which has been constantly quoted in his biographies. The great Huguenot scholar, who had found refuge and high es-

teem at the court of James I, was so charmed by the young Dutchman that he could only describe him as a combination of profound
learning, sincere piety, and divine genius. But his notion that this
enthusiastic admiration was shared by "all learned and good men"
is open to some doubt in view of a letter written at the time by
Abbot, Archbishop of Canterbury. To the Archbishop, Grotius
was an intriguing agent of what he regarded as the dangerous
Arminian sect in Holland, making a display of superficial scholarship in an effort to win the King's support for his side in the
religious and political crisis then brewing in the Netherlands.[1]

Returning home, Grotius was soon up to the neck in the rivalry
of sect and faction which rent the United Provinces after their
victory over the Spanish oppressor. With Barneveld, his patron on
the mission to France in 1598, and long a leading statesman in
Holland, he set himself against the centralizing policy of Maurice
of Nassau, Captain- and Admiral-General and Governor of the
United Provinces. Grotius and his friends of the Arminian persuasion pleaded for the rights of the Cities and Provinces and for
religious toleration. Maurice, taking full advantage of his military
renown and prestige as contemporary head of the House of Orange,
and shrewdly allying himself with the intolerant majority sect of
Calvinists, occupied the more important cities with his troops and
dominated the States-General of the United Provinces. By order
of that supreme body, Barneveld and Grotius were arrested on a
charge of treason. Barneveld was executed, Grotius sentenced to
life imprisonment.

Here enters the story the loyal and heroic woman whom Grotius
had married in 1608. She had been allowed to join him in his fortress prison. He busied himself with much reading and translation
of Greek classics and wrote an *Introduction to Dutch Jurisprudence*, which is still a standard textbook. For these labors he needed
many books, which he was permitted to borrow from his friends,

[1] See W. S. M. Knight, *The Life and Works of Hugo Grotius*, London, Sweet
and Maxwell, 1925, pp. 143-146.

sending them back from time to time in a large chest. His wife, noticing that the guard had ceased to examine this box, persuaded him one day to place himself in it and be carried out. The plot worked. Grotius made good his escape into France, where his wife, who had had the courage to remain behind and take the risk of punishment, was later able to join him.

In Paris, though Louis XIII received Grotius and even granted him a pension, the pair lived in great financial difficulty, eking out the pension, which was only partially paid, with what they were able to salvage from Marie's property. Some of the great French lawyers of the day provided him with books and even a temporary home, and in spite of constant uncertainty and embarrassment Grotius was able not only to complete his chief theological work, *The Truth of the Christian Religion*, but to produce his *Law of War and Peace*. This he wrote in 1623-24, for publication in 1625.

The book brought no immediate economic relief. Nor did the fame which it rapidly achieved win for its author what he most desired, namely freedom to return and live with honor in his own country. He did indeed return to Holland in 1631, after preliminary exploration by his wife, and even settled down to some months of consultative legal practice in Amsterdam. But the second decree of the States-General, offering a reward for his arrest, drove him for refuge to Hamburg. There he made friends who arranged for his introduction to an employer more appreciative of his great qualities than the unrelenting burghers of the United Provinces. At Frankfort he met the Swedish Chancellor, Oxenstiern, and at the end of 1634 was appointed by Queen Christina as Swedish Ambassador to France.

Grotius was not so superbly equipped for diplomacy as for scholarship. He was inclined to be rigid on points of etiquette and precedence, probably to the detriment of his substantive work. In the protracted and difficult business of maintaining and adapting the Franco-Swedish alliance in the shifting combinations of the Thirty Years' War, Richelieu was cold to Grotius, preferring in the main to negotiate directly with Oxenstiern. Even the most skillful diplomat would probably have failed to persuade the penurious French treasury to pay regularly its contracted subsidies to the Swedish contingents fighting against the Emperor. Added to his official difficulties was his familiar but troublesome private financial stringency. As always, Grotius found consolation in study and writing, now principally in the field of theology, and this distraction in turn perhaps reduced his effectiveness as representative of the Swedish government. In any event, Christina finally became dissatisfied and dispatched an auxiliary agent to Paris. Grotius thereupon demanded his recall, hoping to be sent to another capital. The recall was granted, but no word came of another post. Grotius decided to go to Stockholm. There, though received with much pomp and circumstance, he was unable to secure any concrete undertaking of further employment. Anxious and depressed, he left Stockholm in a ship provided by the Queen. The ship was wrecked near Rostock, and Grotius, ill from exposure, hardship and discouragement, died there on August 29, 1645.

Grotius left behind him lasting contributions to the literature, the law, and the theology of Europe. In one field he enjoys, rightly or wrongly, a title which is unique. The world has long known him as "the father of international law." This title rests mainly upon *The Law of War and Peace,* with some support from *Free Sea. The Law of Prize,* published only in 1868, never enjoyed the circulation or prestige of the other two publications.

Why should *The Law of War and Peace* have achieved a renown which is still fresh after more than three hundred years? The book has been habitually described as the first complete and systematic treatise on international law. The words continue to be repeated by many who have never read the text in anything but excerpts. Those who have labored through from one end to the other know that the portion strictly relevant to international law is only a fraction of the whole. They also know that though the author does indeed follow a plan, he is so frequently and at such length

drawn away into winding alleys of legal pedantry that any faithful
modern reader asks himself in periodic amazement, "How did we
reach this point?" Only by painfully retracing his steps does he
find again the boasted "system."

For, by modern standards, this *Law of War and Peace* is a
rambling catch-all. It is quite as much a treatise on religion and
ethics as on law, and these three are almost inextricably inter-
mingled. In many a long passage it is above all a literary scrap-bag,
where the author with jubilant abandon accumulates from jurists,
historians, poets, dramatists, philosophers, and theologians anything remotely supporting a principle which he wishes to see
established.

Yet *The Law of War and Peace* got read. The piling up of clas-
sical tags, which wearies us, was apparently an intellectual feast
for the seventeenth and eighteenth centuries. There was a spreading demand for the book which could only be met by new editions,
at first at three-year intervals. There have been at least thirty trans-
lations, in English, French, German, Dutch. It touched off a train
of publications on the subject of international law. Its author was
revered and quoted, not only in the multiplying treatises, but in
the negotiations of governments and the deliberations of tribunals.
It formed or, perhaps better, it gathered together, the headwaters
of a broad stream of European thought.

True, though kings, judges, and professors have heaped praise
upon *The Law of War and Peace*, the book can hardly be said to
have exercised much visible influence upon events. If, as we may
gather from his own words in his Preface (*Prolegomena*), Section
28, Grotius had at first some thought that his work might induce
rulers to avoid war, or at least to temper its barbarities, we can
well understand the sad disillusionment of his last days. For his
fresh memories in 1624 of the battles by which his own land had
won its independence, and his knowledge of the early campaigns
of the Thirty Years' War, can have contained nothing to equal

the savagery and suffering of the later phases of that complex struggle of religious faiths and imperialistic ambitions.

Students of diplomacy and arbitration nevertheless know that decisions on questions arising in the relations of states have been swayed, and swayed in the direction of peace and decency, by the urbane reasoning and practical common sense of Grotius, with its reinforcements of high morality and flattering historical precedent. If war still flourishes as a human institution, and breaks out into new barbarities when old ones have become demoded, the explanation is not to be found in any lack of nobility or cogency in the arguments of Grotius and his successors. It is to be found rather in the multiplicity of forces shaping the conduct of men, among which reason and the influence of intellectual systems, however skillfully and nobly built, are far from uniformly dominant.

All *systems* are intellectual creations, but some are more closely related than others to observable natural phenomena or the observable conduct of men. The tendency in our day is to rely upon the inductive process, by which rules and principles are formulated as tentative working guides from observed events, and to discount the results of that unfettered speculation which was so characteristic of the science and philosophy of the past. Thus in the "social sciences," including all branches of law, we are increasingly convinced that human conduct can be more effectively directed towards desired ends by principles formulated from the analysis of actual behavior than by any amount of religious and ethical exhortation. The more conservative among us complain about the transformation of churches into social laboratories, which is merely one manifestation of a general trend.

Thus far the literature of international law has shown only minor adaptations to the trend. It continues in the main to present what Grotius and his successors presented—a system constructed by free speculation, which its authors strive to impose upon a recalcitrant reality.

At the core of the system, in the works of Grotius, as in those of our contemporaries, is the dogmatic assertion that the peoples of the world form a "society," "community," or "family" of nations. The assertion indeed goes far back beyond Grotius to the philosophers of antiquity. It was repeated with moving eloquence by those Spanish theological jurists, Victoria and Suarez, whose claims to the paternity of international law vie with those of Grotius.

But for any painstaking analysis of this alleged "society" or "community," for any weighing of its manifested and observed power against the anti-social drives of nations, we look in vain to the classics of international law. Is there indeed such a fund of accepted common values, transcending all the strident particular claims of nation-states, as will justify use of the term "society" or "community" in this context? Is there a firm basis here in actually realized common interests for a system of rules which may be expected to perform for mankind at large the function which law performs within the state? To this fundamental question the authorities on the "law of nations" from the sixteenth to the twentieth century have returned the bland answer—"there is a society of nations."

Grotius was not shut away in academic seclusion from the life of his time. On the contrary, he was a direct participant in national and international politics, and a victim of the clash of faction. And in his work, after many learned preliminaries, he does come to grips with a number of the real problems of his day. His voluminous and searching treatment of the changes in territorial sovereignty resulting from war, his meticulous detail about truces, about booty, about prisoners and their ransom, may come strangely to the modern reader. They are less strange when one remembers that the whole of the writer's life was a period of continuous war, with Spain striving to hold her scattered dominions in subjection, a Holy Roman Empire battling a Protestant Reformation, France torn with bloody religious strife and wrestling with the Hapsburgs for hegemony in Europe, and scores of lay and ecclesiastical princelings snatching at each other's petty possessions and grandiloquent titles.

But why should the reader need to be reminded of the environment? The answer is to be found in the Preface, Section 58—"If anyone suppose I have written with an eye to any controversies of our own age, either already arisen or to be foreseen, he does me an injustice. For I truthfully declare that even as mathematicians view their figures as abstracted from bodies, so I in my treatment of law have held my mind aloof from every particular event."

Strange as it seems to us, Grotius found his data not in his alleged existing society of nations but in the society of the men, gods, and peoples presented by Homer, Plato, Thucydides, Polybius, Livy, Plutarch, Cicero, Caesar, and Tacitus. Only rarely does he mention anything as recent as Charlemagne. The bulk of his moral authority comes direct from the Greek and Roman philosophers, from the Old and New Testaments, and from the great Fathers of the Church. His law, when it is not derived from the Scriptures or from his own and others' speculations on the nature of man and society, is that of Justinian's *Corpus Juris*. For him, as for most European minds of his time, a golden age lay somewhere in the early civilization of Greece and Rome, the model for all legal construction was Roman Law, and the last word on morals was the word of God in the Old and New Testaments as interpreted, where necessary, by Tertullian, Ambrose, Augustine, and Jerome.

From these materials Grotius compiles a righteous guide for the rulers of states and commanders of armies. His "system" recognizes two criteria of what is lawful. One is the outer criterion of judicial approval, the other the inner criterion of conformity with conscience. Only that is fully lawful which satisfies the second standard, though man may do with outward impunity anything which meets the first test. To the jurist of today this is confusion of law and morals, but we find the same dualism in expositors of the law of nations as late and as great as Vattel. It is indeed essentially the same (save that it is more frank) as the confusion, so frequent in the works of our own contemporaries, of what the law is and what the writer thinks it ought to be.

It might have saved centuries of confusion and hairsplitting if Grotius had realized, and had stated with all his authority, that the distinction between the "divine law" and "law of nature" on one side, and the so-called "voluntary law of nations" on the other, is also one between religion, morals, and law. Grotius and his Spanish predecessors knew well that it was not practically possible to impose the law of God or of nature (even if they could have agreed on the relationship and content of these two) upon the governments of states in their mutual relations. They knew that they would do exceedingly well if they could induce more rulers to abide by the much less exacting "voluntary law," resting upon custom and convention. But they did not, as today's legal science does, separate religion and morals off from law as different orders of restraint—orders more or less powerfully influencing the formation of law but not part of it. They mingled all three in one order (all were law, though they occupied different and disputed hierarchical positions in the order) and involved themselves in hopeless and divergent casuistry in the effort to explain away the obvious contradictions between them.

The important thing, then as now, was to devise a means of reducing violence to the lowest possible dimension in the relations of states. The mixture of religion, morals, and law which Grotius concocted for this purpose was probably as effective an influence on the ruling minds of his time as anything that could be produced by scholarship and philosophy. Not the least interesting aspect of his work is its intimate revelation of the thinking habits of that age. Heavy upon it is the authority of the past. One cause of many a long digression in *The Law of War and Peace* is the vital importance to the author and his contemporaries, though not to us, of smoothing out into innocuous harmony the conflicting opinions of equally revered authorities. We have become too much accustomed to seeing the dogmas of great men refuted by the observation of actual phenomena to be troubled by the downfall of seers and their systems. For better or worse, ours is not the mind of the Renaissance.

In this edition, the translator has not "streamlined" *De Jure Belli ac Pacis*. She has left quite enough of what now seems the surplus adornment to remind the modern reader that this work was produced in an intellectual climate very different from ours. But she has cut away much of that tropical luxuriance of quotation and example which has stopped many a reader. In doing so, she has given new prominence to passages recording and explaining the international usage which, from its roots in antiquity or the Middle Ages, had grown into a pattern more or less followed in the fifteenth and sixteenth centuries. The reader who knows something of the routine of today's foreign offices or the present "law of war" cannot but be struck with the extent to which the pattern still holds. But he will also be aware of changes, and will be able to recognize with special clarity the effect of the major "law-making" treaties of the nineteenth and twentieth centuries.

Thus *The Law of War and Peace* will be found quite modern on the acquisition of territory, on freedom of the sea, on the special rights and immunities of ambassadors, on declaration of war, neutral rights, and title by capture. On the other hand, we have abandoned the theory of a universal right to trade. It would no longer be held that a state barring all commerce with the nationals of another state is committing a breach of international law, unless it is specifically bound by treaty. We would therefore not accept the view, as so many appear to have done in the time of Grotius, that Spain's conquests in America were justified by the alleged refusal of the native rulers to enter into commercial dealings with their enterprising visitors. Nor do we admit any duty to permit innocent passage across land territory. On the contrary, a neutral granting such passage to military forces is regarded as committing a breach of neutrality.

One marked change is in the matter of privateering. Our text has a good deal to say about the activities and the rights of those adventurers who, taking out letters of mark and reprisals, levied war for profit. Here, as in the treatment of the wounded and of prisoners, the treaties of this and the last century have had their effect.

In general, the famous *temperamenta* of Grotius, his reasoned exhortations to generosity, mercy, and moderation in the exercise of belligerent rights, will be warmly approved by the contemporary reader. But in some respects, Grotius was more severe than we. He held that certain offenses against common morality, such as impiety towards parents, would justify armed intervention, and that the prohibition of religious teaching was a breach of the law of nations. We have become a little less conscious of a moral or religious mandate, or, shall we say, more tolerant.

Grotius was content to accept much of the working pattern of his time. Some of it he wanted to change, but mostly he wanted to strengthen and expand. He had little hope that war could be abolished; but he did aim to establish a body of principles complete enough and clearly enough defined to provide for the peaceful settlement of disputes and, if through the lack of wisdom or Christian charity on one side or the other war must come, to mitigate its cruelties. It was on precept that he depended. Only in one brief passage does he recommend organization. In Book II, Chapter xxiii, Section 8, he advocates congresses of Christian Powers where neutrals would settle disputes and compel the disputants to accept peace on equitable terms.

The accent today is on organization. And this is a more promising approach in our time. We have learned from repeated failure that precept, inadequately supported by organized power, cannot be relied upon to restrain the ambitions of governments. But we can take yet another lesson from the failure of the collection of precepts so elaborately compiled by Grotius to produce any marked change in the conduct of states. Organization can run as far ahead

of the elements of human community actually existing at a given
time as can precept. Then, when interests held vital come into
conflict with it, the structure crumbles. Law depends in large
measure on organization. Law and organization are indeed aspects
of one social method. Together they constitute one of the cohesive
social forces. But even they cannot perform the whole function
of cohesion. They are conditioned upon a strong sense of community. They can only survive and operate where and to the
extent that agreement exists upon certain values and objectives
which are not to be subordinated to the claims of members of the
given society, whether these be individuals or groups.

The matters in regard to which such a sense of community and
such an agreement exist in the world of nation-states are still much
more limited than they are within the nation-state. The moralist
and the jurist can aid in expanding their scope, but mostly the
growth of an effective world society will depend on the slowly
advancing education of the man in the street. He has learned
already to repeat the easy formulae about the insanity of war, the
brotherhood of man, and the need for world government. But he
has still some way to go before he begins to think and to act as
a world citizen, accepting the subordination of his own and his
nation's interest to a general welfare defined by bodies in which
his nation may find itself outvoted. The time has probably passed
when his education in that direction can be accelerated by the
construction and subsequent ruin of systems spun out of abstrac-
tions.

The law of a world society and the machinery for its enforcement
will remain ineffective in so far as they embody ideals too lofty
for the earthy environment in which they must operate. This
conclusion does not, however, reject ideals. It merely counsels
patience and practical intelligence in the effort to realize them.
The "great society" of which Grotius so often speaks, and to the
realization of which he devoted great faculties three hundred
years ago, is still an ideal. We are laboring, by methods which we

believe more appropriate to our time, to make some measure of it a reality. It was vitally important that the ideal should be communicated and that it should take hold upon more minds in each succeeding generation. No book has rendered greater service to this end than *The Law of War and Peace*.

P. E. CORBETT

The Law of War and Peace

Preface

1. MANY have undertaken to expound or to summarize in commentaries or abridgments the civil law of Rome or of their own states. But few have treated of that law that exists between peoples, or between the rulers of peoples, whether based upon nature, or established by divine decree, or grown out of custom and tacit agreements; and no one as yet has discussed it in a comprehensive and systematic way, important as it is to mankind that this should be done. . . .

3. THE work is all the more necessary because in our own time, as in the past, there is no lack of men who make light of this branch of the law, as if it were nothing but an empty name. On most men's lips are the words of Euphemus, quoted by Thucydides, that for a king or a free city nothing is wrong that is to their advantage.[1] To this may be added a similar saying, that for fortune's favorites might makes right; also, that a state cannot be run without some injustice. Moreover, the disputes that arise between nations or kings are in fact usually decided by Mars. And it is not only the ignorant who believe that war has nothing whatever to do with law, but men who are learned and wise often let fall remarks that support such an opinion. Nothing is more common than a contrast drawn between law and arms. . . .

5. BUT since it would be futile to discuss this kind of law, if actually it does not exist, it is incumbent on us to endorse and de-

3

fend our work by refuting briefly this most serious error. So, to save
us from having to deal with a swarm of opponents, let us appoint
one speaker for them all. And whom better could we choose than
Carneades, who became so skillful in what his school considered
the supreme art that he could muster the full power of his eloquence as easily to defend a falsehood as to defend a truth. He
once undertook an attack on justice—in particular, that type of
justice of which we are now speaking—and used this as his strongest argument: that laws were imposed by men on themselves in
their own interest, varying as customs varied, and often altered by
the same people as the times changed; that, accordingly, there was
no such thing as a law of nature,[2] seeing that all creatures, men as
well as other animals, were inspired by nature to work only for
their own advantage; and that, therefore, there was no justice, or
if there were any, it was the height of folly, because a man who
considered other men's welfare was only doing himself an injury.

6. BUT certainly we must not accept what that philosopher says,
or the poet who follows him:

"And nature cannot tell what's just from what's unjust." [3]

For though man is indeed an animal, he is an extraordinary animal,
differing far more from all other animals than they differ in kind
from each other. To this fact bear witness the many traits peculiar
to the human species. Among these traits peculiar to man is his
desire for society, that is, for life in a community; not any sort of
life, but one that is peaceful and organized to suit the measure of
his intelligence, with persons of his own kind. The Stoics called
this trait 'friendliness.' Therefore we should not grant as a universal
proposition the statement that nature impels every animal to aim
only at his own advantage.

7. THERE are other animals too that in one way or another restrain their desires for their own comfort for the sake, sometimes of
their offspring, and sometimes of their fellow creatures. Such conduct on their part springs, we believe, from some extrinsic, intelli-

gent principle, because when it comes to other acts, no more difficult than those, they do not show the same degree of understanding. The same may be said of children, for even before their training begins, they display an inclination to do good to others, as Plutarch acutely observed.[4] Thus even at that early age they break out spontaneously into pity. The man of maturer years, as a part of his intense desire for society, has knowledge that makes him act in a similar way under similar circumstances. He also, alone among animals, has the special instrument of speech, and the faculty of understanding and conducting himself in accordance with general rules. What belongs to that faculty is not common to all animals but peculiar to humankind.

8. THIS care to preserve society, which we have here roughly outlined, and which is characteristic of human intelligence, is the source of all law which is properly so called. From it come the rules that we must not take something belonging to another, must restore whatever we have that is another's with the profit we made from it, must keep our promises, and must make good a loss incurred through our fault; and also that it is right to punish men who deserve it.

9. OUT of this meaning of law arises another and broader one. For man above all other animals possesses not only the strong social faculty, of which we have spoken, but also the judgment to weigh his joys and pains, both present and future, and whatever conduces to both. Evidently, then, it is part of human nature, as far as the capacity of the human mind allows, to follow in these matters well-framed judgments, and not be led astray by fear or the temptation of present pleasure, or be carried off by reckless impulse. Whatever we do that is plainly contrary to good judgment is contrary also to the law of nature, that is to say, of the nature of man. . . .

11. AND what we have just said would have validity, even if we granted what cannot be granted without great wickedness, that there is no God, or that he has no care for human affairs. But the

opposite belief has been instilled in us, partly by our reason, partly
by an unbroken tradition, confirmed by many proofs and miracles
attested through every age. It follows that we should without exception obey God as our Creator, to whom we owe ourselves and
all that we have, especially since he has shown himself in many
ways most good and most mighty. Thus, being himself eternal, he
is able to offer to those who obey him the greatest rewards, even
those that are eternal. And we must believe he has willed to do
so, all the more since he has explicitly promised it, as we Christians,
who are convinced by the undoubted faithfulness of the testimonies, do believe.

12. HERE, then, is another source of law besides the source in
nature, namely, the free will of God, to which, as our intellect
irresistibly tells us, we must submit. Moreover, the law of nature
of which we have spoken—both that which relates to man in
society and that which may be taken in a broader sense—although
it springs from man's inner, fundamental traits, may rightfully be
ascribed to God, for the reason that he willed we should have such
traits. . . .

13. FURTHERMORE, through the laws he has given us, God has
made these traits still more clear, even to persons whose minds
have feeble powers of reasoning. For he has forbidden us to yield
to distracting passions that would harm either ourselves or others,
effectually checking our more violent impulses and controlling
them within bounds and limits.

14. SACRED history also, besides the commands it contains, does
much to strengthen man's social instinct, since it teaches that we
all are children of the same first parents. In that sense, we may
rightly repeat what Florentinus has said in another connection,
namely, that nature has made us all kindred of one another; [5] and
consequently that it is wrong for man to plot against man. To men
their parents are indeed like divinities, to whom they owe obedience, not unlimited but yet of a special kind.

15. NOW the law of nature requires us to abide by our promises

(since it was necessary that men should have some way of binding themselves to one another, and no other natural way can be
imagined); and this was the origin of civil laws. For all who had
joined a group, or had submitted themselves to some other man
or men, had either expressly promised, or from the nature of the
case must have been understood to have tacitly promised, that they
would conform to any decision taken either by the majority of the
group, or by those to whom authority had been committed.

16. HENCE not only Carneades but others who assert that

"Expediency is the mother of justice and of right," [6]

are not speaking the truth, if what we say is correct. For the mother
of natural law is human nature, which, even if we were not in any
need, would still lead us to desire social companionship. And the
mother of civil law is that bond of consent which derives its force
from natural law, so that nature may be called the grandmother,
as it were, of civil law. However, expediency does enter into natural
law; for the Author of nature willed that we as individuals should
be weak and in need of many things to live properly, the lack of
which would drive us to seek society. Expediency supplied too the
occasion for the rise of civil law; for the formation of groups, of
which we spoke, and the submission to authority took place first
for some reason of expediency. Moreover, those who prescribe
laws for others usually have, or ought to have, some purpose of
expediency in view.

17. NOW just as there are laws in each state that aim at securing
some advantage for that state, so between all or most states some
laws could be and indeed have been established by common consent, which look to the advantage not of single communities but
of the whole great concourse of states. And this is the law we
call the law of nations, whenever we distinguish it from natural
law. . . .

18. CARNEADES is wrong too when he slanders justice by calling
it folly. For he admits himself that the citizen who obeys the civil

law of his country is not a fool, even though in his respect for the
law he may have to forego some advantage to himself. In the same
way, it is not a foolish people that refrains from pushing its own
advantage to the point of disregarding the laws common to all
nations. The reason is the same in both instances. For just as a
citizen who violates the civil law for the sake of a momentary advantage destroys thereby that which safeguards the lasting advantage of himself and his posterity, so a nation that transgresses the
laws of nature and of nations breaks down the bulwarks that guard
its own future peace. Even if no advantage were to be expected
from keeping the law, it would be wise and not foolish to follow the
direction in which we feel our nature leads us.

19. WHEREFORE the saying is not universally true that

> "We must admit it was the fear of wrong
> That caused the making of the laws," [7]

which someone in Plato [8] explains as meaning that men devised
laws for fear of suffering injury, and so were driven by a kind of
force to cultivate justice. That theory applies only to such institutions and laws as have been established to facilitate the execution
of justice. Thus many a multitude of persons, individually weak,
have combined to set up and maintain by their common strength
judicial courts to protect them from oppression by the powerful,
in order that together they might control those for whom singly
they were no match. In this sense, we may even accept without difficulty the saying that law is whatever satisfies the stronger, understanding by it that law cannot achieve its external aim, unless it has
force to back it. Thus Solon accomplished great things, as he said,
"by harnessing force and law together." [9]

20. LAW, however, even lacking the support of force, is not entirely without influence. For justice brings peace of conscience, and
injustice torment and anguish, such as Plato describes as inhabiting the breasts of tyrants.[10] Good men unite in praising justice and
condemning injustice. Most important of all, God is a foe to in-

justice, a protector of justice, and though he reserves his judgments for the next life, yet he often makes their power evident in this, as history teaches by manifold examples.

21. THERE are many who demand of private citizens a respect for justice, but who consider it unnecessary for a nation or the ruler of a nation. The reason for their error is, first of all, that they regard nothing in law but the advantage to be derived from it, which is obvious in the case of citizens who are too weak singly to defend themselves. But great states, which seem to contain within themselves everything required for the adequate maintenance of life, do not, apparently, stand in need of that virtue which looks to something outside itself, and is called justice.

22. BUT, not to repeat what I have already said about law not being based on expediency alone, there is no state so strong that it may not some time need the help of others outside itself, either for purposes of trade or to defend itself against the combined hosts of a number of other nations joined against it. Accordingly we see the most powerful nations and kings working to obtain allies, whose value is not perceived by those who would shut law up within the boundaries of each state. Most true it is that everything becomes uncertain, once men forsake the law.

23. IF no community can subsist without law, as Aristotle showed by his famous illustration of brigand bands,[11] surely the community that embraces the whole human race, or at least a great many nations, needs law. . . .

25. THERE are persons who imagine that all laws lose their authority in wartime, but such a theory we should never accept. Rather, we should declare it wrong to begin a war except for the enforcement of justice, and wrong to continue a war already begun, unless it is kept within the bounds of justice and good faith. Demosthenes well said that wars should be made only against those who cannot be restrained by courts of law.[12] For legal judgments are effective against persons who know they are too weak to resist, and wars are our resort against those who are strong enough, or

who think they are. Nonetheless, in order to be right, wars must be conducted as scrupulously as judicial proceedings habitually are.

26. LAWS may be silenced by the clash of arms, but only those laws of the state that have to do with courts and peacetime affairs; not those other laws that are permanent and applicable at all times. As Dio of Prusa very well said,[13] between enemies, written laws, that is, laws of particular states, have no validity; but unwritten laws, that is, those which nature dictates, or which the nations have agreed to recognize, are valid still.

27. WRITERS of history furnish many instances that show how great is the power in warfare of the consciousness of a just cause; they often attribute the victory chiefly to that influence. Hence the proverbs: that a soldier's strength is increased or destroyed by his cause; that seldom does a man come back unhurt who has gone to an unjust fight; that hope is one's comrade in a good cause; and others of similar tenor. Nor should the success of wicked enterprises make anyone dismayed. It is enough that the justice of a cause brings with it strength, great strength for action, even though, as often happens in human affairs, that strength is prevented by other opposing forces from having its full effect. And for winning the friendships which nations as well as individuals need for many reasons, it is a vast help to have a reputation for making war neither recklessly nor unjustly, and for fighting it honorably, since no one readily allies himself with persons who, he believes, treat justice, uprightness, and good faith as things of little account.

28. INASMUCH, therefore, as I am convinced on the grounds I have now given that there is a common law between nations which is valid for war and in war, there are many grave reasons why I should undertake to write on the subject. Throughout the Christian world I have seen a lawlessness in warfare that even barbarian races would think shameful. On trifling pretexts, or none at all, men rush to arms, and when once arms are taken up, all respect for

law, whether human or divine, is lost, as though by some edict a fury had been let loose to commit every crime.

29. CONFRONTED by this hideous spectacle, many of our best men have concluded that all armed conflicts must be forbidden to Christians, whose chief duty it is to love everyone. Their view seems now to have been accepted by John Wild and by my fellow countryman Erasmus,[14] both devoted lovers of ecclesiastical and civil peace. They have, I think, the same idea as we have, when to straighten something that has gone too far in one direction, we bend it back the opposite way. But their very effort to force a thing back too far toward the other extreme frequently does more harm than good, because the exaggeration in it is easily detected and detracts from the influence of what else they say that is actually true. A remedy must therefore be found for both sets of extremists, that men may neither suppose that nothing in the way of war is lawful, nor that everything is.

30. AT the same time, I have been anxious to contribute by my personal efforts something to the study of jurisprudence, which in former days I practiced in public office with all the honesty of which I was capable; for this now is all the occupation left me, undeservedly exiled[15] from the country to which my many labors had brought distinction. Many men before now have set out to give an orderly presentation of the subject. No one has succeeded. Nor indeed could anyone succeed until—a point hitherto too much neglected—the provisions that belong to positive law were strictly separated from those of natural law. For natural laws are forever the same and hence can be easily assembled into a system. But the provisions of positive law are constantly changing and differ from place to place, and so lie outside the scope of a systematic treatment, as do other notions of particular things.

31. BUT if the apostles of true justice would agree to treat only the various parts of natural unchanging jurisprudence, omitting all that has its source in man's untrammeled will, and if one would write of laws, another of taxes, another of the judge's office, an-

other of the interpretation of intent, another of the establishing of facts—when all these parts were collected, there might then be created a body of jurisprudence.

32. THE method which we believe should be followed we have plainly indicated, by deeds rather than by words, in this present work, which comprises by far the noblest part of jurisprudence.

33. WE have opened the first book by speaking of the origins of law, and have then examined the general question whether there is such a thing as a lawful war. Next, in order to make clear the difference between public and private war, we found we must explain the nature of sovereignty, what nations and what kings possess full sovereignty, who possess it only in part, who with the right of alienation, and who in other ways. Then we had to describe the duty of subjects to their superiors.

34. IN the second book, we undertook to discuss all the questions out of which a war may arise, and explained at length what kinds of property are held in common, what in private ownership, what rights persons may have over other persons, what are the obligations of ownership, what is the rule governing royal succession, what right is established by a pledge or a contract, what force a treaty or a public or a private oath has, and how it is to be interpreted, what reparation is due for damage inflicted, what is the sanctity of ambassadors, what is the law for burial of the dead, and what the proper nature of punishment.

35. THE third book has for its subject, first, what is legitimate in war. After distinguishing what may be done with impunity and what foreign nations assert is lawful from that which is really free of wrong, we proceed to consider the kinds of peace and all agreements relating to war.

36. THE value of the work seems to me greater because, as I have said, no man so far has treated this subject as a whole, and those who have handled parts of it have done it in such a way as to leave much for others to labor over. Nothing has survived from the ancient philosophers on the topic, either from the Greeks—although

Aristotle did write a book called *Rights of War*—or from those whose allegiance was given to the youthful Christianity, though such a book from them would have been extremely precious. Of the old Roman books relative to the law of war and treaties nothing has come down to us but the titles. Those who make collections of cases they call 'cases of conscience' merely put together chapters on war, on promises, on oaths, on reprisals, along with other topics.

[37–38. Faults of treatises by earlier writers, e.g., Victoria, Henry of Gorkum, Ayala, Gentile.]

39. . . . I have now to explain briefly what helps I have used and with what care I have approached the task. In the first place, I have taken pains to refer for proofs of all my statements regarding the law of nature to certain ideas so unquestionably true that no one can deny them without doing violence to himself. For the principles of that law, if only you look at them fairly, are in themselves plain and evident, almost as clear as the things we perceive with our external senses. . . .

40. FURTHER to prove the existence of this law of nature, I have called on the testimonies of philosophers, historians, poets, and, lastly, orators. Not that we should believe these men indiscriminately, for they were accustomed to serving the interests of their sect, their argument, or their cause. But whenever many of them at different times and in different places declared the same thing to be true, their unanimity must be ascribed to a universal cause, which, as we inquire into it, can be nothing else than a correct inference from the principles of nature, or some general consensus of opinion. The former means a law of nature, the latter a law of nations. The difference between these two kinds of law cannot be found in the testimonies just mentioned (for writers are apt to confuse the terms, law of nature and law of nations), but from the character of the content. A rule that cannot be deduced from fixed principles by a sure process of reasoning and that is yet apparently

everywhere observed must have originated in the free will of mankind.

41. so I have endeavored always to differentiate particularly
between these two kinds of law, no less than between them and
civil law. Also, in considering the law of nature I have distinguished
between what really and on every occasion is the law and what
merely produces an external effect resembling that of the original
law, such as a prohibition against violent resistance, or an order for
general defense by public force when it is to someone's advantage,
or when it prevents some serious trouble to issue it. How necessary
in many cases it is to draw the distinction will become apparent in
the course of this work. . . .

42. AMONG philosophers, Aristotle deservedly holds the first
place, whether you take into account his order of treating his material, the acuteness of his distinctions, or the solidity of his reasoning. Would that this preeminence had not for some centuries past
degenerated into such a tyranny that the truth, which Aristotle
labored so faithfully to serve, is now more suppressed by Aristotle's
name than by any other influence![16]

For myself, here as well as elsewhere, I practice the liberty of the
ancient Christians, who swore allegiance to no philosopher's
school, not because they agreed with those who said all knowledge
was impossible—the most foolish view of all—but because they
thought that no school had seen all the truth, and not one but had
seen some bit of it. Accordingly, they believed that to gather into a
whole the truths scattered among the several philosophers and diffused through the sects would surely be to establish a way of teaching that was truly Christian.

[43–44. Criticism of Aristotle's theory of ethics.]

45. . . . WE propose to treat Aristotle with great respect, but
with the same liberty that he in his zeal for truth allowed himself
in dealing with his own teachers.

46. HISTORY has a double value as regards our subjects, for it
provides both examples and judgments. The nobler the times and

the people, the more weight their examples carry; for that reason we have preferred the ancient examples, Greek and Roman, to any other. Nor should the judgments of history be despised, especially when they agree, for the law of nature, as we have said, is proved thereby, in a way. As for the law of nations, there is no other proof.

47. THE sentiments of poets and orators do not carry so much weight. We cite them often, but less as a basis for faith than as a means of adding some beauty from their lines to what we are trying to say.

48. I frequently appeal to the authority of the books written or approved by men under inspiration of God, but draw a distinction between the Old Testament and the New. There are those who maintain that the Old Testament represents the law of nature, but unquestionably they are wrong, for many of its precepts are expressions of God's free will, which, however, never does violence to true natural law. So up to a point the Old Testament may be cited as a source for natural law, provided we distinguish correctly between a law of God, which on occasion he executes through men, and a law made by men for one another. . . .

50. THE New Testament I use in order to find something I cannot learn anywhere else, namely, what is permissible for Christians. Contrary to the practice of many men, I distinguish this from the law of nature, convinced as I am that this most holy law requires a greater holiness on our part than the law of nature alone demands. Nor have I failed to note the things we are advised to do, and not commanded, that we may realize that there are both commands to which disobedience is wicked and liable to punishment, and an exalted good, to which a noble mind will aspire and not lack its reward. . . .

[51–55. Description of legal and doctrinal authorities and texts cited in this book—canon law, writings of church fathers and medieval schoolmen, Roman law and commentaries on it, etc.]

56. THROUGHOUT this work I have aimed at three things above all: to make the reasons for my conclusions as clear as possible, to

set in a definite order the material I had to treat, and to distinguish plainly between things that might seem to be the same and were not.

57. I have refrained from taking up topics that belong to another treatise, such as showing what course of action is practically advantageous. For those matters have their own special science, which is politics. Aristotle rightly treats it alone, without admixture of anything else. With Bodin, on the other hand, that science is mixed with the science of law, which is our subject. In some passages I have indeed touched on the question of expediency, but only in passing and in order to distinguish it clearly from the question of what is lawful.

58. IF anyone supposes I have written with an eye to any of the controversies of our own age, either some that have already arisen or some that may be foreseen as likely to arise in the future, he does me an injustice. For I truthfully declare that, even as mathematicians view their figures abstracted from bodies, so I in my treatment of law have held my mind aloof from all particular events.

[59–60. Aim at conciseness of exposition. Use of direct quotations from the classics.]

61. I ask and adjure all those into whose hands this book will come to use the same liberty with me that I have assumed for myself in judging the opinions and writings of other men. They will not be quicker in advising me of error than I shall be in following their advice.

And now, if I have here said anything at variance with piety, with good morals, with Holy Scripture, with the consensus of the Christian Church, with any phase of truth, let it be unsaid.

BOOK ONE

What Is War? What Is Law?

1. THE disputes that arise between those who are not held together by a common bond of civil law—such as a people who have not yet combined to form a nation—are connected either with times of war or with times of peace. So too are the disputes of persons who belong to different nations, whether they are private individuals, or kings, or persons invested with ruling power, such as an aristocracy, or as the body of a free people. So, because war is waged for the sake of peace, and there is no dispute which may not give rise to war, it will be proper in a discussion of the law of war to treat every kind of quarrel that is apt to arise; and then war itself will lead us to peace, as to its rightful end.

2. IN treating of the law of war, the first point we have to consider is: what is the war which is the subject of our inquiry, and what is the law which we seek to establish. Cicero called war [1] a contest of force, but the custom has been to indicate by that word, not an act but a state of affairs; so that war is the state of forcibly contending parties, considered as such. This general definition comprises all the wars of every description that will form the subject of the present treatise. Nor are private wars excluded from this definition. For in fact they came before public wars and are undoubtedly of the same nature; they should therefore be included

under one and the same term. . . . I do not mention justice in my
definition of war, because the very point we are to decide is whether
any war can be just, and what kind of war is actually so. Therefore,
we must make a distinction between war itself and the justice of it.

3. AS the Law of War is the title we give to this treatise, our
first inquiry, as I have already stated, is whether any war can be lawful, and, in the next place, what is lawful in war. Law here signifies nothing but what is just, and that more in a negative than in a
positive sense; so that a lawful thing is what is not unjust. Now
anything is unjust which is opposed to the nature of a rational
society. Thus, for instance, Cicero says [2] to deprive another of what
belongs to him for one's own advantage is against nature; and by
way of proof he adds that, if the practice were general, all society
and intercourse among men would necessarily be destroyed. . . .
Seneca too remarks [3] that, "just as all the members of a body agree
among themselves, because the preservation of each is to the interest of the whole, so men refrain from injuring one another. For we
are born for society, which cannot be secure except by giving love
and protection to its parts."

There is one kind of social tie founded on equality, as, for instance, that between brothers, citizens, friends, and allies; and another kind on preeminence, as Aristotle styles it, such as that between parents and children, masters and servants, sovereigns and
subjects, God and man. So justice is one thing between equals and
another between the governor and the governed, according to their
difference in rank. The former, if I am not mistaken, may be called
the law or right of equality, and the latter the law or right of
superiority.

4. THERE is another meaning of the word law, or right, different
from this, but yet arising out of it, which has reference to persons.
In this sense, a right is a moral quality annexed to a person, enti-
tling him lawfully to possess some particular thing, or to perform
some particular act. This right belongs to a person, although it is
sometimes attached to things, as servile dues are to some lands. The

latter are called real rights, in comparison to others that are merely personal, not because such rights do not also belong to persons, but because they belong only to those who possess the particular quality. This moral quality, when perfect, we call a faculty; when imperfect, an aptitude. The former corresponds to the actuality, the latter to the potentiality in natural things.[4]

5. JURISTS call a faculty the right which a man has to his own; we shall hereafter, taking it in its strict and proper sense, call it a legal right. This right includes the power we have over ourselves, which is called liberty, and the power we have over others, like that of a father over his children and of a master over his slaves. It includes also the right of ownership over property, either absolute or incomplete, such as rights to usufruct, and to hold pledges until payment is made; also the right of a creditor to what is due him on the other side as a debt.

6. LEGAL rights, again, are of two kinds: private, which have to do with the interests of the individual, and public, which are superior to private rights, because they are the rights of the community over its members and over their property for the common good. Hence regal authority is above that of a father and of a master, and so the king's right over the property of his subjects for the common good is greater than that of the owners themselves. And hence every citizen is more obliged to contribute towards the public expense than to satisfy a creditor.

7. APTITUDE is what Aristotle calls worthiness, that is, suitability. . . .

8. LEGAL rights are the subject of expletive justice, which is known generally as justice, properly or strictly speaking. Aristotle calls it contractual justice, which is too narrow a name, for when a man who holds property that is mine returns it to me, he does it not because of a contract; yet it is an act of the same justice. Attributive justice, which Aristotle calls distributive, has to do with aptitudes. It is an accompaniment of those virtues which aim at the

welfare of other men, such as generosity, compassion, and foresight in government. . . .

It is not true to say, as some do, that attributive justice is concerned with public property and expletive with private. On the contrary, an individual who wishes to give a legacy from his own property is acting in accordance with attributive justice; whereas a state that returns from the public funds what some citizens have spent on a public enterprise is performing a duty of expletive justice. The distinction was correctly drawn by the teacher of Cyrus. For when Cyrus had given to a small boy a small tunic which belonged to another boy, and to a big boy, on the other hand, a big tunic, his teacher told him: [5] "That would have been right if he had been appointed judge of what was suitable for each boy. But when the decision to be made was to which boy the tunic ought to belong, then the question to consider was which boy had the more lawful right to it, the one who had grabbed it by force, or the one who had made or bought it."

9. THERE is a third meaning of the word law, which is the same as right, when law is taken in its widest sense and denotes a rule of moral action, obliging us to do what is good. We say obliging us, for the best counsels or precepts, if they lay us under no obligation to obey them, do not come under the name of law or right. Permission,[6] strictly speaking, is not an act of law but a negation of action, except when it forbids a person to hinder another from doing what the law permits. But as we said, the law obliges us to do what is good, not simply what is just, because law in this sense has to do with matters not only of justice, as we explained it, but of all other virtues. That which is good by law in this sense may be also broadly called just. The best division of law, understood in this way, is to be found in Aristotle,[7] who calls one kind natural law, and the other voluntary, or statutory in the strict sense of the word; or sometimes positive. . . .

10. NATURAL law is a dictate of right reason, showing the moral necessity or moral baseness of any act according to its agreement

or disagreement with rational nature, and indicating that such an act is therefore either commanded or forbidden by the author of nature, God. The acts for which such a dictate exists are in themselves either obligatory or unallowable, and therefore recognized as necessarily being either commanded or forbidden by God. This mark distinguishes natural law, not only from human law, but from ordained divine law, which does not command or forbid things that in themselves and by their own nature are either obligatory or unallowable, but by forbidding them makes them unallowable, or by commanding them obligatory.

Now to understand natural law, we must observe that some things are said to be a part of it not properly, but, as the schoolmen love to say, 'by reduction.' These are things which do not conflict with natural law; as, to repeat what we just said, we call things just in which there is no injustice. . . .

We must further remark that natural law has to do not only with things that exist independent of the human will, but with many things which are a result of the exercise of that will. Thus private property, as now in use, was a creation of the human will. But once it was introduced, the law of nature tells me that it is wrong for me to seize what is yours against your will. . . .

The law of nature also is so unalterable that it cannot be changed even by God himself. For though the power of God is measureless, things can be mentioned to which it does not extend. Yet when this is said, it is said only; it has no meaning in reality but contains in itself a contradiction. Thus even God cannot cause twice two not to make four; nor, again, can he make what is intrinsically evil not evil. And this is Aristotle's meaning, when he says [8] that some things are no sooner named than we perceive their evil nature. . . .

Yet it sometimes happens that in cases coming under some rule of the law of nature, there is an appearance of change that deceives the thoughtless. Whereas in reality there is no change in the law of nature, which is changeless, while in the points that come under it there may be variation. For example, if my creditor gives me a receipt for a debt I owe him, I am no longer bound to pay it, not because the law of nature has ceased to command me to pay my debts, but because what was a debt has ceased to be one. . . . Thus too, if God should command the killing of someone or the taking away of his property, that would not be authorizing murder or robbery, words which always imply a crime. An act performed by command of him who is the sovereign lord of life and of all things would not be murder or robbery. There are also some things allowed by the law of nature, not absolutely but under certain conditions. So it was natural to use things in common, as long as private ownership had not been introduced, and to obtain one's rights by force before laws were enacted. . . .

12. THAT anything is or is not a part of the law of nature may be proved by two kinds of argument, *a priori* and *a posteriori*, the former a more subtle method and the latter more popular. We are using the *a priori* method when we show the necessary agreement or disagreement of a thing with a reasonable and social nature; the *a posteriori* when, without absolute certainty but yet on strong probability, we infer that a thing is part of the law of nature which is accepted as such among all, or at least among all the more civilized nations. For a universal effect demands a universal cause. And the cause for so universal an opinion can scarcely be anything but the common sense, as it is called, of mankind. . . .

I said "the more civilized nations," and not without reason. For, as Porphyry well observes: [9] "Some nations are so savage and inhuman that no fair judges should base a low opinion of human nature on them." Andronicus of Rhodes says: [10] "To men of a right and sound understanding, what we call the law of nature is unchangeable. Nor does it alter the case that men of sick and perverted minds think otherwise. For he who says that honey is sweet is not lying because it does not appear so to men diseased." . . .

13. WE have said that there is another kind of law, which is voluntary [or positive] law, deriving its origin from the will; and this law is either human or divine.

14. WE will begin with the human, as more generally known. Human law is either civil law, or else a law more or less broad in scope than civil law. Civil law is that which issues from the civil power. Civil power is that which governs a state. A state is a complete association of free men, combined in order to enjoy their rights and provide for their common advantage. The law that is narrower in scope and is not derived from the civil power, although subordinate to it, is varied in character, comprising the commands of parents to children, of masters to servants, and the like. The law that is broader in scope is the law of nations, which derives its forceful authority from the will of all, or at least of many nations.

I added "of many nations" because scarcely any law can be found common to all nations except the law of nature, which is itself often called the law of nations. Frequently indeed, in one part of the world, there is a law of nations which does not exist in another. The proof of a law of nations is the same as that of unwritten civil law, long custom, and the testimony of the experts. For this law, as Dio Chrysostom well observes,[11] is "a work of custom and time." In the study of it we derive great help from the eminent writers of history.

15. AS for what voluntary divine law is, the meaning of the words clearly tells us, namely, it has its origin in the divine will. By this fact it is distinguished from natural law, which, as we said, may be called divine also. To voluntary, divine law we may apply what Anaxarchus vaguely said,[12] that God does not will a thing because it is lawful, but that it is lawful, or lawfully due, because God willed it. Now this law was given either to the human race or to one people. We find three occasions on which it was given by God to the human race, the first, immediately after the creation of man, the second, on the restoration of mankind after the Flood, and the third on that more glorious restoration of mankind through Christ. These three bodies of divine law are undoubtedly binding on all men, as soon as they come to a sufficient knowledge of them.

16. OUT of all the nations there is one to whom God vouch-

safed to give laws of a particular kind, and that was the Hebrew
people, to whom Moses thus speaks in Deuteronomy IV, 8: "What
nation is there so great, that hath statutes and judgments so righteous as all this law, which I set before you this day?" . . . Now
it cannot be discovered by any sign that God intended any other
people but the Israelites to be bound by that law. Therefore, as
regards ourselves, we have no need to prove any abrogation of that
law; for it could never be abrogated as touching those on whom it
was never binding. . . .

17. SINCE, then, the law given by Moses, as we have just shown,
can impose no direct obligation on us, let us consider whether it
has any other use, either in this inquiry into the law of war, or in
other inquiries of the same kind. For to know this is important on
many counts.

In the first place, then, it is evident that the Hebrew law enjoins
nothing contrary to the law of nature. For since the law of nature
is permanent and unchangeable, nothing contradictory to it could
be commanded by God, who is never unjust. . . . Whatever the
law of Moses commanded regarding the virtues which Christ demanded of his disciples should be obeyed by Christians now, to an
even greater degree. This for the reason that the virtues of humil-
ity, patience, and charity are required of Christians in a higher
measure than they were of Jews under the Hebrew law; and rightly
so, because the promises of heaven are far more clearly laid before
us in the Gospel. Hence the old law, when compared with the Gospel, is said to have been neither perfect nor faultless (Hebrews VII,
19; VIII, 7), and Christ is said to be the end of the law (Romans X,
4), and the law our schoolmaster to bring us to Christ (Galatians
III, 24). . . .

Is It Ever Right to Go to War?

1. HAVING looked into the sources of law, let us come to the first and most general question, which is this, whether any war is lawful, or whether it is ever permissible to make war. This question, like others that will follow, must, in the first place, be referred to the law of nature. Marcus Tullius Cicero, in the third book of *On Ends*,[1] and in other places, proves with great erudition from the books of the Stoics that there are certain first principles, 'first by nature,' and also certain derived principles which are superior to the first. He calls first principles of nature the care which every animal from the moment of its birth feels for itself and for the preservation of itself, and its zeal for its own well-being, and the things that protect it, as well as its abhorrence of destruction, and whatever seems to threaten it. So, he says, there is no one who, if he had a choice, would not prefer a body that was sound and perfect in all its parts to one that was mutilated and deformed. And it is our first duty to preserve ourselves in a natural state, and then to hold to whatever accords with nature, and reject the opposite.

But after these principles are admitted, there follows a further idea, that our deeds should accord also with reason, which is superior to the body. And the conformity to reason, which is the basis of goodness, should be thought more important than the mere satisfaction of our first instincts; because, though the first principles of nature lead us to right reason, right reason should be dearer to

25

us than the things that led us to it. This is a true statement and readily admitted by all men of sound judgment without any other demonstration. It follows then that in an inquiry into the law of nature we should first see what goes with those first principles of nature, and then proceed to that which, though it develops later, is nobler in quality, and not only to be accepted when it appears, but sought after by all means in our power.

This later principle, which we call goodness, sometimes turns—depending on a variety of circumstances—on a mere point, so to speak, the least departure from which is a deviation into evil. Sometimes more room is allowed, and an act is laudable, if performed, but may be omitted or altered without dishonor. . . .

It is with this latter type of case that both divine and human laws are especially concerned, to make obligatory what by itself was only laudable. We said above, when discussing the law of nature, that the question is whether an act may be performed without injustice, and that by an act of injustice we understand something that is necessarily repugnant to a rational and social nature.

In the first principles of nature there is nothing opposed to war; rather, they all favor it. For as the end of war is the preservation of our lives and limbs, and the retention or acquisition of things useful to life, it accords well with those first principles. And to use force, if necessary, for the purpose, is no way contrary to the first principles of nature, since all animals are endowed by nature with strength, in order to protect and defend themselves. . . .

Nor do right reason and the nature of society, which are the second and more important objects of this inquiry, prohibit all use of force, but only that which is hurtful to society, that is, deprives someone of his right. For the end of society is by a common and united effort to preserve to everyone his own. This rule, it may be readily understood, would hold, even if what we now call private property had not been introduced. For the free use of life and limbs and liberty would still be the right of everyone, and could not be assailed without injustice. So too the use of the common

possessions and consumption of them as far as nature needed them
would be the right of each taker, and for anyone to rob him of that
would be an injustice.

But now that law and custom have established private property
under its present form, the situation is even more easily understood. I will put it in Cicero's words: [2] "If every member of a body
had separate feelings of its own and imagined it would grow strong
by absorbing the strength of a neighboring member, the whole
body would inevitably languish and perish. So if every one of us,
for his own advantage, should seize the property of another man
and take off whatever he could, there would be an end of human
society and community life. For though nature allows everyone to
give preference to himself over another in acquiring the goods of
life, she does not permit us to increase our means, resources, and
riches by robbing other men." It is not, then, contrary to the nature
of society to look out and provide for ourselves, so long as we do
not destroy another's right; hence, the use of force, if it abstains
from violating the rights of others, is not unlawful. . . .

2. OUR statement that all war is not a transgression of the law of
nature may be more amply proved from sacred history. For when
Abraham with his servants and allies had gained an armed victory
over the four kings who had plundered Sodom, God approved his
act by the mouth of his priest Melchisedech, who said to him:
"Blessed be the most high God, which hath delivered thine enemies into thy hand." (Genesis XIV, 20.) Yet Abraham had taken
up arms, as appears from the history, without any special command
from God. Hence this man, eminent for both sanctity and wisdom, had relied on the law of nature. . . .

3. WHAT we are saying is proved also by the consensus of all
nations, especially the wisest. There is a celebrated passage by
Cicero, in which, speaking of force when used in defense of one's
life, he bears testimony to nature.[3] "This law is not written but
born in us; we have not learned it from any teaching, from hearing
or reading, but have got it from nature herself, imbibed it, put it

in words . . . ; a law to the effect that if our lives are threatened
by plots, violence, or weapons in the hands of robbers or enemies,
any means of ensuring our safety is right." He proceeds: [4] "Reason
taught this law to the educated, necessity to the barbarians, habit
to the nations, and nature herself to the wild beasts—always to use
every possible means of repelling any violence offered to their
bodies, their heads or their lives." Gaius the jurist says: [5] "Natural
reason permits us to defend ourselves against danger." . . . This
principle is so obviously fair that even when dealing with brutes,
who, as we said, have no actual laws but only a kind of shadow of
them, we draw a distinction between the force they use to do harm
and that they use for defense. . . .

4. IT is plain, then, that not all wars are condemned by the law
of nature, which may also be designated as the law of nations.
For history and the laws and customs of every people show us
clearly that war is not forbidden by the voluntary law of nations.
Indeed Hermogenianus says [6] that war was introduced by the law
of nations; however, I think his words should be understood
somewhat differently from the way they are generally interpreted.
Rather, that a certain formality in war was introduced by the law
of nations, and wars waged with this formality had by the law of
nations certain peculiar features. Hence we have a distinction,
which there will be occasion to use hereafter, between a war with
the formality of the law of nations, which is called lawful, or complete, and an informal war, which does not for that reason cease to
be lawful, or according to law. For the law of nations neither approves nor disapproves of other wars, provided their cause is just,
as we shall explain more fully hereafter. . . .

5. A greater problem arises when we come to divine voluntary
law. But let no one object that because the law of nature is unchangeable, nothing can be ordained by God contrary to it. For
this is true only as to things which the law of nature positively
forbids or commands; not as to those which by the same law are
merely permitted. For acts of this kind, which do not strictly come

under the law of nature but fall outside its scope, may be either forbidden or commanded.

The first argument which some persons present against war is the law that was given to Noah and his posterity (Genesis IX, 5, 6), where God says: "Surely your blood of your lives will I require; at the hand of every beast will I require it; and at the hand of man; at the hand of every man's brother will I require the life of man. Whoso sheddeth man's blood, by man shall his blood be shed; for in the image of God made he man." Here some take the passage on requiring blood in a most general sense; and the other passage, on the shedding of blood in turn, as a threat, not an expression of approval. Neither of these interpretations can I accept. For the prohibition against shedding blood plainly covers no more than the commandment, "Thou shalt not kill," which obviously has not put a stop to capital punishments or to wars.

Neither the later law nor that given to Noah established anything new; they were only a declaration and a repetition of the law of nature, which had been obliterated by depraved customs. So the words are to be taken in a sense that forbids only something criminal, just as when we denounce murder we do not mean every act of killing a man, but only the premeditated slaughter of an innocent person. As to what follows about blood being shed in return for blood, it seems to be not a bare statement of fact, but a statement of a law. I explain it thus: it is not unjust, according to nature, that a man should suffer in proportion to the evil he has done. . . .

We find too that capital punishment was inflicted on other criminals as well as on murderers, not only among the Gentiles, but also among those who had been taught the sacred doctrines. (Genesis XXXVIII, 24.) . . . We have, I think, said enough to show that the law given to Noah does not have the meaning ascribed to it by those who cite it as an argument against all war.

6. THE arguments against war drawn from the Gospel are more plausible. In examining them I shall not assume, as many do, that,

except for the rules of faith and the sacraments, the Gospel contains nothing more than the law of nature—an assumption which, as generally accepted, is, I think, not true. I readily agree that nothing that is not by nature good is commanded in the Gospel, but I see no reason for saying that the laws of Christ impose no duties on us beyond those imposed by the law of nature alone. It is strange how hard those who disagree with us will labor to prove that certain practices forbidden by the Gospel, such as concubinage, divorce, and polygamy, were offenses also by the law of nature. They are practices, indeed, such as reason alone might tell us it was better to abstain from, but not such as would be marked as sinful without the law of God. And who would say that the Christian precept of laying down our lives for others was an obligation of the law of nature? (I John III, 16.) . . .

7. PASSING over now the less convincing arguments, we cite as chief proof to show that the right to make war was not entirely abolished by the law of Christ, the passage in Paul's First Epistle to Timothy (II, 1–4), where the Apostle says: "I exhort therefore that, first of all, supplications, prayers, intercessions, and giving of thanks, be made for all men; for kings, and for all that are in authority; that we may lead a quiet and peaceable life, in all godliness and honesty. For this is good and acceptable in the sight of God our Saviour; who will have all men to be saved, and to come unto the knowledge of the truth." From this passage we learn three things: that it is acceptable to God that kings become Christians; that, being Christians, they should continue to be kings: . . . and, lastly, that it is acceptable to God that Christian kings secure to other Christians a tranquil life.

How do they accomplish this? Paul explains this in another passage (Romans XIII, 4): "He is the minister of God to thee for good. But if thou do that which is evil, be afraid, for he beareth not the sword in vain: for he is a minister of God, a revenger to execute wrath upon him that doeth evil." By the right of the sword is understood the exercise of every form of compulsion, in the sense used sometimes by the jurists; nor is the extreme form, which is the actual use of the sword, thereby excluded. . . .

The same passage in Romans XIII, of which we have quoted a part, supplies us with our second argument. There the highest power, meaning that of kings, is said to be from God, and is called an ordinance of God; whence it is to be inferred that we are to honor and obey it—and that too from the heart—and that whoever resists it is resisting God. . . . Nor does the question turn upon the characters of the rulers, whether they are godly or not, but whether the office they fill is unrighteous. This, Paul denies, for he maintains that their office was instituted by God, even at that time, and therefore should be honored from the depths of the soul, which, properly speaking, submit to God alone. . . . As once the sacrifices ordained by the law were sacred, even though performed by wicked priests, so sovereign power is a sacred thing, even though in the hands of an ungodly man.

A third argument is to be found in the words of John the Baptist, who, at a time when many thousand Jews were serving in the Roman armies, as appears from the writings of Josephus and others, was asked in all seriousness by some Jewish soldiers what they should do to escape the wrath of God. He did not tell them to renounce their military calling, which he ought to have done, had that been the will of God, but to abstain from violence, extortion and falsehood, and to be content with their wages. (Luke III, 14.) . . .

The fourth argument, which seems to me to have considerable weight, is this: if the right of inflicting capital punishment and of protecting citizens by arms against brigands and robbers were abolished, wickedness would run rampant, and the world would be deluged with crimes, since even now, with our constituted law courts, they are with so much difficulty held in check. If then it had been the intention of Christ to introduce such an order of things as had never been heard of, he would undoubtedly, in the most clear and explicit language, have forbidden all capital punishment and all bearing of arms, which we never read that he did. For his words which are quoted to support such an idea are either very general or obscure. Both justice and common sense tell us not only that general expressions should be taken in a limited sense, and ambiguous sayings given a suitable meaning, but that there may even be some departure from the precise significance and ordinary use of words, to avoid an interpretation that would lead to great disturbance and harm. . . .

The example of Cornelius the centurion gives us a sixth argument. He received the Holy Spirit from Christ, an indubitable proof of his justification; he was baptized into the name of Christ by the Apostle Peter.[7] Yet we do not read that he either gave up or was advised by the Apostle to give up his military profession. . . .

Now that we have proved that after the coming of Christ capital punishments were still rightfully inflicted, we have also, I think, proved that it sometimes may be lawful to make war, on a multitude of armed evildoers, for instance, who can only be brought to justice by defeat in battle. For though the strength and bold resistance of the criminals may have to be taken into account in prudent deliberations, they do not in the least weaken the force of the law.

An eleventh argument may be that Christ's law abolished only those parts of the Mosaic law which made separation between the Jews and other nations. (Ephesians II, 14.) The parts that nature and the consensus of civilized people call good, it not only did not abolish but included under the general precept to do whatever is honorable and virtuous. (Philippians IV, 8; I Corinthians XI, 13–14.) Now the punishing of crimes and the taking up of arms to prevent injustice are by nature counted praiseworthy and are classed among the virtues of justice and beneficence. . . . The property too which a man owns by human law is no less his than if God had given it: nor is his right abolished by the Gospel.

8. LET us see now by what arguments the contrary opinion is

supported, that the conscientious reader may judge more easily which side has the stronger.

In the first place, the prophecy of Isaiah is often cited, who says that the time will come, "when nations shall beat their swords into plowshares, and turn their spears into pruning hooks. Nation shall not lift up sword against nation, neither shall they learn war any more." (II, 4.) But this prophecy, like many others, is to be taken conditionally. We are to understand that such will be the state of the world if all nations accept and obey the law of Christ; to which end God will suffer nothing to be wanting on his part. Certainly, if all people were Christians and lived like Christians, there would be no wars. . . . Whatever way you take the prophecy, no conclusion can be drawn from it against the lawfulness of war, so long as there are men who will not allow the lovers of peace to live in peace but harass them with violence.

From the fifth chapter of Matthew many arguments are often taken. But in order to judge their value it is necessary to recall what we said a little earlier, that if Christ had intended to abolish all capital punishment and all right to make war, he would have done so in words as clear and explicit as possible, because of the importance and novelty of the idea, the more so because no Jew could imagine that the laws of Moses with regard to judicial processes and the state did not bind all Jews as long as their state existed. Bearing this in mind, let us examine the meaning of the separate passages in order.

Our opponents find the second argument for their view in the words: "Ye have heard that it hath been said, 'An eye for an eye and a tooth for a tooth.' But I say unto you that ye resist not evil (in Hebrew, 'the evil man,' which the Greeks translate 'the wrongdoer'), but whosoever shall smite thee on thy right cheek, turn to him the other also." [8] From this some people conclude that no injury should be resisted or penalty demanded, either in public or in private. Yet the words do not say this, for Christ is not here addressing magistrates but the injured persons. Nor is he speaking of all injuries but only of one like a slap on the cheek, for his last words are a restriction on his general words before. . . .

So in the passage which comes afterward: "Whosoever shall compel thee to go a mile, go with him twain." [9] The Lord did not say a hundred miles, a journey that would take a man too far from his business, but one mile, and—if useful—two, a walk of which no one thinks anything. The meaning then is, that in matters which will not inconvenience us much we should not insist on our rights but yield more than the other man asks, that our patience and good will may be manifest to all. . . . In such circumstances, then, Christ bids us have patience, and, lest someone quote in objection that well-worn saying: "By bearing an old wrong you invite a new one," he adds that it is better to bear a second wrong than to resist the first, seeing that it does us no harm, save what there is in foolish men's opinion. . . .

A third argument is frequently drawn from what follows next in Matthew: "Ye have heard that it hath been said: 'Thou shalt love thy neighbor and hate thine enemy.' But I say unto you, 'Love your enemies, bless them that curse you, pray for them that despitefully use you and persecute you.'" [10] There are those who believe that both capital punishment and war are incompatible with such love and good will toward our enemies. But they are readily answered if we consider the actual words of the Hebrew law. The Jews were commanded to love their neighbor, that is, a Jew. . . . None the less, their magistrates were ordered to put murderers and other serious criminals to death; none the less, the eleven tribes made righteous war on the tribe of Benjamin for an atrocious offense (Judges xx), and none the less, David, who fought the battles of the Lord, took rightfully from Ishbosheth by arms the kingdom promised to him.[11]

Let us now widen the meaning of the word 'neighbor' to include all men. For all are now received into God's common grace, and no people is doomed by him to destruction. What was right then for the Jews is now right for all, and as they were bidden to love

one another, so now are all men bidden. And if you believe that
the Gospel law commands a greater degree of love, we will grant
that, provided you recognize also that we need not love all to the
same extent, but may love our father more than a stranger. So too
by the law of a well-ordered love we should choose the good of an
innocent person before that of an evildoer, and the public good
before that of an individual. Now the love of innocent men is the
cause of capital punishment and of righteous wars. . . . The precepts of Christ, then, on loving and helping all men should be
obeyed, except as a greater and juster love stands in the way. We
all know the old saying: "To spare all is as great a cruelty as to
spare none." [12]

In addition, we are told to love our enemies after the example of
God, who makes his sun to rise on evildoers. But the same God
even in this life inflicts punishments on some evil men and hereafter will inflict terrible ones. . . .

As for what Christ said to Peter, "For all they that take the
sword shall perish with the sword," [13]—that does not apply properly to war in general but to private war. Christ too gave as his reason for forbidding or refusing to make any defense of himself, that
his kingdom was not of this world. (John xviii, 36.) These words
will be discussed more properly in another connection.

9. WHENEVER a question comes up as to the meaning of a document, subsequent usage and the opinions of learned men usually
carry great weight; which should be the case also in the interpretation of Holy Scripture. For it is not likely that the churches, which
had been founded by the Apostles, would either quickly or universally have strayed from those teachings which the Apostles briefly
set down in writing, and then more fully explained with their own
lips and introduced in practice. Still there are certain sayings of
primitive Christians which are sometimes quoted by those who
are against all war; as to these I have three things to say.

In the first place, nothing more can be gathered from these sayings than the private opinions of certain individuals, not the pub-

lic opinion of the churches. Also, these sayings for the most part are those of men who liked going their own separate ways and teaching something extraordinary. Such were Origen and Tertullian, who were not even consistent with themselves. . . .

My second observation is that Christians often disapproved of or evaded military service on account of the conditions prevailing at the time, which almost compelled a soldier to perform many acts inconsistent with Christian law. In Dolabella's letter to the Ephesians, to be found in Josephus,[14] we see that the Jews requested exemption from military expeditions, because while mingling with other races they could not well observe the rites of their law and would be obliged to bear arms and to make long marches on the Sabbath. . . .

The third point we make is that the primitive Christians in their burning ardor aimed at such glorious perfection that they often took divine counsels for commandments. "Christians," says Athenagoras,[15] "do not go to law with those who rob them." And Salvian [16] says that Christ commanded us to relinquish the object of dispute rather than engage in lawsuits. But this saying, taken in so general a sense, was rather by way of counsel, to indicate a sublimer mode of life, than a positive command. . . . In the same way Lactantius maintains [17] that a good man, such as he wishes a Christian to be, will not take part in war, nor will even go to sea. How many of the early fathers wrote to dissuade Christians from second marriages! All these counsels are praiseworthy, excellent, highly acceptable to God, yet they are not imposed on us by any binding law. This is sufficient answer to these objections. . . .

But setting individual opinions aside, let us appeal to the official judgment of the church, which ought to have great weight. I say, then, that none were ever refused baptism, or excommunicated by the church merely for bearing arms, as they should and would have been, had military service been irreconcilable with the terms of the new covenant. . . . Tertullian in his *Apology*, speaking in the name of the Christians, says: [18] "We sail with you, and we serve as soldiers with you." A little earlier, he observes: [19] "We are strangers to you, yet we have filled all your cities, your islands, your fortresses, your towns, your council chambers, even your camps." In the same book he relates [20] that rain was obtained for the Emperor Marcus Aurelius by the prayers of his Christian soldiers. . . .

Add to this that the church paid equal honors to some soldiers who had suffered torture and death for Christ and to other martyrs; among them are recorded three of Paul's companions. . . . Hence it is plain what the community of Christians thought of military service, even before the emperors became Christians. . . .

Capital punishments were not abolished even after Constantine accepted and began to promote the Christian religion. He himself enacted among other laws one for punishing parricides, by sewing them in a sack and throwing them into the sea. The law is to be found in the Code, under the title, "Murderers of parents and children." Yet in other cases he was so mild in punishing criminals that he is blamed by many historians for his excessive lenity. Also, the historians tell us, he had at that time many Christians in his army, and had inscribed the name of Christ upon his standard. . . .

Nor among the numerous bishops of the time, many of whom suffered fearful hardships for their religion, do we read of a single one who for fear of divine wrath tried to dissuade Constantine from inflicting capital punishments and making war, or Christians from serving in the army. Yet most of those bishops were strict observers of discipline, who by no means hesitated to point out the duty of the emperors and of others. . . .

Nor do I overlook the fact that bishops and other Christians often interceded to mitigate punishments, especially punishments of death, and that the custom was introduced that persons who had taken refuge in churches should not be given up, save on the promise that their lives would be spared; also that prisoners held for crimes should be released at Easter. But all these instances and others like them, if carefully examined, will be found to be examples of Christian kindness, embracing every opportunity to show

mercy, and not a mind set against all capital punishment. Therefore these acts and intercessions were limited to certain particular
times and places. . . .

Let us be satisfied then with quoting the address of the Theban
Legion [21] to the emperor, which with terse brevity expresses the
duty of a Christian soldier. "We offer our hands to fight against
any enemy, though we hold it a crime to stain them with the blood
of the innocent. Our right hands know how to do battle with an
ungodly enemy, but not how to slaughter our good fellow citizens.
We recall that we took up arms to protect our fellow citizens and
not to do them hurt. We have fought always for justice, for godliness, for the safety of the innocent; and these have been hitherto
the rewards of our dangers. We have fought for the faith; but how
shall we keep it with you, if we do not keep it with our God?" . . .

III

Division of Wars into Public and Private.

Explanation of Sovereignty.

1. THE first and most necessary division of war is that into private,
public, and mixed. Public war is waged by a person who has the
lawful authority to do it. Private war is waged by one without that
authority. A mixed war is that which on one side is public and on
the other private. Let us consider first private war, as the most
primitive.

We have, I think, already said enough to show that since forcible resistance to injury is not contrary to natural law, some private wars may be justified, as far as the law of nature is concerned. But someone perhaps may believe that, at least after public tribunals had been erected, private war was not allowable. For although public courts of justice are not institutions of nature but of men, yet it is much fairer and more conducive to the peace of mankind that a matter in dispute should be investigated by a disinterested person, than that individuals who too often are partial should enforce what they call justice by their own hands. And natural justice and reason teach us the importance of upholding so admirable a system. . . . And the law calls it violence when any man tries to take what he thinks his due without appealing to a judge.

2. THERE is certainly no doubt that the liberty of private redress, which existed before courts of justice were established, has since been greatly abridged. Yet there still are cases in which private redress may be allowed, as in places where there are no courts. For, when the law prohibits anyone from redressing his own wrongs, it must be understood as applying where judicial institutions exist. Now lack of judicial institutions may be either temporary or permanent. Temporary, where the injured party cannot wait for a judge, without certain risk or damage. Permanent, either in law or in fact; in law, when a man is living in uninhabited regions, on the sea, in a wilderness, on a desert island, or in any other spot where there is no civil government; in fact, when persons subject to a judge do not heed him, or he refuses openly to take cognizance of the case. . . . The passage of the Twelve Tables, taken undoubtedly from old Attic law, is well known: "If a thief commit robbery in the night and a man kill him, he is lawfully killed." Thus by the laws of all known nations, a person who defends himself against another, who is threatening his life with arms, is judged innocent. So conspicuous an agreement is evidence to prove that there is nothing in this opposed to the law of nature. . . .

[3. Private war is sometimes permitted even by the Gospel.]

4. PUBLIC war, according to the law of nations, is either formal or informal. What I here call formal is often called legal, in the sense in which a legal will is contrasted with codicils, or a legal marriage with the cohabitation of slaves. This contrast by no means implies that it is not permitted to any man, if he pleases, to make codicils, or to a slave to have a woman living with him, but only that, by civil law, formal wills and marriages have certain special features. It is useful to make this observation because many, from a misunderstanding of the word legal, think that all wars to which that epithet does not apply are to be condemned as unjust or unlawful.

To make a war formal by the law of nations, two things are necessary. In the first place, it must be waged on both sides by the supreme power in the state; and, in the next place, it must be accompanied by certain formalities, on which we shall speak later. Both conditions are so essential in conjunction that one without the other is not enough. An informal public war may be waged without those formalities, and against private persons, and by any official whatever. If, indeed, we consider the matter without reference to state laws, it would seem that every official, in case of resistance, has a right to take up arms to maintain his authority as well as to defend the people committed to his protection. But since a war involves the whole state in danger, it is, in almost all nations, provided by law that no war can be made save by the authority of the sovereign in the state. There is such a law as this in the last book of Plato's *Laws*. And by Roman law, to make war or levy troops or assemble an army without a commission from the prince was high treason. . . .

Yet this, like all rules, however universal, is to be interpreted with equity. For, first, there can be no doubt that an official in charge of a district may, through his subordinates, forcibly reduce a few rebellious persons to submission, provided that to do it does not require a force of great size or endanger the state. Again, if the danger is so imminent as to allow no time for consultation with the chief of state, here too necessity admits an exception to the rule. . . .

5. BUT under what circumstances minor officials have the right to use military force, and whether such warfare should properly be called public or not, is a matter of dispute among legal writers, some affirming and others denying. Certainly, if we call public whatever is done by official authority, there is no doubt that such wars are public, and those who in such cases oppose the official incur the penalties of resistance to superiors. But if public is understood in the loftier sense of something formal, as it undoubtedly often is, those are not public wars, because they do not meet the full legal requirements, lacking the decision of the sovereign and other particulars. Nor do the confiscation of the resisters' property and the assignment of it to the military, in my view, at all affect the question. For those penalties are not inflicted only in formal war, and excluded from all other kinds. It may happen, however, in an extensive empire, for instance, that persons in subordinate posts may have power granted them to commence military operations. In this case it must indeed be supposed that the war is undertaken by authority of the sovereign; for he who gives another the right to perform an act is himself considered the doer of it. . . .

Cicero defended the conduct of Octavian and Decimus Brutus, who on their own initiative had taken up arms against Antony. But even if it were evident that Antony deserved to be treated as an enemy, yet they ought rather to have waited for the decision of the Senate and the people of Rome as to whether it was for the public interest to take no notice of his conduct, or to punish it, to agree on terms of peace with him or to rush to arms. For no one is obliged to exercise a right that frequently is attended with dangerous risks. And even if Antony had been declared an enemy, the choice of persons to conduct the war should have been left to the Senate and the Roman people. . . .

This instance will serve, along with many others, to remind us not to accept everything that authors say, however celebrated.

They are often influenced by their times and their feelings, and fit
'their measuring rod to the stone.' Wherefore we should make an
effort in these matters to use cool judgment, and not take unthink-
ingly as an example something which may be excused but not
recommended. Those who do this are apt to make dangerous
mistakes.

Since, then, we have said that public war should not be waged
save by the sovereign ruler of each state, in order to understand our
argument and the questions connected with formal war, and then
many other matters, it will be necessary to discover what sovereignty is and who possesses it. . . .

6. THE moral faculty of governing a state, commonly called the
civil power, is described by Thucydides [1] under three heads, since
every state that is truly a state, he says, has its own laws, courts,
and officials. Aristotle [2] divides the administration of a state into
three parts: the consultation on subjects of general interest, the
selection of magistrates, and the judicial system. . . .

But if one wishes to make an accurate analysis, he may easily
cover every branch of civil authority, omitting nothing and adding
nothing too much. The ruler of a state exercises his authority partly
in person, partly through others. His personal acts have to do with
either general or particular matters. He acts for the general interest when issuing or repealing laws, on either secular or religious
matters, as far as the latter lie within the province of the state.
The science of dealing with these subjects Aristotle calls 'archi-
tectural.'

The particular concerns of a sovereign are either directly of a
public nature, or are private, in so far as the latter are related to the
public interest. Directly public are acts like the making of peace
and war and treaties, levying taxes, and others of the same sort.
Among these is included the right of eminent domain, which the
state has over the persons and property of its citizens for the public
welfare. The science of dealing with these matters Aristotle calls
'political,' that is, civil, and 'deliberative.'

The private concerns of the sovereign are disputes between individuals, which in the interest of public peace should be settled by public authority. This Aristotle calls 'the judicial science.' The acts of the sovereign that are performed by others are performed by his magistrates or other officials, among whom are included ambassadors. And civil power consists of all these things.

7. THAT power is called sovereign whose acts are not subject to the legal control of anyone else, and cannot be rescinded at the pleasure of another human will. When I say 'another,' I exempt the sovereign himself from this restriction, for he may change his own decision, as may also his successor, who enjoys the same right, having then the same power and no other. Let us see next what is the subject of this sovereign power. Now the subject is either common or particular. As the body is the common subject of the power of sight and the eye the particular, so the common subject of sovereignty is the state, which we have already called a perfect association of men.

We are not now considering peoples who are in a state of subjugation to another people, as the inhabitants of the Roman provinces were. For those peoples are not states in themselves, as we are now using the word, but inferior members of a great state, as slaves are members of a household. Yet it may happen that several peoples, forming each a perfect society, have the same head. For a moral body is not like a natural body, where one head cannot belong to several bodies, since in the former, one person in different capacities may be head of several distinct bodies. A clear proof of this is the fact that whenever the reigning house becomes extinct, the power to rule goes back to each separate people. So too it may happen that several states are joined together in a close confederation, and make what Strabo, in more places than one,[3] calls a 'system,' and yet each retains the status of a perfect state, as has been noted by Aristotle in more than one passage,[4] and by others.

Let us call then the common subject of sovereignty the state, taken in the sense already explained. The particular subject is one or more persons in accordance with the laws and customs of each nation. . . .

8. AND here, first of all, we must reject the opinion of those who maintain that everywhere and without exception, sovereignty lies in the people, so that they have a right to restrain and punish their kings whenever they abuse their power. No wise man can fail to see how much mischief such an opinion, once fully accepted, has brought about and may still bring about. With the following arguments let us refute it.

By both Jewish and Roman law [5] any man may legitimately submit himself in private slavery to whomever he pleases. Why then may not an independent people submit itself to one or more persons, completely transferring to them its right to govern itself, and reserving no portion of that right for itself? Nor can you say that such an act cannot be presumed, for the question is not what act may be presumed in a doubtful case, but what may legitimately be done. Nor is it more to the purpose to cite the difficulties which may, and actually do, arise from such an act. For whatever form of government you devise, it will never be free from imperfections and dangers. As the comedy [6] has it, "You must either take these with those, or let those go with these."

Now as there are many ways of living, one being better than another, and every individual is free to choose from the many kinds what he likes best, so a people may choose what form of government it pleases. Nor is its right to be measured by the excellence of this or that form, on which there is diversity of opinion, but by the people's will.

There may indeed be many reasons why a people should surrender entirely its right to govern itself and transfer it to another. It may, for instance, be in danger of destruction and unable to find a defender on any other terms; or, under pressure of famine, this may be the only way by which it can procure food. . . . It may also happen that a head of a family owning large estates will suffer no one to reside on them on any other terms. Or an owner of many slaves may give them their liberty on condition that they accept his authority and pay rent. There are examples of such things. Tacitus, speaking of the German slaves, says,[7] "Each one manages his own home and his own household. The master demands from him as from a tenant a certain amount of corn, cattle, or wearing apparel; and the slave obeys him to this extent."

Moreover, just as Aristotle says that some men are slaves by nature, that is, fitted for servitude, so some peoples are of a disposition that understands better how to obey than how to govern. This seems to have been the opinion the Cappadocians had of themselves, for when the Romans offered them liberty, they preferred life under a king, saying they could not live without a king. . . .

Some men have been influenced by the example of nations who have for many ages lived happily enough under a monarchy. Livy says [8] that the cities under Eumenes would not have changed their condition for that of any free state. And sometimes a state is so situated that it seems impossible for it to be safe without submitting to the absolute government of a single person. Such was the case, many wise men thought, with the Roman state in the time of Caesar Augustus. For these and similar reasons, it not only may but often does happen that men, as Cicero observes in the second book of On Duty, submit to the power and authority of another.

Again, as private property may be acquired by a lawful war, as we said above, by the same means and with no other title, civil dominion or the right to rule may be acquired. Nor is this rule to be applied only to the support of a monarchy, where one has been established, but the same rule and reasoning apply to a government by nobles, from which the people are excluded. Has there ever been any state so democratic as not to exclude some of its inhabitants, either the very poor or the foreigners, as well as the women and minors, from its public councils?

Some peoples have other peoples under them, no less subject to them than if they were under kings. . . . Nice in Italy, according to Strabo,[9] was assigned to the people of Marseilles; and the island

of Ischia to the Neapolitans. . . . Otho, Tacitus says,[10] gave the
Moorish states to the province of Baetica. None of these arrangements could be allowed to stand, if we accepted the rule that the
rights of rulers depend always on the will and judgment of their
subjects.

In fact, both sacred and secular history tell us that there have
been kings who were not subject to the control of the people as a
body. . . . There were those who, as Plutarch says,[11] "had authority not in accordance with the laws, but over the laws." And in
Herodotus,[12] Otanes describes a monarch as one who does what he
pleases and is accountable to no one. . . . Thus, when the Roman
emperors began actually to exercise royal power, it was said that the
people had transferred all their power and authority to them, even
over themselves;[13] which gave rise to the saying of Marcus Aurelius,
the philosopher, that no one but God alone can judge an emperor.[14] . . .

Hence kings who are subject to their people are said to be improperly called kings. Thus after the time of Lycurgus, and more
particularly after the institution of the Ephors, the Spartan kings
are said by Polybius, Plutarch, and Cornelius Nepos [15] to have been
kings in name but not in reality. The example was followed by
other states of Greece. So Pausanias says [16] of the Corinthians:
"The Argives, who have long loved equality and liberty, have reduced their kingly power very low; so that they have left the posterity of Cisus nothing but the name of kingship." Aristotle says [17]
that such monarchies are not true forms of government, because
they form only parts of what is an aristocratic or a democratic state.

We see too, in nations that are not under permanent royal government, examples of a sort of temporary kingship, exempt from
popular control. Such was the power of the Amymones among the
Cnidians, and of the dictators in the early ages of Rome, when
there was no appeal to the people. Wherefore, Livy says,[18] an edict
of the dictator was obeyed like that of a god. Indeed, there was no

alternative to submission; in the words of Cicero,[19] the dictatorship possessed all the strength of royal power.

The arguments produced on the opposite side are not difficult to refute. In the first place, the assertion that the one who confers authority on another is superior to the one on whom he conferred it is true only in cases where the authority is continually dependent on the will of the conferrer; but not in cases where the authority, though it derives its origin from another person's will, becomes later a necessity, as when a woman has given herself to a husband, whom she must always thereafter obey. The Emperor Valentinian, when the soldiers who had raised him to the throne made a demand of which he did not approve, replied:[20] "Soldiers, when you chose me for your emperor, it was in your power to choose. But now that you have chosen me, it depends on my will, not on yours, to grant what you ask. It is your duty as subjects to obey; it is mine to consider what should be done." Nor is it right to assume that all kings are given their authority by the people, as may plainly be seen from the instances cited above of a householder admitting strangers to his estates on condition of their obedience, and of nations subjugated in war.

Another argument is taken from the saying of the philosophers, that all government was created for the benefit of the governed and not of those who govern. Therefore, since the end is nobler than the means, it is supposed to follow that the governed are superior to their ruler. But it is not universally true that all government was created for the benefit of the governed. For some governments exist intrinsically for the sake of the ruler, such as the rule of a master over a slave, in which the advantage to the slave is only extrinsic and incidental. In the same manner, the pay of a physician has nothing to do with his medicinal art. There are other kinds of government established for the benefit of both parties, like the marriage bond. Then some imperial governments, such as those which are set up by right of conquest, may have been established for the benefit of the monarch; and yet should not be called tyrannies, for

that word, as now understood, implies injustice. Some governments
may be formed for the advantage of both subjects and ruler, as when
a people to defend itself sets up over it a powerful king.

I do not deny that in most governments the good of the governed is the chief object; and what Cicero said after Herodotus, and
Herodotus after Hesiod,[21] is true, that kings were instituted that
men might enjoy justice. But it does not follow from this what they
infer, that the people are superior to the king. For guardianships
were invented for the benefit of wards, yet the guardian has authority and power over the ward. Nor, though a guardian may for
mismanagement be removed from his trust, is it true, as some insist, that the same law must hold for a king. For this is right procedure for a guardian, who has a superior above him; but in governments, because the ranks do not ascend to infinity, there must
certainly be either some individual or some assembly whose misconduct, since there is no judge above them, will be, as God declares,
his own peculiar charge. He either punishes their offenses, if he
deems it necessary, or permits them for the chastisement or the
testing of his people. . . .

There is a remarkable passage in Gregory of Tours,[22] where he
as bishop addresses the king of the Franks: "If any of us, O king,
transgress the bounds of justice, he may be chastised by you. But
if you override them, who will chastise you? We speak to you, but
you listen if you wish; and if you do not, who can condemn you,
except him who has declared that he is justice?" . . .

9. THERE are others who imagine a kind of mutual subjection, in
which the whole people are bound to obey a king who governs well,
but a king who governs badly is subject to the people. If they said
that a thing which is manifestly wrong should not be done because
a king ordered it, they would be saying what is true and admitted by
all good men, but this does not include compulsion of the king or
any right of government. If a people intends to share the government with their king, a case of which we shall speak later, the limits
to the powers of each should be clearly defined, so as to be easily

known in varying circumstances of place, person, or business.

The goodness or badness of an act, especially in political matters, which are often hard to judge, is not sufficient to show which party has the responsibility. The greatest confusion must result if, under the pretext that an act is good or bad, the king on one side and the people on the other, each in the name of his own power, should claim jurisdiction over the same thing. No people, so far as I know, ever thought of introducing so turbulent a state of affairs.

10. HAVING refuted these false notions, let us offer some warnings which may point out the way to ascertain correctly to whom in every nation the sovereign power belongs. The first warning is this, not to let ourselves be deceived by ambiguous terms, or by the outward appearance of things. . . .

The Roman emperors, after they had exercised openly and without any disguise an absolute monarchical power, were still called princes. And in some free states, the chief magistrates are allowed the insignia of royal majesty.

Again, the assembly of the estates, that is, the meeting of those who represent the various classes of people, as Gunther says,[23] "the prelates, the nobles, and the deputies of towns," in some places merely serves as the great council of the king, through which the complaints of his people, which often are unmentioned in his cabinet, reach the royal ears. The king is then at liberty to ordain what he thinks best. In other places, the members have the right to be informed of the prince's acts, and even to make laws by which the prince is bound.

Many think that the difference between sovereign power and something less than sovereign is to be found in whether the power was conferred by election or by inheritance, for they maintain that only hereditary power is sovereign, not elected power. But this view cannot be accepted as universally correct, for succession is not a title to power which prescribes the form of the power, but only a continuation of power already existing. A right conferred originally on a family by election is continued by succession. Hence the

succession conveys just the powers which the first election conferred. . . .

11. ANOTHER warning is this. To know what a thing is is not the
same as to know the mode of its tenure, a distinction which holds
not only for corporeal but for incorporeal possessions. A field is a
thing, and so also is the right of passage or driving or travel through
it. And some hold these things by full right of ownership, some by
right of usufruct, and some by a temporary right. Thus a Roman
dictator held the supreme power by temporary right, whereas most
kings, both those who are elected first of their line and those who
succeed them in lawful order, hold it by right of usufruct. Some
kings, however, hold it with full rights of ownership; as when they
acquire it by lawful war, or when a people, to avoid a greater evil,
make an unqualified surrender of themselves into their hands.

Nor do I agree with those who say that the power of the dictator
was not sovereign because it was not permanent. For the nature of
things moral is revealed by their effects. So powers that have the
same effects should be given the same names. Now a dictator, during his term of office, performed all acts with the same authority as
the most absolute sovereign; nor could his acts be annulled by
anyone else. Length of duration, therefore, does not alter the nature
of a right, although, if it is a question of the dignity which is called
majesty, undoubtedly he whose right to it is permanent has more of
it than he whose right is but temporary, since mode of tenure does
affect dignity.

The same, I maintain, is true of persons appointed regents of
kingdoms before the kings have arrived at their majority, or while
they are incapacitated by insanity or captivity. Neither are they
subject to the people, nor can their power be revoked before the
lawful time. . . .

12. AS for what I have just said, that some rulers hold their powers
with absolute proprietary right, that is, as a patrimonial estate, some
learned men oppose me with the argument that free men are not to
be regarded as property. But as the power of a master is one thing

and the power of a king another, so personal freedom is one thing and civic freedom another, the freedom of an individual and the freedom of a whole body of men. . . . And as personal freedom excludes control by a master, so civic freedom excludes control by a king and any other domination, rightly so-called.

Thus Livy contrasts the two:[24] "Being yet unacquainted with the sweetness of liberty, they called for a king." . . . And again:[25] "The Roman people were not under a king, but were free." Yet again, in another passage,[26] he contrasts nations who were free with those who were living under kings. . . . Arrian, in his book on India,[27] speaks of "kings and free states." . . . Now and again, in Roman laws on war and on suits for recovery,[28] foreigners are distinguished as being under kings or as free peoples. Here, then, it is a question not of individuals but of a people's liberty. . . .

And when a people is transferred to a new king, it is not, properly speaking, a transfer of individuals but of the perpetual right of governing them as a whole people. . . . It may indeed happen that a king in his own right has authority over certain peoples, so that he can transfer them to someone else. Strabo says [29] that the island of Cythera, lying off Cape Matapan, belonged to Eurycles, a Spartan chief, "by his own private right." Thus King Solomon gave to Hiram, king of the Phoenicians, twenty cities.[30] . . .

13. IN the case of kingships which were conferred by consent of the people, we cannot, I admit, assume that it was the people's wish to permit their king to alienate his royal power. . . . Although Charlemagne and Louis the Pious and other monarchs after them among the Vandals and Hungarians did, we read, bequeath their kingdoms by will, their action had rather the force of a recommendation to their people than of a genuine deed of alienation. As to Charlemagne particularly, Ado records that he had his will confirmed by the Frankish nobility. . . .

14. THUS far the point we have been trying to make is that the sovereign power itself must be distinguished from the full possession of it. So true is this that often the sovereign power is not pos-

sessed in full, while many lesser authorities are possessed in full. Accordingly, marquisates and countships are sold or disposed of by will more easily than kingdoms.

15. ANOTHER sign of this difference appears in arrangements for the guardianship of a kingdom, when a king is prevented by age or illness from exercising his power. For in kingdoms that are not patrimonial, the regency goes to those to whom a public law, or failing that, the people's will, commits it. In patrimonial kingdoms, it goes to whomever the father or other relatives have selected. . . .

16. A third thing to be noted is that sovereignty does not come to an end when a new ruler makes promises—even promises regarding his mode of government—to his subjects or to God. Nor am I speaking here of his observance of natural and divine law or of the law of nations, for to that observance all kings are bound, even though they have made no promises. I am referring to provisions by which without a promise he would not be bound. The truth of what I am saying is made clearer by a comparison with a head of a household, who, even though he promises his household that he will do something relating to his government of them, does not for that reason cease to possess supreme authority over the household, so far as the life of the household is concerned. Nor does a husband lose his marital authority because he promises his wife something.

Nevertheless, we must admit that when such a thing happens, the sovereign power becomes in a way restricted, whether the obligation incurred limits only the actual exercise of the power or even, directly, the power itself. In the former case, an act performed contrary to the promise will be unlawful, because, as we shall show elsewhere, a true promise confers a legal right on him to whom it is made. In the latter case, the act will be void, in the absence of power to perform it. Still it does not follow therefrom that the king by his promise has put himself under a superior, for his act in this case is nullified not by any superior force but by the law.

Among the Persians, the king possessed absolute power—"an autocrat and responsible to no one," as Plutarch calls him,[31] adored as the image of God. . . . Yet on his accession to the kingdom he took an oath, as Xenophon [32] and Diodorus Siculus tell us. Also, it was wrong for him to alter laws made with certain formalities, as we learn from the story of Daniel, and from Plutarch's *Themistocles*.[33]

Diodorus Siculus says the same of the kings of the Ethiopians.[34] He says also [35] that the kings of the Egyptians, who like other Oriental monarchs unquestionably possessed absolute sovereignty, were bound to observe numerous rules. If they transgressed them, they could not in their lifetime be charged with it, but on their death an accusation was brought against their memory. If convicted, they were denied ritual burial, as were the Hebrew kings who reigned badly, and whose bodies were interred outside the proper burial place of the kings (II Chronicles xxiv, 25, and xxviii, 27)—an excellent arrangement, by which the sacredness of supreme authority was preserved and yet kings were restrained from breaking faith by fear of future judgment. . . .

What if the provision is added that if the king fails to keep his pledge, he will forfeit his kingdom? Not even then does his authority cease to be supreme, but the mode of his holding it is restricted by the provision and resembles that of a temporary ruler. . . . Thus a landed estate that is held in trust is actually the holder's no less than if it were his in full ownership, but is his subject to chance of loss. . . .

17. IN the fourth place, we must remark that though sovereign power is a unity and itself indivisible, consisting of the parts we enumerated above, along with the supreme right of being accountable to no one, still it may sometimes be divided into sections, either geographically or with regard to subject matter. Thus, although the Roman imperial power was a unit, it often happened that one man took the East and another the West, or even that three men ruled the world in three sections. So also a people, when choosing a king, may reserve to itself certain activities and assign others to the king with full rights.

This is not what happens, however, as we have just shown, when a king binds himself by his own promises. It takes place only when either a provision is made expressly for the division of powers, of which we have just spoken, or when a people still free lays upon the future king something in the nature of a perpetual commandment; or when a condition is added which indicates that the king may be coerced or punished. For to command is to act as a superior, at least in the matter with which the commandment deals. To coerce is not indeed invariably a mark of superiority, for by nature everyone has a right to coerce his debtor, but it is not consistent with a position of inferiority. So from the right to coerce follows at least the equality of the coercer, and hence a division of the sovereignty.

Against such a division, as creating a two-headed state, many have urged numerous objections. However, as we said before, there is no civil institution that is entirely free of faults; and a law is not to be judged by what this man or that considers best, but by the intention of the one who made it. . . .

18. BUT they are much mistaken who suppose that whenever kings declare that certain acts of theirs are not valid unless approved by a senate or some other assembly, the sovereignty is then divided. For whatever acts are rescinded in this way should be taken as rescinded by authority of the king, who has selected this method of ensuring himself from having a measure procured from him by false information treated as an expression of his true will. Of this sort was a rescript of King Antiochus III to his officials, instructing them not to obey him if he gave any order contrary to the laws. . . .

19. AND here I do not accept the view of Polybius, who classed the Roman republic under the mixed type of state,[36] since if we regard not its acts at that time but the law behind its acts, it was a pure democracy. For both the Senate's authority, which he calls aristocratic, and that of the consuls, who, he thinks, resembled kings, were subject to the people. I say the same of the opinions of other political writers, who make it their rule to look at outward

appearances and day-by-day administration rather than at the law
that fixes sovereign power.

20. MORE to the point is Aristotle's statement [37] that between
full kingship, which he calls absolute monarchy, . . . and the
Spartan kingship, which was merely a government of the nobles,
there are several intermediate kinds of monarchy. The Hebrew
kings, I think, may be cited as an example, for in most matters they
ruled indubitably by absolute right. The people had asked to have
a king such as their neighbors had; [38] . . . and Samuel, recounting
the rights of kings, had made it plain that against the wrongful
acts of their king the people would have no power left to resist. . . .

Yet, though this is true, I find that the kings were deprived of
jurisdiction in some cases, which belonged to the Sanhedrin of
seventy men that was set up by Moses at the divine command, and
which lasted, with a permanent right of co-optation, to the time of
Herod. . . . Moreover, the things of God were sharply differentiated from the things of the king; and the things of God, according
to the opinion of the most learned Hebrews, were to be understood
as judgments to be applied according to the law of God. . . . Also,
the king could not exempt from sentence anyone who for whatever
cause had been found guilty by the Sanhedrin. . . .

Something similar, I note, was the rule in the times of the Roman
kings. Almost all the administration was then in the hands of the
king. . . . Nevertheless, Dionysius of Halicarnassus says [39] that
even at that time some matters were reserved for the people's decision. . . .

A like mixture of popular and aristocratic governments existed at
Rome under the interregnum and under the first consuls. . . .
Later on there was still something of that mixture left, as Livy tells
us,[40] as long as the ruling power lay with the patricians, that is, the
Senate, and a means of relief, that is, a right of veto or intercession,
was in the hands of the tribunes, that is, the people. . . .

21. THE next question is whether one who is bound by an unequal alliance can possess sovereign power. . . . An unequal al-

liance is one in which by the very terms of the compact a permanent
advantage is given to one party over the other; when, for instance,
one is bound to uphold the sovereignty and majesty of the other—
as in the treaty of the Aetolians with the Romans—bound, that is,
to work to keep the other's sovereignty intact and to maintain its
prestige, which is what is meant by the word majesty. . . . Under
the same type of alliance come certain rights of the sort now called
rights of protection, of defense, and of patronage, and, among the
Greeks, the rights of mother cities over their colonies. As Thucydides says,[41] the colonists had the same right to liberty as their
mother cities had, but they owed their mother city honor and the
payment of the customary tokens of respect. . . .

We know Proculus' answer to this question,[42] namely, that a nation is free when it is not subject to the power of another, even
though in some treaty of alliance there is a provision that it shall
loyally uphold the dignity of another nation. If, then, a nation
bound by such a treaty remains free as long as it is not subject to
another's power, it follows that it retains its sovereignty. And the
same is to be said of a king, for the situation of a free nation and of
a king who is truly a king are the same. . . .

Clients are under the protection of their patrons. So nations inferior by treaty are under the protection of the nation superior in
dignity. They are "under patronage, not under domination," as
Sulla puts it in Appian.[43] And Cicero, in the second book of *On
Duty*,[44] describing a more religious age of the Romans, says that
their allies then received protection from them, not domination.
. . . Even as private patronage does not destroy personal liberty,
so the patronage of a state does not destroy civil liberty, and liberty
without sovereignty is meaningless.

Contradictory, apparently, to what we have said is a later statement by Proculus:[45] "Among us, allied states are subject to accusation and if found guilty we punish them." To understand this
assertion we must realize that there are four kinds of possible controversies between such states. First the subjects of a popular state

or of a king who is an ally of another may be charged with having broken the treaty of alliance. Second, the states or the kings themselves may be accused of having done so. Third, allies who are in league with the same state or king may quarrel among themselves. Fourth, subjects may complain of wrongs done them by their rulers.

In the first case, if the offense is flagrant, the king or the state is bound either to punish the offender or else turn him over to the party he injured. This rule holds not only between members of an unequal alliance but between members of one that is equal; even between those who are bound by no alliance, as we shall show elsewhere.[46] The king or the state is bound too to endeavor to repair the damage. . . . In the second case, one ally has the right to compel the other to abide by the terms of the treaty and even to punish him if he does not. This right too is not peculiar to members of an unequal alliance, but belongs also to members of an equal one. For in order that one may punish a transgressor, it is enough that one is not his subject, as we shall explain later. Accordingly, the same practice has grown up between kings and states who are not allies.

In the third case, in both equal and unequal alliances, disputes are usually referred to a conference of the allies not involved in the matter, as we read the ancient Greeks and Romans and Germans used to do; otherwise to arbitrators, or to the head of the alliance as the common arbitrator. . . . In the last case, the allies have no right to entertain the complaints. . . . When an accusation was brought against Hannibal by certain Carthaginians at Rome, Scipio said that the senators ought not to intervene in the Carthaginian state.[47] This is comparable to what Aristotle says,[48] that an alliance differs from a state in that the allies may be concerned with preventing wrongs to themselves but not with preventing citizens of one ally from wronging each other. . . .

Yet it is true that most frequently the party having the superior position in the alliance, if in power he also far outranks the other, gradually usurps the sovereignty, properly so called. Especially is this so if the alliance is perpetual and includes the right of introducing troops into towns, as the Athenians did when they allowed appeals from their allies' decisions—a thing the Spartans never did. Isocrates at that time compared the rule of the Athenians over their allies to that of a king.[49] For a similar reason the Latins complained that under cover of a Roman alliance they were in slavery. . . . When these things happen, and turn out so that long-suffering on one side turns into a right on the other—a process which we shall have occasion to discuss later—then either those who were allies become subject, or at least there is a division of sovereignty, such as we said above might occur. . . .

[22–23. Tributary states and feudal vassals may still be sovereign.]

24. IN the case of a governing power, no less than in a case of private ownership, we must distinguish between the right and the exercise of the right, or between the first act and the second. For an infant king has the right but cannot exercise the power. So it is with an insane or a captive king, or with one living in a foreign country and not permitted freedom of action with respect to his domain lying elsewhere. In all these cases guardians or regents must be appointed. . . .

IV

Wars of Subjects versus Their Superiors.

1. WAR may be waged by private persons against private persons, as by a traveler against a brigand; by sovereigns against fellow sovereigns, as by David against the king of the Ammonites; by private

persons against sovereigns who are not sovereigns over them, as by Abraham against the king of Babylon and his neighbors; and by sovereigns against private persons who are their own subjects, as by David against the partisans of Ishbosheth, or who are not their subjects, as by the Romans against the pirates.

The only question, then, is whether war may be rightfully waged by private persons or by officials against those who are either their own sovereigns or have some lesser authority over them. . . . We must ask what measures it is permissible to take against our own sovereign or his subordinates acting under authority from the sovereign.

The following rule is accepted by all good men as beyond dispute, namely, that if ever our rulers command anything contrary to natural law or to divine ordinance, their command should not be obeyed. For when the Apostles said that God was to be obeyed rather than men, they appealed to a sure principle, engraved on the hearts of all men, which you will find expressed by Plato in nearly the same words.[1] But if in such a case or any other, our sovereign, because he pleases to do so, inflicts some injury on us, we should bear that rather than resist him by force.

2. BY nature, indeed, all men possess the right of resistance to defend themselves from injury, as we said above. But civil society was instituted to preserve the public tranquillity. So the state thereby acquires a greater right over us and our property to the extent that it needs it to achieve its end. The state, therefore, can, in the interest of public peace and order, cancel our general right of resistance. And unquestionably, it will will to do so, when otherwise it cannot attain its end. For if, under these circumstances, the general right of resistance persisted, the state would cease to exist; there would be only an unorganized multitude. . . .

So in all states the practice is as I have said. "There is," says Augustine,[2] "a general agreement on the part of human society to obey kings." . . . Hence everywhere the majesty, that is, the dig-

nity of the people, or of the single man who is sovereign, is guarded
by innumerable laws and penalties; it could not be maintained if
the right to resist him was open to all. If a soldier resists a centurion
attempting to chastise him and grabs the officer's staff, he loses his
rank; if he willfully breaks it and lays hand on the centurion, he is
punished by death. . . .

3. BY Jewish law [3] a man who disobeyed a high priest or a ruler
of the people especially appointed by God was condemned to
die. . . .

4. IN the New Testament, when Christ bade us [4] render to
Caesar the things that are Caesar's, he wished his disciples to understand that obedience, coupled, if need be, with patience, should
be paid to all sovereign powers, as much as, if not more than the
Jews had paid to their Jewish kings. And that best of interpreters,
the Apostle Paul, enlarging on Christ's words, describes more fully
the duties of subjects, saying among other things: [5] "Whosoever
therefore resisteth the power resisteth the ordinance of God, and
they that resist shall receive to themselves damnation." Further on
he adds: "For he is a minister of God to thee for good." And then:
"Wherefore ye must needs be subject, not only for wrath but also
for conscience' sake." Under 'subjection' Paul includes the duty of
non-resistance, as a result not only of our fear of a greater evil but
of our sense of the obligation we are under both to man and to
God. He adds two reasons: first, that God has given his approval to
this order of ruling and obeying. . . . And second, that this order
works for our good.

But, someone may say, there is no good in suffering injustices.
To which others may reply—with more truth, it seems to me, than
exact adherence to the Apostle's meaning—that these very injustices have a value for us, since our patience will not fail of reward. To me it seems rather that the Apostle had in mind the
universal end proposed for this present order, which is the public
tranquillity, within which is included that of the individual. And
this good end unquestionably we attain most often through the

functioning of the public authorities; for no one wants to do himself harm, and the well-being of a ruler consists in the well-being of his subjects. . . .

Even if sometimes, in an excess of fear or anger or other emotion, our rulers are impelled away from the straight path which leads to tranquillity, we should regard this as one of the less common occurrences, which, as Tacitus says,[6] are outweighed by the better things that ordinarily happen. . . .

At this point we must quote those never sufficiently remembered words of Pericles, in Thucydides: [7] "I myself believe that even for the individual citizen it is more to his advantage that the state as a whole should prosper than that he in his private fortunes should flourish and the state in general be in a bad way. For a man may have his private means well invested, but if his country goes down, he too will inevitably be lost. Contrariwise, a man who meets with misfortune in a prosperous country is through it much more easily saved from ruin. The state is able to bear the calamities of individuals, but individuals are not able to do the same for the state. . . ." . . . .

5. NOR did the ancient Christians, the best interpreters of the law of the Lord, depart from it in their practice. For though the Roman emperors were frequently the most wicked of men, and there were many who rebelled against them under pretext of delivering the state, the Christians never took part in these uprisings. . . . Ambrose believed that Valentine, Valentinian's son, would do an injury not only to him but to his flock and to Christ. The people were intensely excited, but he would not take advantage of the commotion to stir up resistance. "Though treated with violence," he said,[8] "I know not how to resist. . . ." . . . .

6. IN our time men are to be found of considerable learning, but too much influenced by occasions and places, who first, I think, persuade themselves and then others that what I have just said applies to private persons but not to subordinate officials. These latter, they maintain, have the right to resist wrongs committed

by the sovereign; they are actually guilty if they do not resist. But I do not accept their opinion. . . . For all the governmental authority possessed by officials is subordinate to the sovereign authority. So whatever they do in opposition to the will of the sovereign is devoid of that authority and hence should be counted as the act of a private person. The philosophers' saying is here in point,[9] that order is established only in relation to some head. . . .

Consider Augustine's well-known saying: [10] "Observe the gradations of rank in human affairs. If a guard gives an order, you must obey it; yet not if a proconsul orders the opposite. It is the same if a consul orders one thing and the emperor another. You are not thereby showing disrespect to all authority, but you are choosing to obey the higher. Nor must a subordinate be vexed if his superior is obeyed before him." . . .

7. MORE difficult is the question whether the law of non-resistance should bind us in circumstances of dire and immediate peril. For some of God's laws, though stated in broad terms, contain a tacit exception in a case of extreme necessity. Such an exception was made in the Sabbath law by the wise men of the time of the Maccabees, whence the famous saying: "Peril to life does away with the Sabbath." . . . This exception was endorsed by Christ himself, as was also a breaking of the law which forbade the eating of shewbread.[11] . . . This is not to say that God has not the right to require us to suffer certain death, but that the character of some laws is such that it is incredible that they were imposed on us with so inflexible an intention. The same holds even more true of human laws.

I do not deny that even human law, such as a command not to desert one's post, may demand of a man certain acts of valor in face of certain death. But we are not to assume lightly that that was the intention of the lawgiver, nor does it seem that men would have accepted so stern a regulation for themselves and for others, except as extreme necessity compelled it. For laws are and should be drawn up by men with an understanding of human weakness.

Now the law of non-resistance which we are discussing seems to be an inference from the purpose of the people who first joined themselves together in a civil society, and from them to have passed as a right to the rulers. If these people could be asked whether they intended to impose on everyone the heavy duty of preferring death under all circumstances to armed resistance against the violence of their superiors, I do not know that they would answer that such was their intention, without perhaps adding a limitation to cases where resistance would inevitably involve the state in grave disorders or cause the death of many innocent persons. I do not doubt that we may read into human law also what love would counsel in such a case.

Someone may say that the strict obligation to suffer death rather than ever to resist any act of injustice by a superior came as a principle not from human but from divine law. But we must recall that men first combined to form a civil society not at the command of God but at the prompting of their own free will, after experience of the weakness of isolated households against attack. This was the origin of the civil power, which Peter for that reason calls an ordinance of man.[12] However, it is also called elsewhere a divine ordinance, because God approved of this wholesome institution of men. But when God approves a human law, he is to be thought of as approving it only as human and as applied in a human way.

Barclay,[13] the strongest advocate of monarchical government, yields nevertheless so far as to grant to the people or to an outstanding party of the people, the right to defend themselves against inhuman cruelty, even while he insists that the people as a whole is subject to the king. I easily see that in proportion as the party protected is of greater value, the more equitable it is to admit an exception to the letter of the law. Yet, even so, I should hardly venture to condemn indiscriminately either single individuals or a minority of the people who at the last resorted to the final defense of necessity, as long as they did not meanwhile lose all regard for the common good. . . .

At the same time care should be taken, even in such a crisis, to spare the person of the king. Those who believe that David did this [14] not from a sense of duty but for a more ambitious reason are mistaken. For David himself said publicly that no one could be guiltless who laid hands on the king. . . . It is wrong to circulate false scandal against even a private person. Against a king one should not repeat even scandal that is true, since, as the author of the *Problems* that bear the name of Aristotle says,[15] "Whoever speaks evil of the ruler does injury to the state." If then we should not hurt the ruler by speech, much less certainly should we do so by hand. Thus we read [16] that David was filled with penitence because he had cut off a piece of the king's garment; so well did he understand the sanctity of his person. And rightly so, for the sovereign power is inevitably exposed to the hatred of many and hence the security of him who wields it must be especially protected. . . .

A more difficult question is whether as much resistance is right for Christians as was right for David and the Maccabees, in view of the fact that the Christians' Master bids them again and again to bear the cross, and so seems to require of them a more enduring patience. Certainly when rulers threaten Christians with death for their religion, Christ allows them to flee—allows those, that is, who are not bound by some compulsion of duty to their posts. But he allows nothing more than flight. . . . And the faith of the Christians waxed strong, we read, principally through their long-suffering. . . .

Sovereigns, we have said, cannot lawfully be resisted. But there are things to be taken into consideration, of which we should now inform the reader, that he may not suppose persons guilty of breaking this law who in fact are not guilty.

8. FIRST, then, when kings are held accountable to their people, whether they received their authority thus limited at the beginning, or whether there was later an agreement to this effect, as at Sparta, then, if they transgress the laws or do injury to the commonwealth, they may not only be resisted by force but, if necessary,

punished by death, as happened to Pausanias, king of the Spartans. . . .

9. SECOND, if a king or anyone else abdicates his authority or openly relinquishes it, from that time on everything may be done to him that may be done to a private person. But he is not to be considered to have relinquished it, if he is merely negligent about it.

10. THIRD, . . . a king who actually attempts to alienate his kingdom or subject it to the rule of another man, may, I do not hesitate to say, be resisted in his attempt. For the sovereign power is, as we have said, one thing and the mode of holding it is another. The people may oppose a change in the mode of holding it, for that is not included in the power. . . .

11. FOURTH, as the same Barclay says, the kingdom is forfeit if the king with truly hostile intention sets about to destroy the whole people. This I grant, for the will to govern and the will to destroy cannot exist together, and so a king who declares himself the enemy of all his people by that very act renounces his kingdom. It scarcely seems, however, that such a thing could happen with a king in his right mind and ruling over one people. If he rules over several, it might be that he would choose to ruin one people for the sake of another, in order to plant colonies there. . . .

13. SIXTH, if a part of the sovereign authority is vested in the king and the rest in the people or the senate, and the king attempts to grasp a part that is not his, he may rightfully be opposed by force, because his authority does not extend so far. This rule, in my judgment, holds, even though, as we said, the power of making war belongs entirely to the king, for that rule is to be understood as applying only to foreign wars. Certainly whoever possesses a part of the sovereign authority must possess the right to defend it, and in that defense a king may lose even his own part of that authority through the law of war.

14. SEVENTH, if in the conferring of sovereign authority the statement is made that under certain conditions the king may be resisted, we should not say that under such an arrangement a por-

tion of the sovereignty is withheld from him. Yet certainly some natural liberty is thus retained and exempted from royal control. He who gives away his right can by agreement put a limit on that right.

15. WE have considered one who has or had a lawful right to govern. We have yet to consider the usurper of governing power, not after he has established his right through long possession or by agreement, but while his claim to possession is still unlawful. Now while he is in this position, the acts of government he performs may have a binding force, not for any right on his part, for he has none, but because it is highly probable that the rightful owner of authority, whether that is the people themselves or the king or the senate, would prefer that for the time being his orders should be accepted as valid than that all law and justice should be overthrown and utter confusion follow. . . .

In the case, however, of orders issued by the usurper which are not so essential and which tend to confirm the thief in his unlawful possession, if it is possible to disobey them without serious danger, they should be disobeyed. Whether it is right to use force to overthrow such a usurper, or even kill him, is the next question before us.

16. FIRST, then, if he has seized the power by an unlawful war, one which does not meet the requirements of the law of nations, and if no agreement has since been made with him and no promise given him, but he keeps possession solely by force, it would seem that the right to make war on him still continues, and any measure permissible against an enemy is permissible against him. He may lawfully be killed by anyone, even by a private person. . . .

18. IT will also be right to put a usurper to death, if the deed is sanctioned by the express authority of the true owner of sovereignty, whether that be the king or senate or people. . . .

19. OUTSIDE these cases I cannot believe it is right for a private citizen either to depose by force or to kill a usurper of sovereignty. For it may be that the lawful sovereign would prefer to have him

left in possession than to give occasion for the dangerous and bloody conflicts that are apt to result, when those who have a strong following among the people or supporters abroad are mal-treated or slain. Certainly, when it is uncertain whether the king or the people would wish matters pushed to that extreme, without some knowledge of their desires a resort to force cannot be law-ful. . . .

It is indeed, as Tacitus says,[17] a most serious problem which to choose, liberty or peace. It was a very difficult political question for Cicero to decide [18] "whether, when one's country is oppressed by an unlawful ruler, one should put forth every effort to unseat him, even if in so doing, one must put the state in extreme jeopardy." Individuals ought not to take on themselves a decision that be-longs to the whole people. The following was clearly a wrong act: [19] "We are removing the masters from a city ready to serve them." . . . Plato gives better advice in his letter to Perdiccas, in words which Cicero translated into Latin: [20] "Carry your struggles within the commonwealth only so far as you have the approval of your fellow citizens. You should not use violence against either your parents or your country." . . .

20. ABOVE all, in a case of controversy, a private citizen should not take it on himself to pass judgment, but should obey the possessor of authority. Thus Christ ordered [21] the payment of tribute to Caesar, because the coin bore his image, that is, because he was in possession of the government.

V

Who May Legitimately Make War?

1. AS in other things, so also in acts of the will, there are usually three types of efficient causes,[1] the principal actors, their assistants, and their instruments. In war the principal efficient cause is commonly the party whose interests are at stake; in a private war, a private individual, in a public war, a public authority, most usually the sovereign authority. Whether war may also be made by one party to protect others who are taking no action, we shall see later. Meanwhile we shall maintain that by nature every man is a defender of his own rights. Hands were given us for that purpose.

2. BUT to help other people as far as we can is not only legitimate but honorable. Those who have written on duty rightly say that nothing is more useful to a man than another man. Now there are various bonds that bind men together and call for mutual aid. Kinsmen combine to assist each other. Neighbors ask one another for help and so do members of the same state. . . . Solon taught[2] that commonwealths would be happy when every citizen in them thought of others' wrongs as if they were his own.

When other bonds are lacking mere fellowship in human nature is enough. To a man nothing human is a matter of indifference. . . . Democritus says:[3] "With all our strength we must defend those who are unjustly oppressed, and not neglect them, for this is right and good." Lactantius explains it as follows:[4] "God, who did not give the other animals wisdom, made them more secure from attack and danger by natural weapons. But to man, because he created him naked and frail, so that he might bestow on him wisdom, he gave along with other gifts this feeling of devotion, so that man would defend, love, and cherish man, and in face of every peril would receive and proffer aid."

3. WHEN we say 'instruments,' we do not mean by it arms and things of that kind, but men who in action voluntarily make their wills dependent on another's will. Such an instrument is a son to his father, by nature a part of him indeed. Such is a slave to his master, a part, as it were, by law. . . . And what a slave is in a household, a subject is in a state, and hence an instrument for his ruler.

4. BY nature undoubtedly all subjects may be taken to serve in war, but some are exempted by a special law, as in old times the slaves were at Rome, and now the clergy everywhere. Such a law, however, like all of that sort, should be understood as subject to exception in a case of extreme necessity.

This is sufficient to say in general on the topic of assistants and subjects. Special points will be treated in their appropriate connection.

BOOK TWO

I

Causes of War. First, Defense of
Persons and Property.

---

1. LET us come now to the causes of war, by which I mean the justifiable causes. For there are causes that are merely promptings of self-interest, quite distinct from motives of justice. . . . The subject of our discussion here is particularly justifiable causes, of which Coriolanus, in Dionysius of Halicarnassus, says:[1] "This, I think, should be your first care, to have a righteous and just cause for war." And Demosthenes says:[2] "As in a ship or a house or any other structure, the substructure should be the strongest part, so in the measures we take, our reasons and underlying motives ought to be grounded on truth and justice." . . .

The above is no less true for public than for private wars. Hence the complaint of Seneca:[3] "We penalize homicide and the murder of individuals. But what of war and the glorious crime of slaughtering nations? Greed and cruelty know no bounds. By decrees of the senate and resolutions of the people, savage acts are authorized; and things forbidden to individuals are ordered done by the state." Wars undertaken by public authority are, indeed, marked by certain legal features, as are the sentences of a judge, of which we shall speak later; but they are no less criminal, when undertaken without just cause. Thus Alexander was deservedly called a brigand by the

Scythians, as Curtius states,[4] when without cause he attacked the
Persians and other nations. . . . Augustine has a pertinent remark.[5] "Without justice, what are kingdoms but the spoils of vast
robberies?" . . . A just cause can be only an injury. . . . Thus
the Roman declaration of war says: "I call you to witness that this
is a lawbreaking people which refuses proper satisfaction."

2. THE grounds of war are as numerous as those of suits at law.
For where judicial processes fail, there war begins. Now suits in
law are brought for injuries either not yet committed or actually
committed. In the former case, a guarantee is requested against
possible assault, or security against threatened injury, or an injunc-
tion of some sort against violence. In the latter case, reparation is
sought for an injury sustained, or punishment for an offender. Plato,
in his ninth book *On Laws*,[6] correctly makes the same distinction.
Reparation has to do with what either does or did belong to us, and
so gives rise to suits involving property and to some personal actions; or else with something owed to us, either by contract or in
return for an injury, or by law. . . . A crime calling for punishment leads to accusation and public trial.

Three justifiable causes for war are generally cited: defense, recovery of property, and punishment. . . . The first just cause of
war, then, is an injury, which, even though not actually committed,
threatens our persons or our property.

3. WE have said already that when our bodies are violently attacked with danger to our lives, and there is no other way of escape,
it is lawful to fight the aggressor, and even to kill him. By this instance we showed that by general agreement some kind of private
war is lawful. We must note that this right of self-defense derives
its origin primarily from the instinct of self-preservation, which nature has given to every creature, and not from the injustice or misconduct of the aggressor. Wherefore, even though my assailant may
be guiltless, as for instance a soldier fighting in good faith, or one
who mistakes me for someone else, or a man frantic with insanity
or sleeplessness, as we read sometimes happens, in none of these

cases am I deprived of my right of self-defense. It is enough that I am not bound to submit to the harm he intends, any more than if a wild beast were attacking me.

4. IT is a question whether innocent persons, who by getting in the way obstruct our defense or our flight, without which we cannot escape death, may be cut down or trampled on. There are some, even theologians, who think they may. And, certainly, if we look to nature alone, according to it our own preservation should have far more weight with us than the welfare of society. But the law of love, in particular the Gospel, which puts our neighbor on a level with ourselves, does not permit it. . . .

5. THE danger must be immediate, and, as it were, at the point of happening. If my assailant seizes a weapon with an obvious intention of killing me, I admit too that I have a right to prevent the crime. For in the moral as well as in the natural realm, there is no point without some latitude. But persons who regard any sort of fear as a just ground for the precautionary killing of another person are themselves greatly deceived and deceiving to others. Cicero truly says in the first book of *On Duty*,[7] that the root of most wrongs is fear, as when a person who thinks of hurting another is terrified of danger to himself unless he carries out his scheme. Clearchus, in Xenophon, says: [8] "I have known men who, through misrepresentation or suspicion, came to dread one another, and so chose to strike first instead of being the sufferer, thus committing the most enormous wrongs against persons who had no evil designs, and did not even dream of harming them."

Cato, in his speech for the Rhodians, asks: [9] "Are we to start first doing what we say they intended to do?" . . . There is another passage from Cicero, no less apt:[10] "Whoever made such a rule, or to whom could the right be granted without the most terrible danger to everybody, to kill a person who he says he fears may some day kill him?" . . .

If a man intends no immediate violence, but has apparently formed a plot or scheme either to poison me or, by false accusation and false witnesses, get an unjust judgment against me, I cannot lawfully kill him, if the danger can be averted in any other way, or if it is not certain that it may not be so averted. For often a delay gives a chance for a variety of protective measures or accidents. As the saying goes, "There's many a slip 'twixt the cup and the lip." . . .

6. WHAT shall we say in case of danger of mutilation of a limb? Certainly, the loss of a limb, especially one of the principal limbs, is a grievous injury, and nearly equal to the loss of life; besides, one cannot be sure that it does not bring with it the danger of death. If then the threat cannot otherwise be avoided, I should think it right to kill the person who so threatens me.

7. THAT the same right should be granted for defense of chastity is scarcely a matter of debate, since, both in common estimation and by divine law, chastity is deemed as precious as life itself. . . .

8. WE have already said that though it is lawful to kill a person preparing to kill another, the man is more admirable who prefers to be killed rather than to kill. Some, however, who agree with this last make an exception in the case of a person whose life is valuable to many. But to me it seems unsafe to set for all whose lives are of importance to others a rule so contrary to the law of forbearance. The exception, therefore, in my opinion, should be restricted to those whose duty it is to protect others from violence, such as escorts on a journey, hired for that purpose, or rulers of a state, to whom may be applied the words of Lucan: [11]

"When the lives and the safety of so many nations hang on thy breath,
And so great is the world that has chosen to make thee its head,
Thou art cruel to have chosen to die."

9. ON the other hand, it may happen that the aggressor's life is valuable to many and he cannot be killed without transgressing not only the divine law, of which we spoke when we showed how sacred is the person of a king, but also the law of nature. For the law of

nature, as far as it has the force of law, has to do not only with the principles of what we have called expletive justice,[12] but prescribes other virtues also, as temperance, fortitude, and discretion, making the observance of them in certain cases binding as well as honorable. To observe these we are also bound by the law of love. . . .

11. LET us come now to injuries affecting our property. In expletive justice I do not deny that we may kill a robber, if necessary for the preservation of our goods. For the difference between the value of life and the value of property is overbalanced by the concern men feel for the innocent owner, and their hatred of a robber. Wherefore, if we regard our right alone, we may cut down with our javelin a thief in his flight with our property, if it cannot otherwise be recovered. . . . Nor, apart from divine and human law, does the law of charity forbid it, except where the property is of little value, and so beneath notice—an exception which some writers correctly add.

12. . . . THE laws all agree in making a distinction between a thief who steals by day and one who steals by night, but are vague about the reason for this distinction. Some think it arises from the impossibility of telling by night whether the intruder is a thief or a murderer, and therefore he may be killed as a murderer. Others think the distinction is made because at night the thief cannot be recognized and there is less chance of recovering the goods. I think the framers of the laws had neither of these points in mind. Their idea was that no one should be killed simply for the sake of property; which would happen, for instance, if I struck down a man in flight in order that, by killing him, I might recover my goods. But if my own life is endangered, then I am allowed to avert the danger, even at the hazard of another's life. Nor does it count against me if I ran into the danger while trying to keep hold of my property or recover what had been taken or catch the thief. For no blame can attach to me in any of these instances, since I am engaged in a lawful act, nor am I doing wrong to anyone when I exercise my right.

The distinction, therefore, drawn between a thief at night and a thief by day is based on the difficulty of procuring sufficient witnesses of a deed at night. So that if a thief is found killed, a man who says he killed him in his own defense easily gains credence, particularly if a destructive weapon is found with the body. . . . There is, then, a presumption, as I said, in favor of a person who has killed a thief at night. But if there should happen to be witnesses to prove that the life of the person who killed the thief was in no danger, the presumption in his favor is gone, and the killer is held for murder. . . .

13. . . . THAT the law of the Gospel requires more of us I do not doubt. For if Christ bids us let go our tunic and cloak, and Paul tells us to endure an unjust loss rather than take it to the courts—a bloodless form of struggle—how much more do they expect us to give up property of greater value rather than kill a man, the image of God, a child of the same blood as our own? Therefore, if our property can be defended in a way that seems to involve no danger of causing death, it is right to defend it; but if not, we should let it go, unless, perhaps, it is property of such a kind that our lives and those of our household depend on it, and it cannot be recovered through the courts, because the thief is unknown, and there is some chance that it may be saved without killing the thief. . . .

[14–15. Civil law, though permitting one to kill in self-defense, does not confer a right to kill, but only waives punishment.]

16. WHAT we have said thus far of the right of defending one's person and property relates chiefly to private war, but should likewise be applied to public war, allowing for the difference of circumstances. For in a private war the right of defense is, as it were, momentary, and ends as soon as one can reach a judge. But a public war does not begin except where there are no courts or where they are powerless; hence it is more protracted and perpetually inflamed by the appearance of new wrongs and injuries. Besides, private war is usually only a matter of defense, whereas public authorities have the right not only of defense but of punishment as well. Wherefore

they may act to forestall an aggression that is not immediate, but seems to be threatening from a distance. They may not act directly, for that, we have said, would be unlawful, but indirectly, by exacting penalty for a crime started but not yet completed. The place for discussing this point will come later.

17. BUT quite inadmissible is the doctrine proposed by some, that by the law of nations it is right to take up arms in order to weaken a rising power, which, if it grew too strong, might do us harm. I acknowledge that in councils of war such a question does come up, but not on any ground of justice, only of expediency. If for any other reason a war would be justified, for this reason it may seem prudent to undertake it. The authorities cited on the subject say nothing more. But that the bare possibility that violence may be some day turned on us gives us the right to inflict violence on others is a doctrine repugnant to every principle of justice. Human life is something that can never give us absolute security. The only protection against uncertainty and fear must be sought, not in violence, but in divine providence and harmless precautions.

18. THERE is another opinion, no more acceptable, according to which a war of defense, waged by persons who have deserved to have war made on them, is justified because few are content to take merely such vengeance as is due them for the injuries they received. But the fear of an uncertainty cannot give a right to resort to arms. Nor has a malefactor the right to resist by force the public officers who attempt to arrest him, because he fears his punishment may be too severe. A person who has injured another ought first of all to offer satisfaction to the one injured, through the mediation of some honest man. Only after that will a resort to arms be right. . . .

II

Things Which Belong to Mankind in Common.

1. NEXT among the causes of war we may reckon an injury actually received; and, first, an injury to what belongs to us. Now some things are ours by a right we share with all other men, some by our individual right. Let us begin with the things that are the common right of all mankind. This right covers directly both corporeal objects and certain acts.

Things corporeal are either unappropriated, or are already the property of someone. Things unappropriated may be either reducible to a state of private property or may not be. In order to understand this more clearly, it will be necessary to take a survey of the origin of property, what the jurists call the right of ownership.

2. AT the first creation of the world God gave to mankind in general dominion over all things of inferior nature, a grant renewed upon the restoration of the world after the Deluge. "All things," as Justin says,[1] "were the common and undivided property of all men, as if all were heirs of one general patrimony." Accordingly, every man could take at once for his own use whatever he wanted and consume whatever was consumable; the general exercise of this right supplied the place of private property. For to deprive anyone of what he had taken for himself became an act of injustice. This Cicero has explained by a comparison in the third book of *On Ends*.[2] "Although the theater is a public place, yet it is right to say that the seat which a man has taken is his own."

This condition of affairs could have lasted if men had continued living in great simplicity, and with remarkable charity towards one another. An example of community of goods arising
from extreme simplicity may be seen among some races of America,
who for many centuries have lived in this manner without inconvenience. An example of community of property based on charity
was furnished in the past by the Essenes, and by the primitive
Christians at Jerusalem, and is still to be seen in numerous religious
orders. The nakedness of primitive man is a proof of his simplicity
at creation. Yet, as Trogus says of the Scythians,[3] they were ignorant of vice rather than acquainted with virtue. . . . They lived
easily on the fruits which the earth brought forth of its own accord
without toil.

But in this life of simplicity and innocence men did not long
continue. They used their minds to invent various arts, the symbol
of which was the tree of knowledge of good and evil, that is, the
knowledge of things which may be either used well, or abused.
. . . The most ancient arts, agriculture and pasturage, appeared
with the first brothers, along with some interchange of products.
But from these differences in occupation arose rivalry, even murder.
At length the good men became corrupted by their association with
the bad, and the kind of life that giants live, that is, one spent in
violence, appeared.

However, the world was cleared of this race by the Flood, and
the savage life was succeeded by a greed for pleasure, to which wine
made its contribution; and out of which sprang lawless passions.
But the greatest breach in the harmony of men was made by a
nobler vice, namely, ambition, the emblem of which was the tower
of Babel. Later on, men divided up the land and took possession of
different parts.

Even after this there was still among neighbors a common ownership of lands for pasture, though not of flocks. For while the number of men was small, the wide expanse of land sufficed for the use
of many occupants, without their incommoding each other. "To

mark the bounds of fields, or portion out their limits was a sin."[4]
But as men increased in numbers, and their flocks with them, they
began gradually to divide their lands, not, as formerly, between
tribes, but between families. Then, too, as wells in the dry countries were objects of prime necessity and one did not suffice for
many, all tried to seize and keep them for their own.

We learn these things from sacred history, which agrees with
what the philosophers and poets have told us about the primitive
state of goods held in common, and the distribution of property
that came later. Their testimonies we have quoted elsewhere.[5]
From them we learn why men departed from the primeval state
of common ownership of things, of first their movable and then
their immovable possessions. It was because men were no longer
content to live on the spontaneous products of the earth, or to
dwell in caves, or to go about naked, except when wrapped in the
bark of trees or the skins of wild beasts, and wanted a pleasanter
way of life. Industry then became necessary, and each individual
applied himself to some particular craft. But the remoteness of
the places to which men had wandered prevented them from bringing their products to a common stock, and their lack of justice and
kindliness marked the end of that equality which had been the
rule in both the labor of producing and in the consumption of the
fruits.

We learn also how things passed from common to private ownership, not alone by an act of deliberate planning. For no one
could know what others wished to have for their own, so as not to
encroach on it; many too may have desired to possess the same
thing. But there must have been either some express agreement,
as for a division, or a tacit understanding, as for simple occupation. For as soon as it was found inconvenient to hold things in
common, before any division had taken place, we must suppose
that all agreed that whatever anyone had already taken possession
of, he should keep as his own. . . .

  3. HAVING stated so much, we say next that the ocean, whether

taken as a whole or in its principal divisions, cannot be reduced to a state of private property.[6] Some authorities agree to this principle as far as regards individual owners, but not as regards nations. We will prove its validity, therefore, first on practical grounds, since in this case the reason why men gave up holding their other goods in common does not hold. For the size of the ocean is so vast that it is enough for every use of all nations, for drawing water, fishing, and sailing. The same might be said of the air, if there could be any use of it that did not require the use of the ground beneath, as fowling does. So sports like that are subject to the law of him who controls the land. The same may be said of the sand banks of the seashore, which are completely barren. Their only use is to furnish sand, and that is inexhaustible.

There is a natural reason too which forbids our treating the sea, thus considered, as private property; which is that occupancy can take place only in things bounded by plain limits. . . . But liquids, which have no limits of their own . . . except as they are contained in something else, cannot be appropriated. Thus ponds and lakes, and rivers likewise, are made private property, since they are confined within banks. But the ocean, as it is equal to or greater than the land, is not confined by the land, so that the ancients said the land was confined by the sea. . . . Nor can any division of it be imagined. For at the time the land was first divided, the sea was for the most part still unknown, and afterward by no conceivable method could races so far removed from each other agree on a way to divide it.

Whatever then was once the common property of all, and in the first division of things was not divided, does not now become private property by division, but only by occupancy, nor is it divided up until after it has become private property.

4. LET us come now to things which though not yet made private property may yet become so. Such are the many regions still uncultivated, islands in the sea, wild beasts, fishes, birds. Here two points should be noted. Possession may be taken in two ways: one,

of the object as a whole, the other, in separate portions. The first method is commonly followed by a people, or by the ruler of a people; the second by individuals. The latter is more often the result of a grant than of free occupancy. Any region that has been taken possession of as a whole, even though not yet portioned out among individual owners, is not to be considered ownerless. For it remains the property of the first occupier, whether that is a king or a people. Regions of this sort are rivers, lakes, pools, forests, and rough mountains.

5. AS to wild beasts, fishes, and birds, we must observe that whoever controls the lands and waters where they are found can by his order prohibit anyone from capturing these beasts, fishes, and birds, and thereby acquiring them. His prohibition extends to foreigners also, for the reason that it is practically necessary in the government of any people that foreigners who mingle with them, even temporarily, as they do when they enter the country, should conform to that people's institutions. . . .

6. LET us see next whether men generally have any right to the use of things that already belong to someone else. Some may think this a strange question, since it would seem that the right of the owner had absorbed every right that sprang from the previous state of common ownership. But this is by no means the case; for the intention of those who first introduced private ownership must be taken into account. And that, we must suppose, was to depart as little as possible from principles of natural equity. For if written laws are to be construed in this sense, that is, in accordance with natural equity, much more should we follow the same rule in interpreting usages which are not bound by the letter of written laws. Hence it follows, first, that in case of extreme necessity, the primitive right to the use of things is revived, as if they had remained in common; because in all human laws, and consequently in all the law of ownership of property, a case of supreme necessity patently forms an exception.

Hence again it follows that if on a voyage provisions fail, whatever each person has must be brought out for the common stock. For the same reason I may pull down a neighboring house that has caught fire, in order to save my own. I may cut the cables or nets in which my ship is entangled, if it cannot otherwise be disengaged. None of these rules was introduced by the civil law; they were results of the interpretation of it.

Even among theologians the view is accepted that if in urgent distress a man takes from another what is essential to preserve his life, he has not committed a theft. This rule is not founded, as some allege, on the law of charity, which obliges the owner of goods to give to him who needs; but on the idea that when all things were divided among private owners, there was a benevolent reservation in favor of the primitive common right. For if those who made the first division had been asked their opinion on the matter, their reply would have been what we are saying. "Necessity," says Seneca the elder,[7] "the great protectress of human infirmity, breaks all law," —human law, that is, and all rules made in the spirit of human law. . . .

7. BUT warning should be given not to let this permission lead to excesses. In the first place, every effort should be made to obtain relief in some other way—for instance, by appeal to a magistrate, or by trying whether the use of the property can be obtained by entreaty from the owner. Plato allows the drawing of water from a neighbor's well, but only if one has dug down to the chalk to get water in one's own well. . . .

8. SECONDLY, this right cannot be granted where the owner is in an equal state of need himself. For under the same circumstances, the owner's claim is superior. . . . Cicero, in the third book of On Duty, says:[8] "Should not a wise man, in danger of perishing with hunger, take the food of another man who is good for nothing? Certainly not. For my life is not more important to me than my resolution of mind not to hurt another for the sake of benefiting myself." . . .

9. IN the third place, restitution of property taken should be

made whenever possible. There are some indeed who disagree, on the ground that no one is bound to restore what he took in the exercise of his right. But correctly speaking, his right here was not absolute, but limited by an obligation to make restitution when the emergency was over. Such a right suffices only to preserve some natural equity as against the rigors of private ownership.

10. HENCE we may infer that one who is waging a just war may take possession of a place situated in a country at peace, if there is real danger—and not an imaginary one—that the enemy will attack it and inflict irreparable damage. In that case, nothing should be taken but what is necessary to security, such as the bare guarding of the place; to the real owner should be left his jurisdiction and produce. Finally, this should be done with the full intention of returning the place to his guardianship as soon as the necessity ceases. . . . The Greeks who were with Xenophon,[9] being in great want of ships, by Xenophon's own advice, seized some that were passing, but still preserved for the owners the cargoes untouched, supplied the sailors with provisions, and paid them wages. The first then of the rights that under private ownership survive from the ancient community of goods is what we have called necessity.

11. THE second right is that of harmless use. "For why," says Cicero [10] "should not a man, when he can do so without injury to himself, share with another things which are useful to the receiver and can be shared without detriment to the giver?" Seneca too remarks [11] that it is no favor to allow another to light his fire from your flame. And in the seventh book of Plutarch's *Symposiacs* [12] we read: "It is wicked for us to destroy food when we ourselves have more than enough; or to stop up or hide a spring after we have drunk what we wanted; or to tear down the signs that mark the route for sailors or land travelers, and were of use to us."

12. A river, then, viewed as such, is the property of the people, or of the governor of that people through whose territories it flows. He or they may build a quay out into that river, and to them all the

produce of it belongs. But the same river, viewed as running water, still remains common to all to drink and draw from. . . .

13. so, too, when lands, rivers, or part of the sea belong to some particular people, they ought to be open to those who need to cross for legitimate reasons; if, for instance, they have been driven from their own country or wish to trade with a remote nation, or even are attempting to recover by lawful war some lost possession. The reason here is the same as that given above, that private ownership may have been originally introduced with a reservation of this kind, which benefits one party and does no harm to the other. So we should assume that this was the intention of the founders of private property. . . .

The right view is one between extremes. Permission to pass through should first be asked; if it is refused, the crossing may be made by force. Thus Agesilaus, on his return from Asia,[13] asked the King of the Macedonians for leave to pass through his dominion. But when he answered that he would consider it, Agesilaus said: "Let him consider; meanwhile we shall pass."

No one can rightfully object that he is afraid of a multitude passing through his territories. My right is not destroyed by your fears. Especially as precautions can be taken, such as requiring that the troops be sent through in small bodies or without arms; as the people of Cologne asked of the Germans.[14] . . . Or the one who grants the right of passage may hire suitable garrisons at the expense of the party passing through; or make them give hostages. . . .

Nor is fear of the ruler with whom the one who asks passage is lawfully at war a sufficient reason for refusing to let him go through. No more admissible is it to tell him he can go another way; for every other power might say the same, and thus his right of transit would be entirely annulled. It is enough that he is asking, without false pretense, to pass by the nearest and most convenient way. Obviously, if when he makes the request, he is engaged in unlawful war, or is taking enemies of mine with him, I may refuse him passage. I should even have a right to meet him on his own territory, and prevent his journey.

Free passage should also be allowed not only to persons, but to merchandise. For no one has a right to hinder one people from trading with another at a distance; it is to the interest of human society that it be made possible. Nor is anyone injured by it. For even though a trader may not make an expected profit, so long as it was not owed him, he cannot be considered injured. . . .

14. BUT it is a question whether the ruler of a country can impose duties on goods in course of transit through his land, or across his river, or over an arm of the sea which may be called an extension of his territory. Undoubtedly it would be unjust to impose burdens with no regard for the nature of those goods. Likewise, strangers passing through a country cannot be compelled to pay the poll-tax that is imposed on citizens to meet the expenses of the state. But if the ruler incurs expense in providing security for this merchandise, or in other ways on its account, he may reimburse himself by imposing duties on it, so long as they do not exceed the amount he spent for the purpose. For on this depends the justice of both tribute and taxes. Thus King Solomon collected tolls for the horses and linen that passed over the Isthmus of Suez. . . . The Romans too took toll for crossing the Rhine. "One paid even to go over a bridge," says Seneca.[15] The books of jurists abound in material on river crossings. Frequently the toll is exorbitant, an accusation which Strabo brings against the Arab chiefs, adding: [16] "It is hard for men of that tough and lawless type to fix on any duty that is not oppressive to the merchant."

15. TRAVELERS with merchandise or on their way through a country ought to be allowed to stay there for a time, for reasons of health, or any other just cause. For this too is included among the privileges it is harmless to grant. . . . As a consequence, they should be permitted also to put up a temporary shelter, on the shore, for instance, even though we admit that the shore is the possession of the people of the place. . . .

16. NOR should even a permanent dwelling place be refused to foreigners driven from their own homes, who are seeking a refuge. But this should be on condition that they submit to the established government and to whatever other regulations are necessary to prevent tumults. . . . "To drive away strangers," says Strabo,[17] following Eratosthenes, "is to act like barbarians"; and for conduct like that the Spartans were condemned. . . .

17. AND if within a nation's territory there is any empty or barren soil, this should be granted to newcomers who ask for it. Indeed, they may rightfully take possession of it, because uncultivated land should not be considered occupied, except as regards the governing power, which still rests altogether with the original peoples. . . .

18. AFTER the common right to things comes the common right to acts. This right is either granted simply or conditioned on certain suppositions. It is granted simply to perform the acts by which we provide things essential to a comfortable life. In this case, it is not required to show the same necessity as was demanded for taking another's property, because here it is not a question of what may be done against the will of the owner, but of how to obtain things with the owner's consent; and there must be no obstruction in the shape of a law or a combination to prevent it. Any such obstruction is contrary to the nature of society, as regards the things of which I am speaking. It is what Ambrose calls [18] "depriving men of their share in the goods of a common parent, withholding the fruits lavishly spread for all, and destroying our community in living." For we are not here speaking of superfluities and sheer luxuries, but of things which life needs—food, clothing, medicines.

19. SUCH things, we maintain, all men have a right to buy at a fair price, unless the owners themselves have need of them. Thus, in time of extreme scarcity, the sale of grain is forbidden. Yet not even in such a time of necessity may foreigners who have once been admitted to a country be expelled; but as Ambrose says, in the pas-

sage already quoted, the common calamity must be borne by all in common.

20. OWNERS have not the same right to force the sale of their goods; for everyone is at liberty to decide what he wishes to buy. The ancient Belgians, for instance, would not accept wines or other foreign merchandise. . . .

21. WITHIN this common right of which we speak is included, we think, the freedom to propose and contract marriages among neighboring peoples, as when, for example, a group of men has been expelled from one country and come to another. To live without a woman is not always unendurable to a man's nature, but it is unendurable to most men's natures. Celibacy is suited only to persons of superior mentality. Therefore, men should not be deprived of an opportunity to obtain wives. Romulus, in Livy,[19] asks his neighbors, as men, not to object to mingling their blood and race with other men. . . .

The civil laws of some peoples that forbid marriages with foreigners are either based on the reason that, at the time they were enacted, there were no nations without a plentiful supply of women, or else have reference not to every kind of marriage but only to those marriages that are legal, that is, accompanied by certain special features of civil law.

22. A common right based on a supposition has to do with the acts which a nation allows to foreigners indiscriminately. To exclude any one people then from the right to perform these acts is an injury to that people. Thus, wherever foreigners in general are allowed to hunt, fish, catch birds, gather pearls, inherit property by will, sell their wares, or contract marriages when there is no scarcity of women—these same rights cannot be refused to one people alone, except after some grave misconduct. For such a reason the rest of the Jews debarred the tribe of Benjamin from intermarrying with the other tribes.[20] . . .

24. I recall an inquiry whether one nation may lawfully agree with another to sell to it alone certain products which are not pro-

duced anywhere else. The agreement may be made, I think, if the nation which buys is prepared to sell to others at a fair price. For it is a matter of indifference to other nations from whom they buy what meets their natural wants. Nor is there anything unlawful in one people getting a prior advantage over another, particularly when there is a reason for it, as when the nation that has obtained the concession has taken the other under its protection and incurs expense on that account. Such a business arrangement, for the purpose I have mentioned, is not inconsistent with the law of nature, though sometimes in the interest of the community it is prohibited by the laws of the state.

III

Original Acquisition of Property, with Special Reference to Sea and Rivers.

1. BY individual right a thing becomes ours through acquisition, either original or derivative. Long ago, when the human race could meet together, original acquisition might take place through division of goods, as we have said. Now it can take place only through occupancy. . . .

3. TO the other modes of acquiring property Paulus the jurist [1] adds one more, which seems most natural, that is, causing something new to come into the world. But since nothing in nature can be produced except from materials already existing, it follows that

if the materials were ours, our ownership of them is merely continuing under a new shape; if they belonged to no one, our acquisition comes under the head of title by occupancy; if they were another's, the thing we have made does not, naturally, become our sole possession, as will later appear.

4. SINCE primitive times, then, occupancy has been the only natural and original mode of acquisition, and this we must now consider. There are two forms of taking possession of things that belong to no one, namely, assertion of sovereignty and assertion of ownership, in so far as ownership is distinct from sovereignty. Seneca has described the two:[2] "To kings belongs power over everything, to individuals ownership." . . . Sovereignty is habitually exercised over two classes of subject matter. The first is persons, who in some cases form the whole, as when a host of men, women, and children are on a march to a new country; the second is a region, which is called territory. Although sovereignty and ownership are acquired by one act, yet they are quite distinct. So ownership may pass not only to other citizens but also to foreigners, whereas sovereignty remains with him who took it. . . .

5. IN a place over which sovereignty is already established, the right to occupy and take possession of movables may be abolished by the law of the state. For that right was a permission of the law of nature, not a command that could be perpetually enforced. It is not a requirement of human society. . . .

6. WE should note too that if we consider solely the law of nature, the right of ownership is restricted to persons equipped with reason. But the law of nations has in the general interest introduced a rule that infants and demented persons may receive and own property, the human race meanwhile acting, as it were, as their representative. Unquestionably, human laws can add many provisions to natural law, though they can add nothing contrary to it. So this right of ownership, which by consent of the civilized nations has been set up in favor of infants and persons in similar condition, extends only to the first act, as the schools call it, and cannot go

to the second. It includes, that is, only the right to hold the property but not the right by themselves to use it. For alienation and other acts of that kind imply by their very nature the decisions of a will based on reason, something which in persons of this sort cannot exist. . . .

7. IT is possible to occupy a river, even though neither the stream above nor that below is included in the same territory, and it flows straight from the water above to the water below or to the sea. . . .

8. IN the same manner, it would seem that the sea can be occupied by one who holds the shore on both sides, even though it may spread out above into a bay, for instance, or both above and below, as a strait does; provided, however, that this part of the sea is not so large that, when compared with the lands that border it, it seems not to belong to them. And the right allowed to one people or king may also be allowed to two or three, if they wish to occupy together a sea that lies between them. Thus rivers separating two peoples have been occupied by both, and later divided.

9. WE must admit that in the regions known to the Roman Empire from the earliest times down to Justinian, the law of nations forbade any people to take possession of the sea, even so far as to interfere with fishing rights. . . . Ulpian said [3] that by nature the sea is open to all and belongs to all as much as the air. Celsus said [4] that to all men in common belongs the use of the sea. The jurists, moreover, distinguish plainly between the public property of a nation—among which are rivers—and the things common to every man. Thus we read in the *Institutes*:[5] "Some things by natural law are common to everyone; some are public property. . . . By natural law, the following are common to everyone; the air, flowing water, the sea, and in consequence the seashore. All rivers and harbors, however, are public property." . . .

As regards the shores of the sea, Neratius said[6] that they were not public property in the way that things inherited by a people were, but were like the things that were at first gifts of nature and had never yet come under the ownership of anyone, not even of a people. With this dictum Celsus appears to disagree when he writes:[7] "The shores over which the Roman people hold dominion are in my opinion the property of the Roman people, but the use of the sea is the common right of all men." But the two views can, I think, be reconciled, if we say that Neratius was speaking of the shore, in so far as use of it is necessary for sailors or others passing by, and Celsus was thinking of its being appropriated for someone's advantage, as for the purpose of putting up a permanent building. . . .

11. WE must note too that when in any place the law of nations regarding the sea has not been accepted or has been abrogated, from the mere fact that a people has occupied the land we cannot conclude that they have possession also of the sea. Nor is an act of mind enough for that; there must be an outward act, from which others may understand that the sea is occupied. Then, if possession by occupancy is given up, the sea returns to its previous condition, that is, to the common use. . . .

12. THIS is certain, that whoever takes possession of a part of the sea cannot prohibit unarmed and harmless navigation, since on land such travel cannot be prevented, and there it is apt to be less necessary and accompanied by more damage.

13. TO acquire mere sovereignty over a part of the sea, without any proprietary rights, has not been difficult, nor do I think the law of nations, of which we have spoken, forbids it. The Argives once expostulated with the Athenians, because they had permitted the Spartans, the Argives' enemies, to pass through their sea. They accused them of violating a treaty by which it had been agreed that neither nation should allow the enemies of the other to go "through regions under their rule." [8] . . . It appears also that sovereignty over a portion of the sea is acquired in the same way as other sovereignties, that is, through the medium of persons and the medium of territory: through the medium of persons, when, for example, a fleet, that is, a sea-borne army, is stationed at some point in the sea; through the medium of territory, in so far as ships sailing through

the portion of sea close to the land may be controlled from the land as much as if they were actually on land.

14. so it will not be breaking the law of nature or of nations if he who has taken on himself the burden of protecting navigation and safeguarding it by flares at night, and by marks to warn of shoals, imposes a fair tax on seagoers, such as the Roman toll in the Red Sea, which went to meet the expense of the maritime force that defended the sea against pirate raids. . . .

15. INSTANCES may be found of treaties by which one nation binds itself to another not to navigate beyond a certain limit. Thus long ago, it was agreed by the Egyptians and the kings inhabiting the borders of the Indian Ocean that the former should not enter that sea with a ship of war, or with more than one merchant ship. . . . And in the first treaty which the Romans, immediately after the expulsion of their kings, made with the Carthaginians, it was stipulated that neither the Romans nor their allies should sail beyond Cape Bone, except as they were driven thither by storm, or by an enemy's fleet. Whoever was so driven would take nothing from there but the necessaries, and leave within five days. . . .

But these instances do not prove any actual occupancy of the sea, or proprietorship of the right of navigation. Nations as well as individuals may cede by a compact in favor of someone concerned not only a right that is strictly their own but one which they share in common with all men. When this happens, we may say, as Ulpian did on a like occasion, when an estate had been sold with the reservation that there should be no tunny fishing to the prejudice of the seller. Ulpian declared [9] that the sea could not be subjected to a service, but that the good faith of the contract required that the terms of the sale be observed. Hence the new owners and those who succeeded to their rights were bound by the contract.

16. WHEN a river changes its course, disputes frequently arise between neighboring people as to whether the boundaries of government have changed at the same time, and whether any additions made by the river belong to those to whom they have come.

Such disputes must be settled according to the nature and mode of acquisition. Surveyors tell us there are three kinds of land: first, the divided and assigned land, which Florentinus the jurist calls de-limited,[10] because its limits are marked by artificial boundaries. The second is land assigned as a whole, or specified by a measure, by hundred-acre sections, for instance, or acres. The third is land of defense frontiers, so called, Varro tells us, because it has fron-tiers suited for defense against an enemy, that is, natural bounda-ries of rivers or mountains. . . . In the case of the two first kinds of lands, even if a river changes its course, it occasions no change of territory; and if it adds anything by alluvial deposit, that will come under the rule of the present occupants.

In lands with natural frontiers, where any gradual change in the course of the river makes a change also in the territorial boundaries, whatever the river adds to either side comes under the jurisdiction of the side to which it is added, because the two nations are sup-posed originally to have taken possession of those lands with the intention of making that river the line of separation between them. . . .

17. HOWEVER, this rule holds only in cases where the river has not altered its channel. For a river dividing jurisdictions is not con-sidered simply as so much water, but as water flowing in a par-ticular channel, and enclosed within certain banks. For which reason, any addition, decrease, or similar change of particles which leaves the previous appearance of the whole unchanged, allows us to consider the river as still the same. But if the whole face of the river is changed, the case will be altered. For as a river may be en-tirely destroyed by the erection of dams upstream and a new stream may be formed in an excavated ditch into which the water is con-ducted, so when a river deserts its old channel and breaks through into another, it is not the same river as it was before, but a new one, while the old is gone. And, just as if the river had dried up, the middle of the last channel will still continue to be the boundary between jurisdictions, because it must be supposed that the people

intended the river to be a natural line of separation between them; and if the river had ceased to exist, then each side would have kept what it had. So when a river bed changes, the same rule should hold. . . .

18. ALTHOUGH in doubtful cases the jurisdiction of two nations on opposite sides of a river extends, as we said, each to the middle of the channel, yet it may happen, and in some places has happened, that the whole river belongs to the party on one side, because the government on the other shore was set up later, after the river had already been occupied, or else because the matter was so settled by treaty.

19. IT is also worth remarking that things which have once had an owner, but have ceased to have one, are subject to the right of original acquisition. Such are things abandoned or whose owners have disappeared. They have, therefore, returned to the original state of things.

This too we must observe, that sometimes the original acquisition has been made by a people or their head in such a manner as to give to them or him at first not only sovereignty, in which is included the right of eminent domain, described elsewhere, but also full rights of private ownership in general. And this property later was distributed in small grants to individuals, in such a way that their ownership was dependent on the previous ownership. . . . When private ownerships distributed in this way depend on a previous public ownership, if any property loses its particular owner, it does not become the property of him who seizes it, but reverts to the public or to the superior lord. . . .

IV

Presumed Abandonment of Property and Subsequent Occupancy.

1. A serious problem arises here with regard to rights of ownership based on length of use.[1] For time has no effectual power of itself to create a title. Though everything takes place in time, time itself does nothing. These rights, therefore, were created by civil law, and so, in the opinion of Vasquez,[2] they do not hold as between two independent nations or kings, or between an independent nation and a king; or even as between a king and an individual who is not his subject, or between two subjects of different kings or states. This view would appear, indeed, to be correct, except in so far as the things or acts involved are controlled by the laws of the country. But to accept it would lead to great inconvenience, and prevent disputes over kingdoms and boundaries of kingdoms from ever being settled, a condition which would tend to upset many minds, sow the seeds of wars, and affront the common sense of nations.

2. IN Holy Writ,[3] when the king of the Ammonites claimed as his own the land lying between the rivers Arnon and Jabok, from the deserts of Arabia to the Jordan, Jephthah cited in answer his people's possession of the same for three hundred years, and asked why the king and his ancestors had for so long a period left it neglected. And the Spartans, according to Isocrates,[4] laid it down as a fixed rule, accepted by all nations, that a right to public prop-

erty as well as to private might be so firmly established by length of use that it could not be disturbed; on this ground they rejected the claim of those who demanded back Messene. . . . As for Cicero, he says,[5] in the second book of *On Duty*: "What justice is there in depriving a man of a field which he or his family has possessed for many years, or even generations?"

3. WHAT shall we say? A process of law which depends on a man's intentions can never be founded on the mere act of his mind, unless he has disclosed it by some outward sign. For to grant legal efficacy to mere acts of the mind is not practicable for human nature, which can recognize such acts only by their outward signs; hence inward acts alone are not a subject of human laws. . . .

4. A thing cast away is understood by that act to be abandoned, unless the circumstances of the case are such that we must suppose it thrown aside for a moment only, with intention of recovery. . . . The rules of abandonment are derived not from civil law but from the law of nature, which allows every man to let go of his own, and from the natural presumption that a person wishes to do the thing which he has clearly indicated he intends to do. . . .

5. ALSO under the head of acts, taking all proper circumstances into consideration, come, for practical purposes, failures to act. Thus a person who knows of and is present at an act, and keeps silent about it, seems to consent to it . . . unless the circumstances show that he was hindered from speaking by fear or some other mishap.

A thing is counted lost when all expectation of recovering it is given up. Ulpian, for instance, says [6] that pigs carried off by a wolf and goods lost in a shipwreck cease to be ours, not immediately but when we cannot recover them, that is, when there is no reason to suppose that anyone still has any expectation of owning them, and when no indications of such expectation appear. But if persons are sent out to look for the property, or a reward is offered, we have to judge differently about it.

If a person knows his property is in the possession of someone

else, and for a long time asserts no claim to it, he seems, unless
there appears another reason for his conduct, to have acted thus
because he did not care to keep that property among his possessions. Ulpian has said elsewhere,[7] that a house is regarded as abandoned by its owner, if he is too long silent. . . . But for silence to
be taken as valid ground for a presumption that property is abandoned, two things are required: it must be the silence of one who
knows the situation, and who has free choice. For failure to speak
on the part of an ignorant person can have no legal effect; and if
some other reason appears, the presumption of free choice may be
impossible.

6. THERE are various indications that show when these two conditions may be regarded as present; but with both, length of time
is highly important. In the first place, it can scarcely happen that
over a long period of time a piece of property belonging to a man
should not in some way or other come to his attention, since time
provides many occasions for it. . . .

7. AND as time exceeding the memory of man is, for all practical
purposes, infinite, silence for such a length of time is always thought
sufficient to establish a presumption that the property is abandoned, unless the strongest proofs are produced to the contrary.
Able jurists have correctly observed that time beyond the memory
of man is not the same as a century, although often the two are
not very different. For a hundred years is the limit of ordinary human life, a period which in general covers three ages or generations
of men. The Romans made this point in objection to Antiochus,[8]
that he claimed cities which neither he nor his father nor his grandfather had ever possessed.

8. . . . AS for rights of government, we must know that though
they are highly prized, the burden of them is great and failure to
exercise them aright subjects their possessor to the divine wrath.
Even as it would be dangerous for two who call themselves guardians to carry on a lawsuit at the ward's expense to decide which of
them had the right to be guardian, or—to use Plato's illustration—

for sailors at the risk of sinking the ship to fight over which of them would best take the helm, so men are not always to be praised who at heavy cost, with the shedding of innocent blood, are eager to decide by conflict who should be governor of a people. . . .

It is to the interest of human society that governments should be firmly established, beyond the hazard of controversy, and all presumptions that help promote such a state of things should be favorably considered. For if Aratus of Sicyon [9] thought it a hardship that private property possessed for fifty years should be confiscated, how much more should we respect the words of Augustus,[10] that he is a good man and a good citizen who does not wish the existing condition of the state changed, and who, as Alcibiades says in Thucydides,[11] "will maintain the form of government he received." . . .

9. AND probably it may be said with reason that the practice does not rest on presumption only, but on a rule sanctioned by the voluntary law of nations, namely, that possession beyond the memory of man, not interrupted or challenged by an appeal to court, should actually transfer ownership. It is likely that the nations agreed on this rule as most conducive to their common peace. For good reason I said "possession not interrupted," to signify, as Sulpicius says in Livy,[12] "something held by one lasting tenure of a right continuously exercised, without a break." Or, as the same author, in another place, calls it, "a lasting possession, never called in question." For transient possession creates no title. . . .

10. BUT here another and exceedingly difficult question arises, whether, by such abandonment, persons yet unborn may tacitly lose their rights. If we say they cannot, the rule thus defined would add nothing to the tranquillity of empires and estates, for most of them are so arranged that they must pass to descendants. But if we declare these persons can, it then seems strange that silence could prejudice the rights of those who cannot speak, since of

course they are not yet alive; or that the act of one person could work injury to someone else.

To solve this problem, we must realize that a person not yet born has no rights, even as a thing that does not exist has no qualities. Wherefore, if a people on whose will depends the right to rule them changes its will, they do no injustice to persons still unborn, for as yet they possess no rights. And as a people may expressly declare a change of will, so also they may be tacitly supposed to have changed it. If, then, the people changes its will, while the rights of the expected heirs do not yet exist, and the parents, who might give birth to heirs who in their time would own the rights, fail to assert them, there is nothing to prevent their being taken over by someone else, as abandoned.

We are speaking here of the law of nature: for civil law can provide, along with other fictions, that the law shall protect in the interim the persons of beings not yet alive, and so prevent anyone from taking possession of what should be theirs. However, we should not hastily conclude that such is the law's intention, because the advantage in such a case to the individual is seriously detrimental to the public interest. . . .

Nothing prevents the introduction into civil law of a rule to the effect that a thing which cannot lawfully be alienated by a single act may yet, to avoid uncertainty of ownership, be forfeited by neglect over a given time. The rule may still preserve for persons born later the right to bring personal suit against those who were guilty of the neglect, or against their heirs.

11. FROM what we have said it is plain that a king may in this way acquire a right against another king, and an independent nation against another nation, either by express agreement, or through one party's relinquishment of a right and the other's subsequent taking possession of it, or taking more forcible possession. . . . Similarly also, the rightful king of a people may lose his royal power and become subject to the people; and one who was not truly king but only a citizen leader may become king with full

sovereignty; or the sovereignty that was once entirely in the hands of the people or of the king may be divided between them.

12. IT is important then to inquire whether a law providing for ownership through long use or prescription, and enacted by a supreme ruler, applies even to the right of sovereignty itself and to its necessary parts, which we have explained elsewhere.[13] Many of the jurists who discuss questions of sovereignty in terms of Roman civil law seem to think it does apply. We think otherwise. For in order that a man may be bound by a law, the lawmaker must possess both power and intent, at least presumed. Now no man can bind himself by authority of his own law as by authority of a superior; therefore, lawgivers have the right to alter their own laws. Yet a man may be bound by his own law, not directly but by inference, inasmuch as he is a part of the community and natural justice requires that all parts should adjust themselves to the plan for the whole. . . .

However, this principle does not apply here. For we are here considering the lawgiver, not as a part, but as the one in whom the power of the whole body resides. We are considering sovereignty as such. Nor are we to presume that he had any such intent, for lawgivers are not supposed to intend to include themselves under the rule of their laws, except where the subject matter and purport are general, as they are in regulations fixing prices. But sovereignty is not on a level with other things; instead, it far surpasses them in the nobility of its nature. I have seen no civil statute treating of prescription that either does include sovereignty or could be reasonably construed as designed to include it under its rules.

Hence it follows . . . that no civil statute which prohibits the taking over of property in less than a certain time has any bearing on the matter of sovereignty. However, when sovereignty is actually being transferred, the people may express their will as to how and in what length of time sovereignty may be forfeited by nonuse. And their will would undoubtedly have to be obeyed, nor could even a king who had obtained the sovereignty disregard it, because it would have to do not with sovereignty itself but with the mode of holding it. Of this distinction we have spoken elsewhere.[14] . . .

14. FROM this we may see how far to accept some authors' assertions that it is always legitimate for subjects to recover the people's liberty if they can; since a sovereignty won by force can be overthrown by force, and what the people set up by their will they may repent of, and change their will. But sovereignties that were first won by force may acquire legality by the people's tacit acceptance; and the people's will, either at the establishment or at some later event, may confer a right which in future will be independent of that will. . . . However, I think it indisputably true that prolonged inactivity on the part of the king, such as we described above, can be reason enough for a people to reclaim their liberty on the ground of presumed abandonment of sovereignty. . . .

V

Original Acquisition of Rights over
Persons, including Rights of Parents,
of Marriage, of Organizations, and
Rights over Subjects and Slaves.

1. A right may be acquired not only over things but over persons. It has its source in either procreation, consent, or crime. By procreation parents acquire rights over their children—both parents,

in my opinion, father and mother. If their authorities clash, the father's authority comes first because of the superiority of his sex.

2. IN the treatment of children three stages must be recognized. The first is when the child's judgment is immature . . . ; the second is when his judgment is mature, but he is still a part of his parents' family . . . ; the third is when he has left the family. In the first stage, all the child's actions are controlled by his parents, for it is right that one who cannot govern himself should be governed by another. . . .

3. IN the second stage, when his judgment has ripened with age, only those acts are subject to the parental rule that have some importance for the position of the paternal or of the maternal family. For it is right that the part should adjust itself to the plan of the whole. . . .

4. IN both these stages, the right to govern comprises also the right to coerce, in so far as children must either be compelled to do their duty or be corrected. Later we shall have occasion to decide what to think of the severer forms of punishment.

5. ALTHOUGH paternal authority is so closely attached to the special person and position of the father that it cannot be withdrawn and transferred to someone else, still, by the law of nature, wherever the civil law does not forbid it, a father may pledge his son as security, and even, if necessary, sell him, when there is no other way of having him supported. . . . Nature herself, it is thought, confers the right to do whatever must be done to obtain what she demands.

6. IN the third stage, the son is independent in every particular and a law to himself, though there always remains a duty of filial devotion and respect, the ground of which does not change. So the acts of a king cannot be declared void on the pretext that he has parents.

7. WHATEVER power a parent has beyond this is derived from statute law, which differs in different places. . . . Among Roman citizens, a father had special power, even over sons who were heads

of families of their own, as long as they had not been declared emancipated. . . .

8. RIGHTS over persons, based on consent, come either from association or from subjection. The most natural association is manifestly marriage, but because of the difference in sex the authority is not mutual; the husband is the head of the wife, at least in matters concerned with the marriage and with the family. For the wife becomes part of her husband's family, and so the right to decide questions affecting the domicile belongs to the husband. Whatever further rights are granted to the husband—by Hebrew law, the right to nullify his wife's vows, and, among other nations, the right to sell his wife's property—are not founded on nature but on instituted law.

At this point we must examine the nature of marriage. Marriage, by the law of nature, we understand to be a type of cohabitation of a man with a woman that places the woman under the eye, as it were, and guardianship of the man. Such an association we see even among some dumb animals. But in the case of man, since he is an animate being gifted with reason, an additional tie is created through the pledge by which the woman binds herself to the man. . . .

[9–16. Lawfulness of divorce. Conditions necessary for a valid marriage.]

17. BESIDE this most natural association of marriage, there are others, both private and public. The latter are either within a people or between peoples. They all have this trait in common, that when dealing with matters for which the association was formed, the whole body, or a majority, acting in the name of the whole, may bind every individual in the association. Generally speaking, we must believe that the founders of the association intended there should be some way of transacting business, and obviously it would be unfair to have a majority obey a minority. So naturally, leaving out of account compacts and laws that prescribe forms for conducting business, the majority does possess the rights of the whole. . . .

18. IF the voices are equal, no action is to be taken, because there is not sufficient impulse to warrant a change. Likewise, when votes are equal, a man accused is pronounced acquitted. . . . In the same case, the possessor of a property keeps it. . . .

20. WE must add this, too, that if any members of the association are prevented by absence or some other reason from exercising their right, it accrues in the interim to those present. . . .

21. THE natural order among the members is the order in which each man joined the association. So, among brothers, the same order is prescribed; the first-born takes precedence over the rest, and so on down, disregarding all other qualifications. . . . In ancient times, within the association of Christian kings and peoples, the custom prevailed that those who had first professed Christianity should take precedence in the councils that dealt with Christian affairs.

22. HOWEVER, this too must be said, that whenever an association has as its basis something in which the members do not share equally, such as an inheritance or an estate, where one owns a half, another a third, another a quarter, not only should the order follow the amount of the shares owned by each member, but their votes should count in the same proportion, *pro rata*, as they say. This practice accords with natural justice and was sanctioned by Roman law. . . .

23. AN association in which numerous fathers of families unite to form one nation and one state gives to a body the most far-reaching rights over its members, for this is the most perfect association. There is no outward act of a man that may not bear some relation to such an association, either in itself or through the accompanying circumstances. . . .

24. THE question is often raised whether citizens may withdraw from their state without permission. We know there are nations, like the Muscovites, where such a thing is not allowed; and we admit a civil society may be formed on those terms, and the custom acquire the force of an agreement. By Roman laws—at least the

later ones—a man was allowed to change his domicile; yet none the less, after he had changed, he was subject to the taxes of the town he had left. But those to whom this rule applied were remaining within the borders of the Roman Empire, and the rule aimed chiefly at providing for the payment of taxes.

But we are asking what would naturally be the practice, if no other rule were adopted, and if it were not a matter of leaving one district but the state altogether, or the confines of a wide empire. It is certainly clear from the exigencies of the situation—which in practical affairs constitute law—that citizens could not withdraw in large bodies; for if they were allowed to do so, the civil society could not last. The case of individuals withdrawing is a different matter, as it is one thing to dip up water from a river and another to channel it into a new bed. . . .

However, the rule of natural justice, which the Romans followed in suppressing private associations, should be observed here too, namely, that a thing should not be permitted which is hurtful to the interests of society. . . . It is to a civil society's interest that a citizen should not quit his country when it has contracted a heavy debt, unless he is prepared to pay his share immediately; nor, again, when it has gone to war, trusting in its numbers, particularly if it is threatened with siege, unless he is prepared to furnish an equally competent substitute to defend the community. Outside these exceptions, we believe that nations do agree to the free departure of citizens, because from that freedom they may reap an equal advantage in arrivals from other countries. . . .

25. . . . AN association of several peoples, either of themselves or through their heads, is an alliance. Of its nature and effects there will be a place to speak when we come to obligations arising from compacts.

26. SUBJECTION by consent is either private or public. Private subjection by consent is of many kinds, as the kinds of lordship are many. The noblest kind is adoption, by which a person gives himself to the family of someone else, so that he becomes subject to

him in the way that a son of mature years is subject to his father. . . .

27. THE basest form of private subjection is that by which a man gives himself into complete slavery, as those Germans did who staked their liberty on the last throw of the dice. "The man who was beaten went of his own accord into slavery," says Tacitus.[1] . . . Slavery is complete when a man owes lifelong labor in return for food and the other necessaries of life. If the situation is accepted as such, within natural limits, it contains nothing that in itself is intolerably bitter. For in compensation for the perpetual servitude is the perpetual assurance of maintenance, which often those who work for daily hire do not have. . . .

28. MASTERS do not have rights of life and death over their slaves (I am speaking now of perfect, inherent justice); nor can any man lawfully kill another man, unless he has committed a capital offense. But by the laws of some nations a master who for any reason has killed a slave goes unpunished, as kings do everywhere who have unlimited power. . . .

29. WITH regard to the children of slaves, the problem is difficult. By Roman law and the law of nations for captives, as we shall see later, the offspring of persons in servile condition, like that of animals, follows the mother. Yet this rule does not well accord with the law of nature, in cases where the father can be known with sufficient certainty. For among dumb beasts, fathers no less than mothers tend their progeny and show thereby that it is the common progeny of them both. So then, if the law of the state makes no provision for the case, a child should follow its father as much as its mother.

But let us suppose, to make the difficulty less, that both parents are slaves and see whether their child would by nature be in a state of slavery. Certainly, if there is no other way of raising the child, the parents may sentence their future offspring to slavery along with themselves, seeing that for a similar reason they may even sell their children who were born free. But this right by nature is based on sheer necessity and without that necessity parents have no right to enslave their children to anyone. Hence the rights of masters over slave children in such cases are derived from their providing them with food and other necessaries of life. And as these children must be fed for a long time before their work can be of use to a master, and as their subsequent labors only compensate for their support during their later lives, such children cannot lawfully escape from slavery without paying an amount sufficient to cover the cost of their maintenance.

Indubitably, however, if a master is monstrously cruel, the general judgment is that his slaves, even those who voluntarily submitted to servitude, may save themselves by flight. For the commands of the Apostle [2] and of the ancient canons to slaves, not to leave their masters, are general, intended to oppose the errors of those who denounced every kind of subjection, private as well as public, as inconsistent with Christian liberty.

30. BESIDES the complete slavery of which we have just spoken, there are varieties of incomplete servitude, like one that is temporary, or conditional, or for certain objects. Such is the state of freedmen, of persons in the position of children, of debtor bondsmen, of men under sentence or bound to the soil, . . . and, lastly, of mercenaries. The grades of status depend either on laws or on contracts. Incomplete slavery is apparently by the law of nature the condition of one who has one free and one slave parent, for the reason we gave above.

31. IT is public subjection when a people surrenders itself to a man or to several men or to another people. . . .

32. SUBJECTION as penalty for crime occurs even without the criminal's consent, when a man who deserves to lose his liberty is brought by force under the power of one whose right it is to inflict punishment. To whom that right belongs we shall see further on. In this way individuals may be reduced to private subjection . . . and peoples to public subjection for a public crime. The difference here is that a people's servitude is by its nature a lasting one, be-

cause the passing away of its members does not keep the people from remaining the same. But penal servitude for individuals does not go beyond their own persons, because their crime is on their heads alone. Both kinds of penal servitude, private as well as public, may be either complete or incomplete, depending on the guilt and the penalty assigned. . . .

VI

Derivative Acquisition of Property by Act of Man. Alienation of Sovereignty and of the Properties of Sovereignty.

1. A thing becomes ours by derivative acquisition, through an act of man or of law. Since the introduction of private ownership, it has been a principle of the law of nature that owners of property can transfer their ownership, either as a whole or in part; for this power is inherent in the nature of ownership, that is, of full ownership. . . . Two requirements, however, must be observed, one by the donor, the other by the receiver. For the donor a mere inward act of will is not enough, but along with that there must be either words or some other outward sign, for an inward act is not adequate in human society. . . . So, in some places, we see it is the custom to require a declaration of gift before the people or before

a magistrate, and an entry of it in the records. These are all certainly requirements of the civil law. There must be an act of will expressed by a sign and understood to be an act of rational will.

2. NEXT, there is required of the receiver by natural law, without counting the civil law, a will to receive, expressed by its own sign. This willingness ordinarily follows on the giving, but it may precede it, as when, for instance, a man asks to have a thing given or granted to him. His will is then supposed to stay the same, unless a change becomes apparent. What further requirements there are for the bestowal and acceptance of a right, and how they both may take place, we shall describe below in the chapter on promises. . . .

3. LIKE other things, so sovereignty may be alienated by the legitimate owner, that is, as we explained above,[1] by the king, if he holds it as a property; otherwise, by the people with the king's consent. For as a receiver of the usufruct, he too has some rights, which should not be taken from him against his will. These are the rules of sovereignty as a whole.

4. FOR the alienation of a section of the people something more is required, namely, the consent of the section whose alienation is being considered. For the founders of a state combine to form a perpetual and imperishable society through a union of parts, called integral. Hence it follows that these parts are not so far subject to their body as are the parts of a natural body, which cannot live without the body's life, and therefore, to help the body, may rightfully be cut off. The body of which we are speaking is of another kind, created by an act of will. Consequently its rights over its parts must be measured by the original intention, which we can never believe was to grant the body the right to cut off its parts from itself and give them into the power of another.

5. SO, on the other hand, a part has no right to withdraw from the body, unless it is plainly impossible for it to save itself otherwise. For, as we said above, to all laws of human institution supreme necessity may make an exception and bring the case under the simple law of nature. In the eighteenth book of the *City of*

God, Augustine says,[2] "In almost all nations this word of nature has in some way been heard, that men may choose to submit to conquerors instead of being destroyed in the manifold devastation of war." . . .

6. IT is clear, then, why in this respect the right of a part to preserve itself is greater than the right of the body over the part. For the part is exercising a right which it had before the association was established, but not so the body. . . .

7. BUT I see nothing to prevent an independent people, or even a king with the consent of his people, from alienating their sovereignty over a tract of land, that is, over a part of their territory—for instance, an uninhabited or desert tract. A section of the people, because they have freedom of choice, have also the right of refusal. The tract, however, both the whole and its parts, is the common, undivided property of the people and therefore subject to the people's will. . . .

[8–10. Limitations on a king's right to alienate his inferior powers, or to infeudate or pawn territory.]

11. KINGS may not alienate, either wholly or in part, the public domain, the fruits of which are meant to support the burdens of the state or of the royal dignity. For over this they possess no right greater than that of usufruct. Nor do I allow an exception when the property is of little value, for I have no right to alienate even a tiny part of something that is not mine. However, in small matters more readily than in large the people may be presumed to give consent, if they are informed and keep silent. . . . And the domain was established for the sake of the state. . . .

[12–13. King's right to pledge public domain.]

14. WHILE discussing alienation, we should realize that wills too are included under this head. Though a will, like other transactions, may be given a special form by the law of the state, in essential substance it relates to ownership, and, that being so, comes under the law of nature. By it I can alienate my property not only absolutely but conditionally; not only irrevocably but with

power to revoke; keeping it meantime in my possession, with full right to enjoy it. For a will is an alienation in event of death, until then revocable, and preserving in the interim my right to possess and enjoy. . . .

The fact that the right to make a will is not everywhere granted to foreigners is not due to the law of nations but to the particular law of a state. The habit, if I mistake not, dates from a time when foreigners were considered almost as enemies. So among the more civilized nations it has deservedly died out.

VII

Derivative Acquisition of Property by Act of Law. Intestate Succession.

1. DERIVATIVE acquisition, or alienation, through an act of law, is based on either the law of nature, or the voluntary law of nations, or civil law. Of civil law we are not speaking, for there would be no end to it, and the principal controversies of a war are not settled by civil laws. We may note only that some civil laws are palpably unjust, such as those that consign the goods of shipwrecked persons to the public treasury. To deprive a man of his own property for no reasonable cause is sheer injustice. . . .

2. BY the law of nature, based on the essential character and power of ownership, alienation of property may take place in two ways, through legal compensation and through succession. It takes

place through legal compensation, when, from a person who holds
something of mine or owes me something, I accept, when I cannot
obtain what is mine, something else of equal value, not yet mine
but due me in place of the thing that was mine or was owed me.
For when expletive justice cannot procure the same thing, it takes
something of equal value, which, practically estimated, is the same.
The fact that ownership is transferred in this way is proved by the
results, which in practical matters are the best proof. . . .

We know civil laws forbid us to take the law into our own hands,
so much so that if a man seizes by force what is owed him, it is
called violence, and in many places one who does such a thing loses
his rights as creditor. Indeed, even if the civil law did not explicitly
forbid it, the institution of courts would show it was not permitted.
It is allowable, as we said, where there have never been courts.
How this may happen we have explained above.[1] And where the
absence of courts is only temporary, it will still be lawful to seize
your property, if, for instance, you cannot recover your own in any
other way and your debtor perhaps has absconded. The verdict as
to ownership, however, should wait for a judge, as is usually done
in cases of reprisal, a subject of which we shall have occasion to
speak later. But if your claim is sound, and it is at the same time
practically certain that you cannot get a judge to enforce it, because, perhaps, your proofs are insufficient, under these circumstances the correct opinion is that the law of the courts does not
hold and you are back with your primitive rights.

3. WHAT is called intestate succession to ownership of a given
property has its natural origin, apart from any civil legislation, in
inference as to the will of the previous owner. For the power of
ownership was such that he could at will have transferred it to another in the event of his own death, while he still retained possession
of it, as we said above. And, if a man has given no indication of
his will and yet it is incredible that he intended that after his death
his goods should go to whoever grabbed them, it follows that

they should be understood to belong to the person to whom the deceased most probably wished them to go. . . .

In case of doubt, the presumption is that he wished what was most fair and honorable. Under this head, the first question is, what were his obligations; the next, what, though not an obligation, would be his duty.

4. JURISTS argue as to whether parents are under obligation to support their children. Some think it naturally reasonable that they should support their children, but not obligatory.

We hold that a clear distinction should be drawn between the two meanings of the word 'obligation.' At times, it is used narrowly to mean a duty imposed on us by expletive law; at other times, more broadly, to mean what cannot be left undone without dishonor, though in the latter case the dishonor comes not from expletive justice but from elsewhere. Here we are speaking of obligation in the broader sense, unless some human law adds to its force. So I accept Valerius' dictum: [2] "Our parents by bringing us up have imposed on us a duty to bring up their grandchildren." . . . "Who gives a form gives what is necessary for that form," was a saying of Aristotle. Hence, he who is the cause of another human being's existence should, as far as in him lies and as far as needful, provide it with what is necessary for a human life, that is, for the natural, social life for which man is born.

For this reason, that is, natural instinct, other animals too furnish their young with whatever food they need. . . . Accordingly, the ancient jurists class the bringing up of children under natural law, the law, that is, that the instinct of nature teaches other animals and our reason enjoins on us. As Justinian says,[3] "A natural impulse, that is, affection, prompts parents to bring up their children." . . .

By the Roman law, no property should be left to children born of illegal union, even as the law of Solon declared it unnecessary to leave anything to bastards. But the canons of the Christian religion have mitigated this severity, stating that an amount necessary for support may rightfully be left to children of every rank, and should be left, if they need it. . . .

Not only our descendants of the first generation but also of the second should be provided for, if need be, and beyond that. . . . Provision also should be extended to our descendants in the female line, if otherwise they cannot be supported.

5. TO our parents too we owe support, a duty laid on us not only by law but by the common maxim of 'returning cherishing for cherishing.' . . . Yet this practice is not so widespread as that of supporting children, of which we have just spoken. For children are born bringing nothing with them to live on. In addition, they have longer to live than our parents. So we owe honor and obedience to our parents, not to our children, but owe support to our children more than to our parents. . . .

Hence it is that even without the direction of civil law, the first right of succession to property falls to the children. For their parents are supposed to have wished to provide plentifully for them, the issue of their own bodies, not merely the essentials but the things that help make living more pleasant and honorable, particularly after they themselves can enjoy their possessions no longer. . . .

6. BECAUSE it is generally the rule that the father and mother provide for their children, so, as long as they are living, the grandfathers and grandmothers are not bound to give them support. But when the parents or one of them dies, it is right that the grandfather and grandmother assume the care of their grandsons and granddaughters in place of their own dead son or daughter; and the same rule extends to relatives still further removed. This is the origin of the law that the grandson may succeed in place of the son. . . .

7. WHAT we said earlier as to inference of intention holds unless there is evidence of an intention to the contrary. Evidence of this kind is, first of all, disowning, which was practiced by the Greeks; second, disinheritance, which was the Roman method. Nonetheless, a son who has not deserved death for his sins should be allowed his support, for the reason stated above.

8. HOWEVER, an exception must be admitted to the rule in case
it is not entirely certain who is the child's father. True, there can
be no certain knowledge of the facts. Acts that take place in the
sight of men have certainty of a kind established by witnesses. In
this sense there is said to be certainty as to the mother, because persons are to be found, men or women, who were present at the birth
and rearing of the child. But for the father no such degree of certainty can be obtained, as Homer suggests, when he says: [4]

"No man was ever sure of his own descent." . . .

Thus some method had to be discovered of establishing with
probability who was the father of each child. That method was
marriage, understood in natural terms as an association in which a
woman is put under the guardianship of a man. But if paternity is
ascertained in some other way, or the father accepts it as established, the child in that case naturally succeeds as fully as any other.
Why not, when even an acknowledged foreigner, if accepted as a
son, or adopted, as they say, succeeds on the assumption that his
adoptive parent wished it? . . .

On the other hand, it may happen, either because the law requires it or through an agreement, that some children born in wedlock receive merely their support or at least are excluded from the
principal inheritance. . . . A marriage on these terms is called
morganatic. . . .

9. WHEN there are no children to whom the succession falls naturally, the case is less simple, and on no subject are the laws more
at variance. All these variations, however, may be traced back
chiefly to two different points of view. In one, nearness of relationship is the chief consideration; in the other, a desire to return the
property to those from whom it came. 'Father's goods to father's
people,' as the saying is; 'mother's to mother's.'

We should certainly distinguish between paternal or ancestral
estates—as in the rule that bars a spendthrift from access to them
—and property recently acquired. . . . So Plato says [5] that a pa-

ternal estate should be preserved for the family from which it came. But I should not wish this principle accepted so completely as to make it seem that by the law of nature paternal or ancestral estates should never be disposed of by will. Oftentimes the poverty of a friend makes it not only commendable but necessary to do so. But the principle shows what, in a doubtful situation, may be believed to have been the wish of an intestate deceased. For we assume that he whose wishes we are debating had full ownership over his goods. . . .

. . . If neither the person from whom the property came directly nor any children of his are to be found, then it should be returned to those to whom it is due less immediately but next after the deceased, that is, to a parent of the preceding generation and to his children, especially as in this way it remains among the near relatives both of the one whose estate it was and of the one from whom it last came. . . .

10. IN the case of newly acquired property, what Plato calls [6] "the extras besides the estate," since the duty of returning a benefit no longer exists, the succession may rightly go to the person supposed to be dearest to the deceased; that is, the person nearest in degree of relationship to the deceased. . . . And what we have said of property newly acquired—that naturally it passes to the next of kin—will apply to paternal and inherited estates also, when neither the persons from whom they came nor any children of theirs are living, so that there is no opportunity to return the gift.

11. WHAT we have just said is in close accord with our natural assumptions, but is not an inevitable rule by natural law. So, since a variety of causes move the human will, there is much variation in pacts, laws, and customs. . . . There are countries where the firstborn receive more than the younger children, as among the Jews; there are countries where all children are treated equally. There are countries where only paternal relatives are counted. There are countries where all blood relatives receive as much as paternal relatives. In some places sex matters; in others not. . . .

But this is the rule to follow. Whenever there is no clear expression of will, we are to suppose that for the succession to his property the man accepted the rule laid down by the law or the custom of his people. . . .

12. BUT in the matter of succession to kingdoms, a distinction must be drawn between kingdoms held by absolute right, or as a patrimonial inheritance, and those whose mode of tenure depends on popular consent. Of this distinction we spoke above.[7]

Kingdoms of the first class may be divided between male and female children, as we see was done in the past in Egypt and Britain. . . . Tacitus says [8] of the British: "For they make no distinction of sex in their government." . . .

13. IF there is a rule that the kingdom is not to be divided but no direction as to whom it should go, then whichever child is eldest, male or female, should have it. . . .

14. KINGDOMS that have been made hereditary by free consent of the people are handed down in accordance with the presumed will of the people; and it is presumed that the people want what is most expedient. From this presumption we derive this first principle of succession, namely, that where neither law nor custom orders otherwise, . . . the kingdom is indivisible, since unity conduces most to preservation of the kingdom and peace among its citizens. . . .

15. THE second principle is that the succession continues with the descendants of the first king. His family is supposed to have been chosen for its nobility, and if it becomes extinct, the royal authority reverts to the people. . . .

16. THE third principle is that only those children succeed who by the laws of the country are legitimate. Illegitimate children are excluded, not only because they are open to scorn, since their father did not consider their mother worthy to be married legally, but also because their descent is less certain, and it is important in monarchies that the people should be as certain as possible, in order to prevent disputes. . . .

17. THE fourth principle is that as between those who might be admitted equally to the inheritance, either because they are of the same degree of relationship, or because they have succeeded to their parents' degree, the males should be preferred to the females, for the reason that males are considered more suited than females both for war and for other functions of government.

18. THE fifth principle is that as between male heirs—or between female, if there are no males—preference should be given to the eldest, because he is supposedly either already more mature in judgment or will be the first to become so. . . . But because this advantage of age is only temporary and that of sex is permanent, a priority of sex counts over that of age. . . . So in Xenophon,[9] Cyaxares says that Media should go to his daughter, "because I have no legitimate male child." . . . Whence it may be understood that although in some degree children take the places of their dead parents, it must still be clear that as compared with others they are competent, and that among those competent the priority first of sex and then of age is maintained. . . .

19. . . . THE reason is that the people presumably wish the kingship to be handed down by the best system possible. . . . They desire that there should be certainty and respect created by the heir's blood, and also that his birth and training should warrant expectation of unusual nobility, and that as possessor of the kingdom he should spend more pains on it and defend it more stubbornly, since he will leave it to those for whom he cares most, because of favors received or out of pure affection. . . .

[20–37. Detailed discussion of other problems of royal lineal succession.]

VIII

Acquisitions under What Is Commonly Called the Law of Nations.

1. THE order of our discussion has brought us to acquisitions under the law of nations, what we called above the voluntary law of nations. Such is acquisition by right of war; but of that matter we shall speak more properly below, when we describe the effects of war.

The Roman jurists, when they discuss the acquisition of ownership over things, list a number of methods of acquiring it, which they call acquisition by the law of nations. But if one looks closely into these methods, he will find that none of them, except rights of war, come under that law of nations which we are studying; but that they are all parts of the law of nature, not indeed of the original law, but of the law that followed on the introduction of private property and preceded all civil law. Or else they are parts of the civil law of Rome and of many nearby nations. . . .

But this is not the law of nations properly so called, for it has nothing to do with the mutual relationship of nations with one another but with the well-being of single peoples. Accordingly, it can be changed by a single people without consulting the rest; it may even happen that at different places and times a very different common custom, and hence law of nations—improperly so called—may be set up, a thing which we see actually occurred when the Germanic nations overran almost all Europe. For as anciently the laws of Greece were everywhere accepted, so later were the Germanic institutions, and they are still in force.

The first method, then, of acquiring property, which the Romans call part of the law of nations, is occupancy of things which belong to no one else. But this method is indubitably a part of natural law in the sense I have said.[1] . . .

2. UNDER this heading they put, first, the capture of wild beasts, birds, and fishes. But for how long a time these all may be said to be no one's property is a question. The younger Nerva says [2] that the fish in a fishpond are our property but not those in a lake. So too are the beasts that are shut into a park, but not those that run loose in fenced woods. Yet fish are no less enclosed in a private lake than they are in a fishpond, and beasts are no less under restraint in closely fenced woods than in the parks which the Greeks call 'animal farms.' The only difference is that in one place the confinement is stricter, in the other more loose. So in our time, more correctly, a different opinion has prevailed, and both animals in private forests and fish in lakes are understood to be property, possessed and held in ownership.

3. WHENEVER the animals recover their natural liberty, they cease to be ours, the Roman jurists say. But in every other case the right of ownership that begins with possession is not lost as soon as possession is lost; rather it gives us the right to regain possession. . . . So it is truer to say that our right of ownership is not lost because the animals have escaped from our hands, but because it is a likely assumption that we have renounced it on account of the difficulty of pursuing them; especially as it is impossible to tell what were ours from the others. But this assumption may be invalidated by other assumptions, as when an animal is marked by identity signs or bells, like those we know deer and hawks wear, by which they may be recognized and returned to their owners.

Some kind of bodily possession of a creature is required to obtain ownership. Hence it is not enough to have wounded it. . . .

4. BUT possession may be acquired not only through hands but

by means of tools, such as traps, nets, and snares, provided two conditions are met. First, the tools must be under our control; and, next, the animal must be caught so that it cannot get away. On this principle may be decided the question of a boar fallen into a snare.

5. THESE rules then will apply if no state law interferes. . . .

6. AS wild animals are acquired, so also are other ownerless things, that is, things without a master. For they too, if we follow only natural law, belong to the man who finds and takes possession of them. . . .

7. AMONG unowned things are treasure trove, that is, money whose owner is unknown. And a thing that is unknown is for the time being as if it did not exist. Accordingly, the treasure becomes naturally the property of the finder, that is, of the one who took it out of its hiding place and kept it. There is nothing however to prevent a law or a custom from establishing a different rule. . . . Christ's parable, contained in Matthew XIII, seems to show that among the Jews the practice was to turn the treasure over to the owner of the land. . . . The German peoples assigned treasure trove, like other ownerless things, to their prince. This is now the common rule and a kind of law of nations, for it is observed in Germany, France, England, Spain, and Denmark. Why it cannot be criticized as unjust we have already explained.

8. LET us come now to the matter of lands created by rivers, on which there are many pronouncements by the ancient jurists and whole commentaries by the modern. Their conclusions on the subject are for the most part drawn from the practice of particular nations, not at all from natural law, although they often defend them in the name of that law. Most of their statements are based on the principle that the banks of rivers belong to the owners of the adjacent estates, and the river beds too, whenever they are left bare by the river; therefore, so do the islands that form in the river. . . . All these rules, I admit, may have been established by a law and been justified as useful for protecting the shores, but that they

are laws of nature, as the jurists seem to think, I certainly refuse
to grant.

9. FOR, if we look to see what is usually the case, we find that the
people were the first occupiers of the land, both as rulers and as
owners, before the fields were divided among individuals. . . .
Hence what was originally occupied by the people and was not
later distributed must be regarded as still the property of the people; and even as an island formed in a privately owned river, or its
dried bed, belongs to individuals, so in the case of a public river
they both belong to the people, or to the one to whom the people
gave them.

What we have said of the bed must be held true too of the bank,
which is the outer edge of the bed, that is, of the place where the
river naturally flows. And we see that this is now the common custom. In Holland and the neighboring regions, where in ancient
times there were numerous disputes on the subject because of the
lowness of the land, the great size of the rivers and the nearness of
the sea—which in its changing tides takes up the mud from one
place and carries it to another—it has always been decided that the
islands that were really islands were a part of the public domain.
So too are all the deserted beds of the Rhine and the Meuse, as the
courts have often declared, basing their opinion on the soundest
reasoning. . . .

[10. Flooded land is considered abandoned, if left long neglected
and undrained.]

11. AS for alluvial deposits, that is, the creation of soil, particle
by particle, these can be claimed by no one, because the place from
which they come is unknown; otherwise, by natural law they would
not change owners. Certainly then they must belong to the people,
if the people own the river, as in case of doubt they must be supposed to do. Otherwise they belong to the first occupier.

12. BUT the people may grant to others the right to such lands,
and so may bestow it on the owners of adjacent estates, as in fact
they seem to have done when the fields have no other boundary on

that side but the natural one, that is, the river itself. . . . Some centuries ago in Holland, the judges decided in this way with regard to fields lying on the Meuse and the Issel, because in the deeds and tax registers they had always been described as reaching to the river. . . .

14. BUT, as we have said, the law for an island is one thing and for an alluvial deposit another. So frequently a dispute arises as to which name to apply to a piece of ground rising above the water but connected with the nearest land only by an intervening stretch under water, a thing which, because of the unevenness of the soil, we often see in our country. As to this, customs vary. In Gelderland, if the piece of ground can be reached with a loaded wagon, it goes, with right of occupancy, to the nearest estate. In the district of Putten, it so goes if a man on foot with a drawn sword can walk out to it. If, however, men usually cross over to it by boat, it is quite naturally considered something separate. . . .

[15–17. Rights of feudal vassals over alluvial deposits.]

18. ANOTHER method of acquiring ownership, among those that are called a part of the law of nations, is animal breeding. But the rule established on this subject by the Romans and some other nations, that the offspring follows the mother, is not natural law, as we said above, except where, as often happens, the sire is unknown. But if on probable grounds he has been identified, no reason can be given why the offspring should not in part belong to him. For certainly a part of whatever is born is the father's. . . . This was the rule followed in the old laws of the Franks and the Lombards.

19. IF a man makes something out of material belonging to another, the school of Sabinus calls it the property of the owner of the material; Proculus of the one who made it, because through him a thing previously non-existent came into being. Later, a midway position was taken, that if the material could be restored to its original form, the object belonged to the owner of the material; if it could not be restored, it belonged to the maker. Connan, how-

ever, disagrees with this view and thinks the one point to be considered is which is worth the more, the work or the material, since that which is worth more would draw to it by its superior value what is worth less. . . .

Let us look for the truth of nature. When the materials are mixed, a common ownership is created in proportion to what each man contributes, as the Roman jurists also agreed, because by nature there could be no other solution. Then since objects are made of matter and form, as though of parts, if the material comes from one man and the form from another, it follows naturally that the object is common property in proportion to the worth of each part of it. . . .

21. THAT what is of less value should be absorbed by what is of more—which is the principle by which Connan goes—is natural practice but not law. For the owner of one twentieth of an estate is as much an owner as the man who has nineteen twentieths. So whatever the Roman law provides in certain cases, or what may be provided in others, regarding acquisition of ownership through possession of superior values, is not natural law but a civil enactment for the purpose of expediting business transactions. Yet the law of nature is not against it, because civil law has the right to confer ownership. . . .

22. LIKEWISE it is an established rule that whatever is planted and sown goes with the soil, for the reason that it is nourished by the soil. Hence a distinction may be drawn with regard to a tree, whether it has put out roots. However, the nourishment which a thing already in existence receives is only a part of it; thus even though the owner of the soil acquires a certain right over a seed, a plant, or a tree by nourishing it, the right of its owner by nature is not for that reason entirely lost. So here too there is common ownership. No less is this the rule for a building, of which the ground and the structure are parts. If the building is movable, the owner of the ground has no right over it. . . .

[23–24. In a case where the possessor is not owner, he has no right to all the income.]

25. THE last way of acquiring property by what is called the law of nations is through delivery. However, as we said above, actual delivery is not required by nature for a transfer of ownership. The jurists too in certain cases recognize this truth—as when, for example, a thing is given away but the use of it retained, or the right to it is conferred on one who already has it, or one who has borrowed it keeps it for his own; or when things are thrown out for distributing. In some cases, ownership passes well before possession is obtained, as with bequests and legacies, gifts to churches and holy places, or to cities, or for the support of the poor; or with property on which a general partnership has been founded.

26. THUS far we have carried our observations, so that he who finds the phrase 'law of nations' in the authorities on Roman law may not at once take it as a law that cannot be altered, but may carefully distinguish the precepts of nature from those that are natural under certain conditions, and the laws common to many peoples, regarded separately, from those that compose the chain that binds human society together.

This too must be understood, that if by the law of nations, improperly so called, or by the law of any one people, a mode of acquiring property is established without discrimination as between citizen and foreigner, a right is thereby immediately created for all foreigners. And any obstruction to their enjoyment of that right is an injury sufficient to furnish a lawful excuse for war.

IX

When Rights of Sovereignty or of Ownership Come to an End.

1. WE have said enough of the manner in which rights to private property as well as to sovereign power are originally acquired and transferred; let us see how they are terminated. We have shown already that they are lost by abandonment; for ownership lasts no longer than the will to ownership. Another way in which these rights may be lost is by the disappearance of the person in whom the sovereignty or the ownership resides without his making any transfer of them, express or tacit, as in cases of succession to an intestate. So if anyone dies without any declaration of his will, and leaves no blood relative, all the rights which he had become extinct. His slaves, unless some human law forbids, thereupon become free, and the people who were his subjects become their own masters, because such things are not by their nature liable to possession by occupancy, unless of their own accord they surrender their liberty. Other property goes to the one who takes it over.

2. THE same rule applies when a family that owned some right becomes extinct.

3. THE same applies also to a nation. Isocrates, and after him the emperor Julian, said that states were immortal, or could be so. For a nation is one of that kind of bodies which are formed of separate particles but included under one name, because, as Plutarch says,[1] it possesses one character, or, in the language of Paulus the jurist,[2] one spirit. Now the spirit or character in a nation is its full and perfect union in civil life, the first product of which is sovereign

power, the bond that binds the state together, and, as Seneca says,[3] the vital breath which many thousands draw.

These artificial bodies bear an obvious resemblance to a natural body, which, though its particles change, little by little, does not cease to be the same so long as its form remains unaltered. . . . So Aristotle, in comparing nations to rivers, said[4] that rivers are called by the same name, though one water is always arriving and another flowing on. Nor is it the name alone which continues, but that character which Conon calls 'the constitutional order of the body,' Philo 'the soul that holds it together,' and the Latins 'the spirit.' Thus a people, as Alfenus and Plutarch maintain, in speaking of the tardiness of Divine Vengeance, is thought of as the same now as it was a hundred years ago, though not one of its members then is now alive, "as long as the common spirit which makes a nation and binds it together in mutual bonds preserves its unity." . . . Hence arose the custom, when addressing a people of the present day, of ascribing to them what happened to the same people many ages before; as we see done both in secular histories and in the books of Holy Writ. . . .

But though a change of members cannot cause a nation to cease being what it has been even for a thousand years or more, neither can it be denied that a nation may perish. This may come about in two ways, either by bodily destruction or by the extinction of what I have called its form or spirit.

4. A body dies when the parts without which it cannot exist or else its unifying principle are destroyed. Under the first head may be classed instances of nations swallowed up by the sea, like the people of Atlantis Plato describes,[5] and others whom Tertullian mentioned;[6] or the engulfing of a people by an earthquake or an opening chasm, of which there are examples in Seneca and Ammianus Marcellinus and others. Or a people may voluntarily destroy themselves, as the Sidonians and Saguntines did. We are informed by Pliny that fifty-three nations of ancient Latium had disappeared without leaving a trace.

What if out of a great population so few survive that they cannot form a nation? They may then retain those rights of ownership which they had before as private persons, but not what belonged to their nation as a nation. The same is the case with a corporation.

5. THE unifying principle of the body is gone when the citizens, in terror of a pestilence or out of rebellion, voluntarily withdraw from the community, or else are dispersed by violence so that they cannot come together again, as happens sometimes in war.

6. A nation loses its form as an organized body when it loses all or the fullness of the rights it held in common, when either the individual citizens are reduced to slavery, as were the Mycenaeans who were sold by the Argives, and the Thebans by Alexander, . . . or retain their personal liberty, but are deprived of their sovereignty. Thus, Livy informs us,[7] the Romans determined with regard to Capua that though it might be inhabited as a city, there should be no body politic, no senate, no popular council, no magistrates, but deprived of a political assembly and sovereign authority, the inhabitants should be under the jurisdiction of a prefect sent from Rome. . . . The same is to be said of nations reduced to the form of provinces, and of those subjugated to another nation. . . .

7. BUT if a nation emigrates, either spontaneously or because of famine or any other calamity, or if under compulsion, as the people of Carthage did in the third Punic War, provided it retains its form of organization, it does not cease to be a nation; still less so, if only the walls of its cities are destroyed. . . .

8. NOR does it make any difference how a nation is governed, whether by a monarch, an aristocracy, or the people. The Roman people was the same under kings, consuls, and emperors. Even under the most absolute king, a nation will be the same as it was before, when it governed itself, as long as the king governs it as the head of that people, and not as the head of any other. For the sovereignty which is lodged in the king as head resides in the people, as in the whole body of which the head is a part. So when an

elected king dies or the royal family becomes extinct, the right of sovereignty, as we have already shown, reverts to the people. . . .

We must realize that one artificial system may assume several forms, as an army takes on one form when it is being governed and another when it fights. So the state under one form is a combination of law and governing power, under another is a relationship of the parts that rule with those that are ruled. The latter is the politician's concern; the former the jurist's. . . .

A nation which has set a king over itself does not cease to owe the debts which it owed when free; for it is the same people, retaining ownership of all public property. It even retains the sovereignty over itself, although it is not now exercised by the body but by the head. . . .

9. WHEN two nations become united, their rights will not be lost, but will be shared with each other. Thus first the rights of the Albans and afterwards those of the Sabines, as we are informed by Livy,[8] were transferred to the Romans, and they became one state. The same rule holds good with respect to states which are joined not merely by a treaty or by having a king in common, but in a true union.

10. ON the other hand, it may happen that a nation which previously formed one state is divided, either by mutual consent or by force of war; as the body of the Persian Empire was divided among the successors of Alexander. When this is the case, several sovereign powers arise in the place of one, each with its rights over its own parts. Whatever was common property must either be administered as a common concern or divided into portions pro rata. In this way should be treated the separation which takes place when a nation sends out colonies. For thus too a new nation is created, with its own rights; and, as Thucydides says,[9] "sent out not as slaves but on terms of equality with the mother-country." . . .

11. A famous question among historians and jurists is to whom now belong the rights which once were possessed by the Roman Empire. Many claim that they belong to the German kingdom, as

it used to be called, or empire (which name you give it does not matter), and imagine a kind of surrogateship of the latter empire for the former, although they know well that great Germany, that is, Germany beyond the Rhine, all lay for most of the time outside the borders of the Roman Empire.

For my part, I do not think that an exchange or transfer of rights can be assumed unless it is proved by authentic documents. Accordingly I say that the Roman people is the same as it was in old times, even though mixed with accretions of foreigners, and that the imperial authority has remained in it, as in the body in which it once existed and lived. Whatever the Roman people had the right to do before the rule of the emperors, they had the same right to do as soon as each emperor died, before another took office. Furthermore, the election of the emperor belonged to the people; he was chosen sometimes by the people directly, sometimes through the Senate. The elections that were held by this or that legion were not valid through any right of the legions (for there could be no assured right in a bare name) but through the approval of the people. . . .

Nor did the fact that the emperors later preferred to live in Constantinople rather than at Rome detract at all from the rights of the Roman people, but the people as a whole then ratified the election held by that part of it that dwelt at Constantinople. . . . For all the right that the populace at Constantinople could have to elect a Roman emperor depended on the will of the Roman people. And when, to leave out other considerations, that part went contrary to the design and habit of the Roman people and submitted to the government of the woman Irene, the Romans rightly revoked their grant of authority, expressed or tacit, chose an emperor themselves and announced his election by the mouth of their chief citizen, that is, their bishop. In the same way, in the Jewish state, when there was no king, the person of the high priest came first.

This election was personal in the case of Charlemagne and some of his successors, who themselves drew a careful distinction between the rights of sovereignty they had over the Franks and the Lombards, and their rights over the Romans, as if these last had been acquired on new grounds. . . . But when the Eastern Franks began choosing their own kings by election . . . the Roman people decided, in order to gain surer protection, not to set up their own king but to take the man the Germans elected, retaining, however, some right of approving or disapproving the election, in so far as it touched themselves.

Such approval was usually announced by the bishop and ceremonially attested in a special coronation. So now he who is elected by the seven princes who represent the whole of Germany possesses the right of ruling the Germans according to their customs; and through the Roman people's approval he becomes also Roman king or emperor, or, as the historians often call him, king of the Kingdom of Italy. Under that title he rules over all that once belonged to the Roman people, which has not through treaties or abandonment and occupation or right of victory passed into the control of other nations. . . .

[12–13. Rights of heirs to preserve ownership.]

X

Obligations Arising Out of Ownership.

1. HAVING explained sufficiently for our purpose the rights that may belong to us over persons and things, we must now consider what obligations in turn devolve upon us. Such obligations proceed from

things that either exist or do not exist. Under the name of things I include also rights over persons, as far as may be convenient for us.

From things that exist arises the obligation that binds a person who has our property in his power to do all he can to put us into possession of it. I say, "to do all he can," for no one is bound to do the impossible, or even to restore the property at his own expense. But he is obliged to make his possession known, so that the owner may recover his own. For as in the state of community of goods a certain equality has to be preserved, in order that this man as well as that should be able to make use of the common stock, so on the introduction of private ownership, it became, as it were, a kind of established arrangement between owners, that one who had in his possession anything belonging to another should return it to its owner. For if the power of ownership extended no further than merely a right to have property returned at the owner's request, the owner's right would be too weak and the protection of property too costly. . . .

As to the nature of the ownership, it makes no difference whether it rests on the law of nations, or on civil law, since it always carries with it certain features natural to it, among which is the obligation on every holder of property to restore it to its owner. . . .

2. WITH respect to things non-existent, mankind has adopted the rule that if you have become richer through my property while I am deprived of it, you are bound to return to me the amount of your gains. For to the extent you have enriched yourself from my property, you have more while I have less. And property ownership was introduced to preserve equality, in this respect, at least, that everyone should have what is his.

"It is contrary to nature," says Cicero,[1] "for one man to increase his own advantage at the expense of another," and in another passage,[2] "Nature does not allow us to increase our resources, wealth, and strength from the spoils of others." There is so much justice in these words that many jurists make them the basis of judgments beyond the strict letter of the law, appealing always to their obvious justice.

Whoever puts a slave in charge of his business is bound by the act of that slave, unless he has given notice that he is not to be trusted. And even if such notice has been given, if the slave has made a profit, or some gain has accrued to the master out of the transaction, a suit may be lodged for fraud. . . .

Similarly, if you have treated with my debtor, supposing him not to be indebted to me but to another person, and have borrowed money of him, you are under obligation to pay it to me; not because I have lent you money—for that can only be done by mutual consent—but because it is reasonable and fair that my money, which has come into your possession, should be returned to me. . . .

3. IN the first place, then, it appears that a person who has obtained possession of goods in good faith is not bound to restore them if they are destroyed, because he no longer possesses them or profits from them. A dishonest possessor is chargeable for his wrongdoing besides being accountable for the goods.

4. SECONDLY, a possessor in good faith is bound to return the extant fruits of the property. I say "the fruits of the property," for the fruits of the possessor's industry are not a debt owed to the property, even though without the property they would not have been obtained. . . .

5. THIRDLY, a possessor in good faith is bound to make restitution for whatever of the property and its fruits he has consumed, provided that without them he would have consumed as much. For thereby he is conceived to be the richer. . . .

6. FOURTHLY, he is not liable for fruits which he neglected to collect. For he has neither the property nor anything in place of it. . . .

[7–8. Rules for a possessor who gives away or sells property.]

9. SEVENTHLY, another man's property, even though bought in good faith, must be returned to him, nor can the price paid be recovered. To this rule, however, there seems to be one exception,

namely where the owner probably could not have recovered possession without some expense—as, for instance, when his property was in the hands of pirates. For then a deduction may be made of as much as the owner would willingly have spent in the recovery. . . .

10. EIGHTHLY, a person who has bought from one man something belonging to another cannot, in order to regain the price he paid, return it to the seller, because from the time that the thing came into his possession his obligation commenced to restore it, as we have said, to the lawful owner.

11. NINTHLY, a person in possession of property, the owner of which is unknown, is not by nature bound to give it to the poor; although it would be an act of great piety, and the custom is very rightly established in many places. The reason is that by the theory of ownership, no one except the owner has a right to it. But not to exist and not to be known amount to the same thing for a person to whom the owner is unknown.

12. TENTHLY, whatever a person has received in payment for a base service, or for an honorable one which he was in duty bound to perform, he is not by the law of nature bound to return, although it is not without reason that some laws contain such a rule. The reason is that no one is bound to account for property unless it belongs to another. But here ownership was voluntarily transferred by the previous owner.

The case will be altered, if there was anything wrong in the manner of acquiring the money; if, for instance, it was by extortion. This involves a different principle of obligation, which is not our subject here. . . .

XI

Promises.

1. THE course of our inquiry leads us next to consider the obligation created by promises. . . . Cicero, in his book *On Duty*,[1] ascribes such force to promises that he calls good faith the foundation of justice, while Horace [2] says it is the sister of justice. . . . Simonides [3] too defines justice as not only giving back what one has received, but also as speaking the truth.

But to understand the subject clearly, we should carefully distinguish three different ways of speaking of things to come which are or which, we suppose, will be in our power to control.

2. THE first of these ways is an assertion setting forth our present intention regarding something in the future; and if the assertion is a true expression of our thought at the time, it is no crime if we do not persist in that intention. For the human mind has not only a natural power but a right to change its opinion. So if there is anything wrong in the change of intention, as sometimes happens, it is not inherent in the act of change, but is due to some circumstance, as when, for instance, the original intention was the better.

3. THE second way is when the will declares its course in the future by an outward sign, sufficient to indicate a sense of obligation to abide by its intention. And this may be called a kind of promise which binds us, either conditionally or absolutely, though not by civil law; it conveys no right, properly speaking, to another person. For in many cases it happens that we are under an obliga-

tion, but no one else has a right to compel us, as when we have a duty to show compassion or to return a favor, or, similarly, the duty of constancy or faithfulness. Under such a promise, then, the person promising may keep his property and may not by natural law be compelled to keep faith.

4. THE third way is where to the original declaration of purpose is added a sign of an intention to convey a special right to another. This is a perfect promise, and has an effect similar to an alienation of ownership. It is a first step to the alienation of an object or of some portion of our liberty. Under the former head belong promises to give, and under the latter promises to do. A noble illustration of what we are saying is found in the divine Scriptures, which tell us that God himself, who can be limited by no established law, would act contrary to his own nature if he did not fulfill his promises. . . . Whence it follows that the obligation to keep a promise springs from the nature of that unchangeable justice which is, in its own way, an attribute common to God and to all who have reason. . . .

A promise which is not made with deliberate intent, does not, we believe, have the force of an obligation, as Theophrastus has observed in his book on *Laws*.[4] As for a promise made by deliberate intent, but not with the purpose of conveying a special right to another, that, we say, cannot by natural law give anyone a right to compel its fulfillment; yet it creates an obligation both of honor, and of a kind of moral imperative. . . . Let us consider next what are the requisites of a perfect promise.

5. THE first requisite is the use of reason; consequently the promises of madmen, idiots, and children are null and void. The case of minors is different, for although they are not supposed to have thoroughly sound judgment, any more than women, yet that is not a permanent defect, nor sufficient of itself to invalidate their acts. At what period of life a boy begins to use his reason cannot be absolutely stated, but must be deduced from his daily acts, or from the general custom of his particular country. Among the Jews a

promise made by a boy at the age of thirteen, and by a girl at the age of twelve, was valid. In other nations, civil laws, for good reason, declare void certain promises made by wards or minors. . . .

But such regulations are peculiar to civil law, and have no connection with the law of nature or of nations, except that wherever they are the rule it is natural that they should be observed. So when a foreigner enters into an agreement with a citizen, he is bound by the laws of the country, since whoever makes a contract in a certain place is bound as a temporary subject by the laws of that place. But the case is patently different when an agreement is made at sea, or on a desert island, or by letter between persons at a distance. For such agreements are governed by the law of nature alone, as are those between sovereigns in their public capacity. With regard to the compacts sovereigns make in their private capacity, the laws hold there which make the act void, when that is to their advantage, but not, when it is to their loss.

6. THE problem of promises made under a misunderstanding is one of great intricacy. It is usual to distinguish between a mistake that affects the substance of the promise, and one that does not affect the substance; and to inquire whether the compact was based on a fraud, or not, and whether the other party was privy to the fraud; and whether the act was strictly a matter for law, or only for good faith. For according to these variations in circumstance, writers pronounce some promises void and others valid, though leaving the injured party a choice to have them annulled or amended.

Most of the distinctions originated in the ancient civil and praetorian Roman law, and some of them are not precisely true or accurate. But the way for us to discover the truth according to nature is to refer to what by the general consent of mankind is the accepted view as to the force and efficacy of laws, namely, that if a law rests on a presumption of a fact which in reality has no existence, then that law is not binding. For when the fact is not true, the whole foundation of the law is gone. To decide when a law is founded on such a presumption, we must examine the substance, the words, and the circumstances of that law.

We shall say the same of a promise based on an assumption of a fact which proves not to be true; naturally it has no force, because the promiser's consent to make it was subject to a certain condition which actually does not exist. In this class should be put the case cited by Cicero, in the first book of *The Orator*, of a father who mistakenly believed that his son was dead, and so named someone else as his heir. But if the promiser was careless about investigating the situation, or about expressing his meaning plainly, and the other person suffered damage on that account, he will be bound to make it good, not on the strength of his promise, but because of the injury for which he is to blame, on which subject we shall speak in a later chapter. However, a promise made in error is binding, if the error was not the basis of the promise, for here the consent was a true one. But if the error was caused by fraud on the part of the person to whom it was given, he shall be bound, by that other type of obligation, to indemnify the promiser for any injury sustained as a result of his mistake. If the promise is based only in part on an error, the rest of it shall be valid.

7. PROMISES made in a state of fear are no less difficult to assess. Here also a distinction is usually made between a really serious fear, or one that seems so to the person frightened, and a trifling fear; between one lawfully and one unlawfully inspired; between one inspired by the person to whom the promise is given, and one inspired by someone else; and also between generous acts and those that impose a burden. In accordance with these variations in circumstance, some promises are considered void, others as revocable at the will of the promiser, and others as warranting complete restoration of the things promised. But on each of these points there is great diversity of opinion.

On the whole, I accept the opinion of those who, leaving out of consideration the civil law, which may annul or diminish the obligation, maintain that a person is bound to fulfill a promise, even one he made in fear. For in such a case there was consent, not conditional consent—as in the case we just now mentioned of a man in error—but absolute. For as Aristotle rightly observed,[5] a man who in terror of shipwreck throws his goods overboard would have chosen to keep them had there been no threat of shipwreck; but he has chosen absolutely to part with them, considering the circumstances of time and place.

This, I think, is certainly true, that if the person to whom the promise is made has inspired a fear—not a just fear but an unreasonable one, however slight—and the promise has resulted from that fear, he must release the promiser, if the latter wishes it, not because the promise is not binding but because a damage has been wrongfully inflicted. What exception to this rule may be made by the law of nations I shall explain later, in its place.[6] . . . How great a force oaths have to strengthen a promise we shall see also farther on.

8. TO render a promise valid, it must be one that is or can be in the power of the promiser to perform. Hence, in the first place, no promises to perform an act in itself illegal are valid, because no one has, or can have, a right to do such a thing. A promise, as we said before, derives its force from the right of the promiser to make it, nor does it extend beyond that. . . .

If a thing is not now in the power of the promiser, but may be so at some future time, the validity of his promise will remain in suspense. For it should be thought of as made on condition that it comes into the promiser's power to fulfill it. However, if the promiser has some control over the condition on which it depends whether the thing comes into his power or not, he is bound to do whatever is morally right to fulfill his promise. But in obligations of this kind, too, the civil law, from motives of general utility, often makes promises void that naturally would be binding, such as promises of future marriage made by a man or a woman now married, and many others made by minors and children under the rule of their families.

9. HERE the question is usually raised whether a promise made for a purpose which is by nature iniquitous is by the law of nature valid, as when, for instance, something is promised to a man for committing a murder. Here the promise itself is palpably wicked, because it is made for the purpose of impelling another to commit a crime. But not every wrong act is invalid, as appears in the case of an extravagant gift. There is this difference, that once the gift is made, no further evil is done; for with no more wrongdoing the gift remains in the hands of the recipient. But in promises made for a vicious purpose, the evil influence lasts as long as the crime is un-committed. During all that time, the idea of fulfilling the promise is an inducement to crime, and carries with it the stain of evil, which disappears only after the crime has been committed. . . . However, if the wickedness of the person to whom the promise was given furnished a reason for it, or there is an injustice in the compact, the remedy for such things is another matter, of which we shall treat later.[7] . . .

11. AS to the mode of making a promise, it requires, as we said of the transfer of ownership, an external act, that is, an adequate indication of purpose, such as a nod may be at times, but, more often, a spoken word or a written document.

12. WE are bound by a promise made by another person, if it is clear that we intended to commission him as our agent for this special purpose, or have some general arrangement with him. In case of a general commission, it may happen that our agent binds us while doing something contrary to the instructions we gave him in private. In such a case, there have been two distinct acts of will; one by which we bound ourselves to ratify whatever he did in that type of transaction, the other by which we bound him to do nothing but according to instructions known to him, though not to others. This distinction should be noted in the case of promises made by ambassadors for their kings, in virtue of their credentials, when they go beyond their secret orders.

13. THE actions on contracts entered into by ships' captains and

commercial agents are based on natural law. And so, we may add, it was a wrong provision of Roman law that made the owners of ships individually wholly responsible for the acts of their captains. For it neither accorded with natural justice, which holds it enough if each party is answerable in proportion to his share, nor was it conducive to the public welfare, since men are deterred from employing ships, if they are afraid of being held responsible for the acts of their captains to an unlimited extent. And therefore in Holland, where for a long time commerce has flourished greatly, that law of Rome has not been observed, either now or ever in the past. On the contrary, it is the established rule that all the owners together are not accountable for any greater sum than the value of the ship and its cargo.

14. IN order that a promise may convey a right, an acceptance is no less necessary than when property is transferred. But in this case, a preceding request for the promise is supposed to last over and to be the equivalent of an acceptance. . . . This is not an effect of natural law but of purely civil law, and is like the provision of the law of nations for children and demented persons. It assumes for them an intention to accept, as it does the intention to possess things acquired by possession.

15. ANOTHER question is whether the mere fact of the acceptance of a promise is sufficient, or whether it ought to be communicated to the promiser before the promise is held entirely valid. It is certain that a promise may be made in two ways; either this way: 'I wish this to be valid, if accepted,' or the other way, 'I wish this to be valid when I know it is accepted.' In promises establishing a mutual obligation, the latter meaning is assumed, but purely free promises it is better to take in the former sense, unless there is evidence to the contrary.

16. HENCE it follows that before it is accepted a promise may be revoked without injustice, as no right has yet been conveyed; and even without inconsistency, if the intention was truly to make acceptance the prerequisite condition of its validity. It may be re-

voked too if the person to whom it was made dies before accepting it, because it is plain that the power to accept it was conferred on him, and not on his heirs. For to give a man a right which will descend to his heirs is one thing, and to give it to his heirs is another, since it makes a great difference on whom a favor is bestowed. . . .

17. A promise may be revoked on the death of the person chosen to communicate the intention of the promiser, because the obligation depended on his words. The case is different where a messenger is employed who is not himself an instrument in the obligation, but only the bearer of the obligatory instrument. So letters expressing consent may be carried by anyone. There is a distinction too between a servant commissioned to make known a promise, and one authorized to make the promise himself. In the former case, a revocation will be valid, even though the servant has not been informed of it; in the latter case, it will be void, because the right to promise lay within the power of the servant's will, and his will to promise, as long as he knew of no revocation, was complete. . . .

In case of doubt, it is to be supposed that the authorizer of the promise intended his promise to be kept, unless some great change, such as his own death, should occur. Yet reasons in favor of a different conclusion may appear, which ought readily to be admitted, so long as a donation that was promised to a good cause stands. . . .

19. FROM what has been already said, we can see what to think of the addition of a burdensome condition to a promise. It may be added at any time, so long as the promise has not been completed by acceptance, or made irrevocable by a pledge. And a burdensome condition added to a promise, to the advantage of a third person, may be revoked so long as that person has not accepted it. . . .

20. ANOTHER question discussed is how a promise based on an error can be made valid, if the person who made it, on being informed of the facts, still wishes to adhere to it. The same question may be raised with regard to promises invalidated by the civil law,

because prompted by fear or some other such motive, if that motive is later removed. To confirm such promises, some require merely an inward consent of the mind, which, when joined to the previous outward act, they think sufficient to make the obligation binding. Others disagree with this opinion, on the ground that an outward act cannot be a sign of a subsequent inward act. They require a new verbal promise and an accompanying acceptance. More likely the truth lies between these two opinions. An outward act is indeed required, but not necessarily a statement in words. When the person to whom the promise was made on his part retains the thing promised him, and the promiser on his part relinquishes his right to it, that or something similar is sufficient to signify consent. . . .

22. NOR is a person who has promised that another man should do something responsible for the values involved, provided he himself has not failed to do on his part all that was possible to bring about the promised performance, unless the terms of the agreement or the nature of the business impose a stricter obligation. . . .

XII

Contents.

1. THE acts of men that may be advantageous to other men are sometimes simple, and sometimes mixed.

2. SOME simple acts are favors; others are reciprocal exchanges. Favors are either pure or involve obligations on both sides. Pure

favors are either immediate in their effects or look to some future time. An immediate favor is a beneficial act, of which we do not need to speak, for while it confers a benefit, it has no effect in law. . . . To the future belong promises to give and to do, of which we have just now completed an account.

Favors involving reciprocal obligations are those that dispose of property without complete alienation, or provide for acts in expectation of some results. Under the first head comes a permission to use property, which is called a loan; under the second is a commission to perform some costly work or one involving an obligation. This is called a mandate. One form of mandate is a deposit in trust, which is a requirement of labor to guard and preserve something. . . .

3. ACTS of exchange sometimes keep the parties separate, sometimes bring about a community of interest. Those that are separative are divided by the Roman jurists rightly into the following classes: 'I give that you may give'; or, 'I do that you may do'; or, 'I do that you may give.' On these classes, one may consult the jurist Paulus, in the *Digest*, xix, v, 5. . . .

We say now that when we give in order that someone else may give, one article is given directly for another, as in that exchange which is especially called barter, undoubtedly the most ancient kind of trade. Or else money is given for money, a transaction which . . . merchants today call money-changing. Or an article is given for money, as in selling and buying. Or the use of one article is given for another, or the use of one for the use of another, or the use of an article for money, which last is called renting or hiring. By the term 'use' we understand not only the plain use of a thing, but also use combined with the income from it, whether that be temporary, or personal, or hereditary, or in any other way restricted, as, among the Hebrews, was the contract which lasted only until the year of Jubilee.

We give as a loan, in order that after an interval the same amount and kind of thing may be given back, which may be done

with things measured by weight, number, or size, both money and
other commodities. The exchange of a deed for a deed may assume
countless forms, depending on the variety of the deed. In 'I do that
you may give,' the thing you give may be money, as in arrangements for daily service which we call hiring or renting, or in
guarantees of indemnity against accidental losses, which we call
protection against risk, or, in common speech, insurance, a species
of contract scarcely known to the ancients, but now very usual. Or
you may give an article or the use of an article.

4. ACTS that create a community of interest are those where both
sides share in acts or in property, and so use them for the common
good. These all come under the name of joint enterprises. In this
class we include alliances for war, such as the unions of private
ships so frequently formed among us to fight pirates or other in-
vaders, which are known as admiral's fleets. . . .

5. MIXED actions are either such in themselves, or made so by
some external circumstance. Thus, if I knowingly buy a thing for a
greater price than it is worth, and give the excess price to the seller,
the act will be partly gift and partly purchase. Or if I promise
money to a goldsmith for making me some rings out of his own
gold, that will be partly purchase and partly hiring. So too in a
partnership it may happen that one man contributes labor and
money, the other only money. . . .

7. ALL acts of advantage to others, except such as are pure favors,
come under the name of contracts.

8. IN contracts, natural law requires that there should be equality; insomuch that if one party receives less than the other, that
one acquires a right as against the other from that inequality. This
equality appears partly in the acts involved, and partly in the subject matter of the contract. The acts are both those that precede
the contract and the principal acts specified by it.

9. AS to acts previous to the contract, the person making it is
bound to inform the other of any defects known to him in the subject of the transaction, a rule both widely established by civil laws

and befitting the nature of the act. For between contracting parties there is a kind of league closer than that between men in general. . . . For the nature of the contract, which was invented to be of benefit to mankind, requires something closer than that. Ambrose rightly remarks: [1] "In contracts it is required that the faults of the things for sale be made known; and unless the seller has declared them, even though the property has been transferred to the hands of the buyer, the contracts may yet be voided as fraudulent." . . .

But the same cannot be said of things not entering into the contract, as when a man sells his corn at a high price, knowing that many ships laden with grain are on the way. It would indeed be a praiseworthy act of duty to share the information, and often it cannot be withheld without violating the rule of love. Yet such withholding is not illegal, that is, it does not conflict with the lawful rights of the other party to the deal. . . . The rule of Cicero [2] therefore cannot generally be admitted, that, knowing a thing yourself, to try for the sake of your own advantage to keep others ignorant of it, whose interest it is to know it, amounts to wrong concealment. That is only the case when the facts involved concern closely the subject of the contract; as when the house you are selling is infected with the plague, or has been ordered pulled down by the magistrates, instances of which you may find in Cicero. But it is unnecessary to mention defects known to the person with whom you are dealing. . . . Equal knowledge makes both the contracting parties equal. . . .

10. NOT only in knowledge of the facts but also in power of free choice there should be some sort of equality between the contracting parties. Not that any previous fears, if lawfully aroused, must be dispelled, for that is not a part of the contract; but no fear should be aroused in order to put through the contract, and if so aroused, it should be dispelled. . . .

11. IN the principal act itself, this kind of equality is required, that no more should be exacted than is fair. . . . In all acts of exchange, this rule is to be punctually observed. Nor should it be said

that if one party promises more, it may be looked on as a gift. For such is not ordinarily the intent of persons making such contracts, nor should such an intention be assumed unless it is clearly apparent. For whatever is promised or given should be regarded as promised or given as an equivalent for what is to be received, and so as due for the purpose of equality. "Whenever," in the words of Chrysostom,[3] "in contracts and in buying and selling, we strive and put forth all our efforts to pay less than a fair price, is there not in such conduct a kind of thievery?" . . .

12. THERE should be also an equality in the subject matter of the contract, consisting in this, that in a case where nothing has been concealed which ought to have been made known, nor more exacted than was considered due, and yet where some inequality in the bargain has been discovered, though without either party being to blame—such as, for instance, some hidden defect, or some mistake in the price—there, too, equality should be restored and the party who has more than he ought should be deprived of it, and the one who has less should be indemnified. For in the contract it either was or should have been the intention of both that both should receive the same.

The Roman law established this rule, yet not for every case of inequality, for it passed over trifling instances, because of the likelihood of a multitude of lawsuits; but in serious cases it intervened where the prices obtained exceeded the just value by one half. . . . Persons not subject to civil laws ought to follow the rule that right reason points out to them as fair; so too ought those who are subject to laws, whenever it is a question of what is upright or good, when the laws neither permit nor take away a right, but merely refrain for certain reasons from enforcing it.

13. THERE is, we should note too, a kind of equality to be observed even in agreements to do a favor, not indeed to the full extent required in contracts of exchange, but based on a theory of the transaction, that no one should suffer damage from a kindly act. For which reason a mandatory should be indemnified for ex-

penses incurred and loss endured in carrying out his mandate. A borrower too is bound to make good a thing destroyed, because he is under obligation to the owner not only for the object borrowed, that is, by virtue of the rights of ownership, by which, as we said above, every temporary possessor is bound, but by virtue of his acceptance of a favor. This rule applies unless the thing borrowed would have certainly been destroyed even if it had remained in the house of the owner. For in such a case, the owner lost nothing by his loan. On the other hand, a holder of an object in trust has undertaken nothing but fidelity. If the object he holds is destroyed, he will not be held liable either for it, for it is no longer in existence and he is none the richer, or for his acceptance of it, since in accepting the trust he did not receive a favor but conferred one. In the case of a pledge, as of a thing rented, a middle course should be followed. The person taking it is not answerable, like a borrower, for every accident; yet he must take greater care of it than the holder of a trust. For the acceptance of a pledge is usually not a matter of profit, but a part of a burdensome contract.

All these rules are in conformity with Roman law, though not originally derived from it, but from natural justice. So the same are to be found among other nations. . . . And by the same principles we may pass judgment on other contracts. But now, having discussed the subject in general sufficiently for our purpose, let us run over some special questions pertaining to contracts.

14. THE most natural measure of the value of any article is the need for it, as Aristotle correctly stated.[4] In the exchange of objects among barbarous nations this is the chief consideration. But it is not the only measure, for the desires of men, which dictate their possessions, make them covet many more things than their necessities. "It was luxury," says Pliny,[5] "that set a price on pearls"; and Cicero, in his speech against Verres,[6] talking of statues, says: "The limit of value for such things is the same as the limit of men's desires for them." On the other hand, it does happen that the most necessary things are cheap because of their abundance.

Seneca illustrates this by many instances in the fifteenth chapter of the sixth book of *On Benefits*, and adds the remark: "The price of everything depends on circumstances. Loudly as you may praise them, your things are worth no more now than they can be sold for." . . .

Hence it is that the value of a thing is reckoned as the amount which is commonly offered or given for it, which is not so fixed as to allow no latitude within which more or less may be paid or demanded—except in cases where the law has set a standard price. . . . In setting the common price, the labor and expense of the merchant in procuring the goods are often taken into account, and sudden changes take place depending on the abundance or scarcity of buyers, money, and commodities. Accidents, too, may conceivably happen, owing to which a thing may be legitimately bought or sold above or below the ordinary price, as when, for instance, some damage has occurred, the profit has disappeared, personal prejudice enters in, or an article which otherwise would not have been disposed of is bought or sold as a favor to someone. All such circumstances should be made known to the person with whom we are dealing. We may also take into consideration the damage or absence of gain that results from a deferred or an anticipated payment.

15. IN purchase and sale we should observe that ownership may pass at the very moment of concluding the contract, even without delivery; and that is the most simple way of dealing. . . . But if it is agreed that ownership shall not pass immediately, the seller will be bound to convey it at the time stated, taking meanwhile all the gains and risks. The following provisions, then, of the civil law are not everywhere accepted, namely, that sale and purchase consist in giving to the purchaser the right of possession and eviction, and that the property is at the risk of the purchaser and its profits belong to him, even before the ownership has passed. On the contrary, many lawmakers have assigned to the seller all profit and risk from the property until its actual delivery to the purchaser. . . .

We must understand too that, if an object has been twice sold, of the two sales that one is valid which included an immediate transfer of ownership, either by delivery of the object or in some other way. For by this act the practical mastery over the object passes from the seller, an event which does not take place through a promise alone.

16. NOT all monopolies are contrary to the law of nature. At times they may be authorized by the sovereign power for just reasons and at fixed prices. A famous instance of this we find in the story of Joseph, when as viceroy he governed Egypt. So also under the Romans, the people of Alexandria, Strabo tells us,[7] had a monopoly in Indian and Ethiopian goods.

A monopoly may be established also by private individuals, provided they keep to a fair price. But men who combine, as the oil merchants of the Velabro did, to sell their goods at a price above the top current rates, or who resort to violence or fraud to prevent a larger supply from being imported, or who buy up commodities, in order to sell them again at a price unfair at the time of sale, are wrongdoers and may be required to repair the wrong. And if by any other method they hinder the importation of merchandise, or buy it up in order to sell it at a higher price, even though the price at the time is not unreasonable, they are breaking the law of love, as Ambrose shows by many proofs in the third book of *On Duty*,[8] though they are not, strictly speaking, violating another man's rights.

17. AS to money, we should understand that it performs its functions naturally, not as a result of its material solely, or because of its special name or shape, but because it has a more general character by means of which it forms a measure for all commodities, or for the most necessary. Its value, if not otherwise fixed, should be set at the time and place of payment. . . . Whatever is taken as a standard of measure for other things ought to be in itself of a nature that varies very little. Now in the class of precious things gold, silver, and copper are of that nature, possessing nearly the same in-

trinsic value everywhere and always. But just as other things needed by men may be plentiful or scarce, so the same money, made of the same material and weighing the same, is now worth more and now less.

18. "RENTING and hiring," as Caius justly said,[9] "come very near to selling and buying, and are governed by the same rules." For the price corresponds to the cost of rent or hire, and the ownership of the property to the right to use it. Hence, as the loss of the property falls on the owner, so naturally the renter bears the loss in case of barrenness or other accidents that hinder the use of the property. Nor will the man who lets out the property be, on that account, less entitled to the promised rent, because he gave the other the right of use, which at the time was worth so much. This rule, however, can be changed by law and by mutual agreement. But if the owner, while the first tenant is prevented from using the property, lets it to another, whatever he gains thereby he should turn over to the first tenant, so as not to be made richer at another man's expense.

19. WE said above, when speaking of sales, that an article might be sold for a higher than market price or bought for a less, if it were being sold or bought as a favor to someone else, and would otherwise not be sold or bought at all. The same may be understood of renting or hiring property or services.

And if one service, such as conveyance on a journey, can be useful to a number of people together, and a contractor has pledged himself definitely to several individuals, he can require of each the payment he would have demanded of one, as long as the law does not forbid it. For the fact that the service is useful to a second person as well has nothing to do with the contract made with the first person, nor does it diminish in any way its value to the first.

20. IN connection with a loan the question is frequently raised, by what law is the taking of interest forbidden. . . . Whatever may be thought of this matter, for us the law of God, delivered to the Jews, should suffice, which forbids Jews to lend money on interest to other Jews. For the principles of this law, even if not neces-

sary, are certainly noble from the moral point of view. . . . And precepts of this kind are binding likewise on Christians, who are called upon to furnish still finer examples of virtue; and the duties that a Jew or other circumcised person—whose status was then the same as a Jew's—was commanded to perform, should now be performed by everyone. For the Gospel has removed all distinction between peoples, and the word 'neighbor' has been given a broader meaning, as Christ's wonderful parable of the good Samaritan [10] and other passages teach us. Thus Lactantius, discussing the duty of a Christian man, says [11] he will not lend money on interest, for that is "to reap gain from another's misfortune." . . .

21. WE must note, however, that there are some things which look like interest and are generally considered to be interest but which in reality are agreements of a different nature. Such is an agreement to make good the loss which a lender suffers for going so long without his money, or for missing the profit he might have won from the money he lent, though with some deduction for the uncertainty of expectations and the exertions he would have had to make. So too something may be demanded for the expenses of a person who is lending money to many, and, for that purpose, keeps cash on hand, and also for the risk he runs of losing his principal, in case it is not adequately secured; but this is not truly interest. . . .

22. THERE are indeed human laws that allow compensation to be asked for the use of money or of anything else. Thus in Holland, it has long been permissible for merchants to collect twelve per cent a year and for other persons eight per cent. If such laws actually provide only fair compensation for the money that is or may be out of one's possession, they are not opposed to natural or divine law. But if they go beyond that limit, they may confer immunity: they cannot create a right.

23. CONTRACTS for protection against risk, which are called insurance, will be null and void, if either of the contracting parties knew beforehand that the thing insured had already reached its

destination in safety or had been lost. And this not only on the
ground of the equality required by the nature of contracts for exchange, but because the very essence of this kind of contract is the
uncertainty of the danger. The price of such insurance against risk
should be fixed in accordance with the customary valuation.

24. IN a business partnership in which money is contributed by
both parties, if the contributions are equal, the shares in profit and
loss should be equal also. But if they are unequal, the shares should
be in proportion, as Aristotle has shown at the close of the eighth
book of his *Nicomachean Ethics*. . . . And the same rule holds
good where equal or unequal amounts of labor are contributed.
However, labor may be contributed instead of money, or both
labor and money; as the maxim says: [12] "It's paying one thing for
another when service is given for cash."

But there is more than one way of forming such an agreement. A
man may put in work in return for merely the use of capital; in
which case any loss of capital falls on the owner, and, if saved, it
belongs to the owner. Or one may give labor to obtain ownership
in the capital; in which case the one who contributes labor becomes
a sharer in the capital. . . . What we have said of labor may be
applied to the labor and risks of voyages and similar enterprises.

It is contrary to the nature of partnerships that one partner
should share in the gains and be exempt from the losses. Yet such
an arrangement may be made without injustice. For there may be
a mixed contract, composed of a partnership and an insurance
against risk, in which equality is preserved if the one who takes on
himself the risk of loss receives that much greater share of the gain
than he otherwise would have had. But that one partner should
be responsible for losses without an increase in gains is something
inadmissible; for a pooling of interest is so much the nature of a
partnership that it cannot subsist without it. . . .

25. IN associations of shipowners the common interest is defense
against pirates, though sometimes it is booty as well. It is customary
to set a value on the ships and on their cargoes, and from that to

estimate a total, so that the losses that occur, in which are included
expenditures for men wounded, may be borne by the owners of
ships and goods in proportion to their share in the total.

And what we have thus far said accords with the law of nature.

26. NOR has the positive law of nations made any alteration in
these rules, with one exception, that where unequal terms have
been agreed upon, if no fraud has been used, nor any proper information withheld, they shall be regarded as equal for the purpose of external acts. . . . And this is the meaning of what Pomponius says,[13] that by the law of nature one man is permitted to
overreach another in the price of a sale or a purchase. However, in
this case 'permissible' is not the same as morally right, but is an admission that no remedy exists against a person who insists on the
terms of the contract.

In this passage, as in the others, the phrase 'law of nature' signifies what is widely received as the accepted custom. In this sense
the Apostle Paul says,[14] that nature herself teaches us that it is
shame for a man to wear long hair, though actually it is not repugnant to nature, and is a general practice among many nations. . . .

The advantage, however, of introducing the law I have mentioned is obvious—to put a stop to innumerable disputes, which
would be insoluble where prices of things are uncertain, and between persons who have no common judge, but which could not
be avoided, if men were permitted to withdraw from agreements
on the ground that the terms were unequal. . . .

XIII

Oaths.

1. IN every age and among every people the force of oaths to confirm promises, agreements, and contracts has always been very great. . . . Hence it has always been supposed that heavy punishments would fall on perjurers. . . . "For," as Cicero well says,[1] "an oath is a religious affirmation; what you have solemnly promised, as if before God as witness, you must fulfill." And he adds: "For this is not a matter of the wrath of the gods, which does not exist, but of justice and good faith." . . .

Let us now see from what oaths derive their force, and how far it extends.

2. IN the first place, what we said of promises and contracts applies to oaths as well, that one must have a mind controlled by reason, and a deliberate intent. . . .

3. IF a man deliberately repeats the words of an oath but without any intention of swearing, some authors say he is not bound by it, but that he sinned in swearing thoughtlessly. Yet it is truer to say that he is bound to make good the words he called God to witness. For the act is binding in itself, and it proceeded from a deliberate intention. Accordingly, the saying of Cicero is for the most part true:[2] "To fail to do what you have sworn with full understanding to do is perjury." . . .

There may be, nevertheless, an exception to this rule, in a case where the oath-taker knows or credibly believes that his words are understood in a different sense by the other person concerned. For one who calls God to witness his words ought to make them true in the sense he thinks they were understood. . . . Augustine says: [3] "Persons who keep to the letter of their oaths but deceive the expectations of those to whom they swore are perjurers." . . .

Although in other kinds of promises a tacit condition that releases the promiser may easily be understood, this is not admissible in an oath. On this point the admirable passage of the Apostle's Epistle to the Hebrews has a bearing.[4] "God, willing more abundantly to shew unto the heirs of promise the immutability of his counsel, confirmed it by an oath; that by two immutable things, in which it was impossible for God to lie, we might have a strong consolation." . . . To understand these words we should realize that the sacred writers often speak of God as having human feelings, and rather as he appears to us than as he is. For God does not really change his decrees, although he is said to change them and to repent, whenever he acts otherwise than as his words seem to mean, as he may when some condition, tacitly understood, ceases to exist. . . .

4. FROM what we have said, it can be understood what we should think of an oath fraudulently obtained. If it is certain that the person who took the oath acted on a supposition which actually was false, and if but for that belief he would not have taken it, his oath will not be binding. But if it is doubtful whether or not he would have sworn even without that belief, he must abide by his word, because utter candor is a requirement for an oath. . . .

5. THE meaning of an oath should not be stretched beyond the usual acceptation of the words. So the men who swore that they would not give their daughters in marriage to the Benjamites were not perjured when they permitted the girls who had been carried off to live with their abductors.[5] For it is one thing to give and another not to demand back what has been lost. . . .

6. IN order that an oath may be valid the thing promised should be lawful. Therefore a sworn promise to commit an unlawful act

has no force, either by natural law, or by divine ordinance, or even by human law, of which we shall speak later. As Philo the Jew well said,[6] "He adds guilt to guilt who commits an unlawful deed to keep an oath wrongfully sworn, which it had been better to leave unspoken. Let him then abstain from the unlawful deed, and beseech God to grant him the mercy most suited to his need. For to choose to commit two crimes, when you can be released from one, is incurable madness and folly." . . .

7. FURTHER, if the thing we promise is not actually unlawful, but only a hindrance to some greater practical good, in that case too our oath will not be valid, because we owe it to God to progress in goodness, and have not the right to deprive ourselves of the freedom of doing that. . . . And if we take an oath to the detriment of other persons, we shall be right to say it does not bind us, for it is a hindrance, as we said, to our progress in goodness.

8. THERE is no point in discussing impossibilities. For it is plain enough that no one is bound to do something absolutely impossible.

9. AS for an obligation to do what is at the moment or supposedly impossible, it remains in suspense. But he who took the oath under that supposition should do what he can to make the performance possible.

10. OATHS may differ in form of words and yet agree in substance. For they all ought to include the idea of an appeal to God, such as, for instance, "God be my witness," or "God be my judge," both of which come to the same thing. For when a superior who has a right to punish is invoked as witness, he is at the same time called upon to punish any perfidy. And he who knows all things is the punisher, because he is the witness. Plutarch says:[7] "Every oath ends in a curse on the one who breaks it." . . .

11. IT was a custom also with the ancients to swear by things or by other persons, either calling on them to hurt them, if it was the sun, the heavens, the earth, or their ruler; or asking to be punished in them, if it was their own heads, their children, their country, or

their prince. Nor was this a practice of heathen nations only, but, as the same Philo tells us, it was common among the Jews. . . . But Christ says [8] that he who swears by the temple swears by God who presides in the temple, and he who swears by heaven swears by God whose throne is in the heavens. . . .

12. EVEN if a man swears by false gods, his oath is binding; for although his notions are false, he still has a general idea of deity and reverence for it. So if he breaks his oath, the true God interprets his act as a wrong done to himself. . . . This is what Augustine says: [9] "And a man who swears by a stone, if he swears falsely, commits perjury." And later: "The stone does not hear you speaking, but God punishes your breaking of your oath."

13. THE principal effect of oaths is to cut short disputes. "An oath for confirmation," says the inspired writer of the Epistle to the Hebrews, [10] "is the end of all strife." . . .

14. IF the substance of an oath and the words in which it is phrased are such as to include not only an obligation to God but to a man, unquestionably the man will acquire the same right from the oath as he would derive from a promise or a contract, understood in the simplest way. But if the words contain no reference to another person that confers on him a right, or if they contain a reference, but there is ground for opposing his claim, then the force of the oath will not be to give that person a right, but still to bind the swearer to God to keep his oath. An example of this we have in a person who has extorted a sworn promise by inspiring an unlawful fear. For he obtains no right, or only one he ought to relinquish, because he caused harm. . . .

15. THE same rule applies both to transactions between public enemies and to those between any individuals whatever. For not merely the person to whom the oath is sworn is to be considered, but God, in whose name it is sworn, and who has power to enforce the obligation. For which reason we must repudiate Cicero, [11] when he calls it no perjury to refuse to pay pirates the sum agreed upon as ransom for one's life, even if one has sworn to pay it, because a

pirate is not to be counted in the number of lawful enemies, but is the common foe of all mankind, with whom no faith or mutual oath need be kept. Elsewhere he says the same of a tyrant. . . . It is true that in the established law of nations a distinction is drawn between a public enemy and a pirate, which will be made clear by us later on.[12] Yet here the distinction cannot apply, since, though the person to whom the oath was given has no right to it, God is involved in the transaction. Hence an oath may be called a vow. . . .

16. THERE are the lines in Accius: [13]

"Thyestes: You have broken faith.
Atreus: Faith I never gave nor do I give to the faithless."

This principle may be approved, if the promise sworn by one party had plainly in view a promise made by the other, the latter being implied in the former as a sort of condition; but not if the two promises were different in kind, and had no mutual connection. In that case each party must certainly fulfill his promise. For this reason, Silius, when praising Regulus, addresses him as follows: [14]

"You who through ages long, with evergrowing fame,
Will be remembered as a man who kept his pledge
To faithless Carthage."

[17–19. Cases where an oath may not be binding. E.g. on the heir of the oath-taker, or when the person benefited by it does not wish to be benefited.]

20. LET us see now what are the powers of superiors with regard to oath-taking, that is, of kings, fathers, masters, and husbands, in matters that come under marital rights. The act of a superior cannot annul the obligation to keep an oath, so far as it is truly binding, since that is a part of natural and divine law. But as we are not entirely masters of our own actions, but they in some measure depend upon our superiors, so a superior can act in two ways with re-

gard to an oath, either directly on the person of the swearer or on the person to whom the oath is sworn.

He can control the person taking the oath, either by declaring before he takes it that in so far as the right of the inferior is subject to his authority, the oath shall be void; or else by prohibiting its fulfillment, after it is taken. For the inferior, in so far as he is inferior, cannot bind himself beyond the limits approved by his superior, since he has no power beyond that. In the same manner, by Hebrew law, husbands might annul the oaths of wives, and fathers those of their children who were still under their authority. . . . Or the action may be a combination of the rights of both parties, as when a superior gives orders that an oath of his inferior taken under such and such circumstances—as, for example, when terrified or when feeble in judgment—shall be valid only when approved by himself. On this ground we may uphold the absolutions from oaths which in times past were granted by princes, and now, with the princes' consent, are granted by the heads of the Church, to give more consideration to religion.

The action of the superior may also be directed towards the person of the one receiving the oath, depriving him of the right he has acquired by it, or, if he gets no right, forbidding him to receive anything as a result of the oath. This may be done by two methods, either as a punishment or as a measure for public welfare, through the power of eminent domain. . . .

21. HERE we may incidentally observe that what Christ said in his precepts, and James as well, against swearing,[15] applies properly not to an oath of affirmation, of which there are several examples in the writings of the Apostle Paul, but to oaths promising something in the uncertain future. . . . Indeed Christ says the same thing as Philo: [16] "It is best and most useful and most in harmony with a rational nature to refrain from oath-swearing, and so to habituate oneself to speaking the truth that one's word may be accepted in place of an oath." . . .

22. IN many places, instead of by an oath, we hear that faith

was pledged by giving the right hand—which among the Persians was the firmest form of bond—or by some other sign. These had such force that if the promise was not kept, the promiser was considered as detestable as if he had committed perjury. Of kings and princes in particular it has been said that their pledge was as good as an oath. . . . In heroic times, Aristotle noted,[17] the holding of his sceptre upright was counted an oath for a king.

XIV

Promises, Contracts, and Oaths of Sovereigns.

1. THE promises, contracts, and oaths of kings, and of others who, like them, wield the chief authority in the state, present some special questions, both as to what they may do for themselves by their own acts, and as to what they may do that affects their subjects or their successors. With regard to the first point, the question is whether a king can restore himself to his previous status in full, as he can his subjects, or can declare his own contract void, or can absolve himself from an oath. . . .

We are of the opinion that here as elsewhere we must distinguish between the acts of a king as king and his acts as a private person. For whatever a king does in his acts as king must be considered as if done by the community. And just as laws made by the community would have no power over its acts, because the community is not superior to itself, so the laws made by the king would have no such power. Hence there is no undoing of such royal contracts, for that must come from civil law. And no exception should be admitted in the case of royal contracts made while the king was a minor.

2. OBVIOUSLY, if a people has set up a king without absolute authority, but restricted by laws, any acts of his contrary to those laws can be rendered void by them, either as a whole or in part, because the people has reserved for itself authority to that extent. . . .

But the private acts of a king should be considered as acts not of the community but of a part of the community, and hence as performed with the intention of following the general rule of the laws. Accordingly, the laws which make invalid certain acts, either altogether or in case the injured party desires it, apply here, as if the king's contract were made subject to those conditions. We see too that certain kings have resorted to the remedy of the law to protect themselves against iniquitous interest rates. Yet a king may exempt his own acts, like those of other men, from the operation of the laws. Whether he wishes to do so or not must be judged by the circumstances. If he does, his case will have to be judged by plain natural law.

This should be added, that if any law makes an act invalid not to the advantage of the doer but for his punishment, that law will not apply to the acts of a king, as neither will other penal laws nor any measure of compulsion. For punishment and compulsion can come to him only from wills different from his own. So the compeller and the compelled must be different persons, and separate aspects of one person are not sufficient.

3. A king may render his oath invalid in advance, as a private person may, if by a previous oath he has clearly deprived himself of the power to swear to such a thing. But after he has taken an oath, he cannot invalidate it, for here again two persons are required. . . .

4. WE have shown above that promises which are complete and

absolute and have been accepted do by natural law confer a right. The same is true where kings are concerned no less than where others are; so that in this sense they are wrong who say that a king is never bound by promises he has made without good cause. Yet in what sense this may be true we shall see shortly.

5. . . . WITH regard to the king's private conduct, so far is it from being true that the common laws of the realm have no power over him, that we consider him subject even to the laws of the town where he dwells, for though the king lives there on special terms, it is as a member of that community. However, as we have said, this is the case only unless circumstances prove that the king has been pleased to make his acts not amenable to the law. . . .

6. ALMOST all jurists agree that the contracts which a king enters into with his subjects are binding on him, though merely by natural law, not by civil law. . . . But according to civil law too a person is said to be bound by his act, meaning either that the obligation is derived not only from simple natural law but from the civil law or from both of them, or that an action in court may be based on it. So we say that a true and proper obligation is created by a promise or a contract which a king makes with his subjects, and that it confers a right on his subjects; for that is the nature of promises and contracts, as we explained above, even between God and man. And if the king's acts are such as may be performed by anyone else, the civil laws hold good for him too; but if they are acts of the king as king, the civil laws do not apply. . . . For subjects cannot coerce the man to whom they are subject. . . .

7. THIS too should be understood, that a king can in two ways take away from his subjects even a right they have won,—either as a punishment or by the power of eminent domain. In order to do it by the power of eminent domain, first, the public welfare must require it, and, second, compensation must be made to the loser, if possible, from the public funds. . . .

8. NOR should the distinction ever be admitted here which some make, between rights derived from the authority of the law of na-

ture and those acquired through civil law. For the right of a king over them both is the same; nor can one more than the other be taken away without due cause. . . . If the king violates this rule, he is bound indubitably to make good the harm done, since he has acted against a subject's veritable rights. . . .

10. LET us come now to the king's successors. . . . Unquestionably those who are heirs to all his possessions as well as to the kingdom are bound by his promises and contracts. For the rule that the goods of the deceased are liable for his personal debts is as old as property ownership itself.

11. AS to how far those are bound who succeed to his royal rights only, or to some portion of his possessions and to his royal rights in full, it is worth making some inquiry, for hitherto the subject has not been clearly treated. Quite plainly the successors to the kingship, as such, are not directly bound, because they do not receive their rights from the king just deceased but from the people. . . .

But even such successors may be bound through an intermediary, that is, through the intervention of the state, to be understood as follows. A community, no less than a single individual, has the right to bind itself by its own act, or by the act of the majority of its members. It can transfer this right, both explicitly and as a necessary consequence of other acts; as, for example, when it transfers sovereignty. For in practical matters one who grants an end grants the steps that lead to that end.

12. NOT, however, that this right to bind others goes on indefinitely, or that an unlimited power of so binding them is essential for the right conduct of government. . . . Yet this matter of royal contracts is not, as some writers believe, to be governed by the same rules as an unauthorized agency, whose transactions are to be ratified only if they prove advantageous. For to reduce the ruler of a state to such narrow limits is dangerous to the state itself. Consequently we should not believe the people had any such idea when they conferred authority on him. In the case of a city, the Roman emperors ordained that in a matter of doubt the action taken by

the magistrates was valid,[1] but not if there were no doubt that they had been relaxing what were their obligations. While keeping due proportion, we can and should apply the same principle to answer our question with regard to the people as a whole.

Now not all laws are binding on subjects, for even besides those that prescribe something illegal, there may be some that are patently foolish and absurd. So too the contracts of rulers are binding on their subjects only so far as they are reasonable in character. But in case of doubt, their reasonableness should be assumed on account of their ruler's authority. This distinction is far better than the one suggested by many writers, based on whether the results are more or less harmful. In this instance not the results but the reasonable character of the thing contemplated should be taken under consideration. If it seems reasonable, the people too will be bound by it, even where they happen to have begun to be independent; and also the king's successors, as heads of the people. For if a free people had contracted to do a thing, anyone who later took over their government would be bound to do it, even if his authority were absolute. . . .

We should, however, add here that if by any chance a contract should start to lead not only toward some damage but toward a public disaster, in such a way that if originally drawn up to be extended that far, it would have been judged unlawful and illegal, it may not be exactly revoked but declared no longer binding, on the ground that it was made under certain conditions, lacking which it could not lawfully be made. . . .

And if a contract provides for the alienation of the kingdom, or of a portion of it, or of the royal patrimony, wherever that is not under the king's control, it will be void as disposing of other men's property. The same will be true in limited monarchies, where the people have removed some subjects and types of action from the power of the king. To make such an act valid there the consent of the people themselves or of their lawful representatives is required. . . .

14. NEITHER people nor true kings are bound by the contracts of unlawful usurpers, since they possess no right to bind the people. But the people will be bound for anything spent for their profit, that is, in so far as it has made them richer.

XV

Treaties and Engagements.

1. ULPIAN divided [1] agreements into two kinds, public and private. Public agreements he explained not as some would by a definition but by examples. His first example is agreements 'made in time of peace.' His second is 'agreements made by generals commanding in war.' By public agreements, then, he means those which can be made only by a higher or lower government authority, in which respect they differ both from the contracts of private individuals, and from the contracts of kings about their personal affairs. And although private agreements often furnish causes for war, public agreements do so still more often. So, as contracts in general have already been amply discussed, we must give some account of this higher order of agreement.

2. PUBLIC agreements . . . we may divide into treaties, engagements, and other compacts.

3. ON the distinction between treaties and engagements we may consult the ninth book of Livy,[2] where he informs us that treaties are contracts made by command of the sovereign power, through

which a people is rendered liable to divine wrath, if it fails to keep
its word. Among the Romans such treaties were habitually concluded by the college of Fetiales, accompanied by a ratifying
priest. An engagement is a promise affecting really the sovereign
power, but made by persons without commission for that purpose
from the power. We read in Sallust:[3] "The Senate, as was right,
decreed that no treaty could have been made without their consent and that of the people." . . .

But in monarchies, the king has the power of making treaties.
. . . No subordinate magistrates can bind the people; nor can a
minority of the people do so. . . . It is not possible, as Gellius
says,[4] to treat with a people divided in two. . . .

4. LIVY tells us [5] that Menippus, ambassador from King Antiochus to the Romans, made a classification of treaties, though one
that fitted rather his own purposes than the rules of his art. He said
there were three kinds of treaties which kings and states made with
one another. By one, terms were imposed on a people conquered
in war. In it the victor dictated what properties he wished the conquered to keep and what to forfeit. By the second kind, those who
were equal in war arrived through a fair treaty at peace and friendship. Then property was demanded back and returned, and whatever rights of possession had been disturbed in the war were
readjusted, either under the form of an old law or to suit the convenience of both parties. By the third kind, those who had never
been enemies came together to cement their friendship by a treaty
of alliance. Such people neither imposed terms nor submitted to
them.

5. BUT we must make a more exact classification of treaties, and
say first that some establish merely the rights which are part of the
law of nature, and others add something to them. Treaties of the
former kind are customarily made between enemies at the end of
a war, and in ancient times were also frequently made, and were in
some degree necessary, between peoples who had previously never
entered into any contract. For the principle of the law of nature,

that men are by nature akin to one another, and therefore that it is a sin for one man to injure another, was obliterated before the Deluge, and some time after the Deluge, it was again obliterated by evil habits, so that to rob and plunder strangers, even with no declaration of war, was considered lawful. Epiphanius called it [6] 'the Scythian fashion.' Thus in Homer,[7] "Are you brigands?" is a friendly question. . . .

In the law of the Romans it was a rule that nations with whom no friendship or law of hospitality or treaty of good will had been established were not therefore enemies. But if anything belonging to a Roman fell into their hands, it became theirs, and a free Roman, captured by them, became a slave; and the same would be done to any one of them who appeared among the Romans. . . . Aristotle commends [8] the practice of plundering barbarians, and in ancient Latium the word 'enemy' meant nothing but 'foreigner.'

In this class of treaties I include those that provide for rights of hospitality and of commerce for both parties, as far as such rights come under the law of nature. . . .

6. TREATIES that add something to the law of nature are either equal or unequal. Equal treaties are those whose terms are equivalent for both sides. . . .

Treaties of both kinds are made to secure either peace or some sort of alliance. By equal treaties of peace, agreement is reached for the restoration of prisoners and captured property, and the maintenance of safety, a subject which will be more fully treated hereafter, in connection with the effects and consequences of war. Equal treaties of alliance deal either with trade, or with the joint prosecution of a war, or with other matters. Equal agreements for trade may vary in their terms. They may provide, for instance, that no import duties shall be paid by either side . . . or that no heavier duties shall be levied than at present, or that they shall not exceed a certain amount. . . .

In an alliance for war there may be an arrangement to furnish equal numbers of auxiliary cavalry, infantry, or ships, either for every war—which the Greeks call a complete alliance, and Thucydides describes [9] as a provision for having the same enemies and friends, . . . or for one particular war; or against one particular enemy, or against every enemy except allies. . . . There are other objects too for which, as we said, equal treaties may be made, such as that neither party shall build a fortress in the other's territory, or shall defend the subjects of the other, or allow the other's enemy passage through its country.

7. FROM this account of equal treaties, it is easy to infer what unequal treaties are. The inequality agreed to may be on the side either of the superior or of the inferior party. The superior party, on its side, may promise assistance without stipulating for any in return, or may promise greater assistance. For the inferior party this inequality . . . consists of terms which are called dictates or commands. And such treaties may or may not be attended with impairment of sovereignty. Such impairment of sovereignty marked the second treaty between the Carthaginians and the Romans, by which the Carthaginians were prohibited from making war on anyone without the consent of the Roman people. . . . To this kind of treaty may be added a conditional surrender, except that this implies not an impairment but a total transfer of sovereignty, a subject which we have already discussed. . . .

The burdens attached to unequal treaties, where no impairment of sovereignty takes place, may be either temporary or permanent. Temporary burdens are requirements for the payment of money, demolition of fortifications, withdrawal from certain places, or surrender of hostages, elephants, or ships. Permanent obligations are those which require the recognition of the supreme power and majesty of the other party. How great is the force of such a treaty we have explained elsewhere.

Close to this is a treaty which compels one party to have as its friends or its enemies those whom the other party chooses, or forbids it to allow passage or furnish supplies to the troops of any state with which the other party may be at war. Besides these may be the less important conditions prohibiting the building of fortresses in certain spots, or the placing of armies there, the keeping of ships beyond a specified number, the building of a city, navigation on the sea, raising troops in certain regions, attacking allies or aiding enemies with supplies, or admitting refugees. Or it may demand the annulment of all former treaties with other states. Examples of all such treaties are to be found in Polybius, Livy, and other writers.

Unequal treaties may be made not only between the conquerors and the conquered, as Menippus thought, but also between more powerful and less powerful states, which have never even been at war with one another.

8. IN considering treaties, the question is often asked, whether it is lawful to make them with persons who are strangers to the true religion, a matter which, according to the law of nature, admits of no doubt. For that law is common to all men without distinction of religion. . . .

9. LET us examine first the divine law of the Old Testament and then that of the New. Before the law of Moses, it was permissible to make, with strangers to religion, a treaty to refrain from injury. An example is the treaty of Jacob with Laban.[10]. . . Nor did the law given by Moses change this custom. Take the Egyptians, for instance, who were then undoubtedly idolaters, but the Jews were forbidden [11] to keep apart from them. . . . Trade treaties likewise, and other similar agreements that were to the advantage of both parties or of one, might, according to the law, be made with heathen. For there is nothing to be found against it. As examples we have the treaties which David and Solomon made with Hiram, king of Tyre.[12] . . .

The law of Moses, however, commanded Jews to do good, especially to their own people, to love their neighbors. Furthermore, the peculiar food and system of habits prescribed for the Jews hardly left room for intimate association with other men. . . . The comment of Tacitus [13] about them bears on this point: "Among themselves unflinching good faith and instant charity;

against everyone else enmity and hatred." . . . Later they were
charged with hatred to the human race. In Philostratus,[14] Apollonius of Tyana says of the Jews: "They have set up a way of life
so removed from intercourse with humanity that they will not even
sit at table with other men." . . .

But this was not the intent of the law, as Christ taught us by his
example in not refusing to accept a drink of water from the Samaritan woman,[15] although he was everywhere most punctilious
in observing the law. . . .

There is still the question of alliances for war. Before the law of
Moses, such alliances with heathen peoples were not forbidden, as
appears in the example of Abraham,[16] who aided the wicked
Sodomites in a war. Nor do we read that the law of Moses made in
general any change in this respect. . . .

10. THE law of the Gospel also made no change in this regard;
rather, it gives more support to treaties by which assistance in a
just cause is rendered to strangers to our religion. For the doing of
good to all men, when occasion arises, is now not only permissible
and laudable, but is required of us by precept. In imitation of God,
who makes his sun to rise upon the evil and the good, and refreshes
them both with his rain, we are commanded[17] to exclude no race
of men from our help. . . . This rule we should accept, saving
only some difference in degree, for though we show kindness to
all, we should do so especially to our brothers in the faith. . . .
Even familiar living with men who are strangers to our religion
is not forbidden. Nor is all intercourse prohibited with those even
in worse case, who have fallen away from the rule of Christian
teaching, but simply intimacy beyond what is needed. And even
that is allowed if it gives promise of reforming them. . . .

11. IN such alliances then there is nothing intrinsically or absolutely wrong, but they should be judged by the circumstances.
Care too should be taken lest too intimate a mingling pollute the
weak; for which reason it is useful to keep the housing separate, as
the Israelites lived apart from the Egyptians. . . . However, if by

such an alliance the power of the pagans will be greatly enhanced, we should refrain from making it, unless in extreme necessity. . . . For no right whatever is sufficient to sanction our doing something which we think will prove harmful to our religion, if not directly, then indirectly. For first of all we must seek the kingdom of heaven, that is, the spreading of the Gospel. . . .

12. AND here I shall add that all Christians are members of one body, commanded to feel for one another's pains and sufferings, and that this precept applies both to individuals and to nations as such, and to kings as such. Nor should a man serve Christ by himself alone, but also with the power committed to him. And this kings and people cannot do, while ravaged by an impious enemy, unless they come to one another's aid, which they cannot satisfactorily do without a treaty made to that end. Such a league was once formed, and the Roman Emperor by general consent appointed its head. To such a common cause all Christians ought to contribute men and funds in proportion to their ability. How they can be excused from doing this I do not see, unless they are kept at home by unavoidable war or some other similar calamity.

13. THIS question too often arises; when several states are at war with each other, to which side ought one to give assistance if allied with both? Here, first, we must observe, as we said earlier, that there exists no obligation to support unlawful wars. On which account our ally, who has justice on his side, should have our preference in a struggle with an outsider or even with another ally. . . .

But if our allies are at war for unlawful reasons on both sides, as may happen, we should have nothing to do with either one. . . . However, if two allies are engaged in wars against others, each for a lawful cause, and if we can send aid to both in troops or in money, we should do so, as one does in the case of personal creditors. But if personal assistance, which cannot be divided, is required of us who promised it, reason requires that we give preference to the one with whom we have been longer allied. . . . However, an exception must be made in case the later treaty contains in it something more than a promise of aid, something like a transfer of ownership, that is, some form of subjection. . . .

14. ON the expiration of the time specified, one should not assume that a treaty is tacitly renewed, unless things are done that admit of no other interpretation, for a new obligation is not to be lightly assumed.

15. IF one party violates a treaty, the other is released from it. For every clause of a treaty has the force of a condition. . . . This is true, except where it has been agreed to the contrary, as is sometimes done, so that a treaty may not be abandoned for trifling grievances.

16. ENGAGEMENTS may be made on as many subjects as treaties. The distinction between them is the difference in power of those who make them. But there are two questions usually asked in connection with engagements. First, if the king or the state refuses to ratify it, to what are the negotiators bound—to compensate for the loss, or to restore things to the situation they were in before, or to deliver themselves up in person? The first answer seems to accord with Roman civil law, the second with justice; and it was advocated by the tribunes of the people, Lucius Livius and Quintus Maelius, at the time of the Caudine debate.[18] But the third is that usually adopted, as shown in the instances of the two famous agreements of Caudine Forks and Numantia. This, above all, is to be insisted upon, that the sovereign is in no way bound by such engagements. Postumius rightly said to the Romans,[19] . . . "I maintain that no pledge can be made that will bind the people without the people's consent." . . .

17. THE second question is whether an engagement binds a sovereign who knows of it and keeps silent. Here we should make a distinction between an unconditional engagement, and one made on condition of its ratification by the sovereign. For as conditions ought to be literally fulfilled, such a condition, if not fulfilled, makes the engagement void. . . .

Silence, unaccompanied by some sign or act, does not of itself furnish a sufficiently probable ground for an assumption of intention, as may be seen from what we said above regarding abandonment of ownership. . . .

There remains to be said something about the compacts made by generals and soldiers that have nothing to do with matters of sovereign authority, but only with their private concerns, or affairs entrusted to them. But there will be a more suitable place to speak of these when we come to incidents of war.

XVI

Interpretation.

1. IF we consider only the man who has made a promise, he is bound of his own will to fulfill what he chose to make his obligation. "In good faith," says Cicero, "what you meant, not what you said, is the thing to be considered."[1] But acts of the mind are not of themselves visible, and it is necessary to reach some kind of certainty, if we are to prevent all engagements from being nullified by allowing men to free themselves by assigning any meaning they like to their words. So natural reason dictates that the one to whom the promise was made has a right to compel the promiser to do what a fair interpretation of his words implies. For otherwise the transaction would have no result, a thing that in the practical realm is called impossible. . . . The rule for right interpretation is to gather the intention of the parties from the most probable signs.

And these are of two kinds, namely, words and inferences, which may be considered either separately or together.

2. WHERE there is no inference to suggest something else, words are to be understood in their accepted sense, not in a grammatical sense, based on their derivation, but in accordance with popular usage. . . . The Locrians devised a foolish piece of perfidious evasion when they promised they would hold to their compact as long as they stood on that soil and wore heads on their shoulders, and then threw away the earth which they had put in their shoes, and the heads of garlic which they had laid on their shoulders, as if in that way they could free themselves from their religious obligation. This story is told by Polybius.[2] . . . Tricks like these, Cicero correctly says,[3] aggravate instead of mitigating the perjury.

3. IN the case of technical terms which the people scarcely understand, one should go for explanation to the experts in each art. . . . So when in treaties there is mention of an army, we will define an army as a large concourse of soldiers, capable of openly invading an enemy's country. For historians everywhere make a distinction between a stealthy raid, in the manner of brigands, and the acts of a regular army. To reckon how great a force constitutes an army, one should compare it with the strength of the enemy. Cicero calls [4] six legions and their auxiliaries an army. Polybius says [5] that a Roman army usually consisted of sixteen thousand Romans and twenty thousand allies, but a smaller number can fill the definition. . . . In like manner one may judge how many ships to call a fleet. And thus a fortress is a place able to hold out for a time against the enemy's army.

4. WHEN words or sentences admit of several interpretations, it is necessary to resort to inference. . . . Similarly, it is necessary to fall back on inference whenever a seeming contradiction occurs in the wording of a compact. Then we must try to make such conjectures as will reconcile, if possible, one part with another. If the contradiction is fundamental, a later agreement between the contracting parties will cancel the earlier, since no one could want op-

posite things at the same time. Such, indeed, is the nature of acts depending on the human will that by a new act of will they can be altered either by the will of one party, as in the case of laws and testaments, or by joint consent, as in contracts and treaties. . . .

In all such cases some conspicuous obscurity in the language obliges us to resort to conjectures. These are sometimes so obvious as to suggest themselves readily, even in opposition to the more usual interpretation of the words. . . . Now the principal sources of conjecture as to the meaning are the subject matter, the effects, and the circumstances.

5. IN the subject matter, for instance, may be the word 'day.' If a truce is made for thirty days, it should be understood as meaning legal, not natural days, for this meaning fits the subject matter. . . . So too the word 'arms,' which at one time means weapons of war and at another armed troops, should be interpreted in either this or that sense, according to the subject matter. And one who has promised to surrender men should surrender them alive and not dead. . . . And in a division of ships, 'one half the ships' should be taken to mean whole ships, not ships cut in two. . . . In all similar cases, such should be the judgment.

6. AS to effects, a problem arises chiefly when a word taken in its more usual meaning would lead to consequences contrary to reason. In the case of an ambiguous word, the fair interpretation should be chosen. The quibble of Brasidas [6] therefore should be condemned. He promised to evacuate Boeotian territory, and then declared that the territory which he occupied with his army was not Boeotian, as if the name applied to lands held merely in wartime and not to the ancient boundaries. In that sense the treaty was meaningless.

7. CIRCUMSTANCES are those of either origin or place. Circumstances of origin affect those agreements made with the same intention, according to place and occasion, which furnish ground for inference, since in a doubtful case we suppose the person's intention was consistent with itself. Thus in Homer,[7] the agreement between Paris and Menelaus, that Helen should be given up to the

conqueror, is to be explained by what follows as meaning by 'the conqueror' the one who killed the other. . . .

8. AS to circumstances of place, the reason here for a rule is the strongest. Many confuse this with the intent, whereas it is only one of the indications by which we arrive at the intent. . . . For there are frequently several reasons for an act, and sometimes the will, regardless of reason, through the power of its own liberty, decides for itself, which suffices to create an obligation. Thus a gift presented for a wedding will be canceled if the marriage does not take place.

9. IT is further to be observed that many words have several meanings, one narrower and another broader; which may be due to a variety of causes, either the application of the name of a genus to a single species, as in words of kinship and adoption; or the use of masculine nouns to cover things of common gender, when nouns of common gender are wanting. In technical usage too a word may embrace more than it does in popular usage. So in civil law, the word 'death' is stretched to include banishment, whereas in popular speech its meaning is not that.

10. AS regards promises, we should note further that some are acceptable, some odious, some mixed or indifferent in character. Acceptable promises are those based on equality, which aim at a common good. The greater this good is and the more widely extended, the more acceptable is the promise; hence those are more so that lead to peace rather than to war, or concern a war for defense rather than a war for other purposes.

Odious promises are those that impose a burden on one side only, or on one side more than on the other, or that contain penalties in themselves, or invalidate things already done, or disturb some previous arrangement. A mixed promise may change some earlier arrangement, but in the interest of peace; and it will be considered now acceptable and now odious, according to the amount of good or of change produced. Other things being equal, such a promise may better be called acceptable. . . .

12. THESE principles being established, the following rules should be observed. In agreements that are not odious, the words are to be taken in their full meaning, according to popular usage; and if they have several meanings, the broadest should be taken, even as a masculine gender may be taken to mean a common gender, and an indefinite expression to mean everyone. . . .

In the more acceptable agreements, if the party promising knew the law or employed the advice of a lawyer, the words may be taken still more broadly, including even technical and legal interpretations. But we should not resort to interpretations that are plainly farfetched, unless otherwise the result would be an absurdity, or an end to the usefulness of the agreement. On the other hand, the words may be interpreted more strictly than good usage demands, if such interpretation is necessary to prevent an injustice or an absurdity. Even if no such necessity exists, but either justice or utility manifestly requires a strict interpretation, we should rigidly adhere to it, except where circumstances may influence us to do otherwise. In interpreting odious agreements, some allowance for figurative language may be made in order to lessen the burden. So, in case of a grant, or a surrender of rights, though the terms may be general, they are usually restricted in interpretation to what was probably in the promiser's mind. . . .

13. IT is a famous question whether under the name 'allies' are included only those who are allies at the time of making a treaty, or those who will afterward become so; a question raised by the treaty between the Roman people and the Carthaginians at the end of the war over Sicily:[8] "The allies of each people shall be safe from harm by the other people." For from this the Romans inferred that although their treaty with Hasdrubal, by which he was prohibited from crossing the Ebro, was of no service to them, since it had not been ratified by the Carthaginians, yet if the Carthaginians sanctioned the conduct of Hannibal in attacking the people of Saguntum, whom the Romans had taken as allies after making that treaty, they could declare war on them for having violated it. . . .

What shall we say? Undoubtedly the word 'allies,' with due regard for correctness of speech, means strictly those who were allies
at the time the treaty was made, but may also have a second, wider
meaning covering those who will become allies. Which of these
two interpretations should be preferred must be deduced from the
rules given above. According to those rules, we say that future allies
were not included in that treaty, because a breach of treaty, which
is an odious matter, was thereby involved, and also the destruction of the Carthaginians' freedom to punish by force those who
they believed had injured them—a natural freedom, not to be surrendered without serious cause.

Were the Romans debarred then from making allies of the
Saguntines or defending them after the alliance? No! They were
entitled to do it, though not by virtue of the treaty, but by the principles of natural law, which the treaty had not canceled. With respect to the Saguntines' relation with both parties, they were in the
same situation as if no agreement had been made about allies, in
which case it was no breach of treaty for the Carthaginians to attack them on what they thought were just grounds, or for the
Romans to defend them.

The situation was clarified in the time of Pyrrhus, when the Carthaginians and Romans agreed that if either of them later made a
treaty with Pyrrhus, it should be with a reservation of the right to
send aid to whomever Pyrrhus might attack. . . . This is an example of an equal treaty.

14. FOR an unequal treaty we shall cite another case, where it is
agreed that one of the allied parties may not make war without the
consent of the other. This was a provision of the treaty between the
Romans and the Carthaginians after the Second Punic War, as
we have already stated. . . . As the expression 'make war' may
signify either a war of any description, or else an offensive but not
a defensive war, in case of doubt, we should take it in its narrower
sense, so as not to put too great a restraint on a people's liberty. . . .

16. AND here should be taken up the question that frequently

arises as to compacts that are personal and those that are real. In all transactions with a free people, the engagements entered into with them are indubitably real in their nature, because the subject of them is a permanent thing. Even if the form of the state changes to a kingdom, the treaty will remain in force; for although the head is changed, the body stays the same, and, as we said above,[9] the sovereignty which is now exercised by a king does not cease to be the sovereignty of the people. To this rule there will be an exception if it is evident that the cause of the treaty lay in the special form of the state, as when free states make a treaty to preserve their freedom.

But a compact made with a king is not offhand to be considered only a personal treaty. For, as Pedius and Ulpian rightly say,[10] the name of a person is often inserted in a compact, not to make it a personal compact, but to show with whom it was made. That it is real will be plain enough if a clause is annexed declaring the treaty to be perpetual, or made for the good of the kingdom, or with the king and his successors . . . or for a specified time. . . . Other words, too, and sometimes the subject matter itself, will furnish food for likely inference that it is real.

But if indications are even on both sides, we shall end by regarding acceptable treaties as real and odious ones as personal. Treaties to promote peace or encourage trade are acceptable. Yet all alliances for war are not odious, as some people think; but alliances for defense are more likely to be welcomed, and offensive alliances to seem burdensome. Moreover, in any alliance for war the presumption is that the prudence and loyalty of the other party has been taken into account, and that he seems unlikely to precipitate an unlawful war, or even a rash one. . . .

The position of Bodin [11] we can certainly not accept, which is, that treaties made with kings extend not to their successors, since the binding power of an oath does not go beyond the person who took it. It is true that an oath can bind only the person who takes it; yet the promise itself can be binding on an heir. Nor is it true what Bodin assumes, that oaths are the foundation on which treaties rest, for usually the promise itself is efficacious enough, and the oath is added only to give it greater sanctity. . . .

17. A treaty made with a king continues surely in force, even if the king or his successor is driven by his subjects from the country. For he retains his rights over his kingdom, even though he has lost possession. . . .

18. ON the other hand, if at the will of the true king we attack an invader of another's kingdom, or an oppressor of a free people before he has won popular sanction, that will not be a violation of a treaty, since those persons have possession but no rights. . . .

19. THIS much is enough on the interpretation that has to do with the proper or improper meaning of words.

20. THERE is also another kind of interpretation by conjecture that has nothing to do with the meaning of the words containing the promise. This is of two kinds, either broadening or narrowing the promise. The interpretation that broadens is more difficult to apply and the one that narrows is easier. . . . The difficulty is much greater here than in the case above mentioned, where the words admit of a broad, though less familiar interpretation. For here we are looking for a meaning beyond the verbal promise, which must be very plain in order to make it binding. A similar purpose is not enough; it must be the same. Neither is it always enough to say that reason requires us to extend the meaning; because, as we just said, reason is often so swayed that the will by itself is a sufficient cause, even without reason.

To authorize therefore such a broadening interpretation, it must be evident that the reason covering the case we are trying to understand was the sole effectual cause that influenced the promiser, and that he viewed it in the same comprehensive sense, because otherwise his promise would have been unjust or useless. . . . As an example, take an agreement that a certain place should not be enclosed in walls, made at a time when there was no other kind of fortification. That place cannot even be enclosed by earthworks, if it is plain that the sole motive for prohibiting walls was to keep the place from being fortified at all. . . . In a declamation of Father Quintilian there is the following example: [12] "Murder seems to imply blood and steel. But if a man is killed by any other method, we apply the same law. If he falls into brigands' hands and is hurled into the water or thrown down from a great height, the same law will avenge him and a man stabbed by a sword." . . .

21. HEREWITH we may solve the famous problem found in Gellius,[13] whether a mandate can be fulfilled by doing, not the exact thing ordered by the mandatory, but something equally useful, or even more useful. Such conduct is indeed allowable if it is certain that what the mandatory ordered he did not require to have done in his particular manner, but that he expressed a general idea which might be carried out in some other way. . . . However, where that is not quite certain, we should abide by what Gellius says in the same place, that all duty to the person giving the order would be gone if the one bidden to do something might respond not with due obedience but with an unwanted plan of his own.

22. AN interpretation, restricted more closely than the actual sense of the words of the promise requires, may be based either on some defect in the original intention of the promiser, or on some incompatibility in the situation, as it develops, with his intention. It is considered a defect in the original intention when obviously an absurdity would follow the fulfillment of the promise; or when the sole and effectual reason which furnished the motive for the intention has ceased to exist; or when there is a defect in the subject matter. This first principle is founded on the fact that no man can be supposed to have willed an absurdity .

23. IN the second instance, when a reason is assigned for the promise or is clearly understood, the content of the promise is considered not by itself alone, but to the extent it comes under the reason.

24. IN the third instance, as regards the subject matter, it should

always be looked at from the point of view of the promiser, even if the words signify something broader. . . .

25. IN a consideration of reasons, we should note that they often include things, not on the ground that they actually exist, but as possibilities of a practical sort; in such a case there should be no restriction of meaning. Thus, if there is a provision that no troops or ships shall be brought to a certain place, they cannot be brought there, even with no intention of doing harm. For the purpose of the agreement was to guard not only against positive mischief but against every kind of risk. Another point often disputed is whether promises contain in themselves the tacit proviso that conditions remain as they are. To this question we give a negative answer, unless it definitely appears that the present state of affairs was included in the special reason of which we have spoken. Frequently in histories we read of ambassadors abandoning their missions and returning home after starting on their journey upon learning that things had so changed that the object or cause of their embassy had ceased to exist.

26. INCOMPATIBILITY of a developing situation with the intention of the promiser . . . may come about in two ways. . . .

This should be understood of wills and treaties in one way. For not all contingencies can be foreseen and described in full; hence it is necessary to allow some freedom to make exception of cases which the author of the document would except if he were present. Yet this should not be done lightly, for it would be to make oneself master of another man's acts—but only on sufficient evidence.

The clearest evidence of incompatibility of a promise with the intention of the promiser is when a literal following of his words would involve something unlawful, that is, something contrary to natural or to divine law. For such promises are incapable of creating an obligation and so exceptions must be made. . . . Thus a man who has promised to return a sword left in his care will not return it to a madman, for fear of bringing danger on himself or on other innocent persons. Likewise an article deposited with someone should not be returned to the person who deposited it, if the real owner claims it. . . .

27. A second sign of incompatibility appears when a literal following of the words is not in itself absolutely unlawful, but in the opinion of a fair judge imposes too hard and intolerable a burden, whether one looks at the character of human nature in general, or compares the person and the matter in question with the real purpose of the act. Thus, if a person has lent something for several days, he may ask for the return of it within those days if he has great need of it himself; for the nature of such acts of kindness implies that no one should be supposed to have intended to bind himself thereby to his own manifest inconvenience or hurt. So one who has promised assistance to an ally will be excused insofar as he needs all his troops while he is in danger at home. A grant of exemption from taxes or tribute is understood as applying to the ordinary daily and yearly levies, not to those imposed in an extreme emergency, which the state cannot do without.

From the above instances, it appears that Cicero has worded too loosely his proposition [14] that "promises which are valueless to the person to whom you gave them need not be kept, nor if they are more prejudicial to you than of benefit to the person to whom you gave them." For the promiser must not be the judge as to whether the thing he promised is advantageous to the one to whom he promised it, except, perhaps, in a case of insanity, as cited above. And to release a promiser from his obligation it is not enough that he may receive some damage from it. The damage must be so great that in view of the nature of the event, it would properly be supposed to create an exception. Thus a man who has promised to work certain days for a neighbor is not bound to come, if detained at home by the serious illness of a father or a child. . . .

In the same sense we should accept, but not push too far, what we read in Seneca: [15] " . . . Whatever is in any way changed, gives me freedom to reconsider the whole situation and releases me from my pledge. . . . I promised to go abroad with someone, but it is reported that the road is infested with brigands. I was to come in person to court, but a sick son or a wife in labor keeps me at home. Everything must be the same as it was when I made the promise, if you are to hold me to my pledge." . . .

29. WITH regard to deciding which of the parts of a document should be accepted as authoritative when there happens to be a contradiction between them, Cicero laid down some rules from the ancient authors. They surely should not be disregarded, though in my opinion he set them down not in their proper order. We should list them as follows:

An agreement to permit should give way to a command, because the one who permits a thing seems to be permitting it only in case there is no other objection to it than the one then contemplated. . . .

What must be done at a given time should take preference over what may be done at any time. Whence it follows that prohibitions in a compact generally carry more weight than commands; because a prohibition is binding at all times, whereas it is not so with commands, unless they specify a time, or include a tacit prohibition.

As between agreements which in the above-named respects are equal, the preference should be given to the one that is more specific and comes closer to the point in question. For special agreements are apt to be more effective than general ones.

As for prohibitions, one which has a penalty attached should be given more weight than one which has not; and one which carries a heavier penalty than one which carries less. Agreements that are based on more honorable or more important reasons ought to take first place.

Finally, what was said last should count most.

Here we must repeat what we said before, that the character of sworn agreements is such that they ought to be understood in their most usually accepted meaning, rejecting all implied limitations and such as are not in the nature of the case absolutely necessary.

And whenever a sworn agreement clashes in a particular instance with another not supported by an oath, preference should be given to the one sanctified by an oath.

30. IT is often asked whether in a doubtful case, a contract should be held complete before the written form of it has been finished and delivered. . . . To me it seems plain, unless it has been settled to the contrary, that the written document is admissible as evidence of the contract, but not as part of its substance. Otherwise it is customary to state, as in the truce with Nabis,[16] that the agreement is in effect "from the day the terms are written out and delivered to Nabis."

31. BUT I shall not admit the rule that some writers have accepted, namely, that all contracts of kings and peoples ought to be interpreted as far as possible in accordance with Roman law, unless it appears that among some peoples the Roman civil law has been accepted as the law of nations in matters that come under a law of nations, an assumption which ought not to be hastily granted. . . .

XVII

Damages Unlawfully Inflicted and
Obligations Arising Therefrom.

1. WE have said above that debts due to us have three sources—compacts, injuries, and laws. We have discussed compacts fully enough. Let us proceed to what is due us by the law of nature as a

result of a wrong. By a wrong we mean every fault of commission or of omission in violation of the duties required of all men, either as members of a community or by reason of their particular station. Such a fault by the law of nature creates an obligation to repair the damage if any has been inflicted.

2. BY DAMAGE . . . is meant a diminution, when a man has less than belongs to him, whether it is a right derived merely from the law of nature, or augmented too by some human institution, such as property ownership, a contract, or a law. By nature a man's life is his own, not indeed to destroy, but to preserve; his own too are his body, limbs, reputation, and actions. How property ownership and contracts assure to a man what is his—both goods and a right over other persons' acts—has been shown in the preceding part of this treatise. In the same way, every man derives a right from the law, because the law has as much or greater power over persons and property than individuals have. Thus by law a ward has a right to demand some sort of strict attention to business from his guardian, the state from a magistrate, and not only the state but every separate citizen has that right, wherever the law expressly or by clear enough inference grants it. . . .

3. BUT we must beware here of confusing things of a different kind. A man entrusted with the duty of appointing magistrates is under bonds to the state to choose a worthy person, and the state has a special right to require this of him. So he will be under obligation to repair any damage which the state may suffer from an unsuitable appointment. So also any citizen who is not disqualified, though he has no special right to an office, has a true right with others to be a candidate for it. In the exercise of which right, if he is hindered by violence or fraud, he may recover damages to the value not of the whole office which he sought, but of the possible harm to his chances. . . .

4. A person's possessions may be diminished and damage thereby done him in the matter not alone of his property, but of the produce that rightly comes from it, whether it has been gathered

or not, provided he expected to gather it. But expenses incurred that improved the property or that were necessary for gathering the produce, should be deducted, in accordance with the rule that forbids us to enrich ourselves by another's loss.

5. WE should measure too our expectation of gain from our property not as though we actually had it, but in proportion to our nearness to obtaining it, as in seedtime we expect the harvest.

6. BESIDES the person who himself and directly commits the injury, others too may be liable for acts of commission or of omission. By their acts, some may make themselves primarily liable, others secondarily. Primarily liable is one who issues the order for the crime, who gives the required consent, who aids, who receives the booty, or in any other way is a partner in the offense.

7. SECONDARILY liable is one who gives advice, praise, or approbation. . . .

8. FAILURE to act may also make one primarily or secondarily liable. Primarily, when a man whose duty it is by law, rightly so called, to forbid the wrong by his command, or to succor the injured party, fails to do so. . . .

9. SECONDARILY, when a man whose duty it is does not try to dissuade the wrongdoer, or keeps silent about a deed which he ought to make known. . . .

10. IT should likewise be understood that all the persons we have mentioned, if they have really been a cause of the injury, that is, have given an impetus to it, are liable either for the full amount, or for a part. For it happens often, in cases of commission or of omission of the secondary type, and sometimes too in cases of the primary type, that the injury would undoubtedly have been committed by the offender, even without the others' acts or failures to act. In which case these I have mentioned will not be liable. But this fact must not be taken to mean that if there were still others on hand who might have advised or assisted the wrongdoer, those who did advise and assist him are not liable, as long as without their aid and counsel the injury would never have been committed.

For those others would also have been liable, if they had given advice or help.

11. FIRST of all, the persons are liable who by a command or other means impelled someone to commit the deed. Lacking them, the perpetrator of the crime comes first, and after him, the group of other individuals who prompted the deed, each liable for the whole damage in case they were a cause of the entire offense, though not the sole cause.

12. NOW a man who is answerable for an act is answerable at the same time for the consequences of it. In a *Controversy* of Seneca [1] this point is discussed in the case of a plane tree set on fire, from which a house caught flame. He there makes the following statement: "Although a part of the mischief you did not intend to commit, yet you are liable for it all, as much as if you had done it by design. For a person who defends himself by a plea of not intending a mischief ought not to have intended any part of it." . . .

13. TO take other examples. A man who has unlawfully killed another man is bound to pay the costs of the doctors, if there were any, and to provide for those whom it was the deceased's duty to support—such as his parents, wife, and children—as liberally as their expectation of support was worth, in view of the dead man's age. . . . We are speaking here of an unlawful homicide, that is, by one who had no right to perform an act of which death was the result. . . . No valuation can be put on the life of a freeman. It is different with a slave who could be sold.

14. A person who maims another is likewise liable for the expense involved and for the decrease hereafter in the earning power of the maimed man. . . .

15. SO an adulterer and an adulteress are bound not only to indemnify her husband for the support of their child but also to recompense her legitimate children for whatever loss they may suffer from the participation of that child in their inheritance. A man who violates a virgin by force or fraud is bound to pay her the value of the diminution of her expectation of marriage. He is even

bound to marry her, if by promise of marriage he obtained the enjoyment of her body.

16. A thief and a robber are bound to restore what they took, with all its natural increment, and to make reparation for the loss incurred, and the profit that was not made. If an article has been destroyed, they should pay for it at an estimation neither the highest nor the lowest but fair.

In this class of offenders should be included those who by fraud avoid payment of their lawful taxes; also those who injure others by an unjust judgment, a false accusation, or untrue testimony.

17. A person who has procured a contract or a promise by fraud, violence, or unlawful fear is bound to make full restitution to the other party, because he had a right not to be deceived and not to be coerced. The first right he derived from the nature of contracts, the second from his natural liberty.

With these offenders we may class men in office who refuse to perform their duties without a bribe.

18. BUT a person who has himself given cause why he should suffer coercion or intimidation has himself to blame. For something involuntary that is the result of something voluntary is counted practically as voluntary.

19. HOWEVER, by the consent of nations the principle is admitted that all wars declared and conducted by authority of the sovereign powers on both sides are to be called lawful as far as their external effects are concerned, a subject of which we shall speak later. Consequently, the fear of such a war is regarded as lawful, to the extent that whatever has been obtained through that fear cannot be asked back. In this sense we accept the distinction that Cicero draws [2] between a public enemy, with whom by the consent of nations we have, as he says, many rights in common, and robbers and pirates. For what the latter have extorted from us by terror can be demanded back, unless we have given our oath; what the former have taken cannot. . . .

20. KINGS and state officials are answerable for neglect, if they do

not use all the means they can and should to suppress piracy and robbery. . . .

At a time when the rulers of our country had granted to many persons authority by letters of marque to take booty from the enemy at sea, and some of them had plundered friends, deserted their country, and were wandering loose over the ocean, refusing to return even when summoned, I remember being asked whether the rulers were responsible on the ground either that they had made use of the services of unprincipled men, or had not required security from them.

I said that they were responsible for nothing more than the punishment or surrender of the offenders, if they could be caught; and that, in addition, they should see just compensation paid from the pirates' property. For they themselves had not been the cause of that lawless plundering or shared in the fruits of it. They had even passed laws prohibiting interference with friends. No law required them to take security, since even without letters of marque they could give all subjects the right to seize enemy property—a thing that had previously been done; nor could any such permission be considered the cause of the injury done to our allies, since even without that permission private individuals could arm ships and put out to sea. It really could not have been foreseen that those men would turn out badly, nor could we avoid using the services of wicked men; otherwise we could never collect an army. Nor are kings answerable if contrary to orders their soldiers or sailors do some injury to their friends, a rule approved by testimony of France and England. . . .

21. IT is to be noted too that civil law requires that a slave or an animal that has been a cause of damage or impairment be given up as a penalty. For by natural law an owner who is not at fault is not liable. So neither is a person whose ship, through no fault of his, has damaged another man's ship. However, by the laws of many nations as well as ours, such damage is usually divided between the two parties, on account of the difficulty of proving guilt.

22. DAMAGES, as we have said, may be done also to honor and reputation by blows, insults, accusations, slander, ridicule, and other similar methods. In these cases as well as in a case of theft or other wrongdoing, the criminality of the offense is to be distinguished from its effects. The punishment is the answer to the criminality. Reparation for the damaging effect is made by confession of guilt, conferment of honor, acknowledgment of innocence, and the like. Such damage too may be repaid by money, if the injured party wishes it, for money is the common measure of all valuable things.

XVIII

Right of Embassy.

1. THUS far we have been describing the rights due us by the law of nature, with but a little mention of the voluntary law of nations, insofar as it has added something to the law of nature. We have next to take up the obligations that the law of nations, which we call voluntary, has itself imposed on us. In this class the right of embassy is a most important subject. Everywhere we read of the sanctity of embassies and of ambassadors, the law of nations appointed for them, divine and human law, the right of embassy sacred among nations, alliances sacred to peoples, the alliance of mankind. . . . To violate this right is, by universal admission, not only lawless, but, as Philip said in his letter to the Athenians,[1] impious.

2. BUT first we must understand that this law of nations we are about to examine, whatever it is, has to do only with ambassadors who are sent by rulers with sovereign powers to one another. For besides these there are deputies sent from provinces, cities, and other places, who are governed not by the law of nations that exists between different nations, but by civil laws. In Livy [2] an ambassador styles himself the public messenger of the Roman people. . . .

Nations then connected with each other by an unequal alliance, so long as they do not cease to be self-governing, have the right of embassy. Even those who are partly subject and partly not have that right for the portion that is not subject. But kings who have been conquered in formal warfare and stripped of their dominions have lost the right of embassy along with their other royal privileges. . . .

In civil wars, however, necessity sometimes creates a warrant for this right, regardless of the rule, as when, for instance, a people is divided into two parties so nearly equal that it is doubtful to which of the two the right of sovereignty belongs; or when two claimants, both with dubious rights, are contending for succession to the crown; in such an event, one nation is considered as two nations for the time being. . . . But pirates and robbers, who do not make a state, cannot base any claim to the right on the law of nations. Tiberius, when Tacfarinas sent ambassadors to him, was enraged that a deserter and a bandit should behave as if he were a lawful enemy. These are Tacitus' words.[3] Yet sometimes men of that sort obtain the right of embassy on a pledge of good faith, as in old time fugitives did in the passes of the Pyrenees.[4]

3. THERE are two rights of ambassadors which we see frequently ascribed to the law of nations; first, their right to be admitted; second, their right to be protected from violence. . . .

But the law of nations does not command us to admit everyone. It only forbids us to refuse admission without sufficient reason. The reason may be the person who sends, or the person sent, or the

object of his mission. Thus, at the suggestion of Pericles, Melesip-
pus, a Spartan ambassador, was dismissed from Attic territory
because he came from an enemy in arms. The Roman senate said
that it could receive no embassy from the Carthaginians while
their army was in Italy. . . . An instance of the second reason is
the refusal of Lysimachus to hear Theodorus, who was called "the
atheist," although he was sent by Ptolemy. The same thing has
happened to other ambassadors on grounds of personal offensive-
ness. The third reason we mentioned appears when the object of
the mission is suspicious—as it was when the embassy of Rab-
shaketh the Assyrian [5] was rightly suspected by Hezekiah of
coming to stir up his people; or when the object is not consistent
with dignity or suitable at the time. . . .

With perfect right rulers may refuse to receive the permanent
legations that are now the custom. Ancient practice, to which they
were unknown, shows us how unnecessary they are.

4. THE question of the inviolability of ambassadors is more
difficult and has been treated in a variety of ways by the distinguished writers of our age. We must take into consideration the
persons of the ambassadors, and then their attendants and property.

As to their persons, some writers are of the opinion that it is
only from lawless violence that the law of nations gives ambassadors
bodily protection. For they think that their privileges are to be
interpreted as a part of common law. Others believe that an
ambassador is liable to physical coercion, though not for all
offenses; only if he has transgressed the law of nations, which is
comprehensive enough. For the law of nations includes the law
of nature; consequently an ambassador could be punished for any
crime except for those that are made crimes solely by civil law.

Others again restrict an ambassador's immunity to offenses
committed against the welfare of the state or the dignity of the
person to whom he is sent. Whereas there are some who maintain
that this is a dangerous arrangement and that all complaints ought
to be made to the one who sent the ambassador and the decision

left to him. There are some too who think that kings and nations who have no interest in the matter should be called in for counsel. That might be a policy of wisdom; it is not an obligation by law.

The arguments on which the advocates of these theories base their views lead to no definite conclusion. For this right is not, like the law of nature, definitely a product of fixed causes, but takes its form in accordance with the will of the nations involved. The nations might have laid down rules of security for ambassadors in all cases, or have made certain exceptions. On one side there is the advantage of punishing heinous offenders; on the other, the utility of embassies; exchange of them is best promoted by providing for them every possible security. We should consider therefore how far the nations have reached an agreement. This cannot be discovered by examples alone, for there are plenty of them on both sides. We must turn to the opinions of wise men and to inferences.

I have two especially famous opinions, one of Livy, and one of Sallust. Livy has this to say [6] when speaking of the ambassadors of Tarquin, who had fomented insurrection at Rome: "Although their conduct had evidently been such that they might have been treated as enemies, yet the law of nations prevailed." Here we see the law of nations extended to cover even ambassadors who perform hostile acts. Sallust's statement has to do with the train of an embassy, of which we shall speak shortly, not with ambassadors personally. . . . He says: [7] "Bomilcar, Jugurtha's companion, who had come to Rome under the state's pledge of good faith, was brought to trial on principles of equity and justice, rather than under the law of nations."

Equity and justice, that is, the pure law of nature, allow the punishment of an offender, wherever he is found, whereas the law of nations makes an exception of ambassadors, and those who, like them, come under a pledge of public faith. Wherefore to bring ambassadors to trial is contrary to the law of nations, which prohibits many things that the law of nature permits.

Our reasoning tends to support this view. For privileges should really be understood as additions of something to the common right. Now if ambassadors were protected only against unlawful violence, there would be nothing great, nothing extraordinary in that. Besides, the security of ambassadors is a matter of greater importance than the punishment of an offense. For an ambassador may be punished by the one who sent him, if the latter so chooses. And if he refuses, he may, as a supporter of crime, be compelled by war to inflict punishment. Some writers object that it is better for one man to be punished than for many to be involved in war. But if the one who sent the ambassador approves his conduct, our punishment of that ambassador will not exempt us from a war.

On the other hand, the security of ambassadors would rest on a very slippery foundation if they were accountable for their acts to anyone but the one who sent them. For the views of those who send and of those who receive ambassadors are frequently different, and often even opposed, and almost always some charge can be brought against an ambassador which has the appearance of a crime. And although some instances are so obvious as to admit of no doubt, yet the universal danger is serious enough to prove the justice and utility of a universal law.

For this reason, I am convinced, the nations have agreed that in the case of ambassadors an exception should be made to the common rule requiring everyone living in a foreign country to be subject to that country, since ambassadors by a kind of fiction are identified with the persons who sent them. As Cicero says of a certain ambassador,[8] "He bore with him the majesty of the Senate and the authority of the state." So too by a similar fiction it is held that ambassadors are, as it were, not a part of the country to which they are sent. Consequently they are not subject to the civil laws of the people among whom they are residing. If an offense is such that apparently it can be ignored, it should either be covered up, or else the ambassador should be ordered to leave the country, as Polybius says [9] was done to one who had assisted some hostages at Rome to escape. . . . If the crime is more heinous and aimed at creating a public disaster, the ambassador should be sent back to the one who sent him with a demand that he be punished or else handed over. . . .

But, as we have already more than once observed, all human laws are so arranged that in a case of extreme necessity they may be relaxed, and the same rule holds for the doctrine of the inviolability of ambassadors. However, even this dire necessity does not mean the infliction of punishment which the law of nations prohibits in other cases also, as we shall see further on, when we discuss the effects of formal war. It is much less a concern for place, time, or mode of punishment than for the prevention of a great evil, especially to the state. To avert therefore an immediate peril, if no other proper method can be devised, ambassadors may be detained and questioned. . . . But an ambassador who attempts to raise an armed force may certainly be put to death, not by way of punishment, but as a measure of natural self-defense. . . .

5. THE law that I have mentioned, forbidding violence to ambassadors, should be understood as binding on the one to whom the embassy is sent, at any rate after he has received it, as if from that time a tacit agreement existed between them. But warning may be given, and often is, not to send ambassadors; and if they come, they will be treated as enemies. . . .

This law does not apply to a people through whose territory ambassadors pass without a safe conduct. For if they are going to an enemy of that people, or are returning from him, or are otherwise engaged in some hostile activity, they may be slain; as the Athenians killed the ambassadors passing between the Persians and the Spartans. . . . But if no such excuse exists, then to maltreat ambassadors is deemed not a violation of the law of nations, which is the subject of our discourse, but an offense against friendship and the dignity of the one who sent them or to whom they are going. . . .

6. AN embassy once received is under the protection of the law of nations, even among enemies, and much more so among those

who are only unfriendly. . . . Pomponius says: [10] "A man who strikes the ambassador of an enemy is considered to have committed a crime against the law of nations, for ambassadors are regarded as sacred." . . . Such a statement is well warranted, for in war many matters come up that cannot be dealt with except through ambassadors, and peace can scarcely be made by any other means.

7. THE question is also raised whether an ambassador who comes from a ruler who is guilty of lawless acts can be killed or maltreated by the law of reprisal. There are indeed many instances of such reprisal in the histories. But histories record of course not only lawful deeds but those too that were lawless, wrathful, and passionate. The law of nations protects both the dignity of the sender and the safety of the one sent. So the tacit agreement covers him too. Thus a wrong may be done to him, even if none is done to the one who sent him.

So it was not only a magnanimous answer, but one in conformity with the law of nations that Scipio made,[11] when after the Roman ambassadors had been mishandled by the Carthaginians, the Carthaginian ambassadors were brought before him, and he was asked what should be done to them. For he replied: "Nothing like what the Carthaginians have done." . . .

8. THE aides of ambassadors too and all their valuables have their own kind of inviolability. . . . By the Julian law on public violence,[12] those who injure not only ambassadors, but also their attendants, are pronounced guilty.

But their rights are inviolate only as accessories, and as far as the ambassador thinks right. Accordingly, if any of his suite commit a serious offense, the ambassador may be asked to deliver them up. They cannot be taken away by force. . . . If the ambassador refuses to give them up, the same action may be taken as we have just said might be taken in a case involving the ambassador himself. Whether an ambassador has jurisdiction over his household, and the right to give asylum in his house to whatever fugitives take refuge there, depends on the permission of him in whose territory he resides. That is not a part of the law of nations.

9. NEITHER the movable property of an ambassador, nor anything which is considered attached to his person can, by the best opinion, be seized as security or for the discharge of a debt, whether by order of the courts, or, as some assert, by the hand of the king. For an ambassador must be free from all coercion, both as regards his person and everything needed by him, in order that his security may be complete. If, then, he has contracted a debt, and, as is usual, owns no landed estate in the country, he should be asked in a friendly way to pay; and, if he refuses, the request should go to the one who sent him. Finally, the methods may be used that are customarily used against debtors living outside the country. . . .

11. PROFANE histories abound in instances of wars undertaken because of the ill-treatment of ambassadors. The holy Scriptures too record the war which David waged on that ground against the Ammonites.[13] . . .

XIX

Right of Burial.

---

1. THE obligation to bury the bodies of the dead is a part of the law of nations that has its source in the human will. . . . Seneca the elder [1] ranks the law which bids us spread earth over the bodies of the dead among the unwritten laws that are stronger than all

the written. . . . Whoever hinders a burial casts off his manhood,
says Claudian,[2] disgraces nature, says the emperor Leo,[3] sins against
righteousness, says Isidore of Pelusium.[4]

As the ancients were accustomed to ascribe to the gods as authors
the rights common to civilized men, in order to make them appear
more sacred, so we see that this right, like the right of embassy, is
frequently attributed to the gods. . . .

In Sophocles,[5] Antigone makes the following reply to Creon, who
had forbidden the burial of Polynices:

> "Sure this decree was not the will of highest Jove
> Nor holy law of the gods of the dead world,
> To whom the race of men owes other laws.
> Nor did I think that your commands had power
> Being but mortal, to transgress the laws,
> Unwritten and eternal, willed by gods.
> Not yesterday were they in force, but from all time,
> Their origin unknown. . . ."

2. THERE seems to be no general agreement as to why the custom
was first introduced of covering bodies with earth, whether previously embalmed, as they were with the Egyptians, or burned,
as they usually were with the Greeks, or buried as they are now. . . .
Moschion [6] thinks the cause was the ferocity of the giants in eating
men, and that burial was a sign that that habit had been
stopped. . . .

Others think that in this way men paid, as it were of their own
accord, a debt which otherwise nature would demand of them,
even against their will. For it was not on Adam only that God
passed the sentence that man's body sprung from earth must be
returned to earth. Greeks and Latins also generally acknowledge
it. . . . In Solomon we read [7] that "the dust shall return to the
earth as it was, but the spirit to God who gave it." Euripides, in
the character of Theseus in The Suppliants,[8] touches on this
subject:

"Now let the dead be laid in the earth's lap.
All things return to where they first arose;
Spirit goes back to heaven, body to earth.
For by no right of purchase was it ours,
But lent for a brief use. Earth soon asks back
What she has fed and nourished." . . .

There are some who think that the first parents of the human
race bequeathed to their descendants by this testimonial, as it
were, their hope of a resurrection. For Pliny tells us, in the fifty-
fifth chapter of his seventh book,[9] that Democritus taught that
bodies should be preserved for the promise of living again. And
Christians have often ascribed the custom of honorable burial to
the same hope. . . .

It is simpler to say that inasmuch as man excels other creatures,
it would seem an indignity if his body were to become the food
of the beasts. In order to prevent that as far as possible, burial was
invented. Out of compassion, says Quintilian,[10] the bodies of
men are guarded from the ravages of birds and beasts. . . . And
God, by the mouth of his prophets, warns the kings whom he hates
that they shall have the burial of an ass, and that dogs shall lick
their blood. Lactantius has the same idea of burial when he says: [11]
"We shall not allow the image and handiwork of God to lie the
prey of birds and beasts." . . . Even if our bodies were not mal-
treated, it would still be unworthy of the dignity of human nature
that they should be mangled and trampled under foot. . . . Hence
the office of burial is said to be performed not so much for the dead
man, that is, for the individual, as for humanity, that is, for human
nature. . . . As a consequence, we should not begrudge burial
even to our enemies, private or public. . . . Optatus of Milevis
gives the same reason.[12] "If there was strife between you living, let
the death of your adversary appease your hatred. For he with whom
you contended now lies silent."

3. so everyone agrees that public enemies are entitled to burial.

. . . Examples of this practice are found everywhere. Thus Hercules buried his enemies; Alexander those who fell at Issus. Hannibal tried to bury the Romans, Caius Flaminius, Publius Aemilius, Tiberius Gracchus, and Marcellus. . . .

Many times in histories you may read that a truce was granted to remove the dead. . . . Accordingly, as the old Jewish writers explain, their high priest, who was at other times forbidden to come near a funeral, was commanded to bury a human body, if he found one unburied. The Christians thought burial so important that they believed it right to melt down and sell even the consecrated vessels of the church for that purpose, as they did for support of the poor, or redemption of captives. There are indeed some instances to the contrary, but by universal judgment they are condemned. . . .

4. IN the case of notorious criminals, however, I see there are reasons for doubt. The divine law, indeed, which was given to the Hebrews, and which is the teacher of all virtue and humanity, ordered that even persons hanged on a gallows, the most ignominious kind of punishment, should be buried on the same day. . . . Among the Romans, Ulpian says [13] the bodies of men sentenced to execution are not to be refused to their relatives. . . . We read in the histories, however, of instances of bodies cast out unburied, more frequently in civil war than in foreign. And today we see the bodies of some executed criminals left long in the public view. But whether this practice is to be approved is a question much debated by both statesmen and theologians. Contrarily, we find praise bestowed on those who ordered buried the bodies of men who had not themselves granted the same honor to others. . . .

5. ONE point deserves remark. Even among the Jews, their law for burial of the dead made an exception of persons who had committed suicide, as Josephus tells us.[14] Nor is that surprising, since no other punishment can be inflicted on those to whom death seems no punishment. . . . Aristotle says [15] that it is generally

agreed that suicides should suffer some disgrace. . . . It is no objection to such a custom that, as Homer, Aeschylus, Sophocles, Moschion and others remind us, the dead feel nothing, and so are not affected by loss or shame. For it is sufficient if what happens to the dead so terrifies the living as to deter them from sinning in that way.

The Platonists are right in opposing the Stoics and others who accept the dread of servitude or of sickness, or even ambition for fame as a just excuse for self-destruction, whereas the Platonists maintain that the soul should be kept in the custody of the body, and should not depart this life save at the bidding of him who entrusted it to us. . . . Brutus, following their opinion, once condemned the death of Cato,[16] whom he later imitated, "thinking it at first neither dutiful nor manly to succumb to fate and shrink from threatening misfortunes, which he ought to bear with courage." . . .

Yet there are Jews who make one exception to the law against suicide, calling it 'a praiseworthy departure,' if a man sees that his continued living would be a reproach to God himself. . . Such a case, they say, was that of Samson, who perceived that in his person true religion was an object of derision. . . . In Christian history we read of similar examples of persons who slew themselves so that when put to the torture they might not abjure the religion of Christ, and of virgins who threw themselves into a river that they might not lose their chastity. . . .

But to return to my subject, the ancients with great unanimity agreed that a refusal of burial was justification for going to war. . . .

6. THERE are certain other rights too which owe their origin to the voluntary law of nations, such as the right to things possessed for a long time, the right of succession to one who has died intestate, and the rights resulting from a contract, however unequal. For though all these rights are in some measure derived from the law of nature, they receive from human law a certain confirmation,

against the uncertainties of conjecture and against exceptions that otherwise natural reason would appear to suggest, as we pointed out earlier, when discussing the law of nature.

XX

Punishments.

---

1. WHEN, earlier in this treatise, we started our discussion of the reasons for which wars are undertaken, we said that such action was to be considered as taken for one of two purposes, either to compel reparation, or to inflict punishment. The first of these purposes we have now dealt with; the second, which has to do with punishment, is still to be treated. This subject we must consider all the more carefully because the origin and nature of punishment have not been well understood, with the result that there have been many errors.

Now punishment, taken in its general meaning, signifies an evil of suffering, inflicted in return for an evil of action. Although labor is sometimes imposed on persons as a punishment, the labor is regarded from the point of view of its hardship and is therefore to be classed with suffering. And the inconveniences which men sometimes suffer from a contagious disease or a bodily injury or some impurity—many of which are listed in Hebrew law—such as being excluded from public assemblies or from offices, are not, properly speaking, punishments, although from some resemblance to a punishment they are often, by an abuse of terms, called by that name. But among the things which nature herself pronounces lawful and just, and which the philosophers call the most ancient law and the law of Rhadamanthus, is the rule that one who does evil shall suffer evil. . . .

What we have said of punishment, properly so called, amounts simply to this, that it is a return for crime, as Augustine noted when he said: [1] "Every punishment, if it is just, is a punishment for a sin." This applies even to punishments inflicted by God, although in those cases, the same writer says, because of human ignorance: "The guilt may be hidden while the punishment is not."

2. OPINIONS differ as to whether punishment comes under the head of attributive or of expletive justice.[2] Some class it with attributive justice, because the greater offenders are punished more heavily and the less more lightly, and because the punishment is inflicted by a whole, as it were, upon a part. But their first assumption, that attributive justice operates whenever an equality is established between more than two terms, is not true, as we showed early in this book. Then, as to the fact that more harmful criminals are punished more severely, and less harmful more lightly, that happens merely as an incidental result, and not because it was part of the original and essential aim. For originally and essentially the aim is simply to make guilt and punishment equal. . . . Nor is there more truth in their second assumption, that all punishments are inflicted by a whole on a part, as will appear from what we have yet to say. . . .

Yet those who maintain that expletive justice—which ordinarily they call commutative—is operative in punishments offer no better explanation. For they look on it as a business transaction, as if offenders were being paid something, as they are in contracts. They are deceived by the popular expression we use when we say that punishment is due a person who has committed a crime, which obviously is misleading. For a person to whom something is properly due has some right over another person. But when we say that punishment is due someone, we mean nothing more than that it is fair he should be punished.

Nonetheless it is true that expletive justice is operative in punishment, originally and essentially. For he who punishes, if he is to punish correctly, must have a right to do it, a right growing out of the crime of the offender. And in this there is something approaching the nature of contracts. For just as a seller, even though he makes no special statement to the effect, is understood to have bound himself to perform all the acts natural to a sale, so, punishment being a consequence of serious crime, the criminal seems to have voluntarily subjected himself to punishing. Accordingly, he who directly wills to transgress wills also as a consequence to deserve punishment. In this sense, the emperors say to an offender:[3] "You have imposed this punishment on yourself." . . .

3. BUT who is the possessor of the right to punish, that is, the one to whom the right belongs, is a matter not settled by the law of nature. For though reason declares that a malefactor may be punished, it does not say who ought to punish him, except as nature does clearly suggest that it is most suitable for a superior to do it. Yet this is no proof that such a requirement is absolutely necessary, unless the word 'superior' is taken in a sense implying that the wrongdoer by his very deed is considered to have made himself inferior to everyone else, and to have, as it were, degraded himself from the rank of men to that of brutes, which are in subjection to man; a doctrine which some theologians have proposed. . . .

Whence it follows that in no case should one wrongdoer be punished by another equally guilty. This is the meaning of Christ's saying: "He that is without sin among you, let him first cast a stone." (John VIII, 7.) . . . Here belongs a remark of Seneca's:[4] "No judgment can have any weight when the condemner himself deserves to be condemned." . . .

4. ANOTHER question has to do with the ends proposed by punishment. For what we have said thus far shows only that no injus-

tice is done to malefactors by punishing them. But it does not follow from this that they should invariably be punished. And it is not true that they should. For both God and man pardon the guilty for many faults and are praised on that account. The saying of Plato is famous,[5] that "Punishment is not imposed to do harm"; and elsewhere: "Punishment is not inflicted to undo a wrong done (for what has been done will never be undone), but to protect the time to come." Seneca renders it thus:[6] . . . "We shall not make a man suffer because he has sinned, but to keep him from sinning; nor shall punishment ever have an eye to the past but to the future. It is a measure not of anger but of precaution." . . .

These maxims are true with regard to human punishments, for one man is tied so closely to another by their common blood that he ought not to inflict pain on him save to accomplish some good. But with God the case is different, and Plato is wrong in applying the above principles to him. For the acts of God may be based on his right of supreme dominion, particularly where a man's special deserts are involved, even though the acts have no end in view beyond themselves. . . . But when man punishes man, who by nature is his equal, he should have some clear end in view. The scholastics say that the mind of an avenger ought not find satisfaction in someone else's pain. And even before them, Plato in his *Gorgias* said [7] that persons who punish another with death or exile or a fine should not "desire simply that," but desire it "for some good end." . . .

5. AS for what the comedian said: [8] "The pain of his enemy is healing to a wounded man's woe," and Cicero's remark,[9] that "pain is soothed by punishment"—these befit the nature that man has in common with the beasts. For anger in man, as in beasts, is "a heating of the blood around the heart, caused by a desire to repay pain," as Eustratius rightly defines it.[10] This desire is in itself so irrational that it often strikes out at things that have done no harm, such as the young of a hurtful animal, or at senseless things, such as a stone by which a dog has been hit.

But a desire like this, when regarded by itself, does not fit our rational part, whose duty is to control our emotions. Nor is it sanctioned by the law of nature, since that is a dictate of nature in so far as nature is rational and social. And the dictate of reason to man is to do nothing that may hurt another man, unless it is to bring about some good. But the mere pain of an enemy, considered solely as such, is not a good, except a false and imaginary one, like superfluous riches and many other things of the kind.

In this sense vengeance among men is condemned by both Christian teachers and the philosophers. . . . Indeed, if we are to believe Maximus of Tyre,[11] "The man who takes vengeance is more wicked than the man who did the first wrong." Musonius says: [12] "To plan how one may bite the biter and hurt the one who has done a hurt is the way of a brute, not of a man." . . . So it is against the nature of a man in contention with another man to glut himself on the other's pain, because it is pain. The less use any man makes of his reason, the more eager he is for revenge. . . .

It is plain then that man cannot rightfully be punished by man merely for the sake of punishing. Let us see what useful ends make punishments right.

6. . . . . BUT this question deserves a more minute investigation. We shall say then that in punishing we are to aim at either the welfare of the wrongdoer, or that of him whose interests were injured by the wrongdoer, or that of other people in general.

The first of these three ends is attained by that kind of punishment which philosophers sometimes call correction, sometimes chastisement, and sometimes admonition, . . . Plutarch's 'medicine of the soul,' [13] which acts so as to make the offender better, like medical treatment that operates by contraries. So since all acts, especially those that are deliberate and frequently repeated, produce a certain propensity, which when ripened is called habit, vices should be stripped of their allurements as early as possible, which can best be done by causing them to lose their sweet flavor by following them with pain. . . .

7. THE right to inflict punishment that serves this end is by nature granted to any person of sound judgment, who is not a slave to similar or equal vices, as we see in cases of verbal reproof.

> "To reprove a friend because his fault deserves it
> Is a thankless task, but in due season helpful." [14]

As for cases of flogging and other punishments that include an element of compulsion, the distinction made between those who are allowed and those not allowed to inflict them is not made by nature, but by laws. For nature could not do it, except in so far as reason gives parents a peculiar right to exercise authority over their children because of their close tie. But the laws, in order to prevent quarrels, have passed over the common kinship of the human race, and limited that right to the nearest relatives. . . .

However, this type of punishment cannot be extended to include the death penalty, unless by the way they call reduction, by which negatives are reduced to their opposite positives. Thus Christ said [15] that it would have been better, that is, not so bad, for some men if they had never been born, and so it is better, that is, a less evil, for incurable dispositions to die than to live, when it is certain that by living they will grow worse. Of such persons Seneca is speaking when he says [16] that sometimes it is an advantage to the dying to die. . . . But since the proofs of such a state are not to be depended on, charity bids us call no one incurable too hastily, and punishment for such a reason can but seldom be permitted.

8. THE welfare of the person injured by the crime depends on his being protected in future against any other such injury, either from that offender or from others. . . . There are three ways of saving him from suffering injury again from the same person: first, by removing the offender; second, by depriving him of the power of doing harm; lastly, by teaching him to forsake his evil ways, which is close to the correction we have just spoken of. To save the injured person from more injury from others, the punishment must

be not any kind of penalty, but something public and conspicuous, to serve as an example.

Vengeance, even when inflicted by individuals, provided it is directed to these ends and kept within bounds of justice, is not unlawful, if we consider the bare law of nature by itself, apart from human and divine laws, and from incidental circumstances. It may be inflicted by the injured person or by someone else, for it is in accord with nature that one man should help another. . . . Aristides, the orator, says [17] that poets, lawgivers, proverbs, orators, all agree that "vengeance may be taken on those who have first injuriously attacked us." . . .

But inasmuch as in our own affairs and those of our families we are apt to be biased, as soon as a number of families came to settle in one place, judges were appointed, and to them alone was given the power of avenging injuries, while the rest were deprived of that liberty that nature had allowed them. . . . However, the old natural liberty survives, first, in places where there are no courts, as at sea. Apropos of this, perhaps, is the incident related of Julius Caesar, who, while still a private citizen, pursued with a hastily assembled fleet some pirates by whom he had been taken prisoner, put some of their ships to flight, and sank others. And when the proconsul delayed punishing the pirates who had been captured, he put out again to sea, defeated and crucified them. The same liberty survives in the desert, or where men live as nomads. . . .

This is the origin of the dueling practiced by the Germanic peoples before the introduction of Christianity, and not yet altogether abandoned. Hence, Velleius Paterculus tells us,[18] the Germans were amazed when they saw the form of Roman judicial procedure, because there justice put an end to injustice, and disputes which they were accustomed to decide by the sword were settled by law. . . . But instances of this custom are most frequent among people who have no common judge. So Augustine defines [19] lawful wars as "those that avenge injuries." . . .

9. THE welfare of men in general, which was the third end of

punishment, may be considered under the same heads as the welfare of the person injured. For the object in view is either to prevent the person who wronged one individual from wronging others, which is accomplished by removing or weakening or restraining him, so that he can do no more harm, or by reforming him. Or else it is to prevent others from being lured by the prospect of impunity into molesting people in general. This end is attained by conspicuous punishments, such as the Greeks and Latins call 'examples,' which are inflicted in order that many may be terrified by the punishment of one man, and others may be deterred by the type of penalty, as the laws say; or, as Demosthenes says,[20] "that others may learn wisdom and be afraid." The power and right to punish for such an end by the law of nature belongs to everyone. Thus Plutarch observes [21] that a good man is appointed a magistrate by nature, for the law of nature itself bestows leadership on one who acts justly. . . . Yet within a state this principle is to be understood as extending only as far as the laws sanction it.

As for the law of nature, Democritus says: [22] "What we have written with regard to foxes and dangerous reptiles we think should be applied to men also." He then goes on: "Whoever puts to death a thief or a robber by any method, whether with his hands or by his order or by his vote, is free of guilt." . . .

But since it often requires great care to examine into the facts, and much wisdom and fairness to fix the amount of punishment, so to prevent the rise of quarrels from every man's claiming too much for himself and others refusing to give way to him, in all well-ordered communities men have agreed to select as judges those whom they consider the best and wisest, or who they expect will prove so. . . . But, as we just observed happening in cases of vengeance, so in this kind of punishment for the sake of example, traces and remains of the primitive right persist in those places and among those persons that are subject to no established courts, and in certain other exceptional situations. . . . Among many people too the full right of punishment, even to death, still belonged to masters over slaves, and to parents over children. So the Ephors at Sparta might put a citizen to death without trial.

From what we have now said, it is plain what the law of nature is about punishments, and how far it still remains in force.

10. WE come now to consider whether the law of the Gospel has set narrower limits to our freedom to punish. Surely, as we said in another connection, it is not surprising that some things which are allowed by natural and civil law are forbidden by divine law, since that is nearest perfection, and offers a reward over anything that human nature can bestow. For the attainment of this reward it is not unreasonable that virtues are required exceeding the simple precepts of nature. It is clear from the nature of the matter that chastisements that leave neither loss of reputation nor permanent injury, and are needed because of the age or other condition of the one chastised, provided they are inflicted by those who have the permission of human laws—by parents, for instance, or guardians, masters, or teachers—are in no respect contrary to the precepts of the Gospel. For they are remedies for the soul, no more harmful than distasteful medicines.

But with vengeance the case is different. For in so far as it is merely a gratification of the injured one's resentment, it is not permissible, even by the law of nature, and to the same degree is contrary to the Gospel, as we showed above. . . . The Hebrew law, however, permitted Jews to avenge serious injuries, not with their own hands, but by appealing to a judge. But Christ does not give us the same permission, as appears from the contrast he makes in the passage: [23] "Ye have heard that it hath been said, An eye for an eye," and later, "But I say unto you—." For although what follows deals strictly with resistance to injuries, and to some extent limits our freedom in this respect, yet it should be taken far more as a condemnation of vengeance, canceling the old permission as suited only to a more imperfect age. . . .

And here comes in the command given by Christ to us all without distinction, to forgive all those who have sinned against us—

Matthew VI, 14–15. That is, we should neither do nor wish them harm because we feel we have been harmed. . . . What then shall we say of vengeance, not as retaliation for the past but as precaution for the future? Undoubtedly, Christ wishes us to forbear here too, particularly if the one who wronged us shows any likely signs of repentance. (Luke XVII, 3.) In this passage there is mention of a full pardon, that is, such as would restore the sinner even to the rights of his former friendship; consequently nothing should be exacted of him under the name of punishment. Furthermore, even if there are no such marks of repentance, Christ teaches us, by his command to let go our coat,[24] that we should not take our injury too seriously. . . .

If overlooking an offense involves grave danger, we should be content with such measure of security as inflicts the least possible hurt. For even among the Jews, vengeance was not usual, as Josephus and other Hebrew scholars tell us. But in addition to reimbursement for the expense he had incurred, . . . the injured party accepted a money payment in place of vengeance. . . . Justin, speaking of the accusers of the Christians, says: [25] "We do not wish our calumniators punished. Their wickedness and ignorance of the good is enough."

It remains now to consider punishments that aim at the good not of an individual but of the public, partly by removing or restraining the guilty person to keep him from doing further mischief, partly by deterring others through the severity of his punishment as an example. Punishments like these, we have elsewhere proved beyond a doubt, were not abolished by Christ; for when delivering his own commandments, he at the same time declared that he was destroying nothing in the law. And the law of Moses, which in these matters was to remain in force as long as the Jewish state existed, gave strict orders to magistrates to punish murder and certain other crimes. . . .

11. THERE are those who, in support of the opposite opinion, allege the supreme mercy of God as displayed in the New Testa-

ment, which therefore should be imitated by men, even by magistrates, as the vicars of God. That there is some truth in this we do not deny, but not to the extent which they claim. For the great mercy of God revealed in the New Testament touches chiefly offenses against primitive law, or against the law of Moses, committed before men had received knowledge of the Gospel. . . . But sins committed afterward, especially if marked by a hardened obstinacy, are threatened with judgment much more severe than any that was pronounced by Moses. . . . And God many times punishes sins of that kind not only in the other life, but in the present also. For sins of that kind to obtain pardon, a man must exact some kind of punishment from himself, with heartfelt sorrow. . . .

The same persons argue that immunity from punishment should be granted at least to persons moved by repentance. But to pass over the fact that men can hardly be sure of what is true repentance, and that there is no one who would not procure immunity for his crimes if it sufficed merely to profess some sort of repentance, God himself does not always remit for penitents the whole of their punishment, as appears from the case of David. . . .

12. OTHERS again raise the objection that when a life is cut short, so also is the opportunity for repentance. But they know that conscientious magistrates take great care in this matter and have no one hurried away to execution without allowing him time for realization of his sins and deep abhorrence of them. Such repentance, even though prevented by death from producing good works, may be accepted by God, as is proved by the example of the thief crucified with Christ.

If they urge that a longer life might have led to a more profound reformation, we may reply that there are men who deserve to hear the words of Seneca: [26] "The one good thing left for you is death, which we shall now bestow on you"; and also his other saying: "In the only way they can, let them cease being evil." . . .

These arguments, then, in addition to what we said in the opening of this treatise, shall be our answer to those who think that all punishments, or at least all capital punishments, without exception, are forbidden for Christians. The Apostle teaches us the contrary, when he includes in the office of king the use of the sword as an instrument of divine vengeance, and tells us elsewhere to pray that kings may become Christians, and as kings be a protection to the innocent. Even since the spread of the Gospel, because of the depravity of a great part of mankind, this end can only be attained by holding in check the violence of some by the death of others. In fact, even now, in the midst of so many executions and punishments of criminals, the innocent are scarcely secure.

Nevertheless it will not be out of place for Christian rulers to set before them for imitation, in part at least, the example of Sabacon, king of Egypt, highly renowned for his piety, who, Diodorus says,[27] changed capital punishment into sentences to hard labor, with most successful results. . . . Balsamon observes [28] that the laws of Rome which prescribed a penalty of death were many of them altered by the Christian emperors of later times, and other punishments substituted, so that the condemned might become more deeply imbued with penitence, and the longer duration of their punishment have more effect as an example. . . .

14. FROM what we have said thus far, it may be inferred how unsafe it is for a Christian private citizen, whether for his own or for the public good, to take on himself the punishment of an offender, particularly a punishment of death, even though, as we have said, it is sometimes allowed by the law of nations. Some nations have a laudable practice of furnishing navigators with warrants from the public authority to pursue whatever pirates they meet at sea, so that if occasion offers, they may act as under public orders.

15. A custom not unlike this prevails in many places, of not allowing any individual to bring a criminal charge, but only certain men on whom the public authority has imposed that office, with the result that no one takes any steps towards shedding another man's blood except as obliged by his office. . . .

16. FROM the foregoing it may also be understood that it is not wise or even fitting for a true Christian to undertake of his own accord a public office in which he has to pass judgment on the taking of life, and to think and profess it right that the power of life and death over other citizens should be bestowed on him, as if he surpassed them all and were a kind of god among men. Certainly Christ's warning applies definitely here, that it is dangerous to judge others, for what judgment we pass on them we must expect in like case from God on ourselves.

17. IT is a proper question whether the human laws that permit the putting to death of certain persons confer on their executioners a true right in the eyes of God, or only impunity among men. . . . There is no doubt that in certain cases, as we have said elsewhere, the law can confer either one. Which one it does confer may be deduced partly from the wording of the law and partly from its substance. If the law is lenient towards suffering, it may waive the punishment of the man while it does not deny his crime, as in the case of a husband who has killed his adulterous wife or her adulterous lover. But a law that takes into consideration the danger of future trouble, if punishment is deferred, may confer both the right and the public authority on a private citizen, so that he is no longer simply a private individual. Of this type is the law in Justinian's Code,[29] . . . where permission is granted to anyone to use punishment to put a stop to soldiers' looting. . . .

18. LET us now consider whether all wicked acts are of a kind to be punishable by men. Certainly we must declare that they are not. In the first place, mere acts of the mind, even though by some chance, such as a subsequent confession, they come to other people's knowledge, cannot be punished by men, because, as we said earlier, it is not suited to human nature that mere acts of the mind should furnish cause for any right or obligation among men. And in this sense we should accept the dictum of the Roman law: "No one deserves punishment for his thoughts." However, this does not prevent our taking into account mental acts in so far as they influ-

ence external acts, not for their own sake, but for that of the deeds
that acquire from them the nature of their deserts.

19. IN the second place, acts inevitable for human nature cannot be punished by men. For nothing can be sinful except what is
done of one's own free will, and to abstain always and completely
from any sin is to be above the condition of man. . . . "If," says
Seneca,[30] "everyone who has an evil and malicious spirit is to be
punished, no man will escape penalty." . . . Indeed, it may be
doubted whether such acts should rightly and properly be called
sins, since the free character they seem to have when viewed singly,
they do not possess when considered as a whole. . . .

There are also some actions which are not inevitable for human
nature in itself, but are so for a certain man at a certain time, on
account of some bodily state that affects his mind or some long-
established habit. Actions like these are punished not so much for
themselves as for the guilt that preceded them, because either there
has been a failure to take the proper remedies, or morbid thoughts
have been willingly harbored in the mind.

20. IN the third place, sins are not punishable which neither
directly nor indirectly affect human society or some other individual. The reason is that there is no excuse for not leaving such sins
to the punishment of God, who is the wisest to perceive them, the
most just to weigh them, and the most powerful to punish them.
For men, therefore, to assume the punishment of such acts would
obviously not be beneficial and hence a mistake. We must, however, except from this rule corrective punishments, designed for the
reformation of the offender, even where his conduct does not perhaps involve others. Nor are acts punishable that are simply the
opposite of virtues, the nature of which is incompatible with compulsion. Virtues of this sort are compassion, liberality, gratitude.
Seneca discusses the question [31] whether the vice of ingratitude
should go unpunished, and suggests many reasons why it should.
His chief argument, which may also be extended to cover other
similar cases, is the following: "Whereas to show gratitude is a

most honorable act, it ceases to be honorable when it is compulsory." . . .

21. LET us consider next whether it is permissible at times to grant full forgiveness or pardon. . . .

22. EVEN before the establishment of penal laws, punishment might unquestionably be inflicted, because by the law of nature a wrongdoer is in a state where he may permissibly be punished. But it does not follow therefrom that he must be. For that depends on the connection between the ends for which punishment is instituted and the particular punishment. If the ends themselves are not necessary from a practical point of view, or if ends of a contrary kind, not less useful or necessary, appear, or the ends projected by punishment may be reached in some other way, then, evidently, there is nothing that obliges us strictly to inflict the punishment. Take, for instance, first, a case where an offense is known to very few, and where accordingly a public exposure may be unnecessary, or even injurious. . . . Take, secondly, a case where a man has offset his wrongdoing by his own or his family's services, that deserve compensation. . . . Take, thirdly, a case where a man has been cured by reproof, or has offered satisfaction in words to the injured party, so that there is no longer need for punishment to attain those ends. . . .

23. THREE things then may happen. Either full punishment must be inflicted, as on criminals of the worst sort, or none at all may be inflicted, if it is for the public good to dispense with it, or either course may be open, in which case, as Seneca remarks,[32] clemency has free choice. . . .

24. SINCE the establishment of penal laws a decision to pardon seems more difficult, because a lawmaker is bound, in a way, by his own laws. But this, as we have already said, is true only in so far as the lawmaker is regarded as a member of the state, but not as representing the person and authority of the state itself. As such, he can even entirely repeal the law, for it is the nature of human laws to depend on human wills, not only for their origin but also for their

continuation. Yet a lawmaker ought not to repeal a law except for reasonable cause. Otherwise he will be sinning against the principles of governmental justice.

As, however, the lawmaker has power to repeal a law in its entirety, so in the case of a particular person or act he may suspend its force, while in all other cases it remains binding. . . . Yet this right of suspension too should not be used except for reasonable cause. What reasonable causes are cannot be precisely defined. But we must agree that after the establishment of penal law they should be more weighty than those that were accepted before the law, because to the grounds for punishment has been added the authority of the law, which it is expedient to maintain.

25. THE reasons for releasing a person from the penalties of the law are either internal or external. An internal cause exists when the punishment, though not unlawful, is still severe when compared with the offense.

26. AN external cause exists when some merit or other circumstance, or some fair hope for the future calls for leniency. And this kind of cause will have most weight when the reason for making the law, at least this particular provision, does not apply to the act in question. For although the general reason, when unopposed by any contrary reason, is sufficient cause for enforcing a law, yet where that reason in a particular case does not apply, the law may be suspended more easily and with less danger to authority.

Such a dispensation is most common in the case of offenses committed in ignorance, even though that ignorance is not entirely blameless, or in a state of mental infirmity that could be overcome, but only with difficulty. A Christian ruler should give most careful consideration to all these circumstances, that he may follow the example of God, who even in the Old Testament ordained that many crimes should be expiated by the offering of victims (Leviticus IV and V); and in the New Testament, by his word and example, declared his readiness to pardon the sins of those who repent. . . .

27. . . . WE have considered exemptions from punishment. Let us now consider the assessment of punishment.

28. FROM what has been said above, it appears that in the assessment of punishment two things are to be considered: that for which, and that for the sake of which. That for which is what is deserved; that for the sake of which is the benefit to be derived from the punishment. No one should be punished more than he deserves. . . . But within the bounds of what is deserved offenses may be punished more or less sternly according to the benefit to be derived therefrom.

29. WHEN inquiring into what is deserved, we should take into account the impelling reason for the act, the reason that ought to have prevented it, and the susceptibility of the offender to both. Scarcely anyone is wicked without some reason, or if he delights in evil for its own sake, he has passed outside the nature of human-kind. Most men are led by their desires to commit sin. . . . Under the name of desire I include now the impulse to avoid evil, which is the most natural and therefore the most commendable of desires. Thus wrong deeds committed in order to escape death, imprisonment, pain, or extreme poverty are generally thought very excusable. Here belongs the saying of Demosthenes: [33] ". . . Humane judges make allowance for necessity; but when wealthy men are lawless, they have no acceptable excuse." . . .

Other desires aim at some good, either true or imaginary. True goods, apart from the virtues and their practices which do not lead to sin—for the virtues form a harmony with each other—are either things that give pleasure, or are a cause of the pleasant things we call valuable, such as abundance of possessions. Imaginary goods are not truly good. Such are superiority over other men, when that is not due to virtue or to usefulness, and revenge. The farther these deviate from nature the more detestable they are. . . .

30. THE general cause that ought to prevent men from commit-ting crime is the injustice of it. We are speaking now not of sins of any kind, but of those which affect persons outside the offender

himself. The injustice is the greater the more harm it does to another person.

First among crimes, then, we place those which are completely carried out; and after them those which have gone as far as some action but not to the final step. In this latter class the crime is the more serious the further it has gone. In both classes the most outstanding kind of injustice is that which disturbs the public order, and is therefore harmful to the largest number. After it comes the injustice that wrongs individuals. The worst form of this is a threat to life; the next, a threat to the family, the foundation of which is the marriage contract; and the last is a threat to the desirable property of an individual, either by direct seizure of it, or by fraudulent means diminishing its value.

These topics might be analyzed in greater detail; but we have indicated the order followed by God himself in the Decalogue. For under the name of parents, who are natural magistrates, is rightly to be included the other rulers whose authority holds human society together. Next follows the prohibition of murder; then the sanction of marriage by a prohibition of adultery; then the prohibition of theft, and of false witness; lastly, of unconsummated crime.

Among the reasons that should restrain one from crime should be counted not only the character of the deed actually committed, but the probable consequences of it. If a fire is started or a dike broken, terrible catastrophes and even death for many people are to be expected.

In addition to the injustice of crime, which we have called the general reason for refraining from it, there is present in it sometimes another vice, such as undutifulness to one's parents, or unkindness to neighbors, or ingratitude to benefactors, which aggravates the offense. Frequent repetition too makes the depravity seem greater, since evil habits are worse than evil acts. Hence we may realize the natural justice of the Persian custom of taking into account a man's past life along with his transgression. And this ought to be done in cases where persons heretofore not wrongdoers have suddenly succumbed to some attraction in sinning. . . . The promulgation of a law against an offense adds to it a special kind of enormity. . . .

31. THE capacity of a person to weigh the reasons against crime, or to be aware of the desires impelling him towards it, is usually considered, along with his bodily constitution, age, sex, education, and the circumstances of the act. For children and women and men of dull intelligence and poor education have less understanding of the difference between what is right and what is wrong, what is lawful and what unlawful. Persons with an excess of bile are quick to anger, and those with an excess of blood are prone to lust. Youth too inclines to the latter; old age to the former. . . . The thought of immediate danger increases fear, and fresh and still unallayed pain kindles anger, so as hardly to allow the reason to be heard. Crimes, therefore, committed in such states of feeling are deservedly less abhorrent than those caused by desire for pleasure, because the latter is a less powerful impulse and its gratification can be delayed, and some other harmless object easily found for it. . . .

It should always be kept in mind that the more impediments there are to the judgment of the choosing mind, and the more these are due to nature, the less is the offense committed. . . . And on the basis of these reasons we should measure what the offender deserves, beyond which his punishment should not go.

32. YET we must believe that the Pythagorean doctrine, that justice consists of suffering for suffering, which is to say, of a suffering in punishment equal to the suffering caused by the wrong, should not be taken to mean that one who has deliberately injured another, with no extenuating reasons, should suffer only the same amount of injury and no more. For that law which is the most perfect model of all laws shows us that this is not so,[34] when for a theft it requires fourfold or fivefold restitution. And under Attic law, a thief, besides being sentenced to pay back double what he

had taken, was kept for some days in prison. . . . For it is not fair
that the harm to an innocent and to a guilty person should be
equal. . . . Accordingly, a greater punishment follows a completed crime. But since no punishment is worse than death, and
that can never be repeated, . . . all punishment necessarily stops
there, though sometimes torture is added, as deserved.

33. THE amount of a punishment is to be measured not only in
itself but with respect to the person on whom it is inflicted. The
same fine will be a burden on a poor man and no burden on a rich
one; and to a man of no standing, disgrace will be a trivial injury,
while to a man of high station it will be serious. . . . Such, as we
have said, is the internal standard of measure for punishments.

34. WITHIN the bounds allowed, charity for the one punished
leads us to impose a minimum penalty, except where a juster charity for more people induces us to do otherwise for an external reason. That reason is at times the great menace of the criminal, and
more often the need of making an example. The need is created by
the universal inducements to sin, which cannot be offset except by
sharp remedies. The principal inducements are habit and opportunity.

35. THE divine law given to the Hebrews punished stealing from
a pasture more severely than stealing from a house, on account of
the greater opportunity for the former. (Exodus XXII, 1 and 9.)
Justin says of the Scythians: [35] "With them no crime is more serious than theft; for without roof and walls to enclose their flocks
and herds, what would be safe if thieving were allowed?" . . . A
habit of wrongdoing may somewhat diminish the guilt, . . . but
in a way it calls for more harshness of punishment. . . .

In the law courts, however, clemency should be the aim, in law-
making severity, with allowance made for the time when the laws
are promulgated or the verdicts given. For the value of a punishment resides largely in the universality of its application, which is
a subject for law; but the question of less or greater guilt is a
matter of individuals.

36. THE second type of clemency is, we have said, when great and urgent grounds for punishment do not exist and we should be ready to mitigate it to some extent. The first type of clemency we call dispensing with punishment altogether. . . . Capitolinus says of Marcus Aurelius: [36] "It was Antoninus' custom to punish all crimes with lighter penalties than the laws prescribed." And Isaeus the orator said [37] that it was right that laws should be strictly worded, but that the penalties imposed should be milder than the laws. . . .

37. WE hope we have omitted nothing that would be of much help in clearing up this difficult and obscure subject. We have discussed in turn the four points Maimonides says [38] should be chiefly weighed in punishing, namely, the magnitude of the crime, that is, of the injury done, the frequency of such offenses, the strength of the evil desire, and the opportunity for the deed. . . .

38. WE have shown already, and histories everywhere tell us, that wars are often undertaken to inflict punishment. Frequently this motive is combined with an intention to obtain redress for an injury, when the same act was both wicked and destructive. These two aspects of an act create two different sorts of liability. However, not every injury, obviously, should be taken as excuse for a war. Even the laws, whose vengeance is protective and falls only on the guilty, do not wreak it on every sinner. So, as we just said, there is truth in the remark of Sopater, that trivial and common offenses are better passed over and left unpunished.

39. . . . THE intention that is carried out, the will that proceeds to outward acts—for mental acts, as we said above, are not to be punished by men—is frequently held liable to punishment. "Crimes are punished," says the elder Seneca,[39] "even though they have stopped short of full execution." . . . Hence the Romans thought they should declare war on King Perseus, unless he renounced the plans he had made to prepare for war against them; since already he had assembled arms, soldiers, and fleet. . . .

But not every malicious intention, even though indicated by

some act, is an occasion for punishment. For if even crimes actually committed are not all punished, much less are those that are only thought of and barely started. . . . So wrongdoing merely begun is not to be punished by armed force, unless the case is serious and it has gone so far that the action already taken has resulted in definite harm or at least some ominous danger, though as yet not all that was intended. In such a case, punishment is part of a measure for security against future wrongs, . . . or for protection of injured honor, or for curbing a dangerous example.

40. WE should understand also that kings and those who possess authority equal to theirs have a right to exact punishment not only for wrongs committed against themselves or their subjects, but for those that do not immediately touch them but are brutal violations of the law of nature or of nations, committed against anyone. For the liberty to preserve by punishment the welfare of human society, which originally, as we said, belonged to every individual, now, since the institution of states and courts, resides in the ruling authorities, not, properly speaking, because they are rulers but because they are subject to no man. For subjection has deprived others of that right. It is more noble indeed to avenge others' wrongs than one's own, since in the case of a man's own wrongs, it is to be feared that the sense of his grievance will make him excessive in his claims, or at least prejudiced in his attitude. So we do not doubt that wars are lawful which are made on those who are impious to parents, . . . or who eat human flesh, . . . or on pirates. . . . Thus far we agree with Innocent [40] and others who say war may be waged against those who sin against nature.

A contrary opinion is held by Victoria, Vasquez, Azorius, Molina, and others, who think that a war to be lawful must be waged by one who has either been injured in his own person or in his state, or has jurisdiction over some person who has been attacked. For they consider the power to punish to be properly an effect of civil jurisdiction, whereas we believe it comes from the law of nature, a point we discussed at the beginning of the first book.

Certainly, if we accept the opinion of those from whom we differ, a person will have no right to punish his enemy, even after a war that he undertook for a punitive reason. Yet this right is admitted by many and confirmed by the practice of all nations, not only after the war is over, but even while it is still going on. And it is based not on any civil jurisdiction, but on that natural law which existed before the foundation of states, and even now has force in places where men live grouped in families, not in states.

41. BUT here certain warnings must be given. First, national customs, though accepted for good reason by many people, are not to be taken for the law of nature. . . . To them you may rightly apply the words of Plutarch: [41] "A purpose to make barbarous nations more civilized is a pretext that may cover greed for their possessions."

42. SECONDLY, we should not rashly class with things forbidden by nature other things which are not surely so, or which are instead prohibited by the law of God's will. In this class we may perhaps list the unions of unmarried persons, and some we call incestuous, and also the taking of interest.

43. THIRDLY, we should draw a careful distinction between general principles, such as the duty of living honorably, that is, in accordance with reason, and other principles like them and so obvious as not to admit of question, such as the duty not to grab what belongs to another. Among the inferences from these some are easy of apprehension, such as, given marriage, we should not permit adultery. Others are not so easy to accept, as the inference that vengeance which finds satisfaction in another man's pain is wicked. . . .

As in cases under civil law, we excuse persons who lack knowledge or understanding of that law, so in cases involving the laws of nature, it is fair to pardon persons handicapped by weakness of reasoning power or a poor education. For ignorance of a law, if unavoidable, cancels guilt; and even when partly due to negligence, lessens the offense. . . .

In conclusion, we should add once for all, to avoid repetition, that wars undertaken to inflict a punishment are under suspicion of being unjustified, unless the wrongs committed are atrocious and plain to see, or there is some other accompanying reason. . . .

44. THE progress of our work has brought us to a consideration of offenses against God, since it is a debatable matter whether war may be undertaken to punish them. The subject has been discussed at length by Covarruvias. But he, following others, holds that the power to punish exists only where there is jurisdiction, properly so called. This opinion we have already rejected. Accordingly, just as in ecclesiastical affairs bishops are said to be in a way entrusted with the care of the universal church, so kings, in addition to their peculiar duty to their own states, bear also a general responsibility for the society of mankind.

A stronger argument for the view that denies that such wars are lawful is that God is sufficient to punish sins against himself. . . . Yet palpably the same may be said of other offenses as well, for unquestionably God is able to punish them too. Yet no one disputes the fact that men are right to punish them. Some, however, will argue and maintain that men punish other offenses only in so far as other men are hurt or endangered by them. But, on the other hand, it should be noted that men punish not only offenses which are directly harmful to others, but those too which affect them indirectly, such as suicide, intercourse with animals, and other similar crimes.

Now religion, though it is essentially a means to win the grace of God, has profound effects as well on human society. Plato had reason to call it the bulwark of authority and law, and the bond of good training. . . . And Aristotle calls the support of religion the first of public concerns. . . . All such considerations should be taken into account, and not only in one particular state, as when in Xenophon [42] Cyrus says that the more his subjects fear God, the more devoted they will be to him. They have meaning for human society in general. "Once destroy piety," says Cicero,[43] "and you destroy good faith, the associated life of mankind, and the one most excellent virtue, justice." . . .

A clear proof of this is that Epicurus, when he abolished divine providence, left nothing of justice but an empty name. For he said it originated in agreements only, and lasted only as long as the common advantage from it lasted, and that men could be restrained from hurting others solely by fear of punishment. . . .

But religion is even more useful in the greater society than in the individual state. For within a state, the place of religion may be supplied by laws and the simple execution of laws. In the great community, however, the execution of law is so extremely difficult that it cannot be carried out without an armed force, and the laws are very few. They in fact derive their sacredness chiefly from the fear of the Deity, so that those who sin against the law of nations are everywhere said to be violating a divine law. So the emperors rightly said [44] that an offense against religion is an offense against all.

45. IF we look more deeply into this whole subject, we must note that true religion, which is common to all ages, is founded in the main on four principles. The first of these is that God is, and is one; the second, that God is none of the things that are seen, but something more sublime than those; the third, that God has a care for human affairs and judges them with most upright judgments; the fourth, that the same God is the creator of all things, except himself. These four principles are likewise laid down in the commandments of the Decalogue. . . . And from these contemplative principles are drawn principles of action, such as that God is to be honored, loved, worshiped, and obeyed. . . .

The truth of these principles which we have called contemplative may undoubtedly be proved by arguments drawn from the nature of things. The strongest of these arguments is that our senses show us that some things are made, and things that are made lead us inevitably to something not made. But since not everyone understands this reasoning or more of the same kind, suffice it to say that in all ages and in all lands, with very few exceptions, men have agreed on these ideas, both those who were too dull to try to deceive and those who were too wise to be deceived. And this agreement on such a variety of laws and other ideas shows plainly that the tradition has been handed down to us from the first men, and never positively refuted, a fact which alone is sufficient to make us believe it.

46. WHEREFORE even persons too slow of wit to be able to discover or comprehend the unshakable arguments for these beliefs are not free of blame if they reject them, for they are our guides to goodness, and there are no arguments to uphold a different view. But since we are speaking of punishments, and particularly human punishments, we must draw some distinction between these same beliefs and between modes of deviating from them. The two ideas that a Deity exists—whether one or more I need not stipulate— and that he has a care for humankind are close to being universal, and are absolutely essential to the establishment of any religion, whether true or false. "He that cometh to God," [45] that is, he who has a religion—for the Jews called religion an approach to God— "must believe that he is and that he is the rewarder of them that seek him." . . . Aelian says [46] that none of the barbarians had sunk to atheism, but that all declared there was a divinity, and that he cared for us. Plutarch, in his book on *Subjects of Common Knowledge*,[47] says that to take away God's providence is to take away our knowledge of him, "for God must be conceived and known as not only immortal and blessed but also as loving man enough to care for him and do him good." . . . And really to deny that God exists and to deny that he is interested in human conduct, if we consider the moral consequences, amount to the same thing.

Hence, under something like necessity, these two ideas have been preserved in almost every nation we know, and through these many ages. . . . Dion of Prusa, in his *Twelfth Oration*,[48] calls it "a belief, planted in all men universally, in barbarians as well as in Greeks, necessary and natural to everyone who uses his reason." . . . Therefore, I think that those who first start to destroy these beliefs may be restrained—as they have been in well-ordered states, and as was done, we read, to Diagoras of Melos and to the Epicureans, who were expelled from well-conducted cities—in the name of human society, to which they did violence without reasonable excuse. . . .

47. THE other ideas are not equally self-evident, namely, that there are not more gods than one; that no visible thing, neither the earth, nor the sky, nor the sun, nor the air is God; that the earth and the matter of which it is formed have not existed from all eternity, but were made by God. So, as we see, the knowledge of these truths has faded and almost disappeared among many nations with the lapse of time. And this has happened more easily since their laws made no provisions to preserve these beliefs, because without them some kind of religion at least could exist. The true law of God was given to that people who were instructed in the clear and sure knowledge of these things by the prophets and by miracles, some of which they saw with their own eyes, while some were brought to their ears by reports from indubitable authority. This law, though it expresses the greatest abhorrence of the worship of false gods, still does not punish with death everyone convicted of that crime, but only those whose conduct shows some exceptionally pernicious features. . . .

The Canaanites and the neighboring nations, who had long been sunk in depraved superstitions, were not sentenced by God to immediate punishment, except when on top of this guilt they had heaped up other great crimes. (Genesis xv, 16.) So with other nations God overlooked the times of their ignorance as to the worship of false deities. . . . Where, then, men have not received the law revealed by God they are excusable and certainly not to be punished by other men, whether they worship the forces of the stars or other natural objects, or the spirits in images or in animals or in other things, or the souls of those who have excelled in virtue and in benefactions to the human race, or certain disembodied intelligences, especially if they did not themselves devise these cults or abandon for them the worship of the supreme God. Thus, however, we should count as wicked rather than mistaken those who set up the worship with divine honors of demons they know are evil, of names of vices, of men whose lives were filled with abominations. With them also should be classed those who propitiate their gods with the blood of innocent human beings. . . .

48. WHAT shall we say of the wars that are waged on some peoples for the reason that they refused to accept the Christian faith when it was offered to them? I shall not ask now whether it was offered in the form it should have been. Let us grant that it was. Two things we say are then to be remembered. The first is that the truth of the Christian religion cannot be proved by natural arguments merely, inasmuch as it has made many additions to natural and primitive religion. It rests on the history of Christ's resurrection and of the miracles performed by himself and his Apostles. It is a matter of facts established long ago by irrefutable evidence, but so long ago that the facts in question are of great antiquity. Hence this doctrine cannot be taken deeply into the minds of those who hear it now for the first time, unless God gives them his secret help, help that is not given, to those to whom it is given, as a reward for some work. And when it is withheld from others or less copiously bestowed, it is done for reasons not unjust but generally unknown to us, and hence not punishable by human judgment. . . .

Another thing to be remembered is that Christ, the author of the new law, would have no one compelled to accept his law by punishments in this life or by fear of them. . . .

49. THOSE, however, who subject the teachers or followers of Christianity to punishment for their faith are acting undoubtedly against reason itself. For there is nothing in Christian doctrine—I am speaking of it here in itself and not as it has become mixed with impurity—that is hurtful to human society, nothing indeed that is not beneficial. The doctrine speaks for itself, and even unbelievers are obliged to acknowledge it. Pliny says [49] that the Chris-

tians were bound to one another by an oath neither to commit theft or robbery, nor to break faith. . . .

It is not an acceptable excuse that everything new is to be feared, especially assemblages of people. For doctrines, however new, are not causes for fear, provided they lead to all that is good and to the payment of obedience to those above us. Nor should assemblies of honest men be regarded as suspicious, or persons who do not try to hide, unless they are forced to do so. . . . Those who are cruel to such harmless persons are themselves in a state where they might justly be punished. . . .

50. IT is also extremely wicked to harass with punishments men who accept the law of Christ as true but are in doubt or error on some points which are either outside the law or appear ambiguous in the law, and which were differently explained by the early Christians. This is proved by what we have said above, and by the ancient example of the Jews. For although they had a law which was supported by punishments in this life, they never penalized the Sadducees, who denied the doctrine of the resurrection, a doctrine certainly true but obscurely stated in their law, under a cloak of words and figures.

But what if the error is more serious and one that before fair-minded judges could easily be refuted by sacred authority or the consensus of antiquity? Here too we should take into consideration the power of inbred conviction and the extent to which freedom of judgment is hindered by zeal for one's own sect. . . . Remember too that the amount of guilt depends on the degree of a person's enlightenment and other mental conditions which it is not given to other men fully to understand. . . .

Athanasius, in his *Letter to the Monks*, bitterly reproaches the Arian heretics because they first employed the power of the courts against their opponents and attempted to drag over to themselves by violence, scourging, and imprisonment men whom they could not win by persuasion. . . . In Gaul, long ago, the bishops who had attempted to punish the Priscillianists with the sword were condemned by the judgment of the church. . . . Plato said [50] wisely that the punishment of the erring was to be taught.

51. IT is more like justice to punish those who are irreverent and undutiful to the gods in whom they do believe. . . . Certainly Augustine thought that God had enlarged the empire of the Romans because they had at heart their religion, even though it was false. . . .

XXI

Sharing of Punishments.

1. WHENEVER a question arises of a punishment to be shared, it is a matter either of accomplices in the crime, or of others. Accomplices are punished not so much for the guilt of another as for their own. Who they are may be seen from what we said above regarding damages unlawfully inflicted. For in almost the same way a man comes to share in a crime as he does to share in doing an injury. Yet not always does an obligation to repair an injury mean there has been a crime, but only where there was plainly a malicious intent. But any sort of fault is often enough to create a liability for repairing an injury.

Persons who order a wicked act, or give the requisite consent to it, or assist in it, or furnish asylum, or in any other way participate in the crime; who give advice, praise, or approbation, or who are bound by law, properly so called, to forbid the act, but do not forbid it; or who are bound by a similar law to succor the injured

party but do not succor him; who do not dissuade the criminal
when they should have dissuaded him; or who conceal a fact that
they are required by law to make known, all these are punishable,
if they display the degree of malice that merits punishment, according to the principles we have just discussed.

2. THE subject will be made clearer by illustrations. A civil community, like any other community, is not bound by the acts of
its individual members, except through some act or neglect of its
own. As Augustine well says: [1] "The particular sin of each individual in a nation is one thing, and the sin committed by a nation
as a whole, with one mind and one will, when the people are united
on some object, is another." . . . And the Rhodians before the
Senate drew a line between the case of the people and that of
private individuals, saying: [2] "There is no state that does not sometimes have wicked citizens, and always an ignorant populace." So
a father is not answerable for the misdeeds of his children, or a
master for those of his slave, or other superiors for the acts of those
under them, unless they too have done something wrong.

As for the ways by which rulers over others may become im-
plicated in their crimes, there are two that are extremely common
and should be carefully considered, namely, tolerance and protection.

With regard to tolerance, we must hold that a person who knows
of a crime and is able and bound to forbid it and does not do so,
himself commits a crime. Cicero, in his speech against Piso, says: [3]
"It makes no great difference, especially in the case of a consul,
whether he himself upsets the state by pernicious laws and mis-
chievous speeches, or permits others to do so." . . . Augustine
says with truth: [4] "He who fails to prevent an act, when he can,
consents to it." Hence a man who allows his slave to be made a
prostitute, when he could rescue her, is regarded by Roman laws
as her prostituter. And if a slave commits murder with the knowledge of his master, the master is liable for the whole offense, for
he is regarded as having committed the murder himself. . . .

But, as we said before, a person, besides knowing of the crime, must possess the power to prevent it. And this is what the laws mean when they say that knowledge, when pronounced punishable, is taken as proof of tolerance, when the person could have prevented the crime and did not do so. . . . A master is not bound by the act of a slave who asserts his freedom and refuses to obey his master, because knowledge of a crime without ability to prevent it is not guilt. So parents are accountable only for the misdeeds of children who are under their authority. On the other hand, even if they have them under their authority and in other circumstances might have prevented their wrongdoing, they are not answerable for it, unless they knew of it. For in order to hold any man responsible for the act of another, he must be equally convicted of both things—knowledge and failure to prevent. All we have said may be applied for like reasons to persons under authority, since it is based on natural justice. . . .

3. LET us come next to the second case, that of those who give to criminals protection from punishment. Punishment, as we said above, by the law of nature may be inflicted by anyone who cannot himself be charged with a similar crime. But since states were formed it has been agreed that the offenses of individuals which affect particularly their own community should be left to it, or to the rulers of it, to punish or overlook at their discretion. But these rulers are not allowed the same complete authority over offenses which affect human society at large in some way, and which other states or their rulers have a right to deal with, just as in the separate states the people may take action in certain crimes. Much less has any state full discretion in its treatment of crimes by which another state or its ruler has been especially injured. For such an offense either he or it has a right to exact punishment for the sake of their own dignity and security in accordance with what we said before. Neither the state where the offender lives nor its ruler should interfere with that right.

4. AND as it is not usual or expedient for one state to allow the

armed force of another to enter its territory for the sake of inflicting a punishment, it follows that the state in which the culprit lives
should, on receiving the complaint, do one of two things, either
punish him itself as he deserves or deliver him to the judgment of
the complainant. This latter course means surrendering him, a
thing that in histories happens again and again. . . . So Cato proposed that Caesar should be surrendered to the Germans for having
attacked them unwarrantably. . . . And the Romans themselves
gave up the men who had laid hands on the Carthaginian ambassadors. . . .

Yet all these instances are to be understood not as meaning that
the people or the king are rigidly bound to surrender the offender,
but that, as we have said, they may either surrender or punish him.
. . . Sometimes the choice is left to the aggrieved party, in order
to make its satisfaction more complete. . . . Dio Chrysostom, in
his speech to the Nicomedians,[5] includes among the evils that result from discord between states that "it is then possible for those
who have injured one state to escape for refuge to another." . . .

The surrender here meant is nothing more than delivering up a
citizen to the power of another people to decide on his case as it
wishes. This surrender neither gives nor takes away any right; it
only removes an impediment to the exercise of one. So, if that other
nation makes no use of the right granted it, the person surrendered
is in a position where he may still be punished by his own people—as
happened to Clodius, who was handed over to the Corsicans and
not accepted by them; or may not be punished, for there are many
crimes that may be treated in either way. His right of citizenship,
like his other rights and privileges, is not lost by that event, but
only by a decree or judicial decision, unless some law provides that
the event is to be regarded as equal to a judicial decision, which
cannot be said in this case. . . . But if the surrender is accepted,
and by some accident the person surrendered afterwards returns
home, he will no longer be a citizen, save by some new act of
grace. . . .

What we have said of surrendering or punishing offenders applies not only to those who have always been subjects of the state in whose territory they are now found, but to those also who, after committing a crime, have fled to some other state for refuge.

5. NOR do the views just expounded do away with the rights of suppliants and cases of asylum. For those are a protection to persons who are victims of unmerited hatred, not to persons who have done some wrong to human society or to their fellow men. . . . Thus, by the wisest of laws, asylums were open to one who had killed another man unintentionally, by a weapon slipping from his hand. Slaves too were granted places of refuge; but deliberate murderers of innocent men, or disturbers of the order of the state, found no protection even at the most holy altar of God. Philo, explaining this law, says: [6] "The temple offers no refuge to godless men." . . .

There was at Athens an altar to Mercy, which is mentioned by Cicero, Pausanias, Servius, and Theophilus in his *Institutes*. . . . Aristides calls it [7] a special glory of the Athenians that they were "a refuge and solace to the unfortunate from every land." . . . However, the orator Lycurgus tells [8] of a certain Callistratus, who had committed a capital crime, and who on consulting an oracle received the response that, if he went to Athens, he "would get justice." He then fled to the holiest altar in Athens, confident of impunity, but was none the less put to death by that city, faithful to its religious obligations, and thus the oracle's promise was fulfilled. Tacitus [9] criticizes the custom prevailing in the Greek cities of his day of protecting the evil deeds of men as if they were rites of the gods. . . . Such wrongdoers then ought either to be punished or delivered up or, at least, removed from the locality. . . .

This right we have described of demanding for punishment persons who have fled beyond the territory of their own country has, in most parts of Europe, during our own and recent centuries, been exercised only in cases where their crimes were a threat to the public safety or exceptionally atrocious. Lesser crimes it has been the custom mutually to overlook, unless a more precise agreement has been made by terms of a treaty. We must note too that where robbers and pirates have gained a formidable power, they may rightfully be received and protected from penalty, because it is to the interest of mankind to retrieve them from their wicked ways by assurances of impunity, provided it cannot be done otherwise. Any people or ruler can make this arrangement.

6. THIS too must be remembered, that in the interval while the justice of their cause is being investigated, suppliants are to be protected. . . . And if the deed of which they are accused is not forbidden by the law of nature or of nations, their case must be judged by the civil law of the country from which they come. . . .

7. WE have seen how guilt may pass from subjects, whether old or new, to their rulers. Conversely, it will pass from the sovereign power to the subjects, if those subjects consent to the crime, or if at the command or inducement of the sovereign power they do something they cannot do without sin. But this point it will be better to discuss later, when we are taking up the obligations of subjects. Both a community and individuals may share in a crime; for, as Augustine says in a passage already cited: [10] "Where there is a community there too are individuals; communities cannot exist except as composed of individuals. For it is individuals assembled or considered as a whole that make up communities."

Guilt rests on the individuals who consented to the crime, but not on those who were overpowered by the votes of the rest. Punishments for individuals and for communities are different. The punishment for individuals is sometimes death. The death of a state is its overthrow, which takes place when the body politic is dissolved. Of this we have spoken elsewhere.[11] . . . Individuals, as a punishment, may be reduced to slavery, as the Thebans were by Alexander of Macedon, all but those who had opposed the decree for breaking the alliance with him. So too a state submits to political slavery when reduced to a province. Individuals may lose their property by confiscation. So a state often forfeits whatever it holds as public property—its walls, naval equipment, battleships, arms, elephants, treasury, public lands. But it is not just that individuals should lose their personal possessions because of a crime committed by the community without their consent. . . .

8. THE important question arises here whether punishment may always be inflicted for the crime of a community. As long as the community exists it seems as if that might be done, since the body politic remains the same, although the members change, as we explained elsewhere. On the other hand, we should realize that although some things in a community are said to be a part of it from the start and essentially, such as its possessions of treasury, laws, and the like, there are other things that belong to it only in so far as it derives them from individuals. Thus we say a community is wise or brave which contains many wise or gallant men. Merit is a thing of this sort, for it belongs first of all to individuals, who have the minds which a community of itself does not have. So on the death of the individuals through whom merit was imparted to the community, its merit too disappears; as does likewise any debt it owes of punishment, which, as we said, exists only as merited. . . .

Thus Arrian is to be commended for condemning [12] the vengeance of Alexander on the Persians, when those who had wronged the Greeks had died long before. . . . And everyone laughs at the excuse of Agathocles,[13] who answered the complaints of the Ithacans over the damages he had inflicted on them by saying that in old times Ulysses had done more harm to the Sicilians. . . . Even if it is just that descendants should receive honors and rewards for the good deeds of their forefathers, it is not therefore right that they should be punished for their transgressions. The nature of a good deed is such that it may be credited to anyone without injury, but it is not so with punishments.

9. WE have spoken of the ways by which participation in punishment results from participation in guilt. We must consider next whether without participation in guilt there may still be participation in punishment. In order to understand this matter clearly, and

to prevent a confusion of dissimilar things through a similarity of names, certain points should be recalled.

10. IN the first place, there is a difference between damage directly inflicted and damage that follows as a consequence of something else. I call it directly inflicted when one man deprives another of something to which he has a proper right. I call it a consequence when a man does something that keeps another from having what he otherwise would have had, by destroying the condition which gave him the right to it. There is an example in Ulpian: [14] "If on my ground I have opened a well through which the streams that would have flowed to your lands are cut off." He says that the damage there is not due to anything wrong in my act, for I have merely exercised my right. . . . Thus when the property of their parents is confiscated, it is felt as a loss by the children, though, precisely speaking, it is not a punishment, because the property that was to be theirs would not have become theirs, unless their parents had preserved it to their last breath. . . .

So, when a community is made guilty by misconduct on the part of the majority—which, as we have said elsewhere, represents the person of the community—and as a consequence loses the things we mentioned, political liberty, walls, and other valuables, innocent individuals too feel the loss, though only of things which did not belong to them as individuals, but as parts of the community.

11. FURTHER, we should observe that one man's wrongdoing is sometimes the cause of misfortune or loss to another, and yet the wrongdoing may not be the immediate cause of the damage, as far as the law of damages is concerned. Thus, a man who has pledged security for another's debt may suffer for it; as the old proverb says: "Go surety, and trouble comes." But the immediate cause of his obligation is his own promise. And as a person who has pledged himself for a purchaser is not, strictly speaking, bound by the purchase but by his promise, so one who has undertaken responsibility for a criminal is bound not by the crime but by his own

pledge. Hence the damage he has to incur is measured not by the other man's crime but by his own power to carry out his promise.

It follows, according to the view which we believe correct, that no one can be put to death by the terms of any surety, since we maintain that no one has such power over his life as to take it away himself, or to bind himself to forfeit it for another. The ancient Greeks and Romans, however, thought otherwise and maintained that sureties were liable to suffer a death sentence . . . as may be seen in the well-known story of Damon and Pythias. Hostages too they frequently executed, as we shall note later. . . . If included in the pledge are exile or money loss, and the conditions of the pledge are fulfilled, the man who went surety will suffer the damage, which yet, precisely speaking, will not be a punishment for him. . . .

12. HAVING drawn these distinctions, we will say that no innocent person may be punished for another's crime. . . . For the liability to punishment is a result of desert, and desert is personal, since it originates in the will, than which nothing is more peculiarly our own. . . .

13. "NEITHER the virtues nor the vices of the parents," says Jerome,[15] "are to be imputed to the children." Augustine declares [16] that "God himself would be unjust, if he condemned an innocent man." . . . It is just, says Philo,[17] that the punishments go to those who commit the sins; and he disapproves the custom of certain nations who punished by death the harmless children of tyrants or traitors. Dionysius of Halicarnassus condemns it too,[18] and explains that the reason given, namely, that the children are expected to turn out like their parents, is iniquitous. For it is not certain that they will, and an uncertain fear should not be cause sufficient to put anyone to death. . . .

14. GOD, to be sure, in the law given to the Hebrews, threatens to avenge the impiety of the fathers upon the children. But God has an absolute right of dominion over our property and over our lives, as being his gifts, which he may take away from anyone when-

ever he pleases, without any reason and at any time. Therefore if
he carried off by a premature and violent death the children of
Achan, Saul, Jeroboam and Ahab, he was exercising over them
the right of dominion, not that of punishment; and by the same act
was punishing the parents more severely. . . .

At the same time, we should observe that God does not inflict
this harsher punishment except in the case of crimes that are especially an insult to himself, such as false worship, perjury, or
sacrilege. The Greeks thought the same about this. For the crimes
which they believed were charged against posterity, which they
called pollutions, were all of that kind. . . . However, even if God
has threatened such a punishment, he does not always exercise his
right, particularly if some unusual virtue shines out in the children. . . . But the course of God in these matters is not for men
to imitate. They have not the same justification. For God, as we
just said, without any regard to guilt, has a right over our lives,
whereas men have none except as a consequence of serious guilt,
and guilt belongs to individuals. Wherefore the same divine law
that forbids us to punish parents with death for the deeds of their
children,[19] forbids also the punishment of children for the deeds of
their parents. . . .

[15–16. Children of malefactors may be disqualified for office.]

17. WHAT we have said regarding the penalizing of children for
the offenses of their parents may also be applied to a people that is
really subject, in case the question is raised whether a people can
be made to suffer for the crimes of its king or governors. (A people
that is not so subject may, as we said, be punished for its own guilt,
that is, for failure to act.) We are not asking now whether the
people gave its consent, or did anything else in itself deserving of
punishment, but are thinking only of the tie created by the nature
of a body whose head is a king, while the rest are but members. . . .

18. THE same may be said on the subject of penalizing for a crime
of the community individuals who did not consent to it. . . .

19. AN heir is liable for the other debts of his predecessor, but

not for his punishment. . . . The true reason for this is that the
heir represents the person of the deceased not in his deserts, which
are purely personal, but in his property, to which, ever since the
introduction of private ownership, have been attached the debts
owed to anyone as a result of the inequality of possessions. . . .

XXII

Unlawful Reasons for War.

1. WE said earlier, when we were starting to discuss the reasons for
a war, that some were the plausible excuses and others the convincing reasons. Polybius, who first made this distinction, called the
former 'pretexts,' because they are usually the ones alleged, . . .
and the latter by the generic name, 'causes.' Thus in the war of
Alexander on Darius, his pretext was the avenging of the wrongs
done by the Persians to the Greeks. But the real cause was his desire for glory, empire, and wealth, stimulated by a strong expectation of an easy conquest, based on the expeditions of Xenophon
and Agesilaus. . . .

Similarly, Thucydides calls [1] the real cause of the Peloponnesian
War the growing power of the Athenians and the Spartans' suspicion of it, though the dispute over Corcyra, Potidaea, and other
things was the ostensible pretext. . . .

2. THERE are some who without either kind of reason plunge
into war, because, as Tacitus says,[2] they love danger for its own

---

sake. Their crime is less than human. Aristotle calls it animal ferocity. . . .

3. MOST men going to war have convincing reasons, either with or without plausible pretexts. Some plainly take no pains to find pretexts. To them can be applied the dictum of the Roman jurists, that a man is a robber who, on being asked what reason he has for taking a thing, replies, none but the fact that he is taking it. Aristotle [3] speaks of the promoters of war, as "those who many times do not care whether it is right to enslave their innocent neighbors." Such a man was Brennus, who said all things belonged to the strong.[4] . . . To them you may well apply the saying of Augustine: [5] "To make war on one's neighbors and from that to proceed to more violence, and purely out of greed for territory to crush inoffensive peoples, what must we call this but brigandage on a grand scale?" . . .

4. OTHERS give as excuses causes which when examined by the test of right reason are found to be unlawful. These men obviously want, as Livy says,[6] not a trial of rights, but force. Most kings, Plutarch says,[7] use the two words 'peace' and 'war' as coins, to buy not what is lawful but what is to their advantage.

As to what are unlawful reasons for war, we may form some idea by recalling the lawful reasons which we have already described.[8] For what is straight is a guide to what is crooked. But for clarity's sake we will list the principal types of unlawful reasons.

5. WE said above [9] that fear of a neighbor's power is not a sufficient ground for war. In order that defensive measures should be lawful, they must be necessary, as they are not unless we are certain not only of our neighbor's power but of his intentions, and certain with the certainty required in a matter of morals. Hence we do not approve the judgment of those who call it a just cause for war, when our neighbor, being hindered by no treaty, builds a fortress in his own country or prepares some other military equipment which might at some time be damaging to us. To offset such fears, we may try constructing counter-fortifications and taking other

similar precautions on our own territory, but should not resort to armed force. . . . I like much what Tacitus says of the Chauci.[10] "The noblest people of Germany, who choose to maintain their greatness by justice, showing neither greed nor weakness. They are peaceable and quiet, provoking no wars, laying waste no countries with pillaging and brigandage. . . . Yet they all are ready with their arms, and if the situation demands it, with an army. They have plenty of men and horses, and their reputation remains as high when they are at peace."

6. EXPEDIENCY does not confer the same right as necessity. . . .

8. NOR can a desire to change one's habitation and leave swamps and deserts for a more fertile soil be a lawful excuse for war, though Tacitus says [11] it was an excuse among the ancient Germans.

9. IT is equally wrong to claim for oneself on the ground of discovery what belongs to another, even if the present owner is wicked, has erroneous ideas of God, or is dull of wit. For discovery means that the property belongs to no one else.

10. NEITHER moral nor religious virtue, nor perfect intelligence is required for the ownership of property. However, it does seem possible to argue that if there are races totally destitute of reason, they cannot exercise ownership; yet simply out of charity they should have as much as they need to live. What we said elsewhere regarding the maintenance of ownership, which the law of nations provides for children and insane persons, applies to any people with whom we have exchanged agreements; but such are not people in this category; indeed, I have well-founded doubts if any people are to be found completely destitute of reason. It was wrong, therefore, for the Greeks to call the barbarians their natural enemies, because of a difference of customs, or perhaps what seemed like inferiority of intellect.

But how far serious crimes, striking at nature and all human society, may warrant a forfeiture of ownership is another question, which we treated just now when discussing the right of punishment.

11. A claim to liberty on the part of individuals or of states, that is, to self-government, cannot always furnish a right to go to war, as if by nature and at all times everyone was fit for liberty. For when liberty is said to belong by nature to all men and all peoples, the words are to be understood as meaning a natural right that precedes every act of man. . . . This means that no one is by nature a slave, not that anyone has a right never to be a slave. For in that sense no one is free. Here applies the saying of Albutius: [12] "No one is born free and no one a slave. These are names that fortune imposed on each of us after we were born." And according to Aristotle,[13] "It is law that makes one man a slave and another free." Those therefore who for legitimate reasons have sunk into a condition of servitude, whether personal or political, should be content in that state. . . .

12. IT is equally unjust to attempt to subjugate any people by force on the ground that they deserve to be slaves, and are the kind that philosophers sometimes call slaves by nature. For even if a person is fitted for a particular state, I do not at once have a right to impose it forcibly on him. Reasonable beings should be free to choose what is good or bad for them, unless some other person has obtained a right over them. The case of children is manifestly different, since they have not the right of independent action and management of their own conduct, and nature allots control of them to those who undertake and are fitted for it.

13. I need hardly add that the title of world sovereign, which some persons bestow on the Roman emperor, is absurd, as if he had a right to rule over the most remote and as yet unknown nations. . . . Nor should one be moved by Dante's argument [14] by which he tries to prove that that right belongs to the emperor, since it would be beneficial to mankind. For the advantages he cites are counterbalanced by the disadvantages. A ship may be built so large that it cannot be steered. So the numbers of men and the distances between countries are so vast that they cannot be under one government.

But granting the expediency of such an empire, it does not follow that he has a right to it, as that can be acquired only by agreement or as a form of penalty. The Roman emperor now has not even jurisdiction over all the regions that once belonged to the Roman people. Many lands that were won by war have been lost by war, while some by treaty and others by abandonment have passed under the authority of other nations or kings. Some states too that were once altogether subject have since become only partially subject, or only unequal allies. All these methods of losing or altering jurisdiction are as valid against the Roman emperor as they are against others.

14. BUT there have been persons who asserted the rights of the Church even over peoples in the hitherto unknown parts of the world. . . . Yet though a right of judging belonged to the Apostles, and even in its way extended to earthly affairs, it was heavenly, so to speak, rather than earthly in its character—a right not exercised by scourge and sword, but by the word of God, declared to all men and adapted to the special circumstances, with a displaying or withholding of signs of the divine grace, as it befitted each case; in the last extremity enforced by supernatural punishment, superior to that of nature, and coming directly from God, like the punishments of Ananias, Elymas, Hymenaeus, and others.

Christ himself, the source of all ecclesiastical power, whose life is held up as an example to the Church, as far as it is his Church, said his kingdom was not of this world, that is, was not of the same nature as other kingdoms, adding that otherwise, like other kings, he would have made use of military force. . . . Paul, among other things, forbids bishops to be 'smiters.' (I Timothy III, 3.) "To govern by compulsion," that is, by means of human force, "is for kings but not for bishops," said Chrysostom.[15] . . . And he tells bishops [16] to exercise their office "not by coercion but by persuasion." Whence it is abundantly clear that bishops as such have no authority to rule over men by human methods. . . .

Whether even kings should make war on people who reject the

Christian religion under pretext of punishing them is a question we discussed, as far as was needed for our purpose, in the earlier chapter on punishments.

15. A warning too I have to give, not idly, but because comparing recent and ancient events, I anticipate a great danger, unless we are on guard against it. Hopes based on some interpretation of divine prophecy are no lawful cause for war. For besides the fact that oracles which are not yet fulfilled can hardly be interpreted with certainty without the aid of the prophetic spirit, even the times of events that are sure to happen may be hidden from us. And finally, a prediction, unless it is accompanied by an express command from God, does not confer a right, for God often allows his predicted designs to be accomplished by wicked men or evil acts.

16. THIS too must be understood, that if a person is under an obligation that is not one in strict justice, but is the result of some other virtue, such as generosity, gratitude, pity, or love, his debt can neither be collected by a court of law, nor wrung from him by force of arms. For those courses it is not enough that the thing demanded ought on moral grounds to be paid; we must also have some right to require it. . . .

17. WE should observe too that often when a lawful reason for a war exists, there is evil in the conduct of it, due to the spirit of the person directing it. Either some motive, not in itself illegitimate, actuates him more powerfully than his own right, such as passion for glory, or some advantage, public or private, which he expects to derive from the war, aside from his alleged aim. Or he may be influenced by some quite unlawful emotion, such as the pleasure of watching another man's calamity, without regard for the good. . . . "The one and ancient cause of war," says Sallust,[17] "is the deepseated greed for power and riches." . . . Here too you may well recall the words of Augustine: [18] "The longing to hurt, the cruel desire for revenge, the unappeased and unappeasable mind, the fierce spirit of rebellion, the lust of mastery—these are the things we are right to blame in war."

XXIII

Doubtful Reasons for War.

1. THERE is much truth in what Aristotle wrote,[1] that in the realm of practical morals, certainty cannot be reached to the extent that it can in the mathematical sciences. This comes from the fact that in the mathematical sciences forms are entirely separated from matter, and forms themselves usually have nothing intermediate between them. Thus, between a straight line and a curve there is no intermediate. But in the realm of practical morals, the least circumstances alter the matter, and between its forms, which we are discussing, there is generally something midway, so broad as to approach now this and now that extreme. Thus between what is right and what is wrong there is a mean—what is permissible—which now comes closer to one side, now to the other. Hence many times the situation is ambiguous, as it is at twilight, or when cold water is turning to warm. This is what Aristotle means when he says:[2] "It is often difficult to judge what we should choose first." . . .

2. FIRST, we must assume as a principle, that even if an act is in itself lawful, yet when it is performed by one who, taking everything into consideration, believes it to be unlawful, the act is wrong. . . . For God has given men power of judgment to guide them in their acts, and when this is disregarded the mind becomes brutish. But it often happens that our judgment points us to nothing certain, and is hesitant; and when such hesitation cannot, in

spite of close reflection, be cleared up, it is best to follow the advice of Cicero; [3] "They are wise teachers who tell you that whenever you are in doubt whether a thing is right or wrong you should not do it." . . .

But this rule cannot hold when one of two things must absolutely be done, and we are doubtful whether either one is right. In that case we may choose what seems the lesser evil. For always, when a choice cannot be avoided, the lesser evil takes on an appearance of good. . . .

3. BUT often in doubtful cases, after some investigation, the mind does not remain neutral, but is influenced this way or that by arguments drawn from the facts, or by the respect it has for other men who have pronounced judgment on the question. . . . Arguments from the facts are drawn from causes, effects, and other concomitant circumstances.

4. TO weigh these arguments soundly one must have some experience and skill, and those who do not have them should listen to the counsels of the wise, in order to frame a right decision for action. . . . This method of reaching a decision is followed especially by kings, who have little time to learn or ponder the principles of knowledge. . . . Thus the ancient Romans never undertook a war until they had consulted the College of Fetiales, established for that purpose, and the Christian emperors scarcely ever did so without hearing what the bishops had to say, that they might be apprised of anything that might concern religion.

5. IN many cases of dispute it may happen that reasonable arguments are put forth by both sides, based either on the facts of the situation or on other men's authority. When that happens, if the questions at stake are not important, there may be apparently nothing much wrong in the choice, whichever way it goes. But if the question is one of great moment, such as whether a man is to be put to death, then, because of the wide differences between the courses proposed, the safer should be taken, according to the saying: [4] "Do you, nevertheless, err in this direction." For it is better

to acquit a guilty man than to condemn an innocent. . . . Antiphon says: [5] "If one must err, it is more righteous to acquit illegally than to condemn wrongfully. For in the former instance there is error, but to condemn an innocent man is a crime."

6. NOW war is a matter of supreme importance, since from it flows a multitude of evils, even upon the innocent. Hence when opinions are wavering, we should lean toward peace. . . . There are three methods by which disputes may be prevented from breaking out into war.

7. THE first method is holding a conference. "Whereas," says Cicero,[6] "there are two ways of settling a question, one by discussion and the other by force, and whereas the former is characteristic of man, and the latter of beasts, only when the first of these ways is impossible should we resort to the second." . . .

8. THE second method, when the parties have no common judge, is agreement to arbitrate. . . . The Romans themselves, says Livy,[7] on the occasion of a dispute with the Samnites, appealed to their common allies. And Philip of Macedon, in his quarrel with the Greeks, said [8] he would accept the arbitration of people with whom they were both at peace. At the request of the Parthians and Armenians, Pompey appointed arbitrators to fix their boundaries.[9] . . .

Above all, Christian kings and states are bound to employ this method of avoiding war. . . . And for this and many other purposes, it would be helpful—as a matter of fact, necessary—for the Christian powers to hold conferences, where those whose interests were not involved might settle the disputes of the rest, and even take measures to compel the parties to accept peace on fair terms. . . .

9. THE third method is drawing lots, a practice commended . . . long ago by Solomon, in Proverbs XVIII, 18.

10. SOMEWHAT akin to lot drawing is single combat, a practice which I do not think should be altogether excluded if two men, whose quarrel otherwise might bring terrible calamities on whole

peoples, are ready to fight it out between themselves with arms.
. . . In Livy we find Metius addressing Tullus: [10] "Let us try a
way by which it may be decided which people shall rule the other,
without great slaughter of both peoples." . . .

11. ALTHOUGH in a doubtful case, both sides are bound to search
for every means of avoiding war, yet the side that is pressing its
claim is more bound to do so than the side in possession. For not
only by civil law, but also by natural law, in a case where rights are
equal, the position of the possessor is the stronger. . . .

And here we should add that a man who knows his cause is just
but who has not documents sufficient to convince the possessor
of the injustice of his position may not on that account legitimately
go to war, because he has not the right to compel the other to
relinquish his possession.

12. WHERE the right is uncertain, and neither party has possession, or each is equally in possession, the party who refuses a proposed division of the disputed property may be called wrong.

13. FROM what we have said it is now possible to settle a much
agitated question, whether from the point of view of those who are
the principal movers in a war, that war may be just on both sides.

We must distinguish between the various understandings of the
word 'just.' A thing is said to be just, either through its cause, or
because of its effects. The cause may be just either in the special
meaning of the word, or in the general meaning, which includes
all right behavior under the name. In the special meaning it may
further be divided into the justice which marks an act and the
justice which characterizes the doer, for sometimes the doer is
said to be acting justly, as long as he does not act unjustly, even if
what he is doing is not itself just. . . .

In the special sense and with regard to the act itself, a war cannot
be just on both sides, any more than a lawsuit can be. For, by the
very nature of the case, there can be no moral sanction given us to
do opposite things, such as acting and preventing action. Yet it
may indeed happen that neither of the warring parties is acting

unjustly. For no one is acting unjustly unless he knows that he is doing an unjust thing, and there are many who do not know it. So it is possible for both parties to fight a lawsuit justly, that is, with good faith on both sides. For the numerous things both in law and in fact which established a right are unknown to many men.

In its general meaning an act is commonly called just that is free from all guilt on the part of the doer. Many persons do things with no right to do them, but innocently, because they are unavoidably ignorant. An instance of this is persons who fail to obey a law of which, through no fault on their part, they are ignorant, even after that law has been promulgated and enough time has passed for them to know of it. So too it may happen in lawsuits that neither party is guilty, either of injustice or of any other wrongdoing, especially when each or one of them is acting not in his own name, but in that of another, as when, for instance, he holds the office of guardian, whose duty it is not to abandon even a dubious right. . . .

But in a case of war it is hardly possible that recklessness and a failure in charity should not make their appearance because of the gravity of the issues involved. They are certainly so grave as to require more than plausible reasons for the war. The reasons should be evident to everybody.

If we understand the word 'just' to apply to certain legal aspects, undoubtedly in this sense a war may be lawful for both sides, as will appear in what we have to say later, on formal public war. . . .

XXIV

Warnings against Rashly Engaging in War,
Even for Lawful Reasons.

1. ALTHOUGH it seems not to be properly a part of a treatise entitled *The Law of War* to inquire what instruction or advice the various virtues give us about warmaking, yet there is an error we should anticipate, namely, that of supposing that, after establishing a right to go to war, one ought instantly to start on it, or may at any time do so. On the contrary, it is frequently more highminded and noble to relinquish one's right.

We said earlier, in the proper connection, that it was honorable to be careless of our own life, in order, as far as we can, to secure the life and eternal salvation of someone else. This duty is especially incumbent on Christians, who in practicing it are following the most perfect example of Christ, who consented to die for us while we were yet enemies and ungodly. (Romans v, 6.) His example calls powerfully on us not to insist on our own interests or on what is due us, when they involve the calamities to others that war brings with it. Aristotle and Polybius too tell us that war is not to be undertaken for every lawful cause. . . .

2. THERE are many reasons that urge us not to insist on punishment. Let us note how many things fathers overlook in their children. . . . And whoever sets out to punish another takes on in a way the character of a ruler, which is, of a father. . . .

Sometimes the circumstances are such that to relinquish a right is not merely a praiseworthy act but one obligatory on us, by reason of the love we should feel for mankind, even for our enemies, whether considered in itself or as a command of the most holy law of the Gospel. Thus, as we have said, there are men for whose safety, even though they are our persecutors, we ought to be ready to die because we know they are essential or very useful to the community of mankind. . . .

3. WITH regard to punishments, it is first of all our duty, if not as men, then surely as Christians, to pardon readily and freely offenses committed against ourselves, as God pardons us in Christ. . . . Seneca writes of a prince: [1] "Let him be far more ready to forgive wrongs done to himself than those done to others. For just as a man is not generous who is free with other people's goods, but only the one who takes from himself what he gives to another, so I do not call a prince merciful who is lenient in a case of another's suffering, but only the one who, when harassed by provocations to himself, does not rush into violent action, since he knows . . . that nothing is more glorious than a prince who does not avenge his wrongs." The duty to pardon is most imperative when either we too are conscious of some guilt in ourselves, or the wrong which was done us was a result of some human and excusable infirmity, or the person who wronged us is clearly and sufficiently penitent. . . . These reasons for abstaining from war come from the love we owe or rightly show even to our enemies.

4. OFTENTIMES too for our own sake and that of our friends, we should refrain from taking up arms. Plutarch, in his life of Numa,[2] says that after the Fetiales had declared that a war could be lawfully undertaken, the Senate had still to decide whether it was expedient to undertake it. . . . What Euripides said [3] of the Greek cities you may well apply to everyone else:

> "However oft men vote upon a war,
>> Not one reflects that death hangs over him,
>> But we each plan the slaughter of our foes.
>> In the assembly, if before our eyes

Had been the funeral pyres that would come,
War-frenzied Greece would not have been destroyed."

In Livy you find:[4] "Keep before your mind, along with your own resources, the power of chance and the widespreading nature of war." . . .

5. IN times of deliberation, men consider partly the ends in view, not the ultimate but the intermediate, and partly the means leading to those ends. The end is always some good, or at least the prevention of some evil which might take the place of a good. The means are not desired for their own sake, but only in so far as they lead to the ends. Wherefore in all deliberations, the ends should be compared with one another, and also the effective power of the means to bring about the ends. . . . For this comparison there are three rules.

The first rule: If the course proposed, from a practical point of view, at least, will apparently have an equal effect for good and for evil, it may be chosen if the good has somewhat more of good in it than the evil has of evil. Aristides puts it this way:[5] "When the good is less than the evil, it is better to do without the good." . . . The second rule: If it seems that the good and the evil that may result from the course under discussion are equal, we may choose the course, if its effectiveness for the good is greater than its effectiveness for the evil. The third rule: If the good and the evil look to be unequal, and the effectiveness of the course for them is also unequal, we may still choose it, if its effectiveness for good, when compared with its effectiveness for evil, is greater than the evil itself is, when compared with the good. . . .

6. LET us take as example a question that Tacitus tells us[6] was once debated by the states of Gaul, which they wanted more, liberty or peace. By liberty, understand political liberty, that is, the right of a state to govern itself, a right that is complete in a democratic state but exists within limits in an aristocratic state, especially one where no citizen is excluded from office. By peace,

understand one that averts a deadly war. . . . Everyone knows
how Cato, who preferred to die rather than submit to an autocrat,
would have replied to this. . . . And there are many other instances of the sort.

But right reason dictates otherwise. Life, it says, which is the
foundation for all temporal goods and the opportunity for good
eternal, is worth more than liberty, whether you are considering
them in the case of a single man, or of a whole people. . . . The
slaughter of a people in circumstances of this kind must be considered the most dreadful of evils. . . . As regards Cato, whom
we just mentioned, and Scipio, both of whom refused to yield to
Caesar after his victory at Pharsalia, Plutarch makes the following
comment: [7] "They are to be blamed for bringing about the need-
less deaths of many good men in Libya."

What I have said of liberty I wish to say also of other desirable
things, if the chance of effecting a greater opposite evil is more
likely than not, or is merely even. As Aristides truly says,[8] "It is
customary to save a ship by casting the cargo overboard, though not
the passengers."

7. IN inflicting punishment we should remember this above all,
never on such excuses to start a war with a power whose strength
is equal to our own. For, as in the case of a civil judge, he who attempts to punish a crime by force of arms must be much more
powerful than the other party. Nor is it prudence only, or love for
our own, that should deter us from a dangerous war, but often it is
justice, governmental justice, that by the very nature of government binds the superior to care for his subjects no less than it binds
them to their obedience. The conclusion from this is, as the theologians have rightly stated, that a king who goes to war for light
causes, or in order to exact unnecessary penalties involving serious
risks, is responsible to his subjects for repairing the damage resulting therefrom. For he committed a true crime, if not against his
enemy, yet against his own people, by dragging them on slight excuse into so dire a calamity. . . .

8. IT is seldom that there is a reason for going to war that either cannot or ought not to be disregarded. It is one when, as Florus says,[9] the laws are more cruel than war. . . . "A wretched peace is well exchanged for war," says Tacitus,[10] particularly when, as he also says,[11] "those who dare to fight will either win their liberty, or, if defeated, will be no worse off than before." . . .

9. ANOTHER time for war is when to one studying the situation as he ought it seems lawful, and at the same moment his resources appear adequate—a matter of the highest importance. This is what Augustus said,[12] that war should not be undertaken except when the expectation of gain was plainly greater than the fear of loss. The words of Scipio Africanus and of Lucius Aemilius Paulus [13] about battle apply well here too: "One should never fight save under extreme necessity, or most favorable circumstances." This is particularly true when there is hope that by fear and the strength of our reputation we can accomplish our aim with little or no risk. . . .

10. WAR is a cruel thing, says Plutarch,[14] and drags with it a heap of wrongs and insults. . . . Maximus of Tyre: [15] "Even should you eliminate injustice from war, the very necessity of it is in itself deplorable." . . . If by Hebrew law even one who unintentionally killed a man was obliged to flee, if God forbade David, who is said to have waged righteous wars, to build his temple, because he had shed much blood, if among the ancient Greeks men who had innocently stained their hands in slaughter had need of expiation, who does not see—above all, if he is a Christian—how wretched and ill-omened a thing war is and by what effort, even when it is not unlawful, it should be avoided? . . .

XXV

Reasons for Going to War to Help Others.

1. IN our discussions above of men who make war, we said and showed that by the law of nature everyone is the maintainer both of his own rights and of those that belong to others. The reasons therefore that are lawful for a man whose own welfare is at stake are lawful for those who come to the aid of others. Now a man's first and most necessary responsibility is for those under his authority, whether in the family or in the state. For they are, as it were, a part of their governor, as we said. . . .

2. NOT always, however, does the cause of any subject, legitimate though it be, bind his rulers to go to war, but only when that can be done without harm to all, or to the majority of his subjects. For the duty of a ruler is to look out for the whole more than for a part; though the greater a part is, the nearer it approaches the character of the whole.

3. THUS, if a single citizen, though innocent, is demanded for execution by the enemy, undoubtedly he may be surrendered, if the state is manifestly far from able to resist the enemy's power. This opinion is strongly opposed by Fernando Vasquez,[1] but if we scrutinize not his words so much as his meaning, he seems to be arguing only that such a citizen ought not to be hastily surrendered while there remains any hope of protecting him. . . .

But whether an innocent citizen may indeed be given up into the hands of the enemy to avoid the destruction that otherwise threatens the state, is a question debated by the learned both now and long ago, as when Demosthenes told his fine fable of the dogs who the wolves demanded should be surrendered by the sheep for the sake of peace. . . . Soto holds that such a citizen is bound to surrender himself to the enemy but this too Vasquez denies, for the reason that the nature of political society, into which everyone enters for his own advantage, does not require it. However, no other conclusion follows from this, except that by law, properly speaking, a citizen is not bound to perform such a deed, but that love does not permit him to act otherwise. There are many duties that are not required by law, properly speaking, but are by love— acts that are hailed with praise, which Vasquez admits, and that one cannot fail to perform without guiltiness. Such certainly seems to be the duty of every man to set the lives of a great and innocent multitude above his own. . . .

This being granted, there remains a doubt whether a man may be compelled to do what he ought to do. Soto says he may not, and quotes the case of a rich man, who, though bound by the precepts of mercy to give alms to a poor man, cannot be compelled to do so. We must realize, however, that the relation of parts with each other is one thing, and the position of superiors when compared with their subjects is another. For an equal may not force an equal to do anything but what he is bound by strict law to do. But a superior may force an inferior to do other things, required by some standard of virtue, for this power is included in the right of a superior as such. Thus in a time of great scarcity of grain, citizens may be compelled to bring what they have to the common stock. Hence in this argument of ours, it seems true that a citizen may be forced to do what charity bids him. . . .

4. NEXT to our dependents, even on an equal footing with them as regards rights of protection, are our allies with whom we have a treaty including such a provision, whether they yielded themselves to our guardianship and good faith, or simply made an agreement for mutual assistance. . . . Yet no such agreements can be

stretched to cover their wars for which there was no lawful excuse, as we said above. . . . To which we may now add that not even for a legitimate cause is one ally bound to aid another, if there is no prospect of a successful outcome. For alliances are formed to achieve some good, not harm. . . .

5. THIRDLY, one may go to war for one's friends to whom assistance was not actually promised and yet is due on the score of friendship, provided it can be given readily and without serious trouble. . . . The Romans often made war or threatened to make it not only in support of their allies, to whom they were bound by treaty, but to help their friends.

6. THE last and most far-reaching reason for going to war to help others is the common tie of humanity, which even alone may be sufficient. "Man was born to succor his brother," says Seneca.[2] . . .

7. THE question now is whether a man is bound to defend any man, or a people any people, from injury. Plato thinks [3] that anyone who does not protect another from violence deserves punishment. . . . But in the first place, if it is plainly perilous to do so, one is certainly not bound. For one may value one's own life and property more than those of strangers. . . . In the histories of Sallust we read: [4] "All rulers who in time of their own prosperity are entreated to join an alliance for war should consider whether they may then keep the peace, and, next, whether what they are asked to do is actually right, safe, and honorable, or unfitting." . . .

8. THERE is also the problem whether a war is lawful which is undertaken to protect the subjects of another ruler from oppression by him. Unquestionably, ever since political societies were established, every ruler has claimed a special right over his own subjects. . . . Thucydides includes [5] among the marks of sovereignty "supreme judicial power," as well as "the right to make laws and appoint magistrates." . . . The aim is, of course, as Ambrose correctly explains it,[6] "to prevent men from stirring up war by unwarranted meddling in other people's affairs." . . . All these rights hold when the subjects are really at fault, and also, you may add,

when the case is doubtful. For such situations this distribution of authorities was set up.

But where there is manifest oppression, where a Busiris, a Phalaris, or a Thracian Diomede uses his power over his subjects in ways odious to every just man, his people will not be denied the right of all human society. So Constantine took up arms against Maxentius and Licinius, and other Roman emperors either went or threatened to go to war against the Persians, unless they desisted from persecuting Christians on account of their religion.

Even if it were admitted that not even in direst necessity is it right for subjects to take up arms against their rulers (a point, we see, on which the men who try to defend royal power themselves have doubts), still it does not follow that others may not take up arms for them. For whenever the impediment to an action is personal and has nothing to do with the action itself, then what one man may not do another may do for him, provided the matter is of a kind where one man can assist another. . . . And the impediment that prevents a subject from resisting his ruler is not caused by something that is the same for a subject and for a man who is not a subject, but is a personal status, not transferable to others. . . .

We know, however, from ancient and modern history that greed for other people's possessions looks for pretexts like these to cover its own ends. But a right does not immediately cease to exist when it is misused by evildoers. Pirates, too, sail the seas; robbers wield a sword.

9. WE have said already that military alliances formed for the purpose of ensuring aid for any kind of war, regardless of cause, are wrong. Thus no kind of life is worse than that of men who fight for pay, with no thought of the cause, and for whom.

"The right is there where wages are the highest." [7] . . .

It would matter little actually that they sell their own lives, if they did not sell the lives of others, who are often innocent. They are as

much more detestable than executioners as it is worse to kill without a cause than it is for a cause. . . .

War-making is not one of the honest crafts. Rather it is a thing
so horrible that nothing but absolute necessity or true affection can
make it honorable. How this may be, may be gathered from what
we have said in the last of the preceding chapters. . . .

XXVI

Lawful Reasons Why Subjects of a Ruler
May Go to War.

1. WE have spoken of persons who are masters of their own acts.
There are others in a condition where they must obey, such as children in families, slaves, subjects; also individual citizens, if compared with the body of the state.

2. IF these persons are admitted to deliberations on policy, or
are allowed a free choice between fighting and living in peace, they
should follow the same rules as those do who of their own will engage in war for themselves or for others.

3. BUT if they are commanded to do military service, as usually
happens, and if it is clear to them that the reason for the war is
unlawful, they should absolutely refuse to serve. God is to be
obeyed rather than men, as both the Apostles and Socrates have
declared. . . . In Euripides, when Creon asks: [1]

"Does not right itself command me his orders to obey?"
Antigone answers:

"What justice ordained not it is not righteous to obey." . . .

The very civil laws that readily grant pardon for excusable sins and are lenient to persons who are under the necessity of obeying, are not so in every case. They except from their leniency deeds that have the atrocious character of crimes or outrages, which by their nature are wicked and abominable, as Cicero says,[2] and should be shunned voluntarily, not because of the arguments of the jurists but by natural instinct. . . . The rule is the same for any man who is convinced that the order given to him is wrong. For him the thing is unlawful, so long as he cannot alter his opinion. . . .

4. BUT if he is doubtful whether the thing is right or not, shall he stay where he is or obey? Many writers think he should obey, and should not be stopped by the well-known maxim, "When in doubt, do not do it," for the reason that one who has speculative doubts may have no hesitation in practical decision, for he may believe that in a case of doubt he should obey his superior. And certainly it cannot be denied that this distinction between the two kinds of judgment is applicable in many instances. The civil law, not only of Rome but of other nations, under such circumstances grants immunity to persons obeying orders and does not allow a civil suit against them. The doer of the harm, they say, is the man who orders it done. The man who has to obey is not guilty. The compulsion of power is his excuse; and so on. . . .

There is a saying of Tacitus: [3] "To the prince the gods have given supreme right of judgment; to his subjects is left the glory of obedience." . . . And on this matter of military service in particular, Augustine has the same opinion. For he says: [4] "A good man, therefore, who happens to be serving under an irreligious king, may rightly fight at his command, if he is certain that the command is one that preserves the order of the public peace and is not contrary to the law of God; or if he is not certain whether it is or not. Then for anything wicked in the command the king is probably responsible, while the soldier's position under orders makes him innocent." . . . Hence it is widely believed that as far as the subjects are concerned a war may be lawful on both sides, that is, devoid of unlawfulness. . . .

There are difficulties, however, in this view. Adrian, our fellow countryman, the last man to be elected Pope from north of the Alps, defends the opposite view,[5] which can be supported not exactly by the same argument as he uses, but by the following, which is more convincing, namely, that a man who hesitates while reflecting ought, when deciding on action, to choose the safer course. And the safer course in war is to keep out of it. . . .

It is no objection that in this other course there is the danger of disobedience. For when both courses are dubious, the lesser of the two evils is not sinful. If the war is wrong, there is no disobedience in holding off from it. And disobedience itself, in cases of this sort, by its very nature is less evil than murder, especially the murder of many innocent people. . . . Nor is the contrary argument, which some put forward, of any great weight, namely, that if men were permitted to disobey in this way, the state many times would be wrecked, since it is usually inexpedient to reveal the reasons for its policies to the public. Although this may be true of the inner reasons for a war, it is not true of the alleged reasons, which ought to be clear and visible and likewise such as can and should be openly explained. . . .

What Tertullian said rather indefinitely of laws in general [6] is most justly applicable to laws or edicts on the waging of a war: "No citizen faithfully obeys a law when he does not understand the nature of the thing the law is punishing. No law should keep to itself alone the understanding of its justice, but should impart it to those from whom obedience is expected. A law is suspect if it does not want the people's approval; it is wrong if it controls them without their approval." . . . Similar to this is the remark of the Panegyrist: [7] "So important is a good conscience even on a battlefield, that victory has come now to be as much a matter of righteousness as of valor." . . . In fact, declarations of war, as we shall say further on, used to be made publicly and with a statement of the reasons, so that the whole human race, as it were, might weigh the justice of them. . . .

Altogether then it seems that what we have called Adrian's view is the one to follow, if a subject not merely hesitates but is led by reasonable arguments to incline to the belief that the war is unlawful, especially when it is a question of attacking another people and not of defending his own. It seems reasonable too that even the executioner who is to put a condemned man to death should understand the merits of the case, either by being present at the examination and the trial, or by hearing the criminal's confession, so that he may be sure that the man deserves to die. And this is the practice in some places. . . .

5. THEN if the minds of the subjects cannot be satisfied by a statement of the reasons for war, it will certainly be the duty of a good magistrate to impose extra taxes on them instead of military service, particularly when there will be no shortage of others who will fight. . . . And, even if there can be no doubt as to the grounds for war, still it does not seem right that Christians should be compelled to fight against their will, since to take no part in warfare, even when it is legitimate to do so, is a mark of a higher holiness, which has long been demanded of clergy and penitents, and recommended constantly to everyone else. . . .

6. I think, however, that a situation may arise when a just defense may be made for the subjects who take part in a war not merely doubtful in character but even patently unlawful. For an enemy, though he may be fighting a lawful war, does not have a true and inherent right to kill innocent persons, clear of any blame for the war, except as a necessary measure of defense or as a result of something not a part of his purpose. They are not liable to punishment. It follows, then, that if it is positively established that the enemy has come with the intention of refusing absolutely to spare the lives of his opponent's subjects, whenever he can, those

subjects may protect themselves by the law of nature, of which the law of nations has not deprived them.

But not then shall we call the war right on both sides, for it is not then a question of the war but of certain definite conduct. This conduct, even though it is his who has on other scores a right to make war, is not just, and hence it is justly to be resisted.

BOOK THREE

I

General Rules from the Law of Nature as to What Is Legitimate in War. Trickery and Falsehood.

1. WE have now considered by what persons and on what grounds war may lawfully be declared. We have next to decide what is legitimate in war and to what extent, and what methods may be employed. The question may be viewed by itself or as affected by some prior agreement. By itself, first, as prescribed by the law of nature, and then by the law of nations. Accordingly, let us see what is permissible by the law of nature.

2. IN the first place, as we have said several times already, in the moral field, the means that lead to an end derive their inherent character from that end. It is understood, therefore, that we have a right to do whatever is necessary to the end of maintaining our right, necessity being understood not in the precise, physical meaning but in the moral sense. By a right I mean what is strictly so called, signifying a power of acting, with regard only to the welfare of society. So, if I have no other way of saving my life, I may resist with every kind of violence a person who attacks me, even though, perhaps, he is committing no crime in doing so, as we observed elsewhere.[1] For this right is not properly a consequence of another

269

man's crime, but of the right which nature gives me to look out for myself.

Moreover, I can take possession of another man's property, from which an unmistakable danger threatens me, without considering how far the other man is at fault. But I cannot make myself its owner, for that is not essential to the end in view. I may, however, hold it until my own safety is adequately secured. This matter too we have treated elsewhere.[2]

Thus I have by nature a right to seize my property from one who is keeping it from me; or, if that is too difficult, to take something else of equal value, as I might when recovering a debt. In these cases, ownership follows as well, since by no other means can the equality that was violated be restored. So too when a punishment is just, all the force required to execute it is also just; and everything that is a part of the penalty, such as the destruction of property by fire or in any other way, may be included in what is just and proportionate to the offense.

3. IN the second place, we should realize that our right to make war may be regarded as based not only on the event that started the war but also on causes that develop later, just as in lawsuits, a new right is often acquired by one party after the suit has been begun. So those who join my assailant, whether allies or subjects, give me a right of defending myself against them also. And so those who take part in an unlawful war, especially if they can and should know that it is unlawful, make themselves liable for refunding the expenses and repairing the damages inflicted, because their guilt caused the damage. And so those who join in a war undertaken without reasonable excuse render themselves liable to punishment in proportion to the iniquity of their action. . . .

4. IN the third place, we should note that many a consequence may follow indirectly from a right to act that was not intended by the doer, and to which in itself he has no right. How this applies to a case of self-defense we have explained in another passage.[3] Hence, in order to obtain what belongs to us, when we cannot recover the

precise equivalent, we have a right to take something more on condition that we repay the excess value. So a ship filled with pirates,
or a house with brigands, may be bombarded even though in that
same ship or house there are a few children, women, or other innocent persons, who are endangered by the attack. . . .

But, as we have often remarked before now, it is not always altogether permissible to do what, strictly speaking, is within our right.
Many a time love for our neighbor will not allow us to insist upon
our full rights. Wherefore we should beware of things which happen and which we foresee may happen beyond what we intended,
unless the good which is the aim of our act is much greater than the
harm we fear, or unless, when the good and the harm are equal, the
expectation of good is much stronger than the fear of harm, which
is a question to be left for prudence to reflect upon. But, as always,
in case of doubt we should favor, as safer, the course that protects
the other person's interest more than our own. . . . From these
general rules we may learn how far by the law of nature we may go
against an enemy.

5. A question also apt to rise is how far we may go against those
who are not our enemies and do not wish to be called so, but who
provide our enemies with certain supplies. We know that the point
has been sharply debated in both ancient and recent times. Some
writers maintain the ruthless character of war and others the right
to freedom of trade.

First, a distinction must be drawn between the articles supplied.
For there are some, such as weapons, which are used only in war;
there are some again, such as luxuries, which are never used in war;
and there are some, such as money, provisions, ships, and naval
stores, which are used both in and outside of war.

As to articles of the first class, it is true what Amalasuntha said
to Justinian,[4] that anyone who furnishes an enemy with things
necessary for war is on the enemy's side. Against the articles of the
second class, no objection can be made. . . . As regards articles of
the third class, those with a double use, one must take into con-

sideration the situation. If I cannot defend myself without inter-
cepting supplies that are being sent to the enemy, necessity, as we
explained elsewhere, will give me the right to do so, but on condition of making restitution, unless some new reason appears to the
contrary.

But if the conveyance of these supplies to the enemy obstructs
me in the prosecution of my rights, and the person conveying them
is informed of this—if, for instance, I am besieging a town, or
blockading a port, with expectation of a speedy surrender and a
peace—then the person who sends in supplies will be liable to me
for the injury done me, as one would be who let my debtor out of
prison, or planned his escape, to my hurt. His property may be
seized by way of indemnity to the extent of the damage he has
caused and the ownership of it transferred to me in discharge of
his debt. If he has as yet done me no harm but intends to do so, I
shall have the right to hold his goods, in order to compel him to
give me security for the future in the form of hostages or pledges,
or in some other way. And if, furthermore, my enemy's conduct
toward me is conspicuously lawless, and the other person is supporting him in a war of wickedness, he will be liable for the damage
not only by civil law but by criminal, as a man would be who
rescued a manifest evildoer from a judge about to impose sentence.
And on those grounds I may proceed against him as a criminal. . . .

For these reasons powers at war often issue public manifestoes
to other peoples to make plain the lawfulness of their cause and
their reasonable hopes of securing their rights. This point we have
discussed under the law of nature, since we could find nothing in
the histories established on such cases by the voluntary law of
nations. . . .

When Demetrius [5] was occupying Attica with his army, and had
already taken the neighboring towns of Eleusis and Rhamnus, and
was about to starve out Athens, he hanged both the master and the
pilot of a ship that was attempting to bring in grain, and by this

method frightened off others and made himself master of the city.

6. AS for the mode of operation, force and terror are the most characteristic weapons of war. The question is frequently raised whether it is permissible to employ deceit. . . . In Homer, Ulysses, the model of a wise man, is always full of wiles to cheat the enemy. . . . And in Plutarch, Agesilaus maintains [6] that deceiving an enemy is both right and permissible. Polybius thinks [7] that achieving things by violence in war should be counted a smaller feat than making use of opportunity for a ruse. . . . Among the theologians Augustine says: [8] "When one undertakes a just war, its justice is not affected whether one fights it openly by force or by stealthy ambush." . . .

However, there are ways of judging that lead apparently to an opposite conclusion, some of which we shall mention later on. The solution of the problem depends on whether deceit belongs in the class of things that are always evil, to which applies the rule of not doing evil that good may come; or whether it is one of those things that are not by their very nature always wrong, but may even chance to be good.

7. WE must observe then that one kind of deceit consists of a negative act and another of a positive. I stretch the word deceit, on Labeo's authority,[9] to cover what occurs in a negative act which he calls deceit but not wicked deceit, as when a man by dissimulation protects his own property or that of others. Undoubtedly Cicero is too severe when he says: [10] "From every phase of life remove pretense and deceitfulness." For as you are not bound to tell others everything you know or wish for, it follows that it may be right to dissemble, that is, to conceal some things from some persons. . . . And Cicero himself more than once admits that it is absolutely necessary and unavoidable, especially for persons in charge of a state. . . .

8. THE deceit that consists of a positive act, when practiced in deeds, is called trickery, and when in words is called falsehood. A distinction is drawn by some between these two forms of deceit,

for they say that words are by nature signs of thoughts, but acts
are not. But the contrary is true, that words by their nature and
apart from human intention signify nothing, unless it is some confused and inarticulate word like that of one in pain, which comes
under the head of an act rather than of speech. But when they say
that it is the peculiar nature of man above other animals that he can
express his thoughts to his fellows and for that purpose has invented words, in this they are speaking the truth.

However, to this we may add that such communication may be
made not only by words, but by gestures, like those the dumb use,
whether those gestures have any natural connection with the thing
they signify, or whether they signify it only by agreement. Similar
to gestures are those characters which do not represent words
framed by the tongue, as Paulus the jurist says,[11] but objects themselves, either by some resemblance to them, as in the hieroglyphic
signs, or by pure arbitrary ruling, as among the Chinese.

Another distinction must be made here, like the one we made to
remove the ambiguity in the term 'law of nations.' We said that
by 'law of nations' was meant both rules approved by separate nations, with no mutual obligation to obey them, and rules that carried with them a mutual obligation. Now the words, gestures, and
signs we have mentioned are inventions to convey meaning under
a mutual obligation, by what Aristotle calls a 'convention.'[12] The
same is not true of other things. Hence it is permissible to use
other means to give an impression, even if we foresee that the impression the other man receives will be false. I am speaking of something intrinsic, not incidental. I must give an instance when no
harm followed such an act, or when the harm done, apart from
consideration of the deceit involved, was itself permissible.

An instance of the former kind is the conduct of Christ, who,
with his companions on the way to Emmaus, made as if he would
go farther,[13] that is, gave the appearance of one going on farther.
. . . Harmless too was the act of the Romans during a war, when
they threw bread down from the Capitol into the posts of the

enemy that they might not be thought to be suffering from famine. An instance of the latter kind is the pretense at flight, which Joshua ordered his people to make at the storming of Ai; and other generals have many times done the same. The ensuing damage we should call lawful by the standard of lawfulness in wartime. Flight in itself has no established meaning, although the enemy took it as a sign of fright. But the other party is not bound to prevent him from doing so, and may employ his own liberty to go this way or that, more or less rapidly, with this or that mien or bearing.

Under the same heading we may class the conduct of persons who, we read, have assumed the arms, ensigns, clothing, and tents of their enemy. All these are actions of a sort that anyone can resort to at will, even contrary to the usual custom. For custom itself is a matter of the will of individuals, and was never established by anything like universal consent; and custom such as that is binding on no one.

9. MORE difficult is the argument regarding the use of the signs by which, so to speak, the daily intercourse of humanity is carried on. Under this head comes falsehood, properly so called. There are many condemnations of falsehood in Holy Scripture. . . . "Thou shalt destroy them that speak falsehood." (Psalms v, 6); "Lie not one to another." (Colossians III, 9.) This attitude Augustine invariably maintains, and among the poets and philosophers there are those who evidently agree with him. The lines of Homer [14] are famous:

> "Hateful to me as are the jaws of Hades
> Is he whose mind thinks other than his tongue declares."

. . . Aristotle said: [15] "Falsehood in itself is a vile and odious thing, but the truth is lovely and ever to be praised."

Yet there is authority too on the other side. First, in the Holy Scriptures, there are instances of men lying who are commended with no trace of reproach. . . . Among the philosophers openly supporting this side are Socrates and his pupils, Plato and Xeno-

phon; on occasion, Cicero, and, if we are to believe Plutarch and
Quintilian, the Stoics, who counted among the gifts of a wise man
the ability to lie where and however it was desirable. Nor does
Aristotle in some passages apparently disagree with them. . . . His
commentator, Andronicus of Rhodes, says [16] of the physician who
lies to the sick man: "He deceives, but he is not a deceiver." And
he adds the reason: "For his purpose is not the deceiving of the
sick man but his healing." Quintilian, who, as I said, defends this
view, remarks [17] that many things are made either honorable or
base not so much by what men do as by their reasons for doing
it. . . .

10. WE may perhaps find a way to reconcile these discordant
opinions by using either a broader or a stricter definition of lying.
We do not here take as a lie whatever a foolish person happens to
say, but discriminate, as Gellius does,[18] between speaking an untruth and lying. By lying we mean what is deliberately uttered,
with a meaning that does not match the thought in the mind, as
regards either knowledge or intention. For primarily and directly
words or similar signs are used to express the thoughts of our minds.
Consequently a man is not lying who says something false that he
believes to be true, but he is lying who says something true that he
supposes to be false. So a falsity of meaning is what we look for in
the general nature of a lie. Accordingly, when a word or a phrase has
several meanings, that is, admits of more than one interpretation,
either in popular usage or in the practice of a craft or in some well-
understood figure of speech, if the thought in the speaker's mind
matches one of those meanings, he is not to be charged with lying,
even though he thinks that his hearer may take his words in another sense. It is true that a reckless use of so ambiguous a method
of speaking is not to be approved of, but for special reasons it may
be justified—as when, for instance, it may help in instructing a
youth who has been put under our care, or in evading an improper
question. . . .

On the other hand, it may be not only unseemly but even wicked to resort to such a way of speech, when, for example, either the honor of God, or the love we owe our neighbor, or respect for our superior, or the nature of the situation demands that we make absolutely plain what is in our minds. Thus in discussing contracts, we said that whatever we understand the nature of the contract to require must be stated clearly. . . .

11. TO fit the common notion of a lie it is simply required that what is said, written, indicated, or implied cannot be understood save in a sense different from the mind of the speaker. But to this broad notion of a lie, a closer interpretation must add some peculiar character, which makes a lie a thing forbidden by the law of nature. And this peculiar character, if we look into the matter aright, at least according to the general opinion of nations, seems to be that a lie is a violation of an existing and permanent right of the person to whom the words or the signs are addressed. Obviously no one lies to himself, however great the falsehood he utters.

By a right I mean here not any irrelevant right but one belonging to and connected with this subject. It is nothing else than the liberty of judgment which men who converse are understood by a kind of tacit agreement to owe those with whom they are talking. It is merely the mutual obligation which men intended to introduce at the time they began to use speech and signs of a similar sort. For without such an obligation their invention would have been valueless. We require too that at the time a statement is made this right should exist and continue to be valid. For it may happen that the right has once existed but has later been lost or been canceled by the intervention of some other right. . . .

Here perhaps, you may well recall that Plato, following Simonides, classes truth-speaking with justice; [19] and that Holy Writ often describes the falsehood it prohibits as false witness, or speaking against one's neighbor; and that Augustine, in defining the nature of a lie, calls it an intention to deceive.[20] Cicero also includes the habit of truth-speaking among the foundations of justice.[21]

This right of which we have spoken may be invalidated by the express consent of the person with whom we are dealing, as when one man says beforehand that he will tell an untruth, and the other allows it. It may also be canceled by tacit consent, or by consent assumed on reasonable grounds; or by the opposition of some other person's right, which, in the common judgment of everyone, is of much greater importance. These principles, rightly understood, will furnish us with many inferences which will be of great help in reconciling the differences in the views that we described above.

12. IN the first place, an untruth may be told to a child or to an insane person without incurring the guilt of lying. For by the general opinion of mankind it seems to be allowed, "to sport with childhood's unsuspecting age." [22] . . . The obvious reason is, that as children and insane persons possess no free power of judgment, no injury can be done to them affecting that freedom.

13. SECONDLY, when a statement is made to one who is not thereby deceived, if a third person draws a false conclusion from it there is no lying in the case. No lie has been told to the person addressed, because his freedom of judgment remains quite unimpaired, like that of intelligent people who hear a fable recited. . . . Nor has a lie been told to the person who accidentally heard the statement, since it was not addressed to him, and consequently there was no obligation to him. In fact, if he frames for himself an opinion based on something said to another person and not to him, he has something for which to blame himself and no one else. By right estimation indeed, the statement, so far as he was concerned, was not a statement, but something that might signify anything. . . .

14. IN the third place, whenever it is certain that the person to whom a statement is made will not resent the violation of his right to free judgment, but may even be grateful for it because of some good it may do him, then too a lie, strictly speaking, that is, a hurtful lie, has not been told. Likewise, a man would not be commit-

ting a theft who, presuming on the owner's consent, made use of some small possession of his, in order to secure thereby something very beneficial for him. For in cases where the certainty is so great, a presumed consent is taken as if it were expressed. And clearly no wrong is done to one who consents to it.

Hence it appears that it is no sin to comfort a sick friend with assurances that are not true, as Arria did Paetus on the death of their son. The story is in Pliny's *Letters*.[23] Nor is it a sin to bring false news to encourage a man in peril in battle, so as to inspire him to win victory and his own safety. . . . The reason is given by Proclus [24] in his commentary on Plato: "For the good is better than the truth." . . . We may note also that the violation of the right of free judgment is, in cases like these, of less consequence because it is hardly more than momentary, and the truth is soon afterward made plain.

15. A fourth instance, akin to the one just mentioned, is when one person has a right outtopping all the rights of the other party and makes use of that right for either his own or the public welfare. . . . Quintilian has the saying,[25] "There are times when the public good demands the upholding of falsehoods."

16. IN the fifth place, an untruth may be told when without it the life of an innocent person, or something equally valuable, cannot be saved, or a person be diverted from perpetrating some wicked crime. . . .

17. MANIFESTLY many learned writers have gone further than we have done so far, in allowing the use of falsehood when dealing with an enemy. Thus Plato, Xenophon, Philo among the Jews, Chrysostom among the Christians, add to the rule forbidding lying the exception, 'save to an enemy.' . . . The school of writers in recent centuries do not hold this view, and have chosen on almost all points to follow only Augustine among the ancients. But the same school allows tacit interpretations of one's words that are so repugnant to all past practice that it is a question whether it is not better to permit the use of falsehood against certain persons, in

cases such as we have described, or in some of them (for I take it
that no decision is to be made here), than in so sweeping a manner
to acquit these interpretations of being falsehoods. Thus, when
they say: 'I do not know it,' it may be understood as: 'I do not
know it to tell you'; or: 'I do not have it' may be understood as: 'I
do not have it to give you'; and other things of the sort they say
contrary to the generally accepted meaning. If these things are
sanctioned, we may as well say that a man who states anything is
actually denying it, and a man who denies it is stating it.

Most true indeed it is that there is no word whatever that may
not be used in an ambiguous sense, since they all have, besides a
meaning that is called their primary idea, another that is secondary;
and this varies among the various crafts. They have other meanings
too, in metaphors and similar figures of speech. Nor do I approve
more of the judgment of those persons who, as if shocked at the
word but not at the thing, call 'jokes' utterances which are made
with the utmost seriousness of countenance and tone.

18. IT must, however, be understood that what we have said of
falsehoods applies to assertions and to those only that do harm to
no one but a public enemy; it does not apply to promises. For a
promise, as we lately said, confers on the person to whom it is made
a fresh and special right. And this rule holds even between enemies,
without any exception because of existing hostilities. It holds not
only for promises expressed but for those implied, as in a call for
a parley. We shall explain this when we come to the section on
keeping faith in wartime.

19. WE must repeat too what we said before in our previous
discussion of oaths, both affirmative and promissory, that they have
a force which excludes all exceptions that might otherwise be found
in the character of the person with whom we are dealing, since not
man only but God is involved in the business. And to him we are
bound by our oath, even if the man has no right under it. . . .

20. WE know that some nations and individuals have condemned some kinds of deceit that we have said are permitted by

the law of nature. But they did so, not because they thought them unlawful, but because of the extraordinary loftiness of their own minds, and sometimes because of their confidence in their own strength. There is in Aelian a saying of Pythagoras,[26] that by two roads man comes nearest to God, by always speaking the truth, and by doing good to others. . . . For Plutarch [27] lying was the mark of a slave. . . . It is still more incumbent, certainly, on Christians to be truthful, since they are not only commanded to be simple (Matthew x, 16), but to abstain from idle discourse (Matthew XII, 36); and they have appointed for their example him in whose mouth there was found no guile. . . .

Thus Alexander declared [28] he did not wish to steal a victory. . . . Aelian says: [29] "The Romans know that they are brave, and that not by artfulness nor by tricks have they overcome their enemies." So when Perseus, king of Macedon, had been misled by a hope of peace, the elder senators refused to approve the Roman strategy.[30] . . . And they went on to say: "Sometimes, for the moment, more is achieved by cheating than by valor. But the mind of the man who acknowledges himself defeated in a just and righteous war, not by craft nor by chance but in hand-to-hand contest of strength, is conquered forever." . . .

21. AS to methods of operating, there is this other rule, that it is not lawful to urge or press anyone to do what is unlawful for him to do. For instance, it is unlawful for a subject to kill his king, to surrender towns without public authority, and to plunder his fellow citizens. It is unlawful then to encourage a subject, who continues to be a subject, to do these things. For always the person who causes another to sin sins himself also. Nor can anyone reply that it was lawful for the man who instigated the other to the crime to perform that same act, such as killing an enemy. For it may be lawful for him to do it, but not in that way. . . .

22. IT is another matter if to accomplish something legitimate for me to do, I make use of the services of a man who of his own choice commits a sin and not at my instigation. . . . "By the law

of war we accept a deserter," says Celsus,[31] that is, it is not contrary to the law of war to receive a man who has forsaken the enemy's side and chosen ours.

II

How by the Law of Nations the Property of Subjects May Be Held Liable for the Debts of Rulers. Reprisals.

1. LET us come now to the rules derived from the law of nations. Some of them apply to wars in general; some to a particular kind of war. Let us begin with the general rules.

By the straight law of nature, no one is bound by the act of another, except the person who succeeds to his property, for the rule that encumbrances are transferred along with the property was introduced at the same time as private ownership. . . . Hence the articles in Roman law that a wife may not be sued for her husband, nor a husband for his wife, nor a son for his father, nor a father or a mother for their son.

Nor, as Ulpian clearly says,[1] are the debts of a corporation the debts of its individual members, assuming that the corporation owns property. For if it does not, the members are liable not as individuals but as parts of the corporation. Seneca says:[2] "If a person lends money to my country, I shall not call myself his debtor, nor acknowledge the debt as mine, though I shall contribute my share towards paying it." . . . So there was a special provision in Roman law that no inhabitant of a village should be bound for the debts of his fellow villagers, and elsewhere it was ordered that the property of one person should not be sued for the debts of others, not even for public debts. . . .

2. ALTHOUGH these are correct principles, yet the positive law of nations could and evidently did introduce the rule that all the property, corporeal and incorporeal, belonging to the subjects of any civil society or its head, is bound and liable for any debts which that society or its head may incur, either directly, by their own acts or by pledging themselves for the debt of someone else who has failed to fulfill the law.

This rule too is the result of a certain necessity, for, without it, the door would be wide open for acts of injustice, because the property of rulers often cannot be seized so easily as that of private citizens, who are more numerous. This, then, is one among the laws which Justinian says [3] were established by the nations of mankind as experience and human needs required them. Nor is the rule so opposed to the law of nature that it might not have been introduced by custom and tacit agreement, as men who go surety are bound by no other tie but that of their agreement. It was supposed that members of the same society could obtain their rights from one another and look out for their own indemnification more easily than foreigners could do, who in many places receive scant consideration. So the advantage derived from this rule was common to every people, since those who now felt it a hardship might at another time find it a great help.

That this was an accepted custom appears in the formal wars that peoples have fought against each other. The practice observed in such wars is shown in the formula of declaration: [4] "I declare and make war on the peoples of the ancient Latins and the men of the ancient Latins." . . . We see the same custom obtaining even where it had not yet come to outright war but it was necessary to enforce some right by violent means, that is, by informal warfare. Agesilaus once said to Pharnabazus, a subject of the Persian king: [5] "While, Pharnabazus, we were friends of your king, we treated his possessions in a friendly way; now that we are his enemies, we treat them as foes do. Therefore, since you too choose to be among the king's possessions, we have a right to wound him through you."

3. A form of enforcement of this right the Athenians called man seizure. The Attic law had this provision: [6] "If a man is killed by violence, his relatives and kinsmen have the right, on his account, to seize other men until either punishment is inflicted for his murder, or the murderers are delivered up; they may, however, seize only three men—not more." Here we see that for the debt of a state, which is bound to punish its subjects who have done harm to others, an incorporeal right of its subjects may be held forfeit, namely, the liberty of being where they choose and doing what they choose; so that they are for the time being in servitude, until the state has done what it is bound to do, that is, has punished the guilty. . . .

Similar to this practice is that of detaining the subjects of another state in which a manifest wrong has been done to our fellow countryman, in order to have him compensated. So at Carthage some citizens prevented the arrest of Ariston of Tyre for the reason that [7] "the same thing would happen to Carthaginians at Tyre and in the other trade markets to which they went in great numbers."

4. ANOTHER method of enforcing the right by violence is 'seizure of goods,' or 'taking pledges from different peoples,' which modern jurists call 'the right of reprisal,' the Saxons and Angles 'withernam,' and the French, among whom permission is usually obtained from the king, 'letters of marque.' This method may be followed, the jurists say, when the right is being denied.

5. IT is also understood that this method may be followed not only when judgment cannot be obtained against a wrongdoer or

a debtor within a reasonable time, but when, in a very clear case
—for in a doubtful case the presumption is in favor of the judges
appointed by public authority—the judgment is palpably contrary
to the law. The authority of a judge over foreigners has not the
same force as it has over subjects and even for subjects it cannot
annul a true debt. "A true debtor," says Paulus the jurist,[8] "even
though acquitted, still remains a debtor by the law of nature." . . .

But there is this difference between the two cases. Subjects cannot lawfully resist by violence the execution even of an unjust sentence, nor can they enforce their own rights against it, because of
the effective power of their government over them. Foreigners,
however, have the right of resistance, though they are not justified
in using it so long as they may obtain what is theirs by judicial
award.

The rule, then, that for such a reason either the persons or the
movable property of the subjects of a ruler who refuses to render
justice may be seized, though not introduced by the law of nature,
has been generally accepted in practice. A very ancient example is
given in the eleventh book of Homer's *Iliad*, where we are told that
Nestor had seized the flocks and herds of the men of Elis as a satisfaction for the horses they had stolen from his father. . . .

6. THAT for such a reason the lives of innocent subjects might
be held forfeit has perhaps been the belief of some people, since
they believed that every man had in himself a full right over his
own life, which might be transferred to the state. But this belief,
as we have stated elsewhere,[9] is not reasonable or compatible with
sound theology. Yet it may happen that persons who are trying to
prevent the enforcement of a right by violence are killed not intentionally but accidentally. If such an accident may be foreseen, we
ought instead by the law of love to abandon the prosecution of our
rights, as we showed above; for by that law we Christians especially should put more value on human life than on our property.

7. BUT on this as well as on other points, we must take care not
to confuse the rules that properly are a part of the law of nations

with those that have been established by civil law or by pacts between peoples.

By the law of nations all persons who are permanent subjects of wrongdoers, whether as natives or as settlers—though not those who are passing through a country or are there only for a short time—are liable to furnish surety. For the duty to furnish surety is like the other burdens which are laid on a people for the discharge of the public debts, and from which those persons are immune who are only temporarily subject to the laws of the place. From the number of subjects, however, ambassadors and their property are excepted by the law of nations, but not those sent to our enemies. By the civil law of many countries too an exception is made of the persons of wives and children of men of letters, and of those who come to trade. . . .

By the law of nations ownership of goods seized is ipso facto acquired up to the amount of the debt and the expenses incurred, so that only the balance must be restored. By civil law the persons concerned are customarily summoned to appear, the property is sold or awarded to the parties involved by public authority. But on those and other points one should consult the writers on civil law, and particularly, on this subject, Bartolus, who has written on reprisals.

One thing I will add that may tend to ease this law, so rigorous in itself, namely, that those who by not paying their debts or rendering justice have given occasion for the taking of sureties are bound by natural law and divine law to make good the damages of those who have suffered loss on their account.

III

War That Is Legal or Formal According to the Law of Nations. Declaration of War.

1. EARLIER in this treatise we began by saying that excellent authors frequently call a war legal, not on the ground of its original cause, or, as in other matters, on account of the magnitude of its achievements, but because of certain peculiar legal aspects of it.

What kind of war a legal war is will best be understood by considering the definition of enemies given by the Roman jurists. "Enemies," says Pomponius,[1] "are those who publicly declare war on us or on whom we publicly declare war; all others are pirates or brigands." Ulpian agrees [2] with him that: "Enemies are those on whom the Roman people has publicly declared war or who themselves have declared it on the Roman people. Others are called thieves or brigands. . . ."

We must only note further that by the phrase 'Roman people' is to be understood anyone who holds the supreme power in the state. "An enemy," says Cicero,[3] "is a person who has a state, a senate, a treasury, a united and agreed citizenry, and, if the occasion offers, a right to make peace and conclude an alliance."

2. NOW a commonwealth or a state, though it commits an illegal act, even as a body, does not at once cease to be a state; and a band of pirates or robbers is not a state, even though they may perhaps maintain some kind of order among themselves, without which no society can exist. For pirates and robbers band together to com-

mit crime, whereas the citizens of a state, though not always free from wrongdoing, are associated to live by law and render justice to foreigners. If they do not do this last in all respects according to the law of nature, which, as we have shown elsewhere, has been by many nations partially forgotten, they still do act in accord with the treaties they have made with one another, or with custom. . . .

In morals, the principal element in a thing is its form. As Cicero rightly remarks in the fifth book of *On Ends*,[4] "The whole is called by the name of that which is its chief ingredient, and is most widely diffused through it." . . . So the same Cicero is too hasty when he says in Book III of his *Republic*[5] that where the king or the nobility or the people is lawless, the state is not merely corrupt but has ceased to be a state. Augustine corrects him by saying:[6] "Not for such a reason would I call a people no longer a people or its body no longer a state, so long as there remains some sort of union of a reasonable populace, joined in a harmonious sharing of the things it enjoys." A sick body is still a body; and a state, though seriously diseased, is still a state, as long as it still has laws and courts and what other agencies are necessary in order that foreigners, no less than private citizens, may obtain justice in their relations with each other.

More correctly Dio Chrysostom says[7] that law—especially that law which makes up the law of nations—is in a state as the mind is in the human body, and when it disappears, the state is no longer a state. And Aristides, in the speech in which he urges the Rhodians to harmony, points out[8] that many good laws may exist even under a tyranny. . . .

Among the Germans, acts of brigandage committed outside the borders of a state were, in Caesar's words,[9] counted no disgrace. . . . The Illyrians used to rob and plunder indiscriminately on the sea, yet a triumph was celebrated over them. But over the pirates Pompey got no triumph.[10] Such is the difference between a nation and a band of men, not a nation, united solely for the commission of crimes.

3. HOWEVER, a change may take place not only in the status of individuals such as Jephthah, Arsaces, and Viriathus, who, from being leaders of brigands, became lawful commanders, but in that of communities, so that those who were once nothing but free-booters, by choosing another way of life, may become a state. Augustine, speaking of brigandage, says: [11] "If by accessions of desperate men these pests increase to the point that they hold ter-ritory, set up fixed habitations, take possession of states and subju-gate peoples, they assume the title of a kingdom."

4. WHAT persons have sovereign power we explained above. Hence we may understand that those who share in this power, in proportion to their share, may wage legal war. And those who are not subjects but parties to an unequal treaty have still more right to do so. Thus we learn from the histories that all the forms of legal warfare were observed between the Romans and their allies—Volscians, Latins, Spaniards, and Carthaginians—though they were inferior parties in the alliance.

5. BUT to make a war legal, according to this interpretation, it is not enough that it should be carried on by sovereign powers on both sides, but it must also, as we have heard, be publicly declared, and declared so publicly as to constitute a notification of the event by one party to the other. . . .

6. TO understand these passages clearly, as well as others that deal with the declaration of war, we must draw an accurate distinc-tion between what is required by the law of nature and what is not required by nature, but is nevertheless honorable, what is required by the law of nations to produce the effects proper to that law, and, in addition, what are the consequences of the peculiar institutions of each particular nation. By the law of nature, no declaration is required when one is repelling an invasion, or seeking to punish the actual author of some crime. . . . And no more necessary, by the law of nature, is any declaration where an owner wishes to lay hands on his own property.

But if one thing is being seized in place of another, or the property of a debtor is being taken to pay his debt, and, much more, if someone is proposing to invade the property of the debtor's subjects, a demand must be made first to show that in no other way can we obtain what is ours, or what is due us. For this is not a primary right, but a secondary and vicarious right, as we have explained elsewhere. So too before one attacks a sovereign for the debt or crime of a subject, a previous demand for justice should be made; this will implicate him, so that he may be regarded as involved in the wrongdoing or as a criminal himself, according to the rules we discussed above.

Even when the law of nature does not command us to make such a demand, still it is honorable and praiseworthy to make it, in order, for example, to avoid giving offense, or to allow opportunity for the wrong to be expiated by repentance and redress, in accordance with what we have said about methods to be tried to prevent war. . . . Here belongs the command that God gave the Hebrews,[12] that before they attacked a city, they should first invite it to peace. . . . When Cyrus went into the country of the Armenians, before injuring anyone, he sent messengers to the king, to demand the tribute and troops which were due him by treaty, "thinking this more civilized behavior than to march on without giving notice," as Xenophon tells us in his history.[13] However, by the law of nations, in order to preserve its special features, a previous declaration is required in every case, not from both parties but from one of them.

7. A declaration of war is either conditional or absolute. It is conditional when it is coupled with a demand for restitution. Under the heading of things to be restored, the Fetial Law of Rome included not only things claimed by right of ownership, but also things awarded as dues in a criminal or a civil case. . . . A conditional declaration is cited by Livy: [14] "They will resist that injustice with all their might, unless those who committed it make it good." In Tacitus too we read: [15] "If they do not punish the culprits, he will order a general slaughter." . . .

An absolute declaration of war, which is called particularly a 'proclamation' or an 'edict,' is issued when the other party has either already begun hostilities . . . or has himself committed crimes which call for punishment. Sometimes a conditional declaration is followed by an absolute one, though the latter is not necessary but superfluous. Hence the formula: [16] "I bear witness that this people is lawless and refuses to grant redress." . . . And a third formula: "Whereas the ancient Latin peoples have acted against and done wrong to the Roman people of the Quirites, and whereas the Roman people of the Quirites have given orders for war with the ancient Latins, and the Roman Senate of the Quirites has decreed, consented, and resolved that war should be made on the ancient Latins, therefore I and the people of Rome do declare and make war on the people of the ancient Latins."

A proof that in some cases a declaration is superfluous is that war is frequently declared by both sides, as the Peloponnesian War was declared by the Corcyraeans and by the Corinthians, though a declaration by one party is sufficient.

8. FROM the customs and institutions of certain peoples, not from the law of nations, were derived the use of the herald's staff by the Greeks, of sacred herbs and a bloody spear, first by the Aequicolae, and then, following their example, by the Romans, the renunciation of friendship and alliance, if there had been one, the setting of a thirty-day term after the demand for satisfaction had been made, the second throwing of the spear, and other acts of the kind, which should not be confused with those that are properly part of the law of nations. Arnobius informs us [17] that in his time many of these had fallen into disuse. Even in the time of Varro some of them were omitted.[18] The Third Punic War was begun the moment it was declared. . . .

9. A declaration of war against the sovereign of a people is considered a declaration at the same time against not only all his subjects but all who will join him as allies and thereby become his accessories. This is what the modern jurists mean when they say

that defiance of a prince is defiance of his associates. For a declaration of war they call a defiance. . . .

10. BUT if on the conclusion of the war it should be thought wise to attack another nation or king for having furnished assistance to the enemy, a new declaration of war will be necessary in order to satisfy the rules of the law of nations. For that nation or king is not now regarded as an accessory but as a principal enemy. Therefore it was correctly said that the war of Manlius on the Gallo-Greeks and of Caesar on Ariovistus were not lawful according to the law of nations. For they attacked them not as accessories in another man's war but as principals, and for that purpose the law of nations required a new declaration of war, and the Roman law a new order from the Roman people. . . .

11. THE reason why the nations required a declaration for the kind of war that was lawful by the law of nations was not what some writers state, namely, to keep the war-makers from doing something secretly or treacherously. For that is a matter of displaying courage rather than a matter of law. Accordingly, we read that some nations even fixed beforehand the day and place of battle.

The intention was rather to make it known for certain that the war was not a private undertaking but was to be waged by the will of both peoples or of the heads of the peoples. On this fact were based the special features which are not part of a war against pirates, or of one that a king wages against his subjects. . . .

12. IT is indeed true what some writers have observed and proved by examples, that even in such wars all captures become the property of the captors. Yet this statement is true of one side only and is based there on the law of nature, not on the voluntary law of nations, for the latter is concerned solely with nations, not with persons who have no nation, or are but a part of a nation.

The same writers are mistaken too in the supposition that a war undertaken to defend oneself or one's property needs no declaration. It certainly needs one, not simply to justify itself, but in order to acquire those features to which we have already alluded, and which we shall soon describe.

13. IT is also untrue that a war cannot be begun instantly, on the declaration. Cyrus did it to the Armenians, and the Romans to the Carthaginians, as we have just said, for by the law of nations no length of time is required after the declaration. There may be cases, however, where by the law of nature the character of the transaction calls for some delay, as when, for instance, a restitution of goods or punishment of a wrongdoer is being demanded and has not been refused. Enough time then should be allowed to make it possible to meet the demand without difficulty.

14. EVEN if the rights of ambassadors have been violated, not even then should one dispense with a declaration of war, to ensure the features I have mentioned. But it will suffice to make the declaration in whatever way it can be done safely, as by writing, even as summonses and other notices are customarily issued in unsafe places.

IV

Right of Killing Enemies in Lawful War and Other Bodily Violence.

1. THERE is a passage of Vergil: [1]

"Then to contend in hate, and then to loot
Will become lawful,"

on which Servius Honoratus . . . comments: [2] "If ever a tribe
carried off men or animals from the lands of the Roman people,
the chief priest with the Fetiales, that is, the priests who preside
over the making of treaties, would go forth and standing at the
frontier, declare in a loud voice the grounds for war. And if the
tribe refused to restore the things that had been stolen or to surrender the doers of the injury, he would hurl a spear towards them.
And that act would be the opening of the conflict, and then it
would be lawful to plunder in accord with the usage of war." . . .
Whence we learn that there are certain features peculiar to a war
declared between two peoples or their heads which are not the
result of the nature of war in itself, a conclusion that agrees well
with what we lately found in the Roman jurists.

2. BUT let us see what is the meaning of Vergil's "will become
lawful." For sometimes we call 'lawful' what is right and dutiful
from every point of view, even though perhaps some other kind of
act would be more admirable. Thus Paul the Apostle says: [3] "All
things,"—that is, of the kind of which he had then begun to speak
and was to speak further—"are lawful unto me, but not all are
expedient." Thus it is lawful to contract marriage but single chastity for a pious motive is more admirable. . . . To marry a second
time is lawful, but to be content with one marriage is more admirable. . . .

In another sense an act may be called 'lawful,' not because it can
be performed without violation of one's conscience or of the rules
of duty, but because it is not subject to penalty from other men.
Thus among many peoples prostitution is lawful; among the Spartans and the Egyptians it was lawful even to steal. Quintilian has
the statement: [4] "There are things not by their nature admirable
but permitted by law, as by the Twelve Tables it was lawful for
creditors to divide up the body of a debtor." . . . Yet this is an
accepted meaning, as Cicero shows in his address to the judges on
behalf of Rabirius Posthumus.[5] "You should consider what is right
to do, not how far it is lawful for you to go; for if you are only

looking for what is lawful, you can banish from the state whomever you choose." So all things are said to be lawful for kings, because they are exempt from human punishments, as we said
elsewhere. . . . Musonius reproves kings [6] "who make a habit of
declaring, 'This is lawful for me,' not, 'This is right for me.'"

In this sense we often see contrasted what is lawful and what is
right, as it is more than once by the elder Seneca in his *Controversies*. Cicero again, in his speech for Balbus, says: [7] "There are things
that are not right, even though they are lawful." And in his speech
for Milo [8] he ascribes our idea of what is right to nature and of
what is lawful to the laws. . . .

3. NOW in this sense it is lawful for one enemy to injure another
in both his person and his property; lawful, that is, not only for the
one who fights in a just cause, and who confines his injuries within
the limits allowed by the law of nature, as we said at the beginning
of this book, but for both sides and without distinction. Accordingly, no enemy, even when captured perhaps on the other's territory, can on that score be punished as a murderer or a thief, nor
can his opponent make war on him for such trespass. . . .

4. THE reason why the nations approved this rule was that it
would be dangerous for other people to attempt to decide on the
rights of a war between two nations, since in the course of their effort they might themselves become involved in their neighbors'
struggle. Thus the men of Marseilles said, during the conflict between Caesar and Pompey,[9] that they had neither the judgment
nor the power to determine which party had the juster cause. Furthermore, even in a lawful war it can hardly be ascertained with
assurance from outside indications what is a lawful mode of defense, or of recovering one's belongings, or of inflicting punishment.
Consequently, it has seemed altogether wiser to leave these questions to be dealt with by the consciences of the belligerents than to
call in the verdicts of outsiders. . . .

5. THIS license to injure, which we have begun now to discuss,
extends, first of all, to persons. To this fact, there are many testi-

monies in excellent authors. . . . Thus, according to an ancient
Greek custom, it was not lawful to bathe or drink, much less perform holy rites, in company with anyone who had killed a man,
not in battle; but with those who had killed in battle it was lawful.
Again and again killing is called a right of war. . . . Cicero in his
speech for Marcus Marcellus says: [10] "For although, by the very
terms of the victory we might lawfully all have been slain, by your
merciful judgment we were preserved." Caesar tells the Aeduans [11]
that "by his kindness they have been saved when by the law of
war he might have killed them." . . .

When, however, these writers say 'by the law of war,' we should
not take the law to be one that clears what is done under it of all
manner of blame, but merely one that gives the impunity I have
mentioned. This appears from other passages as well. . . . Seneca
says in his *Letters:* [12] "Deeds which in peace they would atone for
with their lives, we praise them for doing in a soldier's uniform."
Cyprian says: [13] "Murder committed by individuals is a crime. We
call it a virtue when practiced by a people as a whole. Wicked deeds
acquire immunity not because they are harmless but because of the
magnitude of the cruelty they inflict." . . .

6. THIS law of license extends very widely. It does not, in the first
place, cover violence done only to those who are actually bearing
arms or who are subjects of the author of the war, but done to all
persons on enemy territory, . . . because of course damage may
be feared from them also. And that fear, lasting through a prolonged and general war, is reason enough to establish the law of
which we are speaking. . . . And what I have said applies without
question to all strangers who, after the war has started and they
are informed of it, enter the enemy's territory.

7. AS for persons who went there before the war, they too, it
seems, are regarded by the law of nations as enemies after a little
interval has passed, during which they might have left. Thus the
Corcyreans, who were about to blockade Epidamnus, first offered

foreigners an opportunity to depart,[14] announcing that if they stayed, they would be treated as enemies.

8. AS for those who are actually subjects of the enemy, that is, on a permanent basis, the law of nations permits injuring them in their persons wherever they are. For when war is declared on anyone, it is declared at the same time on the persons of his people, as we showed above, in the formula of declaration. . . . Whoever is an enemy may by the law of nations be attacked anywhere. Euripides says: [15]

"The laws permit harming a foe, wherever he is taken."

Such people, then, may be killed with impunity on our own soil, on enemy's soil, on no man's soil, or on the sea. But within a country which is at peace it is not lawful to kill or use force on them. The right to this security does not belong to them personally but is the right of him who is sovereign there. For political societies have been able to establish the rule that no violence should be done to persons in any land at peace, except by decision of a court. . . . And where courts are functioning, there the merits of the persons concerned are taken into consideration, and that promiscuous right of inflicting injury, which, as we say, appears between enemies, ceases to exist.

Livy relates [16] that seven Carthaginian triremes were lying once in a harbor belonging to the domain over which Syphax was ruler, at a time when he was at peace with both Carthaginians and Romans, and Scipio put in there with two triremes. They might have been sunk by the Carthaginians before they entered the harbor, but they were blown in by a sharp wind before the Carthaginians could weigh anchor. And then the Carthaginians dared do nothing in the king's harbor.

9. BUT to return to my subject. How far this rule of license extends may be gathered from the fact that the slaughter of infants and women too is committed with impunity and sanctioned by the same law of war. I shall not cite here the killing of the women

and children of Heshbon by the Jews,[17] nor the command that they
should do the same to the Canaanites and those who were allied
with them. Those were acts of God, whose right over men is greater
than that of men over beasts, as we have elsewhere explained. . . .

But in ancient times, as Thucydides tells us,[18] the Thracians, on
the capture of Mycalessus, put both women and children to death.
. . . Tacitus says [19] that Germanicus Caesar laid waste the villages
of the Marsi, a people of Germany, with sword and fire, and adds:
"No sex and no age found pity." Titus sentenced the women and
children of the Jews to be torn by wild beasts in the arena. Yet
these two men are not supposed to have been cruel by disposition;
but cruelty of that sort had become such a custom. So it is not surprising that old men too were killed, as Priam was by Pyrrhus.[20]

10. NOT even prisoners are safe from this license to injure,
Pyrrhus in Seneca says,[21] in accordance with the custom accepted
at the time:

"No law spares the captive or hinders his punishment.". . .

Hence that line of Horace,[22]

"When you can sell your captive, slay him not,"

for it assumes that you are permitted to kill him. . . . Thus five
thousand prisoners were executed by Hannibal. . . .

Nor, so far as the law of nations goes, has the right of killing
such slaves, that is, prisoners of war, ever been abolished, though
by the laws of individual states it is now restricted, here more,
there less.

11. MOREOVER, there are instances in plenty of the killing of supplicants, as Achilles did in Homer,[23] . . . killing which we note is
described as sanctioned by the law of war. Augustine, when praising
the Goths, who had spared suppliants and people who fled for
refuge to the churches, says: [24] "What the law of war would have
permitted them to do they considered unpermissible for them."
Those who give themselves up are not always accepted. The Greeks

were not, who fought on the Persian side in the battle of Grani-
cus. . . .

12. EVEN those whose unconditional surrender had been accepted have, you may read, been put to death, as . . . the Samnites were by Sulla, the Numidians and Vercingetorix himself by
Caesar. In fact, it was an almost invariable custom with the Romans to execute on the day of a triumph the enemy commanders,
whether captured or surrendered, as Cicero tells us in his fifth
speech *Against Verres*, Livy in Book XXVIII and elsewhere, Tacitus in his *Annals*, Book XII, and many other writers. The same
Tacitus relates [25] how Galba ordered the decimation of the troops
he had taken, at their entreaty, under his protection. . . .

13. HISTORIANS sometimes give as reason for killing one's enemies,
especially prisoners or supplicants, the right of reprisal, or else their
past stubbornness in resisting; but these reasons, as we have explained elsewhere, are more plausible than satisfactory. For a fair
reprisal, properly so-called, should be inflicted on the very person
who committed the wrong, as may be understood from what we
said earlier on the sharing of punishments. In war, on the contrary, what is called reprisal results very often in suffering by persons
who are guiltless of the wrong charged in the accusation. . . .

And no one believes that stubborn loyalty to one's party deserves
punishment. . . . So far is it indeed from being anything criminal
that it is considered a crime to desert one's post. Particularly it was
considered so by the ancient military law of Rome, which hardly
allowed any excuse whether of fear or of peril. "Among the Romans
it is a capital offense to leave one's post," says Livy.[26] Every general
employs this extreme severity when it seems to him best for his
own advantage; and it is sanctioned throughout mankind by the
law of nations, of which we are now treating.

14. THE same right to kill has been exercised too on hostages, not
only on those who had bound themselves, as by some agreement,
but on those who had been surrendered by others. The Thessalians
once put two hundred and fifty to death.[27] . . . We must note also

that boys were sometimes given as hostages, . . . and women, as they were by the Romans in the time of Porsena. . . .

15. HOWEVER, just as the law of nations—by that kind of permission we have now described—permits many things which are forbidden by the law of nature, so it forbids some things which the law of nature permits. For if you are permitted to kill a man, it makes no difference from the standpoint of the law of nature whether you kill him with a sword or by poison. "The law of nature," I say, for certainly it is more magnanimous to kill in such a way that the one who is to be killed has a chance to defend himself. Yet there is no obligation to grant this chance to a man who has deserved to die. But the law of nations—if not of all nations, undoubtedly of the better kind—has now for a long time forbidden the killing of an enemy by poison. The agreement was reached out of consideration for the general welfare, to keep the dangers from war, which had begun to be numerous, from spreading too far. It is likely that it started with the kings, whose lives are more thoroughly protected by arms than other men's are, but are less safe from poison than others, unless guarded by some reverence for law and dread of disgrace.

. . . According to Valerius Maximus,[28] "Wars should be fought with arms not poisons." And Tacitus tells us [29] how when the chief of the Chatti offered to bring about the death of Arminius by poison, Tiberius rejected the idea and by that act of glory raised himself to the level of the generals of old. So those who think it is permissible to kill an enemy by poison, as Baldus does,[30] following Vegetius, are considering only the law of nature, and overlooking the law which rests on the will of the nations.

16. SOMEWHAT different from that mode of poisoning and approaching nearer the method of force is the poisoning of arrow points. . . . But this too is contrary to the law of nations, not of all nations but of the European peoples, and of such others as come near in culture to the higher level of Europe. John of Salisbury made correct note of this fact, in the following words: [31] "Nor do

I read that permission to use poison was ever granted by any law, though I see it has sometimes been employed by unbelievers." . . .

The poisoning of springs also, an act which either cannot be concealed or cannot long remain so, Florus calls [32] a sin not only against the custom of our ancestors but against the law of the gods, for writers, as we have noted, frequently ascribe the laws of nations to the gods. Nor should it seem strange if there were some such tacit agreement between belligerents to diminish the perils of war, as once the Chalcidians and the Eretrians agreed during a war "not to employ missile weapons." [33]

17. HOWEVER, the same rule does not hold against polluting waters, without poisoning them, so that they cannot be drunk, as we read that Solon and the Amphictyons thought it lawful to do in wars with barbarians.[34] . . . For such an act is considered to be like the diverting of a river or the blocking of the streams of a spring, which by the law of nature and by general agreement is permissible.

18. THE question is asked whether the law of nations allows killing an enemy by sending an assassin to murder him. A distinction must absolutely be drawn between assassins who are breaking faith, express or tacit, such as subjects who attack their king, vassals their lord, soldiers their army commander, persons received as suppliants, strangers or deserters those who received them, and persons under no obligation of loyalty. Such a one was Pepin, father of Charlemagne, who, accompanied by one attendant, is said to have crossed the Rhine and killed his enemy in his bedchamber. . . .

It is indeed permissible both by the law of nature and by the law of nations, as we said earlier, to kill an enemy anywhere, nor does it matter how many take part in the deed or how many are slain. Six hundred Spartans besides Leonidas entered the enemy camp and made for the king's tent.[35] A smaller number might well have done the same thing. . . . By the law of nations not only those who do these deeds but those who instigate others to do them are blameless. . . .

Nor should anyone be moved by the fact that assassins, if caught, are often put to excruciating torture, since the reason for that is not that they have transgressed the law of nations but that by the same law anything is permissible against an enemy. But each captor decides on a worse or a lighter punishment as suits his own purpose.

Thus too the law of nations unquestionably permits the sending out of spies, as Moses sent them and as Joshua himself was one; yet if they are caught, they are commonly treated with great cruelty. "It is the custom," says Appian,[36] "to put spies to death." This is lawful when done by those who clearly have a just cause for fighting; others are justified by the license granted them by the law of war. If there are men who refuse to employ the aid of spies, when it is offered them, their refusal must be attributed to loftiness of mind and confidence in their own revealed resources, not to any idea of what is lawful or unlawful.

But when it comes to assassins whose deed is also an act of perfidy, our judgment must be different. Not only are they themselves violating the law of nations, but so also are those who employ them. In other cases, those who make use of the services of bad men are regarded as sinners before God but not before men, that is, not as transgressors of the law of nations, because in such a matter,

"Custom has brought the law under its power," [37]

. . . But a man who makes use of another man's treason is regarded as having violated both the law of nature and the law of nations. . . . Hence that judgment on Perseus: [38] "He does not wage a lawful war with the spirit of a king, but goes about it with all the clandestine crimes of thieves and poisoners." . . .

The reason why the verdict in cases of perfidious assassination has been different from that in other cases is the same as the reason we gave above when condemning the use of poisons, namely, to keep danger from spreading too far, especially among persons of highest prominence. Eumenes said [39] he did not believe that "any general would choose to win by means that would set the worst

possible example for an attack on himself." . . . In formal warfare, accordingly, or between those who have the right to declare
formal war, such a practice is not lawful; outside formal warfare
the same law of nations allows it. So Tacitus declares [40] that a
plot of this sort formed against the rebel Gannascus was not base.
. . . So too perfidy employed against brigands and pirates, though
not guiltless, goes unpunished among the nations because of the
hatred felt for the objects of the perfidy.

19. YOU may read in some places that the raping of women in
war is permissible, and in others that it is not. Those who allow
rape take into account solely the injury to another person's body,
and judge it consistent with the law of war that whatever belongs
to the enemy should be subject to injury. More rightly, others have
regard not merely to the injury but to the act of savage lust itself,
and to the fact that it is no help toward establishing security or
determining punishment. Consequently rape should not go unpunished in war any more than in peace. But this last is law not
among all nations but among the better. Thus Marcellus before he
took Syracuse is said [41] to have provided for the protection of chastity even among the enemy. Scipio says in Livy,[42] that both he and
the Roman people are concerned "that nothing that is anywhere
held sacred should be violated by them,"—"anywhere," that is,
among more civilized peoples. . . .

And among Christians it is right that this rule should be obeyed,
not simply as a part of military discipline, but as a part too of the
law of nations; that is, that anyone who violates chastity by force,
even though in wartime, should everywhere be liable to punishment. Under Hebrew law no man could commit such an act with
impunity, as we perceive from the passage that treats of taking a
woman captive and not selling her afterward.[43] On this passage the
Jewish rabbi Bacchai remarks: "God willed that the camp of the
Israelites should be holy, not given over to harlotry and other
abominations like the camps of the heathen." Arrian after tell-

ing [44] how Alexander, captivated by love for Roxana, "would not mistreat her as a prisoner but thought her deserving of marriage," adds his praise of Alexander's conduct. . . .

V

Devastation and Looting.

1. IT is not contrary to nature, says Cicero,[1] to strip of his possessions a person whom it is right to kill. Hence it is not strange if the law of nations allows us to destroy and plunder the property of enemies whom it permits us to put to death. So Polybius, in the fifth book of his *Histories*, says [2] that the ravaging or destruction of an enemy's fortifications, harbors, cities, men, ships, crops, and everything else of the sort is authorized by the law of war. . . . On almost every page of the historians you will find records of cities totally demolished, walls leveled to the ground, fields laid waste and conflagrations blazing. We should note too that the same treatment is permissible even when the people have surrendered. . . .

2. NOR does the law of nations by itself, apart from other ethical considerations of which we shall have something to say later, make an exception of sacred things, that is, things dedicated to God or to the gods. "When places are captured by an enemy, nothing is any longer sacred," says the jurist Pomponius.[3] . . . The reason is

that the things that are called sacred are not in fact withdrawn from human use but are public, though they are labeled sacred because of the purpose for which they were designed. A proof of what I say is that when any people surrenders itself to another people or to a king it surrenders also the things it calls divine. . . .

Accordingly Ulpian says[4] that the public law covers even things that are held sacred. . . . With this agrees the sentence in Tacitus:[5] "All the rites in the Italian towns, and the temples and statues of divinities are under Roman law and authority." Therefore, the people may change its mind and make secular what was once sacred. . . . In times of emergency, we see that sacred things have been converted to uses of war by the persons who earlier had consecrated them, as we read they were by Pericles, though with promise of restoration . . . and by Sulla, Pompey, Caesar, and others. . . . In the *Controversies* of the elder Seneca, we read: "To meet the need of the state temples are many a time stripped, and we melt down offerings to use as pay." . . . And Cato in a speech in Sallust,[6] describing what usually happens to the conquered, lists the looting of their shrines.

It is, nevertheless, true, that if it is supposed that some deity dwells in an image, it is wicked for those who share that belief to maltreat or destroy it. On this understanding, that is, on the assumption that such is their belief, persons who have committed deeds of this sort are sometimes accused of impiety or even of breaking the law of nations. It is different if the enemy does not hold the same belief. So the Jews were not only permitted but even commanded to smash the idols of the heathen. The reason why they were forbidden to take the images for themselves was to make them detest more thoroughly the heathen superstitions, through being warned against pollution by the edict against contact. . . . The Jews indeed knew through the unerring instruction of God that neither the spirit of God, nor good angels, nor the power of the stars dwelt in those idols, as the benighted heathen thought, but only malicious demons, hostile to the human race. So Tacitus

in his account of the institutions of the Jews said correctly: [7]
"Everything that to us is sacred is profane to them." . . . And
thus when Xerxes destroyed the images of the Greeks, he did nothing contrary to the law of nations, although the Greek writers make
much of it in order to arouse indignation. For the Persians did not
believe there were any divinities in the images; to them God was
the sun, and any fire a part of him.

By Hebrew law, as the same Tacitus rightly observes,[8] "Only
their priests were allowed to approach the threshold of the temple." But Pompey, according to the same author, "entered the
temple by right of victory." . . . He did well in sparing the temple and the furnishings of the temple, though as Cicero acutely
remarks, he did so out of shame and fear of his detractors, not out
of reverence. He did wrong in entering the temple, thereby showing his disdain of the true God. . . . As a consequence some persons think it happened by a special providence of God that this
very Pompey I have just mentioned was slain as it were in sight of
Judaea, near Casius, a promontory of Egypt. Yet if you regard
Roman opinion, he had done nothing in the temple contrary to
the law of nations. When Josephus relates [9] the destruction of
the same temple by Titus, he adds that it was done "in accordance with the law of war."

3. WHAT we have said of sacred things should be understood as
applying also to all dedicated things, since they belong not to the
dead but to the living, whether they are possessions of a people or
of a family. Therefore as sacred places, when captured by an
enemy, are no longer sacred, so dedicated things also are no longer
dedicated, as Pomponius wrote in the passage quoted above. And
Paulus the jurist says: [10] "The sepulchres of the enemy are not
consecrated for us, and so we can put to any use the stones taken
from them." However, these words are not to be interpreted as
meaning that the bodies of the dead may be mishandled, for that
is contrary to the right of burial, which, we have shown elsewhere,
was established by the law of nations.

4. HERE I shall briefly repeat that by the law of nations the property of an enemy may be taken from him, and not merely by force, but that any trickery which does not involve perfidy is considered permissible, even, in fact, the instigation of another man to commit perfidy. Indeed, the law of nations is tending to overlook these frequent minor offenses, even as the civil laws do prostitution and unfair usury.

VI

Right of Acquiring Ownership of Objects Captured in War.

---

1. IN addition to the impunity granted by mankind for certain acts in formal warfare, of which we have now spoken, there is another feature peculiar to such warfare according to the law of nations.

Even by the law of nature, in a lawful war we may acquire ownership of objects which are either the equivalent of things owed to us and which we cannot recover in any other way, or whose loss is a damage to the wrongdoer, not exceeding in amount a fair punishment for him, as we said elsewhere. By this law Abraham offered to God a tenth of the spoils he had taken from the five kings.[1] . . . In the same fashion also the Greeks, Carthaginians, and Romans dedicated to their gods, such as Apollo, Hercules, and Jupiter Feretrius, a tenth of their plunder. . . . It appears too from other passages that God approved of the right of pillage, within the natural limits I have mentioned. Speaking in his law of a city that had been stormed after rejecting peace, he says: [2] "All the spoil thereof thou shalt take unto thyself, and thou shalt enjoy the spoil of thine enemies, which God hath given thee." . . . Indeed, as Seneca declared,[3] it is a fine thing for soldiers to make a man rich out of enemy booty. . . . And Philo calls it [4] one of the hardships of the law that one's field may be reaped by an enemy, whence may follow "a famine for friends and abundance for the foe."

2. BUT by the law of nations not only one who fights in a lawful cause but whoever takes part in a formal war becomes owner without limit or measure of whatever he seizes from the enemy, in the sense, at least, that both he and those who hold title from him are to be protected by every nation in their possession of those things. This right we may call ownership as far as its external effects are concerned. In Xenophon,[5] Cyrus says: "Among men it is forever the law that when an enemy city is captured, the property and money in it belong to the victor." Plato said: [6] "All the goods of the conquered go to the conqueror." . . .

On the word of Aristotle,[7] "The law is a kind of general agreement by which objects taken in war become the property of those who take them." . . . The Roman envoys said to Philip [8] with regard to the cities of Thrace and elsewhere, that if he had taken them in war, by the law of war he should keep them as the reward of victory. . . .

"What is taken from an enemy by the law of nations becomes immediately the property of the takers," says Gaius the jurist.[9] Theophilus, in the Greek *Institutes*,[10] calls this "a natural taking of property," just as Aristotle had called[11] "acquisition in war a natural mode of acquisition," doubtless because they were thinking not of the reason for it but of the bare fact, and from that derived the right. . . . Property too that is taken from people subject to the enemy is regarded as taken from the enemy. . . .

3. FURTHER, with regard to this particular question in warfare, the nations have agreed that a man is understood to have captured an article when he keeps hold of it in such a way that its previous

owner has lost all likely expectation of recovering it, or it has escaped his pursuit. . . . In the case of our movable objects this rule means that they are called captured when they have been transported inside the borders, that is, the defenses, of the enemy. For an object is lost by the same method by which it returns in postliminy.[12] It returns as soon as it is inside the borders of our state, which elsewhere is expressed as within the defenses. This principle Paul stated clearly [13] as regards a man; that is, he is lost to us when he has passed beyond our borders. And Pomponius defines [14] a captive in war as one whom the enemy have taken from our territory and brought within their own defenses, for until he is brought within them, he remains our citizen.

According to this law of nations, the position of a man and of a thing are the same. Hence it is easy to realize that what is said elsewhere,[15] as to objects captured becoming immediately the property of the captors, should be accepted with one proviso, namely, that they continue to the same point in possession of the captors. Evidently then it follows that at sea our ships and other articles are only to be considered captured when they have been brought into the enemy's dockyards or harbors or to the spot where his whole fleet is lying, for then the chance of rescue begins to seem hopeless. However, by a more recent law of nations between the European peoples, we see a rule has been established that such objects may be counted as captured when for twenty-four hours they have remained in the grasp of the enemy.

4. AND land is not considered captured as soon as it is seized. For although it is true that that part of our land which the enemy's army has invaded in heavy force is temporarily possessed by him, . . . still to bring about a change of ownership, mere uncertain possession is not enough, but something stable is required. Thus the Romans were so far from believing that the land outside their gates which Hannibal was occupying with his camp was lost, that at this very time it was being sold for a sum no less than it brought before.[16] So land will be regarded as captured only when it is so

enclosed in permanent fortifications that without storming them
the previous owners can have no open access to it. . . .

5. THIS too is plain, that to make a thing ours by the law of war
it must first belong to the enemy. For articles that are simply on
enemy soil, in their towns, for instance, or inside their defenses,
but whose owners are neither subjects of the enemy nor hostilely
inclined toward us, we cannot acquire by war. . . .

6. ACCORDINGLY, the common statement that goods found in
enemy ships are to be considered enemy property should not be
accepted as a definite rule of the law of nations, but merely as an
expression of a presumption, which may be refuted by valid proofs
to the contrary. In our country of Holland, in the year 1438, while
a fierce war was going on with the Hanseatic towns, a decision to
that effect was reached once, I find, by the full senate and from
that decision passed into a law.

7. THIS, however, is indisputably true, if we are considering the
law of nations, that objects we have taken from the enemy cannot
be claimed by persons who possessed them before our enemy did
and then lost them in war. For the law of nations first made our
enemy the owners by right of external control, and then made us
the owners. . . . Thus David regarded as his own and divided up
what he had taken from the Amalekites, and the Amalekites previously from the Philistines.[17] . . .

By this right, Appian tells us,[18] the Romans kept Syria and did
not return it to Antiochus Pius, from whom Tigranes, an enemy
of the Romans, had wrested it. Justin, citing Trogus, gives this as
the answer Pompey made to Antiochus,[19] "that he had not taken
the kingdom from Antiochus when he held it, but now that Antiochus had yielded it over to Tigranes, he would not give him back
what he did not know how to defend." . . .

8. A more difficult problem is to determine who in a public and
formal war acquires the property of the enemy. Is it the people as
a whole or individuals from or among the people? On this point,
modern interpreters of law differ widely. The majority, who have

read in the Roman law that things captured belong to the captors, and then in the body of the Canons that booty is to be divided in accordance with the people's will, have declared one after another, as their custom is, that first, by the law, the objects do belong to the individuals who laid hands on them, but that then they must be delivered to the commander who will distribute them among the soldiery. This opinion is as generally accepted as it is wrong. It must be refuted by us with the greater care, since it is an example of how little faith in this sort of argument can safely be put in these authorities. Doubtless either one of the two procedures might be approved by consent of the nations, so that the ownership of captured property might pass either to the people who were carrying on the war or to whatever individual laid hands on it. But we are asking what the nations have actually chosen to do, and we say that they have decided that the property of one enemy should be to the other in the same position as ownerless property. . . .

9. NOW ownerless property belongs to those who take it, but as much to those who take it through agents as to those who take it themselves. Hence not only slaves or sons but free men as well, who work for others in fishing, fowling, hunting, or pearl-gathering, acquire what they have got directly for those for whom they are working. . . . And Paulus, writing on the Edict, says:[20] "We may acquire property through an agent, a guardian, or a trustee," which, he explains, happens if they are acting with the intention of doing us such service. Thus among the Greeks, those who contended in the Olympian games acquired the prizes for the people who sent them. The reason is that a man who willingly does the will of another man is naturally his instrument, as we have said elsewhere.[21] . . . Setting aside then the civil law, we may rightfully say that anyone can do through another what he can do by himself, and the result is the same whether he acts by himself or through the other.

10. WE must therefore distinguish in our inquiry between the

truly public acts of a war and the private acts which are committed
during a public war. In private acts the object gained is acquired
primarily and directly by private individuals; in public acts
it is acquired by the people. In accord with the law of nations
Scipio dealt with Masinissa, as Livy tells us.[22] "Syphax was defeated and captured by the power of the Roman people. Hence
he, his wife, kingdom, land, towns and their inhabitants, everything, in short, that belonged to Syphax, is now the booty of the
Roman people." . . .

11. LANDED property is not ordinarily captured except by a public act, invasion by an army and construction of fortifications. So
in the judgment of Pomponius,[23] "land that has been taken from
an enemy belongs to the people." . . . Thus among the Jews and
the Spartans land taken in battle was divided up by lot. Thus the
Romans either kept captured land to be farmed out, leaving sometimes a small tract for the original captor as a sign of honor, or else
sold it in parcels, or distributed it to colonists, or leased it in perpetuity. Examples of such action are to be found in plenty in the
laws, the histories, and the commentaries of surveyors. . . .

12. BUT movable goods or things that can move themselves may
be captured either in the public service or outside it. If outside the
public service, they become the property of the individual captors.
. . . The same rule was followed with regard to men, at a time
when men thus captured were classed with other captured articles.
The passage in Tryphonius [24] is important on this point: "Men
who in time of peace go to other countries, if a war suddenly breaks
out, become the slaves of the persons, now turned their enemies,
among whom it is their fate to be caught." . . .

By the same rule, when soldiers capture anything, not in battle
or in some enterprise under orders, but while doing something by
unspecified right or by permission merely, they acquire it directly
for themselves, since they capture it not in the capacity of servants.
Such are spoils wrested from an enemy in single combat. Such too
are things captured on free and volunteer excursions away from

of himself in a letter to Sallust: [30] "Of my spoils no one save the
city quaestors, that is, the Roman people, has touched a farthing;
nor will anyone touch it." In the old and better days this was the
most usual practice. . . .

Other generals, however, sold their plunder themselves without
a quaestor, and put the proceeds in the treasury. . . . We frequently meet with statements as to how much each commander
brought in to the treasury from his Italian, African, Asiatic, Gallic,
or Spanish triumphs, either personally or through a quaestor, so
there is no need to pile up instances. This point rather should be
noted, that sometimes the plunder or a portion of it was offered to
the gods, sometimes given to the soldiers, sometimes too to others.
To the gods were offered either the objects themselves, as when
Romulus hung up his spoils in the temple of Jupiter Feretrius, or
else the money obtained from them, as when Tarquinius Superbus
built the temple of Jupiter on the Tarpeian Mount from the money
he got for the booty from Pometia.

17. TO the early Romans a gift of booty to the soldiers seemed a
way of courting popularity. So Sextus, son of Tarquinius Superbus,
in exile at Gabii, is said to have given his spoils to his soldiers in
order to win influence for himself by the act. In the Senate Appius Claudius denounced that kind of bounty as being a novel and
ill-advised extravagance.

Booty granted to soldiery is either distributed among them or
taken by them in looting. It may be divided on a basis either of pay
or of merit. . . . Polybius explains carefully [31] the whole scheme
of distribution. For days or for watch periods a half or less of the
army was customarily sent out to collect plunder, and each man
was ordered to bring in to camp whatever he found, that it might
be divided up equally by the tribunes. Those who guarded the
camp too were assigned a share, . . . as well as those who were
absent because of illness or on some service to which they had
been deputed.

Sometimes not the booty itself but the money obtained from the

sale of it was given to the soldiers instead. This was often the practice at a triumph. The following rule of proportion I find was observed. A single share went to a foot soldier, a double share to a
centurion, a triple share to a cavalryman. Or sometimes a single
share went to a foot soldier, a double share to a cavalryman. . . .
Often too some account was taken of special merit, as when Marcius for his courageous action was awarded by Postumius a share
of the plunder of Corioli.

By whichever method the division was carried out, the general
was allowed first choice, to take first for himself as much as he
wanted, that is, as much as he thought fair. The same privilege
was sometimes granted to others as a reward of valor. . . . After
the battle of Plataea, Herodotus says,[32] noble prizes, women,
horses, and camels, were awarded to Pausanias. . . . Fabricius in
his speech to Pyrrhus, given by Dionysius of Halicarnassus, says:[33]
"Of the things captured in war it was lawful for me to take as much
as I wished." . . .

But more praiseworthy were the commanders who relinquished
their rights and took no portion of the loot for themselves. . . .
Their examples were imitated by Marcius Porcius Cato at the time
of his Spanish victory, when he declared[34] he would have none
of the spoils of war except what he consumed in the way of food
and drink; adding, however, that he did not blame the generals
who accepted the privileges allowed them, but that he preferred to
vie with the noblest in virtue rather than with the richest in
wealth. Almost as much praise goes to commanders who helped
themselves to but a little of the spoils, as Pompey did.[35]. . . Sometimes in making the division account was taken of the absent
as well. . . .

But this system of division was already in ancient times open to
scandal, on the ground that leaders used such means to win favor
with individuals. On such a charge Servilius, Coriolanus, and
Camillus were accused of making gifts to their friends and clients
out of the public funds. They defended themselves by answering

that it was for the public good "that men who had taken part in an enterprise should reap the fruit of their labors, and so be more eager for new campaigns." These are the words of Dionysius of Halicarnassus on the subject.[36]

18. I come now to the matter of looting. Either during the ravaging of a countryside or after a battle or the storming of a town, permission was given to the troops to scatter at a given signal. In early times this was seldom done, but instances of it are not lacking. . . . On the defeat of Perseus, the consul Paulus granted the spoils of the beaten army to his infantry, and the loot from the surrounding territory to his cavalry. The same Paulus, by a decree of the Senate, gave the cities of Epirus to his soldiers to sack. When Tigranes was defeated, Lucullus restrained his men from plundering for a long time, but later, when victory was assured, he allowed them the right of ravaging the enemy. . . .

Those who disapprove of this practice say that the hands that are greedy for booty snatch up the rewards of the brave warriors, since it almost always turns out that a sluggish fighter is a plunderer, while the bravest usually wants the chief share of the toil and danger, as Appius says in Livy.[37] Very similar are the words of Cyrus in Xenophon:[38] "I well know that in pillaging it is the scoundrels who enrich themselves most." On the other hand, it is said that a man will like and enjoy more what he has taken with his own hand from the enemy and brought home than many times as much, if he has received it by an award from someone else.

Sometimes too looting was permitted because it could not be stopped. At the storming of Cortuosa, an Etruscan town, Livy tells us,[39] "The tribunes agreed to turn the plunder over to the state, but their authority was slower than the decision. Already the booty was in the soldiers' possession and could not be taken from them without creating resentment." . . .

19. As for the fact I mentioned that booty or the money obtained from booty was sometimes assigned to persons not soldiers, that was usually in the form of an equivalent return to those who

had made a contribution to the war. You may notice too that public games were sometimes paid for out of funds taken in war.

20. NOT only in different wars is one practice sometimes followed and sometimes another, but in the same war the spoils are often treated in different ways, either divided up into portions or separated into different classes of objects. So Camillus gave a tenth of his plunder to the Pythian Apollo, following a custom of the Greeks, which had come originally from the Jews. . . . But when he was again victorious, the greatest share of his plunder he delivered to the quaestor and gave much less to the soldiers. . . . The classes into which booty may be divided are these: human captives, herds and flocks, . . . money and other movable things, valuable or cheap. . . . On the capture of Antium, Lucius Cornelius turned the gold, silver, and money over to the treasury, sold the prisoners and the plunder through the quaestor, and allowed his troops to appropriate articles of food and clothing. . . . When Veii was taken, Camillus gave nothing to the treasury save the money from the sale of prisoners. After the Etruscan defeat and the sale of prisoners, from the money he had then he paid back to the women the gold they had given, and offered three gold libation bowls in the Capitoline temple. . . . When Scipio took Carthage, he gave the contents of the city as loot to the soldiers, saving out the gold, silver, and votive offerings. . . .

21. FROM what we have said it is plain that among the Romans, as among most other nations, booty was the property of the people of Rome, although some decision as to its distribution was left to the generals, but with the proviso, as we said before, that they owed an account of their conduct to the people. This among other things is shown by the case of Lucius Scipio, who was condemned for embezzlement on a verdict, as Valerius Maximus says,[40] that he had taken four hundred and eighty weight of silver more than he had delivered to the treasury. And there were other cases that we have cited earlier.

Marcus Cato, in the speech he composed on the subject of

booty, complained, Gellius says,[41] in vehement and memorable terms of the impunity and license granted to peculators. The following fragment of his speech survives: "Those who steal from private citizens spend their lives in prison and fetters; those who steal from the public, in gold and purple." . . .

Not only generals but soldiers too were arrested on charges of embezzlement of booty, if they failed to deliver it to the public treasury, for, according to Polybius,[42] they were all bound by an oath "that no one would pilfer anything from the booty but would keep his pledge out of reverence for his oath." With this perhaps may be compared the formula of an oath given by Gellius,[43] according to which a soldier inside the army, or within a distance of approximately ten miles, was bound to remove nothing worth more than a silver sestertius, or if he had removed something, to carry it to the consul, or else confess his act within the next three days. . . . All these instances go to show what we have said, that, originally and apart from any ruling by civil law, objects taken in the operations of a war became the property of the people or of the king waging the war.

22. WE inserted the words 'originally' and 'apart from any ruling by civil law,' because such a law may control in the public interest the disposition even of objects not yet actually acquired, whether it is a law of the people, as among the Romans, or a law of the king, as among the Jews and elsewhere. Under the term 'law' also we intend to include well-established custom. The word 'originally' makes us realize that the people can grant booty, as well as other things, to different persons, not merely after it has been acquired but beforehand, so that as soon as the capture takes place the deed is linked immediately with it, as the jurists say. The grant can be made not only to named individuals but to a class—as in the time of the Maccabees a portion of the booty was assigned to widows, old men, and needy orphans—or even to unidentified persons, like the things tossed to a crowd, which the Roman consuls made the property of those who caught them.

However, this bestowal of a right to spoils, conferred either by law or by grant, is not always a pure gift. Sometimes it is the fulfillment of a contract, sometimes a payment of a debt, or a recompense for the damages a person has suffered, or a return for what he spent on the war in money or in services, as when allies or subjects fight without pay, or without enough to compensate them for their exertions. For these reasons we see that grants of booty, either of all or of a part, are customarily made.

23. OUR jurists observe likewise that almost everywhere the tacit custom prevails that both allies and subjects who take part in a war without pay and at their own expense and their own risk, may have as their own whatever they capture. In the case of allies the reason is plain, because naturally one ally is bound to make good to the other the damages he incurred in a common or public enterprise. Besides, services are rarely rendered gratis . . . what Tacitus called [44] "neglecting the care of one's family to busy oneself with other people's affairs." It is probable then that, except where some other factor appears, such as pure generosity or a previous contract, the ally looks on his hope of enriching himself from the enemy as compensation for his damages and his service.

24. IN the case of subjects, their right to booty is not so clear, for they owe their services to their state. On the other hand, it does happen that not all but only some of them engage in a war, so that the body of the state owes them some return for the fact that they are contributing more service or money than the rest and suffering many more losses. In place of some sure reward, the hope of all or an undefined part of the booty may readily and not unreasonably be granted them. . . .

As for allies, there is an instance [45] in a Roman treaty that admitted the Latins to an equal share of the spoils in the wars which they fought under the leadership of the Roman people. . . .

As for subjects, we have an example in the Jewish people, by whom a half of the booty was allotted to the men who had been in battle. So too Alexander's soldiers made their own the plunder they had taken from private individuals, save that things of extraordinary value they would bring to the king. . . . But the property of the enemy public or of the king was not included in this permission. Hence we read that when the Macedonians broke into the camp of Darius on the Pyramus River, they carried off an enormous weight of gold and silver and left nothing intact but the king's tent, "after the traditional custom," says Curtius,[46] "in order that they might receive the victor in the tent of the conquered king." . . . Likewise in the chronicles of Charlemagne we read that after he had vanquished the Hungarians, he left their private riches to his soldiery and took their king's riches for his treasury. . . .

Yet from what we have already said, it is evident that among the Romans, at least under the old republic, so much was not granted to the soldiers. During the civil wars a beginning was made at allowing them rather more license. . . . After the battle of Pharsalia Caesar gave Pompey's camp to his troops to sack. . . . The soldiers of Octavian and Antony looted the camp of Brutus and Cassius. . . . And as discipline grew lax, such permission was more freely given to the men, in order to keep them from neglecting the enemy and loading their arms with spoils before the danger was over, a thing that has many times ruined a victory. . . . According to Tacitus,[47] Suetonius during a battle in Britain urged his troops to keep on with the slaughter and forget the loot, adding that once the victory was won everything would be theirs. Incidents like this you will find reported in many other histories. . . .

There are, however, articles of so little value that they are not worth taking as public property. These things everywhere the captors usually keep by permission of the people. Such things, under the old Roman republic, were spears, javelins, firewood, fodder, wineskins, leather bags, torches, and any small silver coins. We read in Gellius [48] that these exceptions were inserted in the military oath. Not unlike that is the license now granted to seamen, even when fighting for pay. The French call it right of spoliation or pillage, and include under it clothing, and gold and silver worth less than ten crowns. In other places a part of the plunder is assigned to the troops, as in Spain, where sometimes a fifth, sometimes a third, at other times a half remains with the king, and a seventh, or occasionally a tenth, with the head of the army. The remainder belongs to the men who took it, except for ships of war, which all go to the king.

Sometimes too the division is made after account has been taken of services, risks, and expenses, as among the Italians, where a third of a captured ship goes to the owner of the victorious vessel, the same amount to those who owned the cargo in the ship, and the same to those who did the fighting. Often those who at their own peril and expense carry on a war do not receive all the spoils but must pay a part to the state or to him who derives his authority from the state. Thus among the Spaniards, if during a war ships are fitted out at private expense, a share of their plunder is due to the king and a share to the admiral of the sea. . . . On land, however, it is now the general rule that in the sack of towns and in battle each man may keep as his own what he takes, but that on raiding expeditions what is captured should be the common property of the members of the expedition, to be distributed among them according to rank.

25. THESE things make us see that if, within a nation not involved in war, a dispute arises over an object which was captured in war, it should be awarded to the one whose claim is supported by the laws or customs of the people whose men captured it. But if this is quite unacceptable, then by the universal law of nations the object should be pronounced the property of that people as a whole, provided it was taken in actual warfare. . . .

26. WHATEVER is not enemy property, even though found in the enemy's country, does not belong to the captors. For that, as we said before, would be contrary to the law of nature and has not been sanctioned by the law of nations. . . . But where the enemy has some right over such things which is connected with the possessing of them, such as a right of pledge, of holding, or of servi-

tude, there is nothing to keep the captors from acquiring that right.

The question is also asked whether enemy property taken outside the territory of either belligerent party belongs to the captors; it is debated as regards both things and persons. If we are considering solely the law of nations, I think the place need not be considered here, since, as we have said, according to it an enemy may rightfully be killed anywhere. Yet whoever holds the sovereign power in that district can by a law of his own forbid such an act, and if it is committed in violation of his law, he can demand satisfaction for it as for a crime. Similarly, a wild animal captured on another man's land is said to belong to the captor, but access to it may be forbidden by the owner of the land.

27. THIS external right of acquiring ownership of property taken in war is by the law of nations a special feature of formal war and does not exist in other wars. For in other wars between persons of different nations, ownership of property is not acquired by military force, but only as a payment for debts that otherwise cannot be recovered. And in wars between fellow citizens, whether great or petty, no change in ownership can take place except by authority of a judge.

VII

Rights Over Captives in War.

---

1. BY nature, that is, without some act of man, or in the primitive state of nature, no human beings are slaves, as we have already said in another connection.[1] In that sense we may rightly accept the

jurists' statement that slavery is against nature. Yet slavery as a result of an act of man, such as a contract or a crime, is not inconsistent with natural justice, as we have also shown elsewhere.[2] And by the law of nations which we are now discussing, slavery has been extended still more widely, both as regards persons and as regards its consequences. If we consider persons, not merely those who give themselves up or agree to become slaves are classed as slaves, but everyone, without exception, who is taken prisoner in a formal public war, from the moment he is brought within the captor's line of defense, as Pomponius says.[3] No crime is needed, but the lot of all is the same, even of those who by their own ill luck, as we have said, were caught inadvertently by the sudden outbreak of war on enemy territory. . . .

Dio of Prusa, when rehearsing various methods of acquiring ownership, says:[4] "The third method is when a man has taken a person captive in war, and thus holds him as having become his slave." . . .

2. NOT only do they themselves become slaves, but their posterity in perpetuity, that is, those who are born of a slave mother after her enslavement. This is as Marcian said,[5] that by the law of nations children born of our bondwomen are our slaves. Tacitus, referring to the wife of a German chief, said [6] that the womb was subject to slavery.

3. THE scope of this law is unlimited, so that a master may lawfully do anything to his slave, as the elder Seneca said.[7] There is no suffering that he may not inflict on him with impunity, no deed that he may not command or compel him with torture to do by any means. Even savagery on the part of masters to those they hold as slaves goes unpunished, except in so far as civil law sets a limit to it and prescribes a punishment. "Among all nations equally," says Gaius,[8] "we may observe that masters have had power of life and death over their slaves." But then he adds that limits have been set to this power by Roman law, that is, on Roman soil. . . . Further, all property that was captured with the person becomes the

possession of his master. The slave who is himself in the power of another, says Justinian,[9] can have nothing of his own.

4. THEREBY we may refute, or at least modify, the opinion of those who assert that no immaterial rights are acquired by the law of war. It is true that they are not acquired at first hand and directly, but through the medium of the person to whom they previously belonged. However, we must except the rights that accrue to a person because of some special quality in him and which are therefore inalienable, such as his rights as a father. For if these rights can persist, they persist in the person; if not, they become extinct.

5. NOW all these rights over captives were established by the law of nations, of which we are speaking, for no other purpose than to attract the captors by their many advantages and make them willing to refrain from the supreme cruelty, which is the killing of their captives, either on the spot or after a delay, as we have said before. . . . I said "make them willing to refrain," for if you look at this law of nations it is not as it were a bargain, by which captors may be forced to refrain, but it is a method of persuading them by offering them something more to their advantage.

For the same reason this right, like the ownership of property, may be transferred to others. It is agreed also that this ownership covers children, because otherwise, if the captors had exerted their utmost rights, the children would not have been born. Accordingly, children born before the calamity do not become slaves, unless they are taken captive themselves. The nations agreed too that children should follow the status of the mother, because the unions of slaves were not controlled by law or by any reliable overseer, with the result that no sufficient presumption existed to indicate the father. In this light we are to understand Ulpian's statement: [10] "It is a law of nature that a child born outside lawful wedlock follows its mother." That is, it is a law of universal custom, based on natural reason. . . .

From examples taken from civil wars we may perceive that the nations achieved something when they established these rights. In civil wars, we see, prisoners have often been put to death, because they could not be made slaves. . . . Whether they become the property of a people or of individuals should be decided by the rules we have given with regard to spoils. For in this matter the law of nations treats men in the same way as it does goods. . . .

6. THERE are theologians who think that captives taken in an illegal war or the children of captives do wrong in trying to escape, unless to their own people; but I believe them mistaken on this point. There is indeed this distinction. If, while the war is still going on, they escape to their own people, they obtain their freedom by right of postliminy; [11] but if they escape to other people or to their own after peace has been made, they must be returned to their master, if he claims them. However, it does not follow from this that their minds are to be shackled by conscientious scruples. There are many rules that consider only external judgments, and such are these laws of war which we are now expounding. Nor is there any ground for arguing that the nature of the ownership is such as to create a sense of obligation in the captives' minds. For I shall reply that there are many kinds of ownership, and one may be set up that is valid by a human and coercive judgment only. . . .

As to our question, no reason can be imagined why the nations should have had in mind anything but external compulsion. The power of claiming a slave and using force on him, and further of confining him in bonds and seizing his possessions, has been enough to make captors willing to spare his life. Or if they were so brutal as not to be influenced by these advantages, they would certainly not have cared for any scruple imposed on the slave's mind. If they had thought such a thing at all necessary, they could have demanded from him a pledge or an oath.

In this case of a law which was founded not on natural justice, but on the need of preventing a worse evil, we should not thoughtlessly accept an interpretation that would make sinful an act in other cases legitimate. The jurist Florentinus says: [12] "It makes no difference how a captive has returned; whether he was released, or escaped by force or a trick from the enemy's power." This is true because the right of holding men captive is a right that in another sense is often a wrong, a word that is applied to it by the jurist Paulus.[13] It is a right so far as certain results go, a wrong, if one considers the intrinsic character of it.

Whence follows, clearly, this conclusion. When a man is taken prisoner in an illegal war and falls into the power of the enemy, his conscience is not to be stained with the sin of theft if he conveys away stealthily property belonging to him, or pay given him for his labor, in case it is right he should receive pay over and above the cost of his support, provided that neither in his own name nor in that of his people does he owe anything to his master or to a person whose claim his master has taken over.

As for the fact that there are canons that forbid persuading a slave to desert the service of his master, if you apply them to slaves who are undergoing a just penalty or who put themselves in bondage by voluntary agreement, they are ordinances of justice. But if you have in mind slaves captured in illegal warfare, or the children of the slaves, it shows merely that Christian authorities believe that Christians ought to have patience rather than do something which, though legitimate, might be a cause of offense to persons not Christians or weak in some way. . . .

7. BUT I believe these same theologians, whom I have just mentioned, are right in saying that a slave cannot resist his master in the exercise of his external right over him without failing in his lawful duty. Between this case and those we have just discussed there is an obvious difference. For the master's external right consists not only of a right to act with impunity but also of the protection given him by the courts. It will be but an empty name if the slave, on the other hand, retains a right to resist. For if it is lawful for him to resist his master, it will be lawful for him to resist the magistrate who protects his master, even though by the law of nations the magistrate must defend a master in that kind of own-

ership and in the exercise of it. The master's right accordingly resembles the right which we have elsewhere ascribed to the supreme authorities in a state, in that it is unlawful and wrong forcibly to resist it. . . .

8. HOWEVER, it must also be recognized that this law of nations on the position of captives has not always been accepted, and not among all nations, although the Roman jurists speak of it as a universal law, giving to a well known portion the name of the whole. Thus among the Jews, who were separated by their peculiar institutions from the common life of other peoples, there was a place of refuge for slaves, at any rate, as the commentators correctly point out, for slaves who had fallen into their wretched plight through no fault of their own. On some such ground may have been based the right of asserting their liberty, granted to slaves on the soil of France, although we see it now granted not only to prisoners of war but to other slaves as well, of every sort.

9. MOREOVER, Christians as a whole have agreed that in warfare between themselves captives are not to be made slaves so far as to be liable to sale, to compulsory labor, or to other ills that are the lot of slaves. A worthy agreement surely, since Christians have been, or should have been, taught better by him who approved all charity than to need to be kept from killing unhappy human creatures by permission to commit a lesser cruelty. And Gregoras writes [14] that this same rule was handed down in the past from ancestors to descendants among those who professed the Christian faith, nor was it peculiar to those who lived under the Roman empire but was common also to Thessalians, Illyrians, Triballians, and Bulgars. So this much, at least, little as it is, has been accomplished by reverence for the law of Christ, whereas when Socrates told the Greeks long ago that they should obey such a rule, he produced no effect.

In this matter the Mohammedans follow among themselves the practice of the Christians. However, even among Christians, the custom has lasted of holding prisoners under guard until a ransom is paid for them, the amount of which is decided by the victor, unless there has been an agreement on some fixed sum. And this right of holding prisoners is ordinarily granted to the individuals who captured them, except when the prisoners are persons of lofty rank. In those cases the custom of most nations gives that right to the state or to its head.

VIII

Rulership over Conquered Peoples.

1. IT is not surprising that a man who can subjugate individuals to himself in a personal servitude can also subjugate whole peoples—whether they were once a state or a part of a state—in a subjection that may be purely civil, or purely proprietary, or a mixture of both. . . . Tertullian said [1] that empires were fought for in war and enlarged by victories, Quintilian [2] that the fate of kingdoms and peoples, the boundaries of nations and of cities, were fixed by the law of war. . . . Justin, citing Trogus, tells us [3] that those who waged war before the time of Ninus aimed not at empire but at glory for themselves, and being satisfied with victory, did not take over the realm. Ninus, he says, was the first to extend the boundaries of his empire and subjugate other peoples by war, and from him the practice passed into a custom. . . .

The victor may acquire either just so much authority as belonged to the king or other ruler, and then he succeeds to just that man's right and no more. Or he may acquire an authority like that of the people, in which case he possesses so much that he can even alienate it, as the people could. And so it has come about, as we said elsewhere,[4] that some kingdoms have become patrimonies.

2. SOMETHING still more important may happen, which is that what has been a state may cease to be a state. It may either become an addition to another state, as the Roman provinces did, or it may not be attached to any state, as when a king, after conducting a war at his own expense, subjects the conquered people to himself so completely that he has them ruled not chiefly for their good but for that of the ruler. This is proprietary rulership, not civil. . . . A people that falls under such a rule will for the future be not a state but a great household. . . .

Tacitus contrasts these two forms of rule as follows:[5] "He was thinking not of owner and slaves but of governor and citizens." Xenophon says of Agesilaus:[6] "All the cities he brought under his sway he exempted from the services that slaves perform for their masters and required from them only the obedience that free men pay to their governors."

3. HENCE we may understand the kind of rulership that I have called a mixture of civil and proprietary, that is, where some servitude is mingled with some personal liberty. In such cases we read that the people have been deprived of arms, or forbidden to own anything iron, except implements for agriculture, while others have been compelled to change their language and mode of life.

4. AND just as the objects which were the property of individuals are by the law of war acquired by the persons who subjugate their owners, so too the property of an aggregation belongs to those who subjugate it, if they wish for it. As Livy said,[7] speaking of persons who surrendered themselves: "Where everything has been surrendered to the one who is the superior in war, it is the victor's special right to decide what he wishes his subjects to keep and what he will take from them." The same rule holds for the vanquished in formal warfare; for surrender means to let go voluntarily what otherwise would be seized by force. . . . Hannibal in a speech to his soldiers in Livy, says:[8] "All that the Romans possess, won and

amassed by them in so many triumphs, all that will be ours, along with the owners as well." . . .

So too the immaterial rights that belonged to a people as a whole become the property of the conqueror as far as he wants them. . . . Hence the Thessalians were freed completely from their debt of a hundred talents, a sum they owed the Thebans, when Alexander the Great, having made himself master of Thebes, by right of his victory presented the Thessalians with their debt. Nor is the argument for the Thebans in Quintilian [9] correct, that to the victor belongs only what he actually holds; an immaterial right cannot be grasped in the hand; the situation of an heir and of a conqueror are quite different, because a right may pass to an heir, but only objects to a conqueror. But he who is master of persons is master also of all the property and rights which the persons possess. One who is himself a possession possesses nothing for himself, and he who is not in his own power has nothing in his power.

Accordingly, even if a conqueror leaves to a defeated people the right to remain a state, he may still appropriate for himself certain things which before belonged to the state. It is for him to choose what he wishes the measure of his benevolence to be. . . .

IX

Postliminy.

1. ON the right of postliminy professors of jurisprudence in modern times have produced no sound opinion, any more than they have on the subject of things captured from an enemy. The ancient

Romans discussed the problem more carefully, but often too confusedly, so that the reader could not tell what rules they made a part of the law of nations and what of the Roman civil law. As for the word 'postliminy' . . . we should follow Scaevola, who taught that it was a compound of *post*, a returning, and *limen*, threshold. . . .

2. POSTLIMINY then is a right derived from a return to the threshold, that is, to the boundaries of the state. Pomponius says [1] that a man has returned by postliminy once he is within our lines of defense; and Paulus, when he has crossed our frontiers.[2] By similar reasoning the nations have gone on to agree that postliminy is possible also whenever the man, or an object of the kind for which postliminy is granted, has reached "our friends," as Pomponius says in the passage cited, or, as Paulus puts it in his illustration, has reached "an allied or a friendly king." But in these passages 'friends' or 'allies' are to be taken as meaning not simply persons with whom we are at peace but persons who are on our side in the war. Whoever reaches them, as Paulus says, is safe at once in the name of his state. It makes no difference whether the man or the object reaches them or his own people.

On arrival among people who are friends but not on the same side in the war, escaped captives do not change their status, unless by some special agreement. So, in the second treaty arranged between Romans and Carthaginians, it was settled that if any prisoners taken by the Carthaginians from people who were friends of the Romans arrived in harbors subject to Rome, they might be claimed as free; and the same right would hold for friends of the Carthaginians. . . .

3. AN old Roman statement declared that free men too were taken back by postliminy. Aelius Gallus, in the first book of his *Expressions That Have To Do With Law*, says that "by postliminy is taken back"—for this is the reading we must follow—"one who, as a free man, has gone from one state to another and returned to the first state, in accordance with the law established on post-

liminy." Likewise, a slave who has gone from us into the enemy's power and later come back to us, by the law of postliminy, returns to the hands of the master who owned him before. The same rule as for a slave holds for a horse, a mule, or a ship, in a recovery by postliminy, whether we ourselves return, or we receive something back.

4. WE should remember also the view of Tryphonius,[3] who says that the right of postliminy is valid both in war and in peace. . . . But in peace this right, unless a different agreement has been made, belongs not to persons who were conquered by feats of arms but to those who were caught by their own bad luck, like those found in an enemy country, when war unexpectedly breaks out. For other captives there is no postliminy in peacetime, unless such a provision was included in the treaties. . . . Paulus says:[4] "If a prisoner of war escapes after the conclusion of a peace, by postliminy he must return to the one who captured him in the recent war, provided no agreement was made in the peace for the return of prisoners."

Tryphonius, following Servius, asserts that the reason why that rule was made for prisoners taken in war was this:[5] "The Romans wanted their citizens to pin their hopes of returning home on their prowess in war rather than on a peace." Certainly, as Livy says,[6] their state from of old was not easy on prisoners. However, this reason, peculiar to the Romans, could not have been the basis for a law of nations, though it might have been among the reasons why the Romans themselves accepted the law when introduced by other nations.

The truer reason is that kings and peoples who went to war wished others to believe that they had lawful reasons for doing so, and that contrariwise those who took up arms against them were doing wrong. But since both sides wished this to be believed and it was not safe for the people who desired to keep at peace to intervene in the dispute, those who were at peace could do nothing better than accept the outcome as right, and so regard the prisoners taken in actual combat as prisoners for lawful cause.

Yet the same could not be said of those who were caught by the outbreak of war, for in their case no intention to commit injury could be imagined. However, it seemed not unlawful to hold them as long as the war lasted, in order to reduce the enemy's forces; but when the war was over, no pretext could be offered for refusing to release them. Therefore, it was agreed that such persons, when peace came, should always obtain their liberty, as being innocent by admission of both sides. But to the other prisoners each ruler might apply what he chose to consider his right, except in so far as agreements made some definite provision for them.

For the same reason slaves and articles taken in war are not returned in peacetime, unless it is stated in the agreement that they should be, because the victor wishes all to believe that he had a right to appropriate them, and to oppose him would be really to produce war out of war. . . . In wartime, men who were free before they were taken prisoner may return by postliminy; slaves and other things may be recovered.

5. A free man returns by postliminy when he comes back to his own people with the intention of following their fortunes, as Tryphonius puts it,[7] because a slave to become free must, first, so to speak, acquire himself, which happens only by an act of his own will. But whether the man is recaptured from the enemy by armed strength or makes a crafty escape is no matter. . . . It will be the same if the enemy voluntarily gives him up. . . .

6. A free man, then, after his return to his people, acquires not only himself for himself but also all the property, material and immaterial, that he had before, among the peoples at peace. For the peoples at peace accepted the fact of his capture as lawful and do the same for his liberation, thus showing themselves fair to both sides. Therefore the rights of ownership, which his captor by the law of war possessed over his property, were not entirely free of condition, for they could be lost against that captor's will, if he

who had been the prisoner arrived at his own country. The captor then loses the property by the same means as he loses the man to whom it was an accessory.

But what if the captor has previously alienated that property? Will he who received the title to it from the person who was by the law of war at that time its owner be protected by the law of nations, or will these articles too be recoverable? I am speaking of articles in the country of a people neutral in the war. We must here, I think, distinguish between articles of a class that may return by post-liminy and those outside that class, a distinction that we shall explain shortly. Articles of the former class should be recognized as alienated only with some limitation and conditionally, and those of the latter class absolutely. By articles alienated I mean also articles given away and acknowledged as gifts.

7. BUT just as his rights come back to a man returning by post-liminy, so too are rights against him restored, and maintained, as Tryphonius says,[8] as if he had never fallen into the enemy's hands.

8. TO this rule for free men Paulus correctly makes the following exception: [9] "Men defeated in battle who then surrendered themselves to the enemy have no right of postliminy." This is evidently because pacts made with an enemy are valid by the law of nations, as we shall say later, and no right of postliminy breaks them. Thus in Gellius,[10] the Romans who had been taken prisoners by the Carthaginians said "they had no lawful right of postliminy, because they were bound by an oath." So in a time of truce there is no right of postliminy. . . .

9. WHAT we have said of individuals applies in my opinion to peoples as well. Those who were previously free recover their liberty, if it comes about that the forces of their allies deliver them from the hold of the enemy. But if the mass of the population which made up the state has been scattered, I consider it more correct to pronounce them no longer the same people, and not qualified to have their possessions restored by postliminy in accordance with the law of nations, since a people, like a ship, is ob-

viously destroyed by the dispersion of its parts, for its whole nature consists of a permanent union. It was not, then, the same city of Saguntum that it had been, when in the eighth year after its destruction its site was returned to the old inhabitants. And it was not the same Thebes, when the Thebans had been reduced to slavery by Alexander. . . .

10. FROM the foregoing we may understand what by the law of nations is the right of postliminy for free persons. By civil law, however, the same right, since it touches things taking place within a state, may be restricted by the addition of exceptions or conditions, and may be extended to furnish other advantages. Thus by the civil law of Rome deserters were excepted from the number of persons who may return by postliminy. . . .

The right of postliminy is to some extent also limited by the provision first of Attic law and then of Roman, that a man ransomed from the enemy should serve his ransomer until he had paid back the cost. However, this provision was inserted apparently to encourage liberation, to prevent many soldiers being left in the enemy's hands because there was no hope that the ransomer would recover the money spent for them. And servitude to the ransomer was lightened in many ways by the same Roman laws; by the latest law of Justinian it was ended after five years' service. By the death too of the person ransomed the right of recovering the money was extinguished, even as it was considered all repaid by a marriage contract between the ransomer and the ransomed, and all lost by the prostitution of a ransomed woman. There were many other provisions in Roman law in favor of persons paying ransom and penalizing near relatives who did not ransom their kin.

Again, the right of postliminy was extended by civil law to cover not only the property that is included in postliminy by the law of nations, but all property, and all rights were thenceforth regarded as valid as if the man who had returned had never been in the enemy's power. This was also the rule by Attic law, for in the *Fifteenth Oration* of Dio of Prusa we read that a certain man, calling himself the son of Callias, who had been taken prisoner in the disaster at Acanthus and had been a slave in Thrace, on his return by postliminy to Athens claimed the inheritance of Callias from its possessors, and the only question raised in the court was whether he was really Callias' son. . . . Even what has been lost to a property through the right of long use or through liberation, or has been forfeited by non-use, may be restored by an action of annulment. . . .

The Cornelian Law provided even for the heirs of persons who died in captivity among the enemy, protecting their property just as if the man who was not returning had died at the time he was taken prisoner. If you abolished these civil laws, unquestionably the property of anyone taken by an enemy would belong immediately to whoever seized it, on the ground that a man in enemy hands is regarded as non-existent. And if, after being a prisoner, he came back home, he would recover only the objects which by the law of nations have the right of postliminy. By a special law of Rome, the property of persons taken prisoner goes to the treasury, if there is no heir.

We have looked into the case of persons who return; let us look now into the things that are recovered.

11. AMONG these in the first place are their slaves and bond-women, even though they may have been several times alienated or actually set free by the enemy, for emancipation by the enemy's law cannot interfere with the right of our fellow citizen, the owner of the slave, as Tryphonius well observes.[11] But in order to recover the slave, it is necessary that he be either in the possession of his former master or within easy reach. So although in the case of other articles it is enough to have them brought inside the borders, that is not enough to give the right of postliminy over a slave unless his whereabouts too are known. For a slave in the city of Rome but in hiding is not yet recovered, in the opinion of Paulus.

In this respect a slave differs from an inanimate object. So in turn he differs from a free man in that to be recovered by postliminy it

is not required that he return with the intention of following our
fortunes. That is a requirement for one who is to recover himself
but not for one who has to be recovered by another. . . .

The Roman law did not except fugitive slaves from this law of
nations. Over them too the master recovers his former right, as
Paulus teaches us,[12] since a contrary right would not be so injurious to the one who always remains a slave but would be damaging to the master. In general, with regard to slaves retaken by our
soldiers' valor, the emperors made a statement [13] which some persons apply erroneously to all recovered property: "We should regard them as recovered, not as captured, and our soldiery should
be their defenders, not their owners."

By Roman law slaves ransomed from the enemy became at once
the property of the ransomer; when their former owner repaid
their price to the ransomer, he was said to have recovered them.
But to explain all this in more detail is the duty of the interpreters
of civil law, for some points have been changed by later laws. To
induce captured slaves to return, liberty was offered at once to
those who had had a limb broken, and to others after five years, as
we may read in Rufus' collection of military laws.[14]

12. OF more interest to us is the question whether peoples who
have been subjected to foreign rule on release lapse back into their
former situation. The question may be debatable, if it is not their
previous ruler but one of his allies who has delivered them from the
enemy. The same rule, I think, should hold in their case as in the
case of slaves, unless by the treaty of alliance some other terms
were agreed upon.

13. AMONG other objects recoverable by postliminy, land comes
first. "It is true," says Pomponius,[15] "that once the enemy has been
expelled from the land he has captured, the ownership of it returns
to its former proprietors." The enemy should be counted as expelled from the time when he can no longer enter it openly, as we
have explained elsewhere. Thus the Spartans returned the island
of Aegina to the Athenians, its previous owners, from whom it had

been taken. Justinian and other emperors restored to the heirs of
the old proprietors the lands they recovered from the Goths and
the Vandals. . . .

The rule for the recovery of every right that is connected with
the soil is, I think, the same as the rule for the recovery of land.
Religious or consecrated places which have been seized by the
enemy, when they are liberated from that disaster, are restored as
if by a kind of postliminy to their earlier status. . . . So too the
usufruct of land that has been recovered we should consider re-
turnable to its previous owner, after the precedent set by the
response of Pomponius [16] to a question on inundated land. . . .

14. AS to movable objects, the rule in general is the opposite.
They do not return by postliminy but are included in the booty.
. . . Hence articles which have been purchased in a business transaction, wherever they are found, remain the property of him who
bought them. Even if found among people at peace, or if brought
inside the frontier, the former owner has no right to claim them.

In ancient times, however, we see that articles used in warfare
were excepted from this rule, because, as the nations seem to have
agreed, the expectation of recovering such articles would make men
more keen to obtain them. The institutions of many states at that
time were planned with a view to warmaking, so that it was easy
to reach an agreement on the point. . . . Such articles were ships
of war and freight boats; but not pleasure or swift-sailing boats,
designed for amusement; mules, but only pack mules; horses and
mares, tame under the bit. . . . Weapons and clothing are indeed
useful in war but they did not return by postliminy, because those
who lost weapons or clothing in war were granted no favors. In
fact, to lose such things was considered a disgrace, as appears in
many passages in the histories. In this connection we observe that
weapons were differentiated from a horse, because a horse can
break away through no fault of the rider. And this distinction between movable objects persisted, we see, in the West even under
the Goths, down to the time of Boethius. . . .

15. IN more recent times, however, if not earlier, the distinction seems to have been abolished. For those who are acquainted with prevailing customs inform us generally that no movable goods return by postliminy. That this rule has been established for ships we note in many places.

16. ARTICLES which, although seized by the enemy, have not yet been brought within the enemy's lines do not stand in need of postliminy, because by the law of nations they have not yet changed owners. And articles which pirates and brigands take from us do not need postliminy, . . . because the law of nations has not granted such persons the power to alter a right of ownership. . . . Accordingly, articles taken from them may be claimed wherever they are found, except that, as we have pointed out elsewhere,[17] a man who has bought possession of a thing with his own money is entitled to get back as much as the true owner of the article would have been willing to pay to recover it.

17. A different rule, however, may be established by civil law. Thus by Spanish law ships recaptured from pirates become the property of those who took them from the pirates; nor is it unfair that private claims should give way to the public interest, especially when the difficulty of recovery is so great. But such a law does not prevent foreigners from claiming things that belong to them.

18. A stranger thing is proved by the testimony of Roman laws, namely, that the right of postliminy existed not merely between enemies but between Romans and foreign peoples not at war. But, as we said in another connection,[18] these laws were the relics of an age of nomads, whose habits had blunted the sense of the natural association that exists among men. Hence among the nations, even when they were not fighting a public war, there existed a kind of license for war between private individuals, sanctioned as it were by their own habits. So to prevent this license from going as far as the killing of men, it was agreed that the right of taking prisoners should be introduced among them, as a consequence of which postliminy appeared too. But this is different from extending it to

brigands and pirates, for the violence of the times led these early men to make honest agreements, which brigands and pirates habitually scorn to do. . . .

A distinction, I think, should be drawn between treaties. Those that are made simply for the purpose of settling or preventing a public war should not in the future stand in the way of the rights of holding captives and of postliminy. Whereas those that provide that persons crossing from one side to the other shall be protected in the name of the state may mark an end to the holding of captives and the right of postliminy. Pomponius seems to me to be implying this when he says: [19] "If with any nation we have no relations of friendship or hospitality, and no treaty made to establish friendship, those people are certainly not our enemies, but anything of ours going to them becomes theirs, and one of our free men captured by them becomes their slave. The same thing happens if something of theirs comes to us; so, in a case like this, postliminy is allowed." When he says "treaty to establish friendship," he shows that there may be other treaties which include no right of hospitality or friendship. . . .

19. HOWEVER, in our time not only among Christians but also among most Mohammedans the right outside of war of holding prisoners as well as of postliminy has disappeared, since the necessity for both these practices has been removed by the restoration of the influence of that common kinship which nature meant should exist between men. But the old law of nations can be revived, if ever we have to do with a people so barbarous that without a declaration of war or cause for war, it considers it lawful to treat all foreigners with their possessions as enemies.

And while I write these words, a verdict to this effect has been rendered in the highest court of justice at Paris, under Nicholas of Verdun as president of the session. It is that the property of French citizens which has been captured by the Algerians, a people used to preying on all others by plundering sea raids, has by the law of war changed owners, and so when retaken by anyone else

becomes the property of those who recovered it. In the same trial
it was also decided that, as we just said, ships today are not among
the things that may be recovered by postliminy.

X

Warning as to Acts Committed in an
Unlawful War.

---

1. I must now retrace my steps and deprive the warmakers of almost all the privileges I may seem to have conferred, but did not
confer, on them. For when first I started to explain this part of the
law of nations, I declared that many things are said to be lawful or
permissible because they may be done with impunity; in part too
because coercive courts sanction them with their authority. They
are things, however, that either are far from the rule of right—
whether that rule is based on law strictly so called, or on the dictates of other virtues—or at least, with more piety and more applause from good men, they would be left undone.

In the *Trojan Women* of Seneca,[1] when Pyrrhus says:

"No law the captive spares or punishment prevents,"

Agamemnon replies:

"What law does not forbid, this let shame forbid."

In this passage 'shame' means regard not so much for men and
reputation as for justice and goodness, or at any rate for what is

more just and more good and honorable. . . . And in this sense you may often see justice linked with a sense of honor. . . . Plato says: [2] "The god, in fear that the human race might perish utterly, bestowed on men a sense of justice and honor, as ornaments for cities and bonds to unite men in friendship." And Plutarch in similar vein calls justice [3] "fellow-dweller with honor." . . .

The lines we quoted from Seneca fit well with what he says in his philosophical writings: [4] "How narrow is the righteousness that is good merely by law! How much broader the rule of duty than the rule of law! How numerous are the demands of religion, humanity, generosity, justice, good faith, all of which lie outside the tables of the law!" Here you see law distinguished from justice, because law accepts what is enforced by external judgment. The same author makes the point excellently again in an example drawn from the law on the master's power over his slaves.[5] "In the case of a slave you should think not of how much he may be made to suffer with impunity, but of how far the nature of justice and goodness, which bids you show mercy to captives and men bought for a price, allows you to go." And then: "Although all things are permissible against a slave, there is something that the universal law of living beings says is not permissible against any man." In this passage we note again the different interpretations of the word 'permissible'; one in an exterior sense, the other in an inward sense.

2. . . . Aristotle implies the same distinction in discussing the question [6] whether the slavery which results from war should be called just. "Some persons, considering only one aspect of justice (for a law is something just), say that slavery growing out of war is just. But they do not call it absolutely just, since it may happen that the cause of the war was unjust." . . . So the very Roman jurists who often speak of the right of holding captives, at other times call it a wrong, and contrast it with natural justice. . . . Lactantius says of the philosophers: [7] "When they discuss the

duties connected with a military career, their whole talk is taken up not with justice or true virtue but with the kind of life and the habits of states." A little later he says that the Romans legally committed wrongs.

3. IN the first place, then, we say that if the cause of a war is unlawful, even if the war is started with due formalities, all the acts which result from it are unlawful by an intrinsic unlawfulness. Consequently those who knowingly perform such acts or take part in them must be counted in the number of those who cannot attain to the heavenly kingdom without repentance. And true repentance, if time and means allow it, demands absolutely that the man who has done harm, either killing someone, or ruining his property or carrying it off as booty, should compensate for it.

Hence God says [8] that unpleasing to him are the fasts of those who hold captive men unlawfully taken. And the king of Nineveh, proclaiming a public mourning, ordered [9] that hands should be cleansed of rapine, recognizing, under the leading of nature, that without restitution their repentance would be false and empty. And we see that not only Jews and Christians feel alike on this matter but Mohammedans also.

4. IN accordance with the principles we have explained in general elsewhere, the authors of such a war, whether they were that through their use of power or by offering counsel, are bound too to make restitution, that is, for all the usual consequences of a war; and for unusual injuries as well, if they gave orders for any such acts, or advised them, or did not put a stop to them when they might have done so. Commanders too are accountable for deeds committed under their command; and so are all the soldiers severally who united to carry out some common undertaking, such as the burning of a city. In the case of separate acts, each man is responsible for the damage of which he was the sole cause or indubitably one of the causes.

5. NOR should I allow the exception which some persons make in the case of men working for others, provided that some of the

guilt belongs to them themselves. Guilt, even without malicious intent, is sufficient to call for restitution. There are persons who appear to think that property taken in war, even in war with no lawful cause, need not be returned, because when the belligerents began the war they had a mutual understanding that they gave their possessions to those who took them. But no one may be presumed to have disposed of his property so lightly, and the nature of war is very different from that of contracts.

But so that the peoples at peace might have some settled rule to follow and not become involved in war against their will, it was of service to introduce the right of external ownership, of which we have spoken, and which can exist along with an internal obligation to restore what was taken. . . . Thus in Livy [10] the Samnites say: "We have given back the property of the enemy which we took as plunder and which seemed to be ours by the law of war." "Seemed," the man said, because the war had been unlawful, as the Samnites had already previously admitted. . . .

6. HE too who has done no damage himself or has done it without any fault of his own, but who has in his possession an article captured by someone else in an unlawful war is bound to return it, because there is no naturally lawful reason why its former owner should be deprived of it. He did not give his consent, or deserve the bad treatment, or owe it in payment for something.

Valerius Maximus has a story [11] that bears on this subject. "After Publius Claudius had sold at auction the people of Camerina who had been taken prisoners under his leadership and command, the people of Rome, even though they knew that their treasury had profited by the money and their country was enlarged by the new lands, still went to the greatest pains to search out and ransom those captives and restore to them their estates, because they thought their general had not acted in frank, good faith." . . . The Senate passed a similar decree [12] regarding the people of Abdera, adding as their reason that war had been made on them unlawfully.

However, if the person who has an article has spent money or labor on it, he may, in accordance with the rules we have given elsewhere,[13] deduct as much as it was worth to the owner to get back a possession which he had despaired of recovering. Or if the man who has it, has, without fault on his part, consumed or alienated it, he will not be called to account for it, except to the extent that he has been made richer by it.

XI

Moderation in Exercising the Right of Killing in Lawful War.

1. NOT even in lawful war should we accept the maxim: [1]

"He gives up all who does what is not right."

Cicero says with more truth: [2] "There are some duties you must fulfill even toward those from whom you have received an injury. For there is a limit to revenge and punishment." . . . Aristides, in his second speech on Leuctra declares: [3] "Men may, indeed they may, be wrong in avenging themselves, if they pass beyond a fair limit. For he who in punishing goes to the point of committing injustice starts a second wrong." . . . In a speech of Isocrates [4] the people of Plataea ask: "Is it just to inflict such heavy and unfair penalties for such trifling offenses?" . . .

2. WHEN in a lawful war it is lawful to put men to death in accordance with internal justice—for we must start at this point—

and when it is not, we may infer from our discussion in the first part of this book.

A man may be killed intentionally or unintentionally. No one can lawfully be killed intentionally save as a lawful punishment, or when necessary to protect our lives and property. Actually, to put a man to death for paltry reasons, even if, strictly speaking, it is not against the law, is a transgression of the law of love. To make the punishment lawful it is required that the man who is put to death should himself have committed an offense, and one so serious that by any fair judge he would be sentenced to the death penalty. But we shall not now enlarge further on this matter because we think we have explained fully enough what needs to be understood about it in the chapter "Punishments."

3. EARLIER, when we were discussing suppliants [5]—for there are suppliants both in war and in peace—we distinguished between cases of misfortune and of wrongdoing. . . . An example of unfortunate persons are those who are on the enemy's side but without hostile intent, as the Athenians were in the time of Mithridates. Velleius Paterculus says of them: [6] "Whoever blames the Athenians for this period of rebellion, during which Athens was stormed by Sulla, is extremely ignorant of the facts and of antiquity. Up to that time the loyalty of the Athenians to the Romans had been so unwavering that always and on every occasion the Romans used to call any act of good faith 'Attic faith.' But at that particular time, crushed by the troops of Mithridates, the Athenian people were in a most wretched situation. They were in the hands of their enemies and besieged by their friends. Their hearts were outside their walls, but their bodies, compelled by necessity, remained inside." . . .

An old commentator on the passage of Thucydides describing the sale of the captives from Corcyra, says: [7] "It showed a clemency worthy of the Greek character. It is cruel after a battle to put the prisoners to death, especially the slaves, who are not in the fight by their own choice." . . . Alexander, as Arrian tells us,[8] spared the Zelites, "because they had been forced to take the side of the barbarians." . . .

4. BUT we must note that between outright wrongdoing and pure misfortune there is often a midway state, made up as it were of both, an act which can be called not altogether that of a man who understands and deliberately intends it, not altogether that of one who does not understand or does not intend it.

To this kind of act Aristotle gave the name 'error.' In Latin it may be called 'culpa.' Thus in the fifth book of his *Ethics* and the tenth chapter, he says: "Some of the things which we do of our own accord we do deliberately, others without deliberation. The things which we do after some amount of previous reflection are called deliberate acts; things done without that, not deliberate. Now in human society harm may be inflicted in three ways. That which is committed in ignorance is called an accident—as when a man does something to a person who is not the one he intended to hurt, or does not do what he planned, or not in the way he planned, or not with the expected result. . . . Then if some harm is done different from what he could have anticipated, it is an accident. But if the harm might to some extent have been expected and foreseen, and yet he had no malicious intent, it is an error. A man is liable to err who has the spring of action in himself; whereas he whose spring comes from outside is simply unfortunate.

"Whenever a person acts, quite aware of what he is doing, yet without reflecting beforehand, we must admit he does wrong. Men are apt to act that way in anger and similar states of excitement, either natural or compelled, and those who under such emotions do harm, even though they acknowledge their fault, are not guiltless. Yet we do not call them lawless or wicked, though if anyone commits the same deed deliberately, he is rightly called wicked and lawless. Acts committed in anger are correctly judged not as acts of malice aforethought. For the mischief is started not by the man who acts in a passion but by the one who provokes him to anger. . . . A just man is one who deliberately acts justly, whereas anyone may act justly merely on impulse, without deliberation. . . ."

I have given this very fine and much quoted passage in Latin complete, because it is often mistranslated, and hence not properly understood. Michael of Ephesus, commenting on it,[9] gives as an instance of what could not have been foreseen the case of a man who has struck his father when opening a door, or has wounded somebody when practicing javelin throwing in a solitary spot. As an instance of what might have been foreseen but yet was not the result of malice, he cites a man who threw his javelin on a public road. The same author gives as an instance of a man forced by necessity, one compelled by hunger or thirst to do something wrong; and as instances of natural disturbances, cases of love, grief, and terror. A deed is done through ignorance, he says, when the doer is ignorant of a fact, as when a man does not know a woman is married. It is done by an ignorant man but not through ignorance, when the doer does not know the law. And ignorance of the law is sometimes excusable, sometimes inexcusable. All this agrees perfectly with the statements of the jurists.

There is a passage not unlike this, by the same Aristotle, in his book on the art of oratory.[10] "Justice commands us not to treat in the same way crimes and errors, or error and accidents. Accidents are things which could not be foreseen and take place with no evil intent. Errors are things which could be foreseen, but yet are not the result of intentional malice. Crimes are things done advisedly and with malicious intent." . . . The two kinds of wrong—that which is committed deliberately and that which is committed impulsively—are differentiated by Cicero as follows: [11] "In every case of wrongdoing it is very important to know whether the injury was committed in a state of mental excitement, which is usually brief and transient, or deliberately after reflection. For things which take place in some sudden burst of emotion are less serious than things which are done after premeditation and preparation." . . .

Chief among offenses of this middle class are those for which necessity is an excuse if not a justification. For, as Demosthenes

says in his speech against Aristocrates,[12] "The pressure of necessity
makes impossible any discerning judgment as to what ought or
ought not to be done. Therefore, a fair judge should not judge too
severely acts committed under such circumstances." . . . Thucydides, in his fourth book, says: [13] "It is likely that with God too
there is pardon prepared for those who do wrong under compulsion
of war or some similar necessity. For the altars of the gods stand
open as a refuge for unintentional sinners, and only those are held
guilty of crime who are wilfully wicked, not those who are driven
to desperation by their extremity." . . . So in the judgment of
Isocrates,[14] a man who robs to save his life "has necessity as a cover
for his wrongdoing."

   . . . Themistius, in his praise of the Emperor Valens, applies
these same distinctions to support our argument, as follows: [15]
"You have marked the difference between crime, error, and misfortune. Though you neither study the words of Plato nor ponder over
Aristotle, in your acts you do follow their precepts. For you did
not think everyone deserved the same punishment, those who
originally stirred up the war, those who later were swept along in
the rush to arms, and those who merely submitted to a man who
then seemed conqueror of the country. The first you condemned,
the second you reproved, the last you pitied." . . . Pure misfortunes do not deserve punishment, nor do they obligate anyone to
make good the damage. Wrong acts do both. Error, midway, calls
for reparation but often does not deserve punishment, particularly
capital punishment. . . .

   5. AS for what Themistius suggests, that a distinction should be
drawn between persons who instigated a war and those who follow
the lead of other men, there are many instances of it in the histories. In a passage of Livy,[16] . . . " 'Since those responsible for
the rebellion have received their deserved punishment from the
immortal gods and from you, conscript fathers, what do you wish
done with the innocent multitude?' They eventually were par-
doned and granted citizenship." . . . And the Athenians, as

Thucydides tells us,[17] repented of their decree against the people of Mitylene, "to put the whole city to death instead of merely the leaders of the revolt." . . .

6. AND in considering even the instigators of a war we should distinguish between their reasons for action. For there are reasons, not indeed right, but still of a sort to mislead honest men. The author of *To Herennius* [18] gives as an entirely just subject for a pardon a man who has committed a wrong for motives not of hatred or cruelty but of duty and righteous zeal. The wise man of Seneca [19] "will let his enemies go in safety, even, at times, with praise, if they entered the war with honorable motives, to maintain their loyalty, their treaty, or their freedom." . . . Aristides, in his second speech on Leuctra, says that the Thebans who had followed the lead of the Spartans against the Athenians, "had indeed taken part in an unlawful enterprise, but one that they might cover with a cloak of lawfulness, that is, loyalty to the heads of their league." . . .

Thucydides says plainly [20] that acts deserve forgiveness if they are committed "not out of wickedness but through an error of judgment." . . . Sallust in his histories writes: [21] "The rest of the populace, instead of using their judgment, followed, as mobs do, one after the other, as if after someone wiser than themselves." What Brutus wrote of civil wars [22] may, I think, be well applied to most other wars. "More vigor should be shown in preventing them than anger wreaked on the defeated."

7. EVEN when justice does not demand this clemency, it is often a mark of goodness, of moderation and of highmindedness. "The grandeur of the Roman people was increased by pardoning," says Sallust.[23] . . . According to Seneca,[24] "It is characteristic of wild beasts, though not of the noble kinds, to tear and worry the animals they have struck down; but elephants and lions leave what they have overthrown." . . .

On this same topic there is a famous passage in the fourth book of *To Herennius*: [25] "Our ancestors did well in establishing the rule

352 GROTIUS: THE LAW OF WAR AND PEACE

not to put to death a king captured in battle. Why so? Because it was unfair to utilize the chance fate gave to punish a man whom the same fate shortly before had set in the most exalted position. What of the fact that the king had led his army against us? I have forgotten that. Why so? Because a brave man regards as enemies those who are still wrestling with him for victory, but judges as human beings those whom he has conquered. Thus courage may shorten the war and mercy strengthen the peace. But would the king, if he had been the victor, have behaved in this way? Why then are you sparing him? Because it is my habit to despise stupidity, not to imitate it."

However, if you take this passage to refer to the Romans (an uncertain point, since the author makes use of foreign and fictitious illustrations), it conflicts directly with the sentiment expressed in the panegyric addressed to Constantine, son of Constantius: [26] "Though he who holds his enemies bound to him by a pardon may be the more prudent, he is yet the braver who tramples on his opponents. You have, Emperor, revived that ancient assurance of the Roman Empire which inflicted the penalty of death on captive enemy leaders. For then, after the captured kings had served to adorn the chariots of the triumphing general from the city gates as far as the Forum, as soon as he began turning his chariot towards the Capitol, they were dragged off to prison and executed. . . ."

Josephus too, in his account of the killing of Simon Barjoras, speaks in the same way of the severity of the Romans. . . . The gist of his story, in Latin, is as follows: [27] "The end of the triumph came after it had reached the temple of Jupiter on the Capitoline. There by an ancient custom of the country the generals had to wait until the death of the enemy commander was announced. He was Simon, son of Joras, who was led among the prisoners in the triumph, but at this point had a noose thrown over him and was dragged to the Forum, while his guards meantime plied their scourges on him. In that place the Romans are accustomed to inflict punishment on men condemned for capital crimes. When word was brought that Simon was dead, there followed the favorable omens and then the sacrifices." Cicero describes almost the same procedure in his account of punishments in his speech *Against Verres*.[28]

There are many instances of commanders thus punished, and several of kings, such as Aristonicus [Aristobulus], Jugurtha, Artabasdus. . . . Hence Marcus Aemilius Paulus in Diodorus Siculus gave wise counsel to the Roman senators, when he said, speaking in the case of Perseus [29] that "if they felt no fear of man, they should still dread the divine vengeance, which hangs over those who make too callous a use of victory." . . .

An enemy, then, who wishes to show respect not for what human laws permit him to do but for what is his duty and what is right and godly, will spare the blood of his adversary. He will sentence no one to death unless by so doing he escapes death himself or something like it, or because his enemy has himself committed crimes which measure up to capital offenses. And even to some who deserve such punishment he will extend pardon, either in full or from the death penalty, moved perhaps by the promptings of humanity, perhaps by other good reasons. . . .

8. AS for the killing of persons who are slaughtered incidentally, without intention, we must maintain what we said above, that mercy, even if not justice, requires that except for grave reasons affecting the safety of multitudes, nothing should be done that may threaten the destruction of innocent people. Polybius agrees with us here, for he says in his fifth book: [30] "Good men should not wage a war of destruction even on the wicked, but go only so far as to correct wrongs. Nor should they mingle the innocent and the guilty together in one punishment, but for the sake of the innocent spare the guilty too."

9. WITH this understanding it will not be difficult to arrive at a decision in more special cases. "Let a boy be excused by his age, a woman by her sex," says Seneca in the book in which he expresses his anger with anger.[31] In the wars of the Jews, God himself or-

dained that the women and children should be spared, even after
a peace had been offered and refused. A few tribes only were excepted by a special law, since the war against them was not a war
of men but of God, and was so called. . . . Seneca has another saying to the same effect.[32] "Does anyone show anger to children
whose age has not yet learned the difference between things?" . . .
If God has so done and so decreed—God who can without injustice
slay human beings of any sex or age for no reason but because he is
the lord and giver of life—what is it just for men to do, to whom
he has granted no right over humankind which is not essential to
preserve its safety and its existence as a society?

First then, with regard to children, we have the judgment of
those peoples and eras on which the idea of right had greatest influence. "We have arms," Camillus says in Livy,[33] "to use, not
against that age which is spared even when cities are taken, but
against armed men." He adds that this is one of the laws of war,
that is, the laws of nature. Plutarch, commenting on the same subject, says: [34] "Among good men there are certain laws, even in
wartime." Note here that he says, "among good men," so that you
will distinguish this kind of law from one based on custom and
immunity. . . .

What is always the rule for children who have not attained the
use of reason holds usually for women, that is, unless they have
committed some act that calls particularly for punishment, or are
themselves performing the duties of men. . . . In Curtius, Alexander says: [35] "It is not my habit to make war on captives and
women. The person I hate must be an armed man." In Justin,
Gryphus says [36] that "no one of his ancestors, with all their domestic and foreign wars, was ever brutal to women after victory, since
their sex in itself protects them from the perils of battle and the
cruelty of conquerors." . . . Papinius [37] has something similar to
say about old men:

> "the crowd of old men
> Not to be harmed in war."

10. THE same rule should everywhere be applied to men whose way of life is opposed to warmaking. "By the law of war death is for armed men and those who offer resistance," as Livy says; [38] that is, by the law which agrees with nature. And Josephus calls [39] it just that in a fight the men who have taken up arms should suffer punishment, but the peaceful should not be hurt. . . .

In this class of men to be spared should be put, first, those who have charge of sacred things, for from ancient times it has been the custom in every nation that such persons should have nothing to do with arms. Thus the Philistines, the enemies of the Jews, did no harm to the school of the prophets which was at Gaba, as we may see in I Samuel x, 5 and 10. . . . Strabo notes [40] that in old times, when all Greece was blazing with war, the Eleans, as sacred to Jupiter, and their friends lived in deep peace. In this class, together with priests, are included deservedly all who have chosen similar ways of life, such as monks and novices, that is, penitents. . . . Add to them, as is fitting, all who devote their time to literary studies, which are honorable and useful to the human race.

11. NEXT, the workers on the land, whom the canons also mention, should be spared. Diodorus Siculus tells us approvingly of the Indians [41] that "in battle the enemies slay one another but leave unhurt the tillers of the soil, as workers for the whole community." . . . Of Belisarius Suidas says: [42] "He took such pains to spare farmers and to look out for their welfare that under his command none of them ever suffered any violence."

12. THE canon also takes in merchants, and should be understood as applying not only to those who are temporarily in residence on enemy soil but to those who are the enemy's permanent subjects. For their life too has nothing to do with war. And under this heading are included at the same time other workmen and artisans, whose callings demand peace, not war.

13. TO come now to those who have carried arms, we have already reported the words of Pyrrhus in Seneca, that a sense of shame, that is, a respect for justice, forbids us to put a captive to

356 GROTIUS: THE LAW OF WAR AND PEACE

death. We have cited the similar remark of Alexander, grouping
prisoners and women together. Let us add this saying of Augustine: [43] "Necessity may compel us to destroy a fighting enemy, but
it is not our desire. And as we return his violence while he fights
and resists, so immediately he is vanquished or taken prisoner we
must show him pity, especially if we fear from him no disturbance
of the peace." . . .

Sallust, in his history of Jugurtha,[44] after telling how he put
to death young men who had surrendered, calls it a violation of the
law of war, which you should interpret as a violation of the nature
of justice and the practice of more civilized peoples. . . . Diodorus
Siculus calls the sparing of captives, "a universal law," and says
that those who do anything else indisputably commit a sin. . . .
And we see that the histories praise those commanders who, when
they might be overburdened or endangered by an excessive horde
of prisoners, preferred to let them all go rather than kill them.

14. FOR the same reasons, those who surrender either in battle
or during a siege, on condition that their lives be spared, should not
be rejected. Arrian says [45] that the Thebans' slaughter of enemies
who had surrendered did not accord with Greek custom, was "not
a Greek slaying." . . .

In the case of cities under siege, it was the rule of the Romans
to accept their surrender if offered before the battering ram had
shaken their walls. Caesar told the Aduatuci [46] that he would not
hurt their city if they surrendered before his battering ram had
struck their wall. At present too the same custom holds for un-
fortified places before the cannon begin firing, and for fortified
towns until the assault is made on the walls. . . . Jewish commentators observe that it was the habit of their ancestors, when
besieging a city, not to enclose it in a ring but to leave a section
open for those who wanted to escape, so that the final action might
take place with less bloodshed.

15. THE same rule of justice bids us spare those who unconditionally give themselves up or come as suppliants to the conqueror.

"To cut down men who have surrendered is brutal," in Tacitus' opinion.[47] . . . Certainly we should use all efforts to make men surrender out of fear rather than let themselves be killed. Brutus is praised [48] for his conduct in "not permitting a charge to be made on his enemies, but surrounding them with his cavalry and giving orders to spare them, as likely to become his men ere long."

16. TO these precepts of justice and natural law, unfair exceptions are often proposed, as when reprisals are called for, or there is a demand for terrorizing when resistance is stubborn. But one who remembers what has already been said of the lawful reasons for killing will readily perceive that such excuses do not suffice to justify slaughter. There is no danger from prisoners or from persons already surrendered or anxious to surrender. Hence to make their killing lawful they must previously have committed a crime, and one so serious that a fair judge would pronounce it punishable by death. Yet we see cruelty sometimes vented on prisoners, or on persons who have surrendered. Or else their surrender on condition their lives be spared is not accepted, on the ground that some who knew the war was unlawful still remained in their army, or had slandered the good name of their enemy with gross insults, or had broken faith or violated some other rule of nations, like the right of ambassadors, or else were deserters.

But the law of nature does not allow inflicting reprisals, except on the actual persons who committed the offense. Nor is it enough that by a kind of fiction the enemy may be regarded as forming a single body, as we can see from our previous discussion on the sharing of punishments.[49] We read in Aristides: [50] "Is it not absurd for you to want to imitate as right the things you condemn and say were crimes?" . . . Even the advantage that is expected for the future from terrorization is not a thing that gives the right to kill; though if one has the right, that may be among the reasons for not waiving the right.

Then a stubborn devotion to one's party, provided its cause is not wholly unworthy, does not deserve punishment. . . . Or if there is to be a penalty it should not go so far as death, nor would a just judge give such a sentence. When Alexander ordered all the young men of a town which had set up an especially fierce resistance to be put to death, the Indians felt he was conducting war like a bandit; and the king, in fear of such a reputation, began making a more merciful use of victory. He did better when he decided to spare some Milesians, "because," in the words of Arrian,[51] "he saw that they were noble and loyal to their countrymen." . . .

Much less is killing justified by wrath at some calamity that has befallen oneself, as Achilles, Aeneas, and Alexander, we read, avenged their friends, in the blood of captives or of men who had surrendered. So Homer is right when he sings: [52]

> "A wicked deed he pondered in his soul."

17. EVEN where the offenses are so grave that they may seem to deserve death, it will be an act of mercy to let go something of one's full right when many are involved. . . . Applicable here is the saying of Seneca: [53] "A general may vent his severity on individuals, but when a whole army has deserted, he must pardon it. What appeases a wise man's wrath? A multitude of sinners." . . . "The drawing of lots was instituted," says Cicero,[54] "to keep too many from suffering punishment." . . .

18. AS for hostages, we may learn from the things we said earlier what by the law of nature should be our rule with regard to them. In the past it was commonly believed that every man had the same right over his own life that he had over other objects which were included in his property, and that this right by tacit or express consent passed from individuals to the state. It is not so surprising then when we read that hostages, personally innocent, have been put to death for a wrong committed by their state, whether on the ground that it was committed with their special consent, or with public consent, in which their own was included. But now since a truer wisdom has taught us that lordship over life belongs only to God, it follows that no man by his consent alone can give to

anyone a right over either his own life or that of a fellow citizen. Thus Narses, the good general, thought it atrocious, Agathias tells us,[55] to punish harmless hostages. And other historians say the same of other commanders. . . . Obviously, however, if a person who comes as a hostage either is or has previously been one of a group of serious offenders, or has broken a pledge he previously gave on a matter of importance, it may be that punishing him will not be unjust. . . .

19. THIS, in addition, should here be said, that all strife which does not help toward maintaining a right or putting an end to a war, but has as its object purely a show of strength, that is, as the Greeks say, "a display of power rather than a struggle with the enemy," is an offense against the duty of a Christian man and against humanity itself. It should therefore be sternly forbidden by the rulers, who will have to render an account of blood uselessly spilt to him in whose name they wield their sword. Sallust praised [56] commanders who won their victories with armies unstained by blood. . . .

XII

Moderation in Devastating a Country, and Similar Matters.

1. IN order to be able to destroy another man's property without wronging him, one of the following three situations must first exist. Either there must be an emergency of the sort that should be re-

garded as creating an exception to the original institution of ownership, as when a man, to escape peril to himself, throws into a
river the sword of a third man, which a lunatic is about to lay hands
on. In such a case, however, as we have said elsewhere,[1] there remains, according to the correct view, an obligation to make good
the loss inflicted. Or there must be a debt, originating in some inequality, of such a sort that the object destroyed may be counted
as if taken in payment for the debt; otherwise there would be no
right. Or there must be a crime deserving punishment, for which
the destruction is a fair penalty, or amounts to as much as the
penalty, for, as a theologian of sound judgment remarks, justice
does not countenance laying waste a whole kingdom because some
flocks have been driven off or some houses burned. . . . These are
reasons that warrant such destruction, provided it is kept within
limits, so that no wrong is done.

But unless considerations of utility lead one to take such action,
it is foolish to injure someone else for no good to oneself. Wise
commanders accordingly usually decide on a policy of devastation
on the grounds of its utility. Its chief advantage is what Onesander
points out: [2] "Let him remember to wreck the enemy's country,
burn it and leave it desolate. For a shortage of money and produce
puts a check on war, just as abundance encourages it." Similar is
a saying of Proclus: [3] "A good general weakens the enemy's resources wherever they are." . . . The method of devastation then
should be used, if by it the enemy is reduced quickly to suing for
peace. . . . However, if you look properly into the subject, you
will find that such methods are more often employed out of hatred
than for reasons of prudence. It is usually the case that there are no
reasons to warrant laying waste a country, or that there are other
and stronger reasons against it.

2. THIS will be true, in the first place, if we ourselves are occupying the enemy's fruitful territory so that it can produce nothing
for him. Such is the special purpose of the divine law [4] which orders
the use of wild trees for building palisades and military structures,

but the preservation of fruitbearing trees for food. . . . By similar reasoning Philo extends the rule [5] to cover fruitful fields, adding to the law the following words: "Why vent anger on inanimate things, which are themselves kindly and bring forth kindly fruit? Do trees, like the men who are your enemies, display signs of hostility, so that for the things they do or threaten to do they must be uprooted? On the contrary, they are valuable to conquerors, and provide them with a supply of the things they need, and even with things to enjoy. . . ." Unless I am mistaken this passage is the source of the Pythagorean maxim in Iamblichus: [6] "Let it be a law never to injure or cut down a cultivated and fruitful tree." . . .

The writers of the Talmud and the Jewish interpreters say further that the law should be stretched to protect everything that is liable to be destroyed without justification, as when buildings are set on fire, or food spoiled which can be eaten or drunk. In harmony with this law was the wise moderation of the Athenian commander, Timotheus, who as Polyaenus tells us,[7] "would not permit a house or a farmstead to be destroyed or a fruit-bearing tree cut down." We have too the law of Plato in the fifth book of the *Republic*: [8] "The land is not to be devastated nor the houses burned."

Still more should this rule hold after a complete victory. Cicero did not approve [9] the razing of Corinth, even though the Roman ambassadors had been disgracefully treated there; and in another passage he calls horrible, wicked, and utterly hateful the war that is waged against walls, roofs, columns, and the posts of doors. . . .

3. IN the second place, what we said will be true even if our hold on the territory is uncertain, as long as we have good hopes of a speedy victory, and the prize will be both the land and its fruits. Thus, as Justin says,[10] Alexander the Great forbade his troops to devastate Asia, telling them they must spare their own property and not destroy the things they had come to take. . . . On this score Alexander Isius finds fault with Philip, in the seventeenth book of Polybius, which Livy translates into Latin as follows: [11] "In war, he [Philip] does not fight on an open field nor engage in

pitched battles, but retreats, burning,and sacking cities, and if defeated, ruins the prizes of the victors. But this was not the way
of the old kings of Macedon, who used to fight it out in battle and,
as far as they could, spare the cities, so that their realm might be the
richer. For what kind of sense is it to destroy the things for whose
possession one is fighting and leave nothing for oneself but the
war?"

4. THIRDLY, the same will be true if the enemy can procure
means of supporting himself from another source; if, for example,
he has access to the sea or to some other country. Archidamus, we
learn from Thucydides,[12] in the speech in which he advised his
fellow Spartans against a war with the Athenians, asked what
hopes they had of carrying through a war. Did they expect perhaps
that because they were superior in number of soldiers they could
easily lay waste the land of Attica? But, he said, the Athenians have
other lands too under their dominion (meaning Thrace and Ionia)
and by marine transport can bring in whatever they need.

In such a situation then the wisest thing to do is to leave agri-
cultural lands untouched, even on a common frontier. This we
have lately seen done over a long period during the Belgian and
German war, the sole requirement being for tribute to be paid to
both sides. It is not unlike the ancient custom of India, where, as
Diodorus Siculus says: [13] "Farmers are left undisturbed, as if they
were sacred; even close to camps and armies they go about their
business free from danger." . . . And later: "No enemy harms a
farmer, but for the general good that class of men is kept immune
from all injury." . . . The same policy we saw most reasonably
and advantageously followed, to the admiration of foreigners, in the
war we spoke of, the Belgian and German war.

The canons, teachers of humanity, call on all Christians, as persons who profess and should practice a greater humanity than
others, to imitate these methods and save from the peril of war
not merely the farmers but the beasts with which they plow and
the seed which they carry to their fields. For a similar reason, prob-

ably, civil laws prohibit the taking as pledges of articles used in
plowing. Among the Phrygians and the Cyprians of ancient times,
and among the Athenians and the Romans later, it was a sin to
kill a plow ox.

5. FOURTHLY, it is a fact that the nature of some objects makes
them useless for carrying on or conducting a war. Such objects
reason bids us spare, even while the war is in process. Apropos at
this point is the plea for the portrait of Ialysus addressed by the
Rhodians to Demetrius, the captor of cities, as translated by Gellius into Latin: [14] "What reason have you for wishing to destroy
the portrait by burning down the temple? If you conquer us all
and take this whole town, by your victory you will obtain the pic-
ture too, safe and unharmed. But if you are unable to take us by
siege, we ask you to consider if it would not be a disgrace to you
to have made war on dead Protogenes, because you could not defeat the Rhodians." Polybius calls it [15] the mark of a crazed mind
to destroy things whose destruction neither detracts from the
strength of the enemy nor adds to that of the destroyer,—things
like temples, galleries, statues, and the like. . . .

6. THIS reasoning, while it holds true for other objects of beauty
on the grounds we have already given, has a special argument to support it in the case of buildings dedicated to religious uses. For although, as we said before, these structures are public property in
their way, and hence by the law of nations may be violated with impunity, yet, if there is no danger from them, our reverence for divine things tells us that they and their appurtenances should be protected, particularly by those who worship the same God, under the
same law, even if by chance they differ on certain doctrines and
forms of ritual. . . . Livy says [16] that Quintus Fulvius the censor
was adversely criticized because he "made the Roman people guilty
of impiety by wrecking temples, as if the immortal gods were not
everywhere the same, but some gods could be worshiped and decked
out in others' spoils." . . .

To come to the Christians, Agathias reports [17] that the Franks spared the churches, since they were of the same religion as the Greeks. It has, in fact, been customary to spare men for the sake of their churches, and—not to mention the examples of pagan peoples, which are numerous . . . —Augustine for that reason praised the Goths [18] who captured Rome. . . .

7. WHAT I have said of sacred buildings should be understood as applying also to all consecrated objects, also to monuments erected in honor of the dead. For although the law of nations grants immunity for the wreaking of wrath on such objects, they cannot be profaned without showing some contempt for humanity. It is the highest reason, say the jurists, that pays respect to reverence. . . . In Statius,[19] Hannibal is called sacrilegious for setting torches to the altars of the gods. . . . Caesar, as Dio tells us,[20] "did not dare to pull down" the trophy built by Mithridates, "because it was consecrated to the gods of war." . . . Florus says of Philip: [21] "Philip went beyond the rights of victory in committing outrages on temples, altars, and tombs." . . .

8. IT is not properly a part of our purpose here to inquire what kind of behavior is the more profitable, but rather to reduce the unprincipled license of war to conduct permissible by nature, or to the best of permissible conduct. Yet virtue herself, held cheap in this present age, ought to forgive me if, at a time when on her own account she is despised, I cause her to be more valued for her profitableness.

In the first place, then, this moderation, shown in preserving objects which do not hinder the war, deprives the enemy of one powerful weapon—despair. Archidamus, in Thucydides,[22] says: "Look on enemy territory as nothing else than a hostage, the more valuable the better its state of cultivation. Therefore spare it as far as possible, that desperation may not make the enemy harder to subdue." Agesilaus had the same idea, when he opposed the views of the Achaeans and let the Acarnanians sow their fields, saying that the more they sowed the more anxious they would be for peace. . . .

Furthermore, moderation in the midst of a war gives an appearance of great confidence of victory. Clemency also is apt of itself to break down determination and win over the enemy's heart. . . . For a similar reason, Augustus Caesar refrained from plundering the Pannonians. Dio explains his motive: [23] "He hoped it would turn out that in that way he could win them over to himself without force." . . . Plutarch, after describing the orderly behavior of Quintius and the Romans who were with him, goes on to say: [24] "It was not long before they reaped the fruits of their moderation, for as soon as they reached Thessaly, the cities came over to him. Next, the Greeks who lived below Thermopylae were calling enthusiastically for Quintius; and the Achaeans renounced their alliance with Philip and made a league with the Romans against him." . . .

Opposite methods have produced opposite results. Livy gives an instance in the case of Hannibal: [25] "By disposition he was inclined to avarice and cruelty, apt to pillage what he could not keep, so as to leave only ruined wastes to the enemy. It was wretched policy, both at the start and also in its results, for it antagonized both the persons who suffered undeserved catastrophe and others besides, since the news of his behavior affected more people than the destruction did."

I most truly believe what certain theologians have declared, that it is the duty of sovereigns and commanders who wish to be regarded as Christians by God and man, to prevent the violent sacking of cities and deeds of that sort, which cannot take place without terrible hurt to multitudes of innocent persons and often have little effect on the outcome of the war. Hence Christian goodness almost always, and plain justice very often must abominate such doings. Certainly the bond which unites Christians is stronger than that which once united the Greeks, and during their wars a decree of the Amphictyons forbade the destruction of a Greek city. . . .

XIII

Moderation with Regard to Captured Property.

1. THE seizure of enemy property, even in lawful war, should not be considered a blameless practice or exempt from the obligation to make reparation. Indeed, if you consider what is right, you ought not to seize or hold anything of more value than is justified by the enemy's debt to you, except that property beyond that amount may be retained when required for security. But when the danger is past, it should be restored, either itself, or its equivalent in value, in accordance with the conclusions we reached in Book Two, Chapter II.[1] What we considered legitimate use of goods owned by persons at peace is much more legitimate in the case of enemy goods. Here then is a certain right of seizure, but without a right of acquiring ownership.

However, a debt may be due us either because of an inequality in our position or as a penalty. So for either reason we may acquire ownership of enemy property, yet still with a distinction. In a debt of the first sort, as we said above, the property of not only the debtor but of his subjects becomes liable according to the established law of nations, as if in a case of surety. And this law of nations we take to be of another kind than that which merely confers immunity or relies on the external force of the courts. For just as a man with whom we have dealings, by our personal consent acquires not merely an external but an inner right over our possessions, so a similar right over a people's possessions may be acquired by a sort of public consent, which has power to include in itself the consent of individuals. In such a sense a law is called "a common agreement of the state." It is likely that the nations approved of such procedure in this kind of situation, because this law of nations was set up not only in order to prevent a greater evil but also to assure to every man his right.

2. BUT in a case of the second type of debt, which is a form of punishment, I do not find that the nations have agreed that a similar right over the property of the debtor's subjects has been created. Any such claim on the possessions of other men is odious, and it therefore should not be carried further than there is proof of their actual misconduct. There is not the same advantage in insisting on this latter form of indebtedness as there is in insisting on the former; for the former is a question of property dues but not so the latter. Hence we may refrain from insisting on it without loss. . . . Therefore the goods of enemy subjects should not be taken over on the score of punishing their rulers, but only those of persons who have themselves been offenders, among whom we include magistrates who fail to punish crime.

3. HOWEVER, the property of subjects may be seized and kept either as payment for the original debt which was the source of the war, or for one which was created later, as we said at the beginning of this book. Thus we must interpret the theologians' saying that the seizure of property in war is not to be looked on as compensation for the original debt. We must understand this to be true, up to the point where a sound judgment would declare that satisfaction had been given for all the damage inflicted by the war itself. So, in their dispute with Antiochus, the Romans, as Livy tells us,[2] judged it fair for the king to pay all the expense incurred for the war, since he had been guilty of provoking it. . . . In Thucydides,[3] the Samians are sentenced "to pay the costs of the war." There are many other instances. Whatever penalty then it is just to impose on the conquered may be justly extorted from them in war.

4. BUT we must remember what we have called to mind else-

where, that the rules of love are broader than the rules of law. A man abounding in riches is guilty of callousness if he strips a poor debtor of all his small possessions in order to wring from him his last farthing. Much more is this true if the debtor has fallen in debt through his own goodness—if, for instance, he has gone security for a friend, and has spent none of the money for his own profit. . . . Yet a creditor so hard-hearted does nothing contrary to the law, strictly speaking.

So humanity requires that we leave to those who are guiltless of the war, and who are liable on no grounds other than as sureties, all articles which we can go without more easily than they can, especially if it is obvious that they will not recover from their own government what they have lost in the war. . . . We must observe too that since our right over the goods of innocent subjects was established to aid us in recovering our dues, as long as there is hope that we can recover them easily enough from the original debtors, or from those who through their failure to render justice have made themselves debtors by their own acts, so long it is inhuman to descend on guiltless people, even though admittedly it is legal in the strict sense.

Instances of such humanity are frequent in history, particularly in Roman history, as when lands were granted to a conquered enemy on condition that they went to the state, that is, went to the defeated state; or when a portion of land was left to the previous possessor as a mark of honor. . . . Thus you may often read of cities surrendered that were not looted. So, as we said above, it is commendable to spare both the persons and the property of tillers of the soil, in accordance with the righteous precept of the canons, subject at most to a tribute; and subject to similar tribute, merchandise is frequently granted immunity from attack in war.

XIV

Moderation with Regard to Persons Captured.

1. AS for countries where it is customary to hold men prisoners or slaves, if we have any respect for inner justice, we must limit that practice, first, as we did in the case of property, that is, by permitting acquisition of ownership only so far as the amount of either an original or a subsequent debt warrants it, unless it happens that the same men have committed some special crime which should justly be punished by loss of liberty. Thus far then and no farther does a person fighting a lawful war have a right over the captive subjects of his enemy; and this right he may validly transfer to others.

Here too it will be the duty of justice and goodness to maintain the distinctions we described above, when we were discussing the killing of enemies. Demosthenes, in his letter on behalf of the children of Lycurgus,[1] praises Philip of Macedon because he did not make slaves of everyone on his enemy's side; "for," he says, "he did not think it right or fair to give the same treatment to all, but looked into the matter, considering also what each man deserved, and so, even in cases like those, acted as a judge."

2. IN the first place, we must note here that a right derived from the captives' position as surety for their state does certainly not extend so far as a right which originated in a crime over persons who are slaves as punishment. Wherefore a certain Spartan said he was a captive but not a slave. For if we view the matter correctly,

369

the general right over captives taken in lawful war is equivalent to the right that masters have over men who under pressure of poverty have sold themselves into slavery, except that even more pitiable is the plight of those who have fallen on their misfortune, not through any special act of their own, but through the fault of their rulers. . . .

Now this kind of slavery is a perpetual obligation to labor in return for maintenance, likewise perpetual. The definition of Chrysippus [2] well fits this type of slave: "A slave is a perpetual mercenary." . . . There is a wide difference between what by the law of nations may be done with impunity to a slave and what our natural reason allows us to do. We have already quoted Seneca: [3] "Although against a slave all things are lawful, yet there are things that the universal law of living beings declares unlawful to do to a man." . . . In another passage, Seneca says: [4] "They are slaves, no, men; they are slaves, no, comrades; they are slaves, no, lowly friends; they are slaves, no, fellow slaves." . . . Clement of Alexandria bids us [5] treat our slaves as our other selves, since they are men no less than we. . . .

3. NOW the right over a slave, which is called the right of life and death, confers on the master a domestic jurisdiction, but one that should be exercised with the same scrupulousness as a public jurisdiction. . . . "Our ancestors," says the same Seneca,[6] "thought of our households as miniature republics." And according to Pliny: [7] "For slaves the household is a kind of republic, and a substitute for a state." Plutarch tells us [8] that Cato the censor would not punish a slave who had apparently committed a capital offense, until after he had been condemned by the verdict of his fellow slaves as well. . . .

4. AND as for minor punishments, such as the flogging of slaves, justice should be displayed there but also clemency. "Thou shalt not oppress him; thou shalt not be a harsh master to him," says the divine law, with reference to a Jewish slave, a command which now, through the extension of the tie of kinship, should be

stretched to cover all slaves. (Deuteronomy, xv, 17, 45, 53.) On this passage Philo remarks as follows: [9] "In their fortunes indeed slaves are inferior to their masters, but by nature they are equal; and by divine law the rule of justice is not what accords with fortune but with nature. Therefore masters ought not to use their power over their slaves insolently, or make it a matter for pride, arrogance and brutal cruelty. . . ." "Is it right," asks Seneca,[10] "to govern a man more severely and harshly than we govern dumb beasts? A skillful horseman does not terrify his horse by constantly beating him. You will make him timid and unruly unless you soothe him with a gentle touch." . . .

5. LABOR too should be required of slaves in moderation, and with humane consideration shown for their state of health. Among other aims of the Jewish law for the institution of the Sabbath was the securing of a respite from toil. . . . In this connection, Seneca calls attention to the humanity of the ancients: [11] "Do you not see how our ancestors protected masters against any resentment and slaves against any abuse? They called the master 'father of the family' [paterfamilias] and his slaves 'members of the family' [familiares]." . . . Tacitus praises the Germans,[12] who treated their slaves like tenant farmers. Theano says in a letter: [13] "This is the just way to treat slaves, not to have them worn out with toil or unable to bear their work because of poverty."

6. IN return for his labor, as we have said, a slave should receive maintenance. In the words of Cicero: [14] "They are good counselors who tell us to treat our slaves like hired servants. Labor should be demanded of them, but they should be paid what is fair." . . . "There are things," says Seneca,[15] "which a master is bound to furnish his slave, such as food and clothing." In the food was included four pecks of grain a month, which, according to Donatus,[16] was the supply for slaves. . . .

Furthermore, in the same passage,[17] Seneca argues that for certain purposes a slave is free, and has the means too of conferring a favor, when he does something which goes beyond the limit of

GROTIUS: THE LAW OF WAR AND PEACE

his duty as a slave, and which he performs not under orders but voluntarily; he passes then from being a dutiful servant to an affectionate friend. On this topic Seneca expands at length.

In accordance with the same idea, if a slave, like the one in Terence,[18] by a course of self-denial has saved up something or has earned it by working in his spare time, that in a way belongs to him. . . . . Ulpian too speaks of his savings [19] as his little patrimony. It makes no difference that his master can at will take it wholly or in part away, for if he does so without good reason, he will be committing an injustice. By a 'reason' I mean not only a punishment, but also the master's necessity; because the slave's welfare is subordinate to that of his master, even more than the interests of citizens are subordinate to that of the state. . . . Accordingly, we read that just as clients have made contributions for the use of their patrons, and subjects for the use of their kings, so slaves have contributed to their masters' aid, as when his daughter must have a dowry, his captive son be ransomed, or some similar event occurs. Pliny, as he tells us himself in his letters,[20] allowed his slaves even to make wills of a kind, that is, to divide, give away, and bequeath their belongings inside the household. Among some nations an even fuller right of acquiring property has been granted, we read, to slaves, just as there are several grades of slavery, as we have already explained.

In many countries the laws reduced the external rights of masters to conform to this inner justice which we are describing. For with the Greeks, slaves too harshly treated might demand to be sold, and at Rome they might take refuge with the statues, or call for the protection of the officials against cruelty or starvation or intolerable abuse. It happens sometimes too, not for any strictly legal reason but out of humanity and kindliness, that after long or very great service a slave is given his liberty, as he should be. . . . Salvianus says [21] that it was a daily occurrence for slaves to be given their freedom, even though their service had not been the best, so long as it had not been bad; and he adds: "and the goods they had acquired during their servitude they were permitted to take from their master's house." Many instances of this benevolence appear in the martyrologies.

Here we should praise the mercifulness of the Jewish law,[22] which ordained that a Jewish slave, after a fixed time had elapsed, should be set completely free, with gifts. The prophets complain loudly of the neglect of this law. Plutarch blames Cato the elder [23] because he sold his slaves when feeble with old age, forgetting the nature that is common to all men.

7. HERE arises the question whether it is right for a man who has been taken prisoner in lawful warfare to try to escape. We are not speaking of one who through his own misdoing deserves that punishment, but of one who through an act of his state has fallen into that plight. The more correct answer is that it is not right, since by a general agreement of the nations, as we have said, he is under obligation to labor in the name of his state. This rule, however, should be understood as applying only if no intolerable cruelty imposes on him a necessity to escape. . . .

8. ELSEWHERE we have raised the question whether and how far the children of slaves are bound to their master by an inner right, and here, because of its special bearing on prisoners of war, we must raise it again. If the parents by their own crimes deserved the death penalty, then the offspring who were to be expected of them may be bound to slavery in return for the preservation of their lives, since otherwise they would not have lived at all. . . .

If the parents are enslaved for the debt of their state, their children already born, no less than they, as members of the state may be bound by its debt. But for children not yet born this does not seem a sufficient reason for slavery and another is required. Either the express consent of their parents, together with their need of being supported, makes them slaves, and that for life; or else the mere furnishing of their support makes them so, but in that case only until their work cancels out all that has been spent on them. If any right more than this is allowed the master over these children, it comes, we see, from the civil law, which does bestow on masters more than is fair.

9. FOR people who do not exercise the right of taking slaves in war the best practice is to exchange prisoners; the next best is to release them for a fair ransom. What that ransom may be we cannot state precisely, but humanity bids us not to raise it beyond the point where the payment of it will leave a captive destitute of the necessaries of life. Even civil laws frequently make a similar provision for persons who have fallen into debt by their own act. In other places the amount is fixed by covenant or by custom, as among the ancient Greeks, where it was a mina, and now, among soldiers, where it is a month's pay. Plutarch tells [24] how in old times the wars between the Corinthians and the people of Megara were fought "decently and as befitted two peoples of the same blood." A man who was taken prisoner was treated by his captor as a guest, his pledge to pay a ransom was accepted and he was allowed to go home. . . . So Xenophon applauds Cyrus for releasing his prisoners. Polybius praises the conduct of Philip of Macedon after his victory at Chaeronea, and Curtius Alexander's treatment of the Scythians. . . .

XV

Moderation in the Assumption of Governing Power.

1. THE justice that is necessary and the humanity that is praiseworthy in the treatment of individuals are all the more necessary and praiseworthy in the treatment of populations or of sections of

populations, as injustice and clemency in the treatment of multitudes are more conspicuous. In a lawful war, among things which may be won are the right of a ruler over a people and the right of rulership which the people themselves possess, though we may win only as much right as the amount of punishment due us for their wrongdoing or some other indebtedness warrants. To this should be added what we need for protection against extreme danger.

This last consideration is often combined with others, though both in drawing up the peace and in the use made of victory it is the one to which attention is chiefly given; for the penalties may be remitted out of compassion. Even in time of public danger, excessive measures of security are unmerciful. Isocrates, writing to Philip, said: [1] "The barbarians should be subjugated only to the point where you will have your realm sufficiently secure."

2. CRISPUS SALLUST says of the ancient Romans: [2] "Our ancestors, most scrupulous of mortals, took nothing from the people they conquered but their ability to do harm," a statement worthy to have been made by a Christian. . . . Aristotle said more than once [3] that "War was instituted to bring peace, business to bring leisure." And Cicero has the same idea, which he expresses in the following lofty words: [4] "Let war be so waged as to make clear that nothing but peace is its aim." . . .

These views are no different from those which the theologians of the true religion instill in us, namely, that the purpose of war is to remove the things that disturb peace. Before the age of Ninus, as we remarked earlier, citing Trogus, it was the custom simply to defend the boundaries of a realm rather than to push them forward. Each man's kingdom was confined to his own country. Kings fought not for an empire for themselves but for the glory of their people, and, satisfied with victory, refrained from enlarging their domains. Augustine, as far as he can, would take us back to that time, when he says: [5] "But they should observe that it is not, apparently, a characteristic of good men to gloat over the breadth of their empires." . . .

3. TO this model of ancient virtue the nearest approach was made by the wise moderation of the old Romans. "What would our empire be today," asks Seneca,[6] "if a sagacious foresight had not mingled together the conquered and the conquerors?" . . . Claudius said too [7] that the ruin of the Spartans and the Athenians was due to nothing else but the exclusion of the people they conquered, as if they were foreigners. Livy says [8] that the Roman empire grew by the admission of enemies into the state. . . . Cerialis in his speech to the Gauls, to be found in Tacitus,[9] tells his audience: "You yourselves often command our legions; you yourselves are governors of these and other provinces. No post is barred or closed to you." And a little later: "Then love and cherish the peace and the life which we, conquerors and conquered, all enjoy under the same law!"

Finally came that most extraordinary event, when all inhabitants of the Roman world by a decree of the Emperor Antoninus [Caracalla] became citizens of Rome, as Ulpian puts it.[10] Thenceforth, as Modestinus says,[11] Rome was the common fatherland; and Claudian writes of her: [12]

> "To her pacific customs we every one owe this,
> That we are all one nation."

4. ANOTHER form of moderation in victory is to leave to the vanquished, either the king or the people, the governing power they had. . . . Thus the Persian kings would leave their royal authority to the kings they conquered. Thus Cyrus left it to the Armenian king, and Alexander to Porus. . . . Polybius commemorates the goodness of Antigonus,[13] who, when he had Sparta in his power, left her citizens "the government and liberty of their ancestors." By that act, we are told, he won great applause throughout Greece. In the same way, the Romans permitted the Cappadocians to keep whatever form of government they chose, and left many other nations free after war. . . .

5. AT times, however, the grant of governing power is coupled

with some provision for the security of the victors. So Quintius ordered that Corinth should be returned to the Achaeans, but on condition that a garrison should be stationed on Acrocorinth, and that Chalcis and Demetrias should be held, until his misgivings with regard to Antiochus were over.

6. A levy of tribute too is often useful, not so much as a reimbursement for expenses incurred in action as a means for providing security for both victors and vanquished in the future. Cicero, speaking of the Greeks, says: [14] "At the same time, let Asia reflect on this, that there is no calamity of foreign war or domestic discord that would not have descended on her, if she were not held fast in this empire; and inasmuch as this empire cannot possibly be maintained without taxes, she should be willing to purchase everlasting peace and quiet for herself with a fraction of her produce." In Tacitus,[15] Petilius Cerealis addresses the Lingones and other Gauls in the name of the Romans, as follows: "Though often provoked, we have laid on you, by right of victory, only this burden as a measure to preserve the peace. For there can be no quiet for the nations without armies, nor armies without pay, nor pay without tribute." To this same end are designed other measures, which we described when discussing unequal treaties,[16] requirements for the surrender of arms, fleet, and elephants, and bans on keeping battle troops and armies.

7. TO leave to the conquered their power of government is not only a policy of humanity; it is often one of wisdom as well. . . . Florus says rightly: [17] "It is more difficult to hold provinces than to gain them; they are taken by force, they are held by justice." . . . And there is the saying of Augustus in Plutarch: [18] "A greater achievement than acquiring a vast empire is governing one that you have." . . . The difficulty of holding an empire, the Hindu Calanus,[19] and before him, Oebarus, the friend of Cyrus,[20] illustrated by comparing it to a leather hide which rises up in one spot as soon as you press down another spot with your foot. . . . In Scipio Africanus' opinion,[21] Rome already in his time possessed so

much that it would be gluttonous to want anything more. She would be more than fortunate if she lost none of what she had. . . .

8. THE Spartans, and at first the Athenians, claimed no governmental right over the cities they took. They merely asked them to set up a form of government which harmonized with their own. The Spartans wanted one ruled by nobles, the Athenians one subject to the popular will. . . . Tacitus says [22] that Artabanus at Seleucia followed a similar course. "The common people," he says, "he turned over to the aristocrats for his own advantage, because a popular government inclines toward liberty, while an oligarchy comes closer to the arbitrary rule of a king." Whether changes like this do add to the conqueror's security is not a part of our investigation.

9. IF it is not safe to take no hand in the government of a conquered people, still one's participation may be limited, so that some authority is left to them or to their kings. Tacitus calls it [23] a practice of the Roman people to keep kings as instruments of subjugation. . . . And after the defeat of Darius, Alexander several times proposed to him the condition that he should continue ruling over others, but himself obey Alexander. We have spoken elsewhere of ways of distributing governmental power.[24] To some kings a part of their royal power was left, just as to some former owners a part of their lands.

10. BUT even when the conquered are stripped of all sovereign power, it is possible to leave them their laws and customs with regard to private and petty public concerns, and also their magistrates. Thus, in the proconsular province of Bithynia, the city of Apamea had the privilege of administering its government as it chose, as we learn from the letters of Pliny; [25] and elsewhere the Bithynians had their own magistrates and their own senate. . . . The Goths left the conquered Romans their Roman laws.

11. A feature of this considerate policy is not to take from a conquered people the right to practice its ancestral religion, unless it

has been persuaded to change it. Such a concession is precious to the conquered and harmless to the conqueror, as Agrippa proves in his speech to Gaius.[26] . . . And in Josephus,[27] both Josephus himself and the Emperor Titus remonstrate with the rebellious inhabitants of Jerusalem on the ground that through Roman be-nevolence they were enjoying rights so great in the practice of their religion that they could shut strangers out of their temple, even on pain of death.

However, if the conquered people have a false religion, the con-queror may rightly take measures to protect the true faith from being oppressed, as Constantine did after crushing the partisans of Licinius; and, following him, the Frankish and other kings.

12. OUR final advice is this. Even in the most absolute and, as it were, masterful empire, conquered peoples should be treated with leniency, and in such a way that their interests are linked to the interests of the conqueror. Cyrus bade[28] the vanquished As-syrians be of good heart, for their lot would be the same as it would have been, with only a change of king. Their houses, their lands, their rights over their wives and children would remain the same as they had been before. Furthermore, if anyone did them a wrong, he, Cyrus himself, and his troops would be their avengers.

In Sallust we read:[29] "The Roman people thought it better to win friends than slaves, and believed it safer to rule over willing subjects than over subjects by coercion." . . . The man from Privernum, when asked in the Roman Senate what kind of peace the Romans might expect from his people, replied:[30] "If you give us a good peace, it will be a faithful and a permanent one; if a bad peace, it will not last long"; adding as his reason: "Do not suppose that any people, or even any man, will remain longer than neces-sary in a position he resents." So Camillus said[31] that government was most stable where the people obeyed it gladly. . . . In a letter of Caesar the dictator[32] are the words: "Let this be our new policy of conquest, to arm ourselves with mercy and generosity."

XVI

Moderation with Regard to Articles Which by the Law of Nations Have no Right of Postliminy.[1]

1. HOW far goods taken in lawful war become the property of the takers we have explained above. From these goods, however, must be deducted articles recoverable by the right of postliminy, for they are regarded as not having been taken. Goods seized in an unlawful war must all be restored, as we said; not only by the persons who seized them but by any others into whose hands, by whatever means, they have come. For no one can transfer to another more right to a thing than he himself possessed, as the authors of the Roman law state it. And Seneca puts it briefly:[2] "No one can give away what he does not own." The man who first seized these goods had no intrinsic right of ownership; hence the one who receives them from him will not have it. So the second or third possessor obtains a form of ownership that for the sake of our explanation we call external. It has this advantage, that everywhere the possessor is protected as owner by the authority and power of the courts. Yet if he makes use of his advantage against the one from whom the goods were wrongfully taken, he is not doing right.

On the question of the status of a slave who had been captured by brigands and later came into the enemy's hands, the noble jurists gave as their opinion that the truth was he had been stolen, and that neither the fact that he had later been in enemy hands or had come back by postliminy altered his position. . . . And Gregory of Neocaesarea gave an opinion like theirs,[3] when he was consulted on the fact that certain citizens of Pontus had accepted property belonging to their fellow citizens, which had been captured by barbarians.

2. SUCH objects then must be returned to those from whom they were taken, as we see has often been done. Livy, after relating [4] the defeat of the Volscians and Aequians by Lucius Lucretius Tricipitinus, says that the booty was displayed in the Campus Martius, so that for three days anyone might take away what belonged to him. . . . The same writer, in another passage, speaking of the spoils which Cornelius Scipio took at Ilipa, a city of Lusitania, says: [5] "They were all displayed outside the city and opportunity was given to owners to identify what was theirs. The remainder was delivered to the quaestor for sale, and the proceeds divided among the soldiers."

Of Lucius Aemilius, conqueror of the Gauls, Polybius writes: [6] "The booty he returned to those from whom it had been taken." Plutarch and Appian describe [7] similar conduct on the part of Scipio, when after the capture of Carthage he found there numerous temple offerings which the Carthaginians had brought in from the cities of Sicily and other places. . . . The Rhodians returned to the Athenians four of their ships, which had been seized by the Macedonians and recovered by the Rhodians. . . . The Romans even restored to their original position articles which had once been dedicated to the gods at Ephesus, and which the kings had appropriated.

3. BUT if any such article comes into a man's possession by way of business, can he charge the person from whom it was taken the price he paid for it? In accord with what we have said elsewhere, he can charge as much as the recovery of the article considered lost will be worth to the one who lost it. And if that much expense may be got back, why should not some account be taken of labor and

danger incurred, as when a man by diving brings up a piece of someone else's property lost in the sea?

Pertinent to this question seems to me the story of Abraham, when he returned to Sodom as victor over the five kings. "He brought back all the goods," says Moses,[8] that is, the goods he had taken from the kings, as previously narrated. The arrangement which the king of Sodom then proposed to Abraham must have been based on reasoning like ours. He was to restore the captives but keep everything besides for himself, as payment for his labor and danger. However, Abraham, being a man not merely dutiful but also magnanimous, would take nothing whatever for himself, but as though by a right of his own dedicated a tenth of the captured spoils . . . to God, deducted his necessary expenses, and asked that some portion be awarded to his allies.

4. AS property then should be returned to its owner, so peoples and sections of peoples should be returned to those who had the right of government over them, or to themselves, if they were self-governing before the advent of the lawless power. . . . The Greek cities which the Macedonians had invaded were restored to liberty by Flaminius. Flaminius too, in a conference with the envoys of Antiochus, pronounced it right to set free the cities of Asia which had Greek names, but which Seleucus, great-grandfather of Antiochus, had taken in war and which, when lost, had been retaken by this Antiochus. "For the colonies were not sent to Aeolis and Ionia," he said,[9] "to be in servitude to a king, but to increase the race and to spread their ancient nation over the world."

5. A question is raised likewise as to the length of time beyond which the inner obligation to restore such goods may be considered extinguished. But this question, if arising between citizens under the same government, should be answered by their own laws, provided the laws admit an inner right and do not count only the external right, a thing to be gathered from a discerning study of the wording and purport of the laws. But if it is a question between men who are foreigners to one another, it can only be de-

cided by supposing it to be a case of abandonment. Such cases we discussed earlier,[10] as far as sufficed our purpose.

6. BUT when the lawfulness of a war is extremely doubtful, it is best to follow the plan of Aratus of Sicyon, who in some instances persuaded the new possessors to accept money and give up their acquisitions, and in other instances convinced the original owners that it would be more to their advantage to be paid what their property was worth than to get it back.

XVII

Neutrals in Wartime.

1. IT might appear unnecessary for us to talk of the people who remain outside a war, inasmuch as obviously there is no right of war over them. But since in times of war much damage is done to them, especially to neighbors, under pretext of necessity, we must here repeat briefly what we have said before, that the necessity, in order to give anyone a right over other men's property, must be extreme. Furthermore, the same necessity must not exist in the case of the owner. And even where the fact of necessity is clear, more must not be taken than need be. That is, if the holding of an object is sufficient, it should not be used; if the use of it is enough, it should not be spoiled; if it must be spoiled, then the cost of it should be returned.

2. WHEN Moses and his people were obliged by extreme necessity to pass through the lands of the Edomites, he promised [1] beforehand that he would go by the king's highway and not turn
aside to the plowed fields or the vineyards; and if he had need of
their water, he would pay the price of it. Renowned commanders
of both Greeks and Romans have given similar assurances. In
Xenophon,[2] the Greeks with Clearchus promised the Persians that
they would march through without doing any mischief; and that
if they were supplied with provisions to buy, they would rob no one
of his food or his drink. . . . Of the army of the Spartan Agis,
Plutarch says: [3] "They were the wonder of the cities as they crossed
the Peloponnesus considerately, doing no harm and almost without
a sound." . . .

Of Domitian, Frontinus writes: [4] "When he was building forts
along the borders of the Ubii, he gave orders that the price of the
produce of the lands which he was enclosing in his fortification
should be paid; and the report of that act of justice won everyone's
allegiance to him." . . . Of the Goths, Huns, and Alani who
served under Theodosius, the Panegyrist says: [5] "There was no
rioting, no confusion, no pillaging, as was customary with barbarians. Whenever there was difficulty in procuring supplies they bore
the scarcity patiently. . . ."

This good order was brought about by strict care in providing
for the necessities, prompt payment of wages, and energetic discipline. The rule for it you find in Ammianus: [6] "The soil of people at peace must not be trampled down." And in Vopiscus' life
of Aurelian, we read: [7] "No man shall steal another man's fowl, or
touch his sheep, or pick his grapes, or tread down his grain, or demand of him oil, salt, or wood." Likewise in Cassiodorus: [8] "They
are to live with the provincials under civil law. The man who knows
he is armed is not to become insolent, for our army should be a
shield to ensure peace to all Romans." . . . With the aid of such
passages you can rightly interpret the words of the great prophet,
or rather, the one greater than a prophet: [9] "Do violence to no

man, neither accuse any falsely, and be content with your wages." . . .

Nor is there any reason to think that these are only fine words, which cannot be put into practice. For the divine man would not have given us this admonition, nor the wise authors of the laws these rules, if they had believed them impossible to carry out. Indeed we have to admit that what we see was done can be done. For that reason we have cited our instances, to which we may add the remarkable incident which Frontinus relates of Scaurus,[10] that an apple tree which a survey had included in the grounds of his camp, on the following day, when his army had departed, was left with its fruit untouched. . . .

However, there is another well-known passage of Livy,[11] where he describes the march of Philip through the land of the Dense-letae: "They were allies, but because the Macedonians were out of supplies, they plundered the country as if it had belonged to an enemy, pillaging everywhere and sacking, first, country houses and then some villages, to the great shame of their king, when he heard the voices of his allies entreating in vain their guardian gods and himself by name." Tacitus tells us [12] . . . how the troops of Vitel-lius were left in idleness through all the municipalities of Italy, to be a terror only to their hosts. . . .

And here I cannot refrain from citing the judgment of the theo-logians, which I consider absolutely correct, and which is that a king who does not pay his soldiers the wages he owes them is re-sponsible not only to his soldiers for the hardships they suffer thereby, but to his subjects and neighbors whom the soldiers under pressure of their hunger maltreat.

3. ON their side, it is the duty of those who stay out of war to do nothing that may add strength to the champion of a bad cause, or may hinder the movements of one who is fighting a lawful battle, in accordance with what we said above.[13] In case of doubt, they should treat both sides impartially, permitting passage through their territory, furnishing supplies to the legions, refusing to assist

places under siege. In Thucydides,[14] the Corcyreans declare it is the Athenians' duty, if they propose to be neutral, either to forbid the Corinthians to raise troops on Attic soil or else to allow the Corcyreans to do the same. . . . The praetor Lucius Aemilius reproached the people of Teos [15] with having aided the enemy's fleet by giving them supplies and promising them wine, and added that unless they did the same for the Roman fleet, he would regard them as enemies. And there is on record a saying of Caesar Augustus: [16] "A state that receives my enemy loses its right of peace."

It will be to the neutrals' advantage also to have treaties with both parties to a war, so that with the good will of both sides they may be permitted to stay out of the battle and perform the common offices of humanity for both. In Livy, we read: [17] "They should desire peace, as befits the friends of both; they should not mix in the war." . . .

XVIII

Conduct of Private Individuals in a Public War.

1. MOST of what we have said thus far applies either to those who have the chief command in a war or who are carrying out public orders. We must see now what is permissible for private individuals in wartime, by the law of nature, by divine law, and by the law of nations.

In the first book of *On Duty* [1] Cicero says that the son of Cato the Censor saw service in the army of the general Pompilius, but that later the legion in which he fought was discharged. The young man, nevertheless, was in love with fighting and stayed on in the army. Cato thereupon wrote to Pompilius that if he wished his son to remain in the army, he should have him renew his allegiance by a second military oath, giving as the reason that since his first oath was now invalidated, he could not lawfully fight the enemy. Cicero adds too the very words of Cato in a letter to his son, in which he warns him to beware of going into battle, because it was unlawful for a man who was not a soldier to fight the enemy. . . .

But they who think this rule was based on the external law of nations are mistaken. For if you are considering that law, it permits anyone to seize enemy goods, as we showed above, and in the same way permits him to kill an enemy, since by that law enemies are counted as nothing. So Cato's words of warning were taken from the Roman code of military discipline, one rule of which, according to Modestinus,[2] was that a man who did not obey orders should be punished with death, even if his action turned out to be successful. And a man who fought the enemy outside the ranks without his commander's orders was considered not to have obeyed orders, as the ordinances of Manlius inform us.[3] And reasonably so, because, if such rash behavior were permitted, posts would be abandoned; and as the lawlessness spread, the whole army, or a part of it, would be involved in battles for which no plans had been made, a thing to be avoided at all costs. Hence Sallust, when describing the Roman discipline, says:[4] "In wartime, punishment is often inflicted on men who have fought the enemy contrary to orders, or who, when summoned to retreat, have been too slow leaving the battlefield." . . . And Plutarch gives the reason[5] why a man discharged from service cannot kill an enemy. He is not bound by military law, by which men who are to fight should be bound. . . .

But if we turn to the law of nature and the inner law, we see that in lawful warfare any man is permitted to do what he believes will benefit the innocent party, within the limits of lawful methods of combat. However, he is not to appropriate captured property for himself, because he has nothing owing to him, unless, possibly, he is imposing some penalty, legitimate by the common law of mankind. Yet how this last right has been restricted by the law of the Gospel we may perceive from our previous discussion of the matter.

Now an order may be either general or special. A general order, for instance, is what the consul used to give during times of rioting at Rome: [6] "Those who wish the republic to be safe, follow me." So individual subjects are sometimes granted the right to kill, when it is a case not of self-protection but of the public welfare.

2. A special order may be given not only to paid soldiery but to men who are in the war at their own expense, to men, furthermore, carrying on a branch of the war at their own expense, such as those who equip and maintain ships at their own cost. It is customary to grant such men in place of pay the right to keep for themselves what they capture, as we have said elsewhere.[7] But how far this practice may be carried without violating inner justice and the law of love is rightfully a question.

Justice has regard both for the enemy and for a state with which an agreement has been made. We have said already that to ensure our own security we may strip the enemy of all his possessions that can be useful in war, but that this is done under obligation to return them. Actual ownership comes only as compensation to a state fighting a lawful war, for either a debt owed to it at the beginning of the war or some later misdeed. The property may belong either to the enemy state or to private individuals, even to persons harmless in themselves. The property of harmful persons, however, may be seized as punishment and appropriated by the captors. Enemy goods, accordingly, may become the possession of men who are carrying on a branch of the war at their own expense, as long as that has an effect on the enemy, provided only they do not go beyond the limits I have stated, a matter to be decided by impartial judgment.

3. AS far as the relationship of these men with their own state is concerned, it will be legitimate by inner justice, if there is fairness in the arrangement, that is, if their expenses and risks are as great as their chances of plunder. If their expectations of booty are much greater than their costs, they should turn the excess over to their state, for in that case they are like a man who has bought the cast of a fish net at a low price. The value of it is indeed uncertain, but it is easy to get and very promising.

4. BUT even when there is no violation of legal justice, strictly speaking, there may be sinning against the duty which consists of loving other men, particularly as the law of Christ commands us, if, for instance, it appears that such plundering by private individuals damages chiefly not the enemy as a whole, nor the king, nor those personally guilty, but innocent people; and to such an extent as to plunge them into the depths of catastrophe, into which it would be heartless to thrust even our personal debtors. And if, in addition, such plundering has no notable effect on bringing the war to an end or on cutting down the enemy's public strength, then certainly the gain derived from pure wretchedness at the time should be considered unworthy of a good man, especially of a Christian.

5. IT happens sometimes that a private war grows out of an incident in a public war, as when, for example, a man falls among enemies and is in danger of losing his life or his property, in which case the rules may be followed which we have given already when speaking of allowable methods of self-defense.[8] Public authority often comes to the support of private interest, as when a man who has suffered a serious damage from the enemy obtains the right to reimburse himself from enemy property. But such a right should be defined in accordance with the principles we laid down above [9] with regard to the taking of surety.

6. BUT if a soldier or any other person, even in a lawful war, without orders sets fire to buildings belonging to the enemy, lays waste his land, or causes other damages of that sort, when no necessity

or lawful cause warrants his doing it, he is bound to make good the
harm done, as the theologians rightly maintain. But I add properly
what they omit, which is, "when no lawful cause warrants it." For
if there is such a cause, the man will perhaps be called to account
by his own state, whose laws he has broken, but will not be accountable to the enemy to whom he has done no injustice. . . .

XIX

Good Faith between Enemies.

1. WHAT and how much is permissible in war we have said may be
considered either absolutely or as dependent on some previous
promise. We have finished our discussion of the first topic and have
still left the second, which involves the question of good faith between enemies. . . . Xenophon, in his speech on Agesilaus, says: [1]
"So great and so excellent a thing it is in all men, but particularly
in generals, to be and to be known as respecters of piety and good
faith." . . .

Public good faith, as the elder Quintilian tells us,[2] is what makes
truces between armed adversaries and upholds the rights of states
which have surrendered. In another place, he says: "Good faith is
the strongest bond in human society; the praise of religion is given
to good faith between enemies." Thus too Ambrose:[3] "Plainly
then good faith and justice are to be maintained even in war." And

Augustine: [4] "Faith must be kept even when promised to an enemy with whom one is at war."

Certainly those who are enemies do not cease to be men. And all men who have arrived at the use of reason are capable of acquiring rights from a promise. . . . On this connection between reason and the spoken word is based the binding force of a promise of which we are speaking. Nor because many writers, as we said earlier, think it permissible, or not wrong, to lie to an enemy, should we suppose that by the same reasoning we can disregard truth in making a promise. For the obligation to tell the truth comes from a reason that existed before the war and may, to some extent, possibly, be removed by war, but the promise itself establishes a new right. . . . Pausanias, speaking to the Arcadians, says of Philip of Macedon: [5] "No one could rightfully call him a good general, who made a habit of disregarding his oath and breaking his pledge on every occasion, so that no man's good faith was more worthless than his." . . . In Homer, the Trojans, beset by their consciences, accuse themselves: [6]

> "And now our holy bonds and our sworn faith
> We break and fight for what no more is good."

2. ALREADY we have declared [7] that the dictum of Cicero,[8] "We should have no association with tyrants, but maintain rather a complete separation," is not to be accepted. He says also: "A pirate is not counted in the number of public enemies; with him no faith need be kept nor mutual oath." . . . From this source came the error of Michael of Ephesus, who, in his commentary on the fifth book of the *Nicomachean Ethics*, said [9] that an assault on the wife of a tyrant was not an act of adultery. By a similar error some Jewish teachers have spoken in the same way of foreigners, whose marriages they consider null.

Yet Gnaeus Pompey won a large part of his war with the pirates by treaties in which he promised them their lives and abodes where they might live without brigandage. And tyrants, after receiving assurance of immunity, have sometimes given back liberty. In the third book of his *Civil War*, Caesar writes [10] that the Roman commanders had reached an agreement with the brigands and fugitives in the Pyrenees mountains. Who will say that once they had made a compact, no obligation would exist to fulfill it?

Such agreements indeed do not have that special binding character on both sides which the law of nations has conferred on treaties between enemies in formal and total war. But because the parties' are men, their agreements have the binding character of the law of nature, . . . whence it follows that they must be kept. So Diodorus informs us [11] that Lucullus kept his pledge to Apollonius, the leader of the fugitive slaves. . . .

3. LET us see then whether some more reasonable view—not the one suggested by Cicero—may be proposed instead. The first argument for his view is that atrocious criminals, who are not members of any state, may, if we consult the law of nature, be punished by anyone, as we have elsewhere explained.[12] And men who may be punished by loss of life may also be deprived of their property and rights; as the same Cicero says correctly: [13] "It is not against nature to strip of his possessions, if you can, a person whom it is right to kill." Now among a man's rights is the right he derives from a promise. Consequently this right too may be taken from him as a punishment.

I reply that this argument will hold if we have not been dealing with the man as a malefactor; but if we have so dealt with him, we must consider such action as at the same time a remission of his punishment, as far as that phase of it is concerned. For always, as we have said elsewhere, we should accept an interpretation which prevents an act from becoming futile.

Nabis, in Livy,[14] made a pat answer when Quintius Flaminius accused him of being a tyrant: "As for the name you apply to me, I can reply that whatever I am, I am the same as I was when you yourself, Titus Quintius, made an alliance with me." . . .

4. NEXT, one might argue, as we said before,[15] that a person who

by terrifying another person has obtained a promise from him is bound to release the promiser, because he has harmed him by an unlawful act, that is, by an act which violates both the nature of human freedom and the nature of a deed which ought to be free.

We admit that this reasoning sometimes applies; but it does not apply to all promises made to brigands. For in order that the person to whom a promise has been made should be bound to release the promiser, he must have extorted that promise by unlawful fear. Accordingly, a man who promises payment to ransom a friend from imprisonment will be under obligation to pay, since he was not terrorized if he came of his own accord to make the bargain.

5. FURTHERMORE, even one who was compelled by unlawful terrorizing to make a promise may be bound to keep it, if with his promises was coupled the sanction of an oath. For by an oath, as we have noted elsewhere, a man is bound not merely to another man but to God as well; and as regards him the fear is no ground for an exception. . . . Yet that which we said before we must repeat again, that a man who breaks a pledge given to a brigand, either with or without an oath, will not on that account be liable to punishment from other nations, since because of their hatred for brigands the nations have agreed to overlook wrongs done to them.

6. WHAT are we to say when it comes to wars of subjects against kings and other sovereign powers? In these cases, even if the subjects' reasons for war are not in themselves unlawful, still their right to employ force is lacking, as we have shown elsewhere.[16] And at times the grounds are so far from being lawful or else the rebellion itself is so wicked that it may be severely punished. However, if there have been dealings with the deserters or the rebels as such, punishment cannot be inflicted on them contrary to a promise, as we have just said.

The scrupulous ancients thought that faith should be kept even with slaves. They believed that the Spartans had incurred the wrath of the gods for putting the Taenarians, their slaves, to death, contrary to their agreements. And Diodorus Siculus mentions the fact [17] that a pledge made to slaves at the shrine of the Palici had never been broken by any master. . . .

7. BUT at this point a special difficulty, besides those already mentioned, is created by the right of making laws and the right of eminent domain over the property of subjects, which belongs to the state and in its name is exercised by the wielder of supreme power. For if that right covers all the property of subjects, does it not cover too any right based on a promise in wartime? If we concede that it does, then apparently all agreements made then will be invalid; hence there will be no hope of putting an end to a war except by a victory.

Yet, on the other hand, we must observe that under any government which is civil but not autocratic, even a monarchy, the right of eminent domain is not exercised indiscriminately, but only so far as it serves the general good. And usually it is for the general good that such agreements be kept. Pertinent here is what we said earlier on the subject of preserving existing conditions. When the situation requires the use of this right of domain, some compensation should be arranged, as we shall explain later.

8. FURTHER, compacts may be sanctioned by an oath of not only the king or the senate but of the state itself. In this way Lycurgus had the Spartans swear to keep his laws, and Solon had the Athenians do the same; and in order that through the changes in personalities the oath might not become obsolete, it was to be repeated every year. If such a ceremony is repeated it will be absolutely impossible to disregard the promise, even in the interest of the public welfare, since a state can grant away its own advantage and the wording be so explicit as to allow no exception to it. Valerius Maximus says to Athens: [18] "Read the law which keeps you bound by oath." . . .

The tribunes were protected by the public religious spirit of the people of Rome, because an oath had been sworn which could not be broken by those who had taken it without violence to this spirit. . . . So good men disapproved the act of Tiberius Gracchus, when he deprived Octavius of his office as tribune, though he said that the tribune's power had its sanctity from the people, and was not to injure the people. Hence, as we said, both the state and the king can be bound by an oath, even in their dealings with subjects.

9. A valid promise may be made to a third party who has not inspired fear. Into the question of what or how great may be his interest in the matter we shall not inquire, for those are subtle details of Roman law. But by nature it is to every man's interests to show consideration to other men. Accordingly, we read [19] that by the peace Philip made with the Romans he was deprived of the right of savagely punishing the Macedonians who had deserted him in the war.

10. ALSO, as we have shown elsewhere,[20] states of mixed type sometimes exist, which by an agreement, may be passing from one pure type to another, or to another mixed type. Then those who were subjects may be beginning to acquire sovereign authority, or, at least a part of it, along with the liberty to defend that part by force.

11. A formal war, that is, a public war, declared as such by both sides, has, besides its other special features of external law, this feature as well, that promises made in the course of such a war or for the purpose of ending it are so completely valid that even though made under influence of fear unlawfully inspired, they cannot be nullified without the consent of the one to whom they were made. For just as many other things, even though wrong in some respects, are treated as lawful by the law of nations, so too is the fear which in such times of war is inspired by either side.

If this had not been the law, neither limit nor end could have been set to these wars, which are exceedingly frequent; and that a limit should be set is a matter of concern to the whole human race. This then may be taken to be the law of war which Cicero says [21] should be kept with an enemy. Elsewhere he says [22] that an enemy retains some rights in wartime, which means not only natural rights but some of those derived from the consent of nations.

Yet it does not follow that a person who in an unlawful war has extorted a promise can without violation of conscience or the duty of a good man keep what he has won by it, or compel the other party to abide by the agreement, whether confirmed by an oath or not. For inwardly and by its very nature the transaction remains unlawful, nor can the inner unlawfulness of it be removed except by a fresh and truly free consent to it.

12. BUT what I have said, as to a fear which is inspired by formal war being considered lawful, must be understood of a kind of fear permitted by the law of nations. For if a promise has been extorted under terror of rape or by means of some other form of unscrupulous intimidation, it will be more correct to consider the case as coming under the law of nature, since the law of nations does not extend its authority to permit that kind of fear.

13. EARLIER, in our general discussion, we said [23] that faith should be kept, even with the faithless. Ambrose too teaches the same doctrine,[24] that is, that it should unquestionably be kept, even with perfidious enemies such as the Carthaginians, with whom the Romans religiously kept faith. . . . Appian, writing of the treaty-breaking Lusitanians,[25] whom Sergius Galba deceived by a new compact and then slaughtered, says: "By punishing treachery with treachery, contrary to Roman standards of honor, he was imitating the barbarians." . . .

14. AT the same time, we must recognize that under two circumstances a man may be guiltless of perfidy and yet may not do what he has promised; namely, some condition may not be fulfilled, or some compensation may be legal. The fact of non-fulfillment of a condition does not really release the promiser, but the result is that there is no obligation, since the bargain was made subject to a proviso.

To this rule we should refer a case when one party has not performed what on his side he was bound to perform. For the separate articles of one and the same contract are considered as depending on each other as if they were conditions; as if one of them said,

wronged by a neighbor who was his pledged ally, "would not break his sworn promise, saying that so holy to him was his oath that he would not injure the other man, even after he had done him a wrong."

Almost every question that is apt to arise regarding faith pledged to enemies can be answered by following the rules stated above [34] in our discussion of the force of promises of all sorts and of special oaths, treaties, and agreements, as well as of the rights and obligations of kings and of interpretations of ambiguous statements. In order to make clearer, however, the application of the said rules, and to take up whatever else is a matter of dispute, I shall go on now to say something on the commoner and best known of certain special questions.

XX

Public Good Faith in the Ending of a War; in Particular, Treaties of Peace, Decisions by Lot and by Single Combat, Arbitration, Surrender, Hostages and Pledges.

1. AGREEMENTS between enemies consist of promises, either expressed or tacit. A promise expressed is either public or private. A public promise is made either by the sovereign rulers or by their

subordinates. The promise of a sovereign ruler either puts an end to the war or is in force for the duration.

In agreements that put an end to a war there are both principal and accessory provisions. The principal provisions are those which put a stop to the war, either by their own action, as treaties do, or by referring the decision to something else, such as to a lot to be drawn, to the outcome of a battle, to the verdict of an arbitrator. The first of these three is a matter of pure chance, the last two combine chance with strength of mind or of body, or judicial ability.

2. THE right to propose agreements which will end a war belongs to those whose war it is, for each is manager of his own affairs. Hence it follows that in a war which is public on both sides the right belongs to those who possess the right of exercising supreme authority. In a true monarchy, then, it belongs to the king, provided the king's own right is not restricted.

3. A king who is of an age which does not yet possess maturity of judgment (an age defined by law in some kingdoms, in others left to be determined by credible estimates), or who is feebleminded, cannot make a peace. The same is true of a captive king, provided his royal authority is derived from the consent of his people. For no one can believe that a people would confer authority on such terms that it could be wielded by a man who was not free. So, in such a case not the whole right to the authority but the exercise and as it were the guardianship of it devolve on the people, or on the one to whom the people commit it. However, if a king, even in captivity, pledges any part of his own private property, that pledge is valid, after the model of the private agreements we shall discuss later.

But can a king who is in exile make peace? Yes, if it is clear that he is not living under restraint. Otherwise his lot will differ little from that of a captive, for there are captives loosely guarded too. Regulus refused to state his views in the Senate,[1] saying that as long as he was bound by an oath to the enemy, he was not a senator.

4. IN governments of the nobles or of the people the right of making peace belongs to the majority—to the majority of the council of state in the aristocracy, to the majority of the citizens who by custom have the right to vote in the democracy. This is in accord with what we said earlier.[2] The treaties so made will be binding even on those who voted against them. Says Livy: [3] "When once the decision is announced, everyone, even those who previously opposed it, must defend the treaty as good and advantageous." . . . A peace is advantageous to those on whom it is binding, if they wish it to be.

5. LET us now consider the subject matter of a treaty. Kings, such as most of them are now, who hold their realm not as patrimony but, so to speak, in usufruct, have not the power to alienate by a peace treaty either the whole or a part of their sovereignty. Indeed, even before they receive their kingship, while the people is still their superior, any such act in the future can be rendered wholly void by a public statute which forbids their making such a pledge in their own interest. And it is reasonable to suppose that would be the people's will, for otherwise, if the act of a treaty-maker were valid for his own interest, the property of subjects might be taken for a debt of the king, and so the principle of not alienating his kingdom would be ineffective.

In order then to transfer the sovereignty as a whole and validly, it is necessary to have the consent of the entire people, which can be given by representatives of the sections, which they call the Estates. In order that any part of the sovereignty may be alienated validly, there must be two consents, the consent of the whole body, and, in particular, the consent of the part in question, which cannot be rent against its will away from the body to which it has belonged. In case, however, of extreme or in other ways inevitable necessity, a part may by itself transfer to other hands the sovereignty over itself without the consent of all the people, because it reserved that power, we may believe, when the civil society was formed.

But in kingdoms held as patrimonies there is nothing to prevent a king from alienating his kingdom. It may be that such a king is unable to alienate a part of his realm, if, for example, he received it as his property on condition that he would not divide it. And the possessions which are called royal possessions may likewise be included in the king's patrimony in either of two ways, either separately, or as an indivisible part of the kingdom. If in the latter way, they may be transferred, though only together with the kingdom; if in the former way, they may be transferred by themselves. But kings who do not hold their kingdoms as patrimony seem scarcely to have granted them the right of alienating the royal possessions, unless such a right appears clearly established in their earlier law or in a custom which has never been reversed.

6. TO what extent the people, and also the king's successors, are bound by his promise, we have explained elsewhere;[4] namely, as far as the power to bind them is included in his sovereign authority. And that power is neither to be indefinitely extended nor restricted within too narrow limits but understood as valid as far as it is based on reasonable grounds. Obviously the case will be different if the king is at the same time lord over his subjects and has received an authority less political than paternal, as the kings have who have reduced to slavery a people they have conquered in war. . . . For here a right added to the royal right makes possible measures that otherwise, by the royal right alone, could not be taken.

7. THE following question too is often debated. How far can those kings who have no other right than the royal right over their subjects' property for the sake of peace make decisions affecting the property of individuals? We have said already that the property of subjects under the law of eminent domain belongs to the state, so that the state, or the person who represents the state, can make use of that property, can even destroy or alienate it, not merely in a case of extreme necessity, which gives private individuals too some right over another man's possessions, but whenever it is to the public advantage. For we must suppose that those who united

to form a body politic were willing to give up their individual possessions for the public good.

We must add, however, that when this happens, the state is bound to make good out of the public funds the damage to those who have lost what was theirs, and to that fund the persons who suffered the loss will contribute, if need be. Nor will the state be relieved of this obligation, even if at the time, it is not perhaps equal to making the payment in full; but whenever there is enough, the debt will assert itself, as if it had been only dormant for a while.

8. NOR do I accept without discrimination the view of Fernando Vasquez [5] that the state is not obliged to take cognizance of damage inflicted by war, on the ground that the law of war permits such damages. For that law of war is referring to other nations, as we explained elsewhere; [6] in part also to enemies, in their relations to one another. But it does not refer to citizens and their relations with each other, for they are associates together and it is fair that they share the common losses which befall them because of their association. The civil law, however, may expressly provide that no action shall lie against the state because of property lost in war, so as to make each citizen more determined to defend his own. . . .

[9–10. Foreigners accept the right of kings to dispose of their subjects' property as bestowed on them by the law of nations.]

11. AS for the interpretation of peace treaties we must state again what we remarked above,[7] that the more favorable a provision is, the more broadly we should construe it, and the less favorable it is, the more narrowly we should take it. If we consider the law of nature, the most favorable principle seems to be that each should obtain what belongs to him. . . . Hence it appears that ambiguous provisions should be interpreted to the end that the party who fought a lawful war should receive what he fought for and be recompensed for his losses and expenses, but should not be awarded anything on the score of punishment, for that way creates more hatred.

Since men seldom arrive at peace by a confession of wrongdoing, treaties should be interpreted in such a way as to put both parties, as far as possible, on a level with regard to the lawfulness of the war. And this is usually done by one of two methods. Either the ownership of the property which was disturbed by the war is settled on terms of the previous right to it; . . . or else things are left as they actually are; which the Greeks call "keeping what they have."

12. OF these two methods, the presumption, in a case of doubt, should be in favor of the second, because it is the easier and introduces no change. Hence the statement of Tryphonius [8] that when peace comes, the right of postliminy should be allowed to those captives only who were specified in the treaty. . . . Accordingly, deserters are not to be given up, unless it is so agreed. For we receive deserters by the law of war; that is, we are allowed by the law of war to take in and enroll in our forces a man who changes sides. Other property under such a treaty remains in the hands of the possessors.

The word 'possessor' is here understood not in the civil law sense, but in that of natural law, for in wartime actual possession is sufficient and nothing else matters. Land, we have said, is possessed if it has been enclosed by fortifications; temporary occupation, as for a camp, does not count in this instance. Demosthenes, in his speech in defense of Ctesiphon,[9] says that Philip made haste to seize all the places he could, knowing that, as matters were, when the business of peacemaking was over, he would keep what he held. Immaterial things are not possessed except through the objects to which they are attached, as servile dues are to lands; or through the persons to whom they belong, provided they do not have to be employed on enemy soil.

13. AS for the first method of peacemaking, by which possessions disturbed by the war are restored as they were, we must note that the restoration is to their last possessor before the war, with the understanding, however, that the individuals who are thus dis-

possessed may bring suit in court by a possessory or proprietary action.

14. BUT if a free people has voluntarily submitted to one of the belligerents, the right of recovery will not be extended to it, since that is allowed only for things done under coercion or fear, or else through trickery, which is permissible only against an enemy. So when peace was made between the Greeks, the Thebans kept Plataea, saying [10] that "they had obtained that place not by force, not by treachery, but by the free will of the people to whom it belonged." . . .

15. IF no different agreement has been made, every peace treaty should be taken as providing that there should be no legal action on the score of damages caused by the war. This is to be understood as well of damages inflicted on private persons, for those too are the results of the war. In case of doubt, it may be assumed that the belligerents intended to make an agreement by which neither side would be labeled as guilty of wrongdoing.

16. BUT we should not suppose that debts which were originally owed to individuals at the time the war started have been canceled. For cancellation of debts is not obtained by the law of war; simply, the collection of them is prevented. So when the obstruction is removed, they are as valid as before. . . .

17. THE same is not so true of the right to impose penalties. For that right, as far as it is a matter between kings or peoples, ought to be relinquished, for fear that the peace may not be peaceful enough, if it leaves standing the old reasons for war. Accordingly, even wrongs not previously known about will come under the general rule of being left unpunished, as they did in the case of the Roman merchants who the Romans did not know had been drowned by the Carthaginians, as Appian tells us.[11] "The best reconciliations," says Dionysius of Halicarnassus,[12] "are those which wipe out anger and the memory of injuries." "Peacetime," says Isocrates in his *Plataic Oration*,[13] "is not the time to rehearse old wrongs."

18. THERE is not so much reason for private individuals to give up their right to demand punishment, for such a right can be enforced by the courts without a war. However, the right to punish is not ours so fully as the right to compensation for an unfairness, and there is always something hateful about a punishment, so that a slight stretching of our words will suffice to make them mean that it too is to be given up.

19. WHAT we have said to the effect that a right which existed before the war should not lightly be considered forfeit, should be steadfastly maintained in a case of private right, but in a case of the rights of kings or of peoples it is simpler to suppose that they are waived to some extent, provided there are words or plausible conjectures to support such a view. Especially is this so if the right in question was never clear, but had been a matter of controversy. It is merciful to hold it has lapsed and so removed the seeds of war. The same Dionysius of Halicarnassus whom I have just cited says: [14] "We ought to give less thought to strengthening our present friendships and take more steps to keep us from being involved again in war. For we have met not to postpone our evils but to make an end of them." . . .

20. EVERYONE knows that property captured after the signing of peace treaties must be returned, because the law of war is no longer in force.

21. AS to the treaties which provide for the returning of objects captured in wartime, in the first place, the articles which are binding on both sides should be interpreted more broadly than those which are one-sided. Secondly, those which deal with human beings should be construed more favorably than those which deal with things; those which deal with land should be more favorably interpreted than those which deal with movable goods; and those which deal with public property more favorably than those which deal with private. And as between the articles dealing with private property, those which order the return of property held by inherited title should count for more than those which deal with property

held by a burdensome title, such as one acquired by purchase or as a dowry.

22. A person to whom property is granted by a peace treaty has the revenue from it conferred on him from the date of the grant, but not from before it. This rule Caesar Augustus correctly maintained against Sextus Pompey, who, when granted the Peloponnesus, at the same time claimed the tribute too which was owing for years past.

23. THE names of regions should be taken from the usage of the present time, not so much the vulgar usage as that of the well-educated. For matters of that sort are ordinarily handled by the well-educated.

24. THE following rules are often applied. Whenever reference is made to a previous or an ancient treaty, the qualifications or conditions stipulated in the earlier treaty are to be regarded as repeated. And a party who was willing to perform an act should be considered to be performing it, if he is hindered from doing so only by the other party to the dispute.

25. BUT the statement of some authors, that delay for a short time is excusable, is not true, unless an unforeseen necessity formed the impediment. The fact that some of the canons sanction such an excuse is not to be wondered at, since their duty is to urge Christians to a course consistent with mutual charity. But in this discussion of the interpretation of treaties we are not now inquiring which is the better course, nor what religion and a sense of reverence demand of each of us, but how much can be enforced, a matter which concerns wholly the law we call external.

26. IN a case of ambiguous wording, the interpretation should be adverse to the person who dictated the provisions, because he commonly belongs to the more powerful party. . . . In the same way, interpretations are made against a seller. For the man has himself to blame for not expressing himself more clearly. The other party also has the right to construe a thing capable of several meanings in the sense more advantageous to himself. . . .

27. EVERY day there are debates as to when a treaty of peace
should be considered broken. . . . A peace treaty is broken in
three ways, by an act contrary to what is in every peace treaty, by
one contrary to the plain terms of this treaty, or by one contrary to
what should be understood from the nature of every peace treaty.

28. AN act contrary to what is in every peace treaty is committed
when one party makes a military attack on the other, of course
without fresh provocation. If such provocation is credibly alleged,
it is better to suppose that it was not a treacherous offense than
that it was. We hardly need the warning of Thucydides: [15] "The
breakers of a peace are not those who resist violence with violence,
but those who first use violence." Having noted this point, we
should see by whom and on whom the armed attack is made which
breaks a treaty of peace.

29. THERE are some, I see, who hold that if any one of those who
were allies commit such an offense, the treaty is broken for all. And
I do not deny that it is possible to make an agreement, not exactly
that one nation should be liable to punishment for another's deed,
but that the treaty should not at first be regarded as fully in force
but conditional, depending partly on power [to enforce it] and
partly on chance. But unless it is unmistakably clear that the treaty
was phrased in such terms, we should not believe it was, for that is
irregular, and not in accord with the general desire of those who
make a peace. Accordingly, it is the party who attacked, provided
the others did not assist him, who is responsible for breaking the
treaty, and it is lawful to make war on him but not on the rest. . . .

30. IF the subjects commit an act of armed violence without
orders from their state, it will be necessary to discover whether the
act of private individuals can be called officially approved. From
what we said earlier,[16] it may readily be seen that three things are
needed to constitute such approval—knowledge of the acts, power
to punish them, and negligence to do so. Knowledge is proved by
the fact that the acts were open or generally known. Power is assumed, unless the lack of it is evident. Negligence is shown when

the time has passed which is usually taken in any state for the punishment of crimes. Such negligence is equivalent to a command. . . .

31. THE question is often asked whether this rule holds, if the subjects of a ruler are not taking up arms on their own account but are serving under other rulers, who are at war. . . . It is correct to say that such service should not be permitted, unless there are plausible arguments in favor of a different course. This does happen now sometimes, following the ancient example of the Aetolians, who thought it their right "to take plunder from a plunderer." [17] The force of the custom with them, says Polybius,[18] was so strong that "even when they were not themselves at war, but others were, who were friends or allies of theirs, the Aetolians nonetheless thought it right to fight on both sides, without public permission, and to take plunder from both." . . .

32. AGAIN, a peace treaty should be considered broken if an armed attack is made not on the entire body of a state but on its subjects, that is, without fresh provocation. For a peace is made in order that all subjects should be safe, since a peace is an act of the state to protect the whole and to protect the parts. In case of fresh provocation, indeed, a peace treaty permits one to defend oneself and one's property. For it is natural, as Cassius says,[19] to resist arms with arms; so it is not easily to be believed that this right has been renounced between equals. But the treaty does not permit punishing or recovering lost property by force, except after judicial proceedings have been refused. These latter grievances can stand delay, and self-defense cannot.

If, however, the vicious behavior of some subjects is so persistent and so contrary to the law of nature that we are compelled to believe they are acting quite without their rulers' approval, and we cannot call for a judgment against them, since they are behaving like pirates, it will be permissible both to recover property and exact punishment from them, as if they had been surrendered to us. But on their account to attack innocent persons is certainly a breach of the peace.

33. AN armed attack on our allies is also a breach of the peace, but only if those allies are attacked who are included in the treaty. . . . If the allies themselves did not agree to the treaty, but others did it for them, the same rule will hold, after it is thoroughly established that those allies considered they had ratified the treaty. As long as it is still uncertain whether they intended to ratify it, they are in the position of enemies. The case of other allies, also of relatives and kindred, who are neither our subjects nor named in the peace treaty, is different, and violence used on them cannot be taken as a breach of the treaty. Yet it does not follow, as we said above, that a war cannot be started on that score, but it will be a war for a new reason.

34. A peace treaty is also broken, as we said, by doing something contrary to the terms of the treaty. Under 'doing something' is included likewise a failure to do what one was bound to do, or at the time one should have done it.

35. I shall not admit here any distinction between the terms of a treaty, as to which are more important and which less. Everything contained in a treaty should seem important enough to be kept. Goodness, however, especially Christian goodness, will readily overlook minor violations, particularly when followed by penitence. . . . But in order to safeguard the peace more effectively, it will be wise to add to the less important provisions a statement that any violation of them will not break the peace; or else, that arbitration shall be tried before it is admissible to resort to arms. . . .

36. THIS, I am sure, is the intention when a special penalty is provided for breach of the treaty. Not that I do not know that a treaty may be drawn so as to leave a choice to the injured party as to whether he prefers to demand the penalty or to withdraw from the compact, but the nature of the business must be what I have said. This certainly is plain; we have said it before, and the authority of history proves it, that a treaty of peace made without penal-

ties is not broken by the party who does not abide by its terms
when the other has failed to do so; for he was bound only conditionally.

37. BUT if some necessity keeps one party from carrying out his
promise—if, for instance, an object has been destroyed or stolen,
or an act by some accident has been rendered impossible—the
treaty will not be considered broken, since, as we said, a treaty does
not usually depend on a chance situation. The other party will
choose whether he prefers to wait, if there is some hope that the
promise can be carried out later, or to accept an estimated equivalent, or to be released from the mutual engagements connected
with that particular provision of the treaty or their equivalent.

38. CERTAINLY, even after an agreement has been broken, it is
honorable for the innocent party to keep the peace, as Scipio did
after the Carthaginians had committed many acts of perfidy, because no man frees himself from an obligation by violating it. And
if a provision has been added to the effect that the treaty shall be
considered broken by such acts of violation, it should be taken as
added purely for the convenience of the innocent party, to avail
himself of if he chooses.

39. LASTLY, we said that a peace treaty may be broken by an act
incompatible with the special nature of a treaty.

40. HENCE acts which are infractions of friendship break a treaty
which was drawn up under the law of friendship, since whatever
the simple obligation of friendship demands of other men should
by the law governing this treaty be performed by these men as
well. To this kind of treaty, though not at all to every other kind,
. . . I think applies much that the legal authorities are accustomed
to say on the subject of offenses other than those of armed violence,
such as insults. . . . But in such cases too we should discount as
far as possible any intentional malice in the act.

A wrong done to another person, however close a relation, or to
a subject, is not to be regarded as done to the person with whom
the treaty was signed, unless it was done openly as an affront to

him. This principle of natural justice was observed by the laws of Rome in cases where slaves had been cruelly hurt. An act of adultery too, or of rape, is to be ascribed to the passion of lust, rather than to a feeling of enmity. . . . But threats which are really vicious, when there has been no new provocation, are violations of friendship. Under these I shall include the building of fortresses on frontiers, not for defense but for the doing of mischief, and an unusual levying of troops, if it appears from reliable indications that they are being raised against no one but the person with whom the treaty was made.

41. IT is no offense against friendship to admit to our country individual subjects who wish to migrate from one realm to another, since liberty to move about is not only natural but advantageous, as we have said elsewhere.[20] In the same class I put the granting of asylum to exiles, for over its exiles, as we then said, citing Euripides, a state has no rights. Perseus, in Livy, says reasonably: [21] "What comes of sending a man into exile, if there is never to be a place for an exile?" . . .

Obviously, as we said earlier,[22] it is not permissible to admit towns or large masses of people, who form an integral part of a state, any more than it is to receive persons who by oath or otherwise owe service or servitude in another state. As to those who are slaves by the fortunes of war, the law of nations among some people has made the same ruling, as we remarked above. With regard to the surrender of persons who were not sentenced to exile but are fugitives from just punishment we have spoken elsewhere.[23]

42. THE outcome of a war cannot always legitimately be made dependent on a chance drawing of lots, but only when the matter at stake is one absolutely at our disposal. For a state is under too heavy obligation to protect the lives, chastity, and other rights of its subjects, and a king to protect the welfare of the state, for them to be able to disregard those considerations which most naturally have to do with their own and others' safety. Nevertheless, if by an accurate estimate, a people assaulted in an unlawful war is so far

the inferior in strength that it has no hope of resisting, it may seem that it could propose a drawing of lots, in order to escape a sure peril through an uncertain one. For that is the lesser of the two evils.

43. THERE follows the much-disputed question of combats, to be fought by a fixed number for the purpose of ending a war, between, for instance, one man for each side, as between Aeneas and Turnus, Menelaus and Paris; between two for each side, as between the Aetolians and the Eleans; between three for each side, as between the Roman Horatii and the Alban Curatii; between thirty for each side, as between the Spartans and the Argives.

If we consider only the law of nations, undoubtedly, according to it, such combats are legitimate, for that law permits the killing of enemies indiscriminately. And if the view of the ancient Greeks, Romans, and other nations was correct, that every man has a supreme right of mastery over his own life, then inner justice too would countenance these combats. But as we have already said more than once,[24] this view is contrary to right reason and to the commandments of God. . . . We shall add now that a man who holds so cheaply the life granted him by God as a great gift sins both against himself and against God. If the object at stake, such as the safety of many innocent persons, is worth a war, it should be striven for with all available strength. To resort to set combat as proof of a good cause, or as an instrument of divine judgment, is senseless and not really reverent.

There is one situation which can make such a combat lawful and right, and that is when without it the prospects are all that the champion of an unlawful cause will be victorious, with heavy slaughter of innocent people. No man then should be blamed who chooses to fight by a method that offers him the most likely hope of victory. It is true too that some wrong deeds are rightly considered by other persons not as good but as permissible, in order to prevent more serious evils which otherwise could not be avoided. Thus, in many places, unscrupulous usurers and prostitutes are tolerated. So, as we said earlier,[25] when it is a matter of preventing a war, if two men who are rivals for a kingdom are prepared to fight it out between them, the people may allow it as a way of preventing a greater calamity which otherwise threatens them. The same may be said when it is a matter of ending a war. . . .

45. FREQUENTLY in such combats it is a question which side should be considered the victor. Only those can be regarded as vanquished who have either every one fallen or taken to flight. Thus in Livy,[26] retirement to one's own territory or cities is a sign of defeat. . . . The acts which in the said passages, and again in Livy [27] you now and again find mentioned as signs of victory—the gathering of spoils, the giving up of corpses for burial, the challenging to a second battle—by themselves are proof of nothing, except insofar as together with other indications they go to show that the enemy is in flight. Certainly, in case of doubt, the one who retreated is likely to be supposed to have fled. But when there are no sure evidences of victory, the situation stands where it did before the combat, and the parties must resort either to war or to new agreements.

46. ARBITRATIONS, Proculus tells us,[28] are of two sorts. One sort is the kind we are bound to obey, whether fair or unfair. This holds, he says, when men go to an arbitrator under a mutual agreement to accept arbitration. The other is the kind we may use when a matter is referred to the judgment of a good man. . . . It is true that an arbitrator may be called upon in either of two capacities, as a mere reconciler, as we read the Athenians were between the Rhodians and Demetrius, or as one whose dictum must be absolutely obeyed. The latter is the kind we are discussing here, and of whom we had something to say earlier [29] when speaking of methods of preventing war.

But although civil law may provide for such arbitrators, whose decision both sides promise to accept, in some places it has provided that an appeal may be made from them and a complaint of injustice entered. No similar arrangement can be made for arbitration between kings and between peoples. For in this case there is no superior power that can either make fast or loosen the fetters of their promises. Accordingly, the arbitrators' verdict, whether fair or unfair, would have to stand without question. . . .

47. IN considering the duty of an arbitrator, one must ask whether he was chosen in place of a legal judge, or with somewhat broader power. . . . Aristotle says [30] that a fair-minded and good-tempered man "prefers to go to an arbitrator rather than to court," giving as his reason, "for an arbitrator looks out for what is fair, a judge for the law. In fact, the arbitrator was procured for the purpose that equity should prevail."

In this passage 'equity' does not really mean, as it does elsewhere, that side of justice according to which the general drift of a law in the mind of its author is narrowly interpreted; for a judge is commissioned to see to that. But it includes everything which it is more right to do than not to do, even outside the rules of justice, strictly speaking. Arbitrators of this type often decide between private citizens of the same state, and are especially recommended to Christians by the Apostle Paul (I Corinthians, VI). Yet in a case of doubt we should not assume that so wide a power has been granted them, since in doubtful instances we follow the strictest rule. This is especially true when the parties are sovereigns, for they have no common judge, and should therefore be considered to have bound their arbitrator by the same rules as those by which the judge's office is regularly bound.

48. THE following observation, however, should be made. Arbitrators chosen by peoples or by rulers should pronounce a decision on the main issue but not on a question of possession, for decisions regarding rights of possession come under the civil law. By the law of nations the right to possess follows on ownership. So, while a case is under consideration, nothing should be changed, both in order not to create prejudice and because recovery is difficult. . . .

49. THE acceptance of an arbitrator is a different matter when a man allows his own enemy to decide about him, because that is

sheer surrender, making a subject of the man who surrenders, and
conferring supreme power on the one to whom the surrender is
made. . . . Appian tells us [31] that Lucius Cornelius Lentulus at
the end of the Second Punic War gave the following advice as to
the disposition of the Carthaginians: "Let the Carthaginians," he
said, "commit themselves to our discretion, as vanquished peoples
are used to doing, and many have done before now. We shall then
look into their case, and if we grant them some privilege, they will
be grateful to us, but they will not be able to call it a treaty. . . ."

But here we should distinguish too between what the conquered
should have to endure, and what the conqueror may lawfully do
to him; what he may do, and yet fulfill every duty; and what, finally,
it most becomes him to do. The conquered, after his surrender,
may suffer anything, since he is now a subject and, if we go by the
external law of war, is in a position where he may be stripped of
everything, even of his life, his personal liberty, and, still more, of
his property, not only public property but private. . . . Elsewhere
we have quoted the following: [32] "When everything has been surrendered to a superior in arms, it is for the conqueror to judge and
decide what of their property he wishes the defeated to keep and
what they are to lose as punishment." . . . We have shown too
that persons who have surrendered may sometimes lawfully be put
to death.

50. HOWEVER, if the conqueror is to do nothing unlawful, he
must first make sure that he puts no man to death, unless by some
crime on his part he deserves it; also, that he takes nothing from
any man except as a legitimate penalty. And within the limit of
how far considerations of security allow one to go, it is always
honorable to incline toward clemency and generosity. Sometimes,
depending on the circumstances, such conduct is even required by
rule of custom.

We have said elsewhere that wars come to an excellent close
when they end with a pardon. Nicholas of Syracuse says in Diodorus: [33] "They surrendered themselves with their arms, trusting

to the clemency of the victor. Therefore it would be unworthy to deceive them in their expectation of humanity from us." . . . And in Appian [34] Octavius Caesar says to Lucius Antony, who had come to give himself up: "If you had come to make peace by treaty, you would have found in me a conqueror, and one angered by his wrongs. Now that you are submitting yourself, your friends, and your army to our will, you are taking away my anger; you are taking away too the power which in a treaty you would have been compelled to yield me. For now, besides considering what you deserve to suffer, I must consider also a second thing, what it is right for me to do. And I shall think more of the latter." One meets often in Roman histories the phrase 'surrender themselves to the good faith,' or 'surrender to the good faith and clemency.' . . . We must realize that these words mean nothing but complete surrender, and the words 'good faith' in these passages signify only the honor of the conqueror, to which the conquered surrenders himself.

In Polybius [35] and in Livy [36] there is told the famous story of Phaneas, an ambassador for the Aetolians, who in his speech to the consul Manius went so far as to say that "the Aetolians," as Livy puts it, "commit themselves and their possessions to the good faith of the Roman people." When the consul questioned him, he repeated his statement, whereat the consul demanded the surrender to him without delay of certain instigators of the war. Phaneas objected to this, and said: "We are surrendering not to slavery but to your good faith," and added that the consul's demand was not in accord with Greek custom. But the consul replied that he did not care what the Greek custom was, and that by the Roman custom he had full authority over persons who surrendered to his discretion and he gave orders to have the ambassadors put in chains. . . . From his words it is plain with what impunity, with no violation of the law of nations, a man may act to whose good faith a people has entrusted itself. Nevertheless the Roman consul made no use of his power but let the ambassadors go free, and gave the Aetolian council the right to discuss the matter over again. . . . In my opinion it makes no difference whether the party surrendering says it surrenders to the conqueror's wisdom, or to his moderation, or to his mercy, for these are all terms of blandishment. The fact remains that their conqueror is now their judge.

51. THERE are, however, conditional surrenders as well. These either provide protection for individuals, by which their lives or their bodily freedom are guaranteed, or some of their property is exempted from confiscation; or else they do the same for an entire people. Such surrenders may even sometimes set up the mixed kind of government of which we have spoken elsewhere.[37]

52. APPENDAGES to treaties are hostages and pledges. Hostages, we have said, may be given with their own consent or at the command of their ruler. For included in civil sovereignty is the right over the movements as well as over the property of subjects. But the state or its ruler will be bound to pay compensation to the sufferer or to his relatives for the harm he suffers. If there are several persons available and it makes no difference to the state which one goes as a hostage, it should, I think, see to it that the question is settled by lot. . . .

53. WE have said that by the external law of nations a hostage may be put to death, but not by the inner law, unless he is guilty of some offense which deserves it. Hostages too are not made slaves. Indeed, even by the law of nations, they are capable of holding property and bequeathing it to their heirs, although in Roman law there is a provision [38] that their property may be confiscated for the public treasury.

54. WE are sometimes asked whether a hostage may try to escape. It is agreed that he may not, if at first or later he pledged his word that he would not, in order to receive easier treatment. Otherwise, we think it was not the intention of his state to bind its citizen not to escape, but merely to afford the enemy an opportunity to keep him in custody, as it chose. . . .

55. THE obligation to go as hostage, however, is hateful, both be-

unless it clearly has reference not to a state of war, but merely to its operations.

On the other hand, any provision made for peacetime will not apply in time of truce. . . . Thus the scholiast on Thucydides calls a truce [3] "a transitory peace, in travail with war," and Varro [4] "a peace of camps, for a few days." All these are not definitions but descriptions of a sort, and figurative. . . . But Gellius rightly criticizes Marcus Varro [5] for adding to his description, in which he follows Donatus, the words "for a few days." He shows that truces are frequently made for hours. And I shall add that they are made too for years, twenty, thirty, forty, even a hundred years; and there are instances of them in Livy. . . .

It may, however, happen that if the sole and determining purpose of a truce was obviously to bring about a complete cessation of warlike acts, then a provision made for peacetime may become valid during the truce, not by force of its wording but by a sure inference as to its intention, a procedure of which we have spoken elsewhere.[6]

2. . . . A truce then is a respite in wartime, not a peace. So the historians are speaking accurately when they tell us, often, that a peace was refused but a truce was granted.

3. ACCORDINGLY, there is no need after a truce of a fresh declaration of war, for once the temporary obstruction is removed, the state of war by its own right reasserts itself, since it was not dead but sleeping, even as the rights of ownership and paternal authority revive in a man cured of insanity. Yet we read in Livy of declarations of war made by direction of the Fetiales on the termination of a truce. Doubtless the Romans wished by those unnecessary proclamations to show how much they were in love with peace and for what legitimate reasons they were drawn into war. . . .

4. THE duration of a truce is usually fixed either as a continuous length of time, such as a hundred days, or else by specifying the date of its end, such as up to the first of March. In the former instance, the reckoning of time must be made precise to the moment.

This is a natural method, for the counting of time by civil days is derived from the laws and customs of peoples. In the second instance, it is often doubtful whether, when a day, a month, or a year has been set as the boundary of a truce, that day, month, or year should be taken as excluded from or included in the truce.

In natural objects certainly there are two kinds of boundaries, one included in the object, like skin, which is the boundary of the body, and one outside the object, like a river, which is a boundary of land. Boundaries which are fixed at will may be fixed in either of these ways, though it seems more natural to take as boundary something which is a part of the object. "The outermost part of everything is called its boundary," says Aristotle,[7] nor does the common usage of men differ from him. "If a man says that a thing will happen by the day of his death, he is counting the day itself too on which he dies."[8] Spurina had given Caesar warning of a danger that would befall him not later than the Ides of March. When reminded of it on those very Ides, Caesar said that the day had come but was not yet over. Such an interpretation should all the more certainly be adopted when the prolongation of the time has something in its favor, as it has in the case of a truce, which halts the shedding of human blood.

But the day from which some period of time is said to begin is not included in that period, because the force of the preposition 'from' is to separate, not to unite.

5. I shall add further that a truce, or anything else of the same kind, is binding at once on the contracting parties as soon as the contract is signed, but that the subjects on both sides begin to be bound only when the truce has taken the form of a law, for which is required some public proclamation of it. When that has been made, the truce immediately begins to have binding force on the subjects; but if the proclamation was made in one locality only, the force does not extend at the same moment through the whole domain, but only in such course of time as is needed to convey the news to the several localities. Hence if meanwhile the subjects com-

mit some act infringing the truce, they will not be subject to punishment. The contracting parties nevertheless will be responsible for making good the damage.

6. WHAT is lawful and what is not lawful in time of truce may be understood from the bare definition. Unlawful are all acts of war against either persons or property, that is, acts of violence against the enemy, since all acts of that kind in time of truce are contrary to the law of nations, as Lucius Aemilius explained during an address to his troops, in Livy.[9] Also, whatever enemy property by any chance comes into our hands during a truce must be returned, even if previously it was ours, because as far as external rights are concerned, according to which these matters must be decided, it has now become theirs. This is what the jurist Paulus said,[10] that in time of truce there is no right of postliminy, because postliminy requires that first there should be the right of capture in war, which in time of truce does not exist.

Both sides have a right to pass back and forth from one to the other, but bringing only such equipment as does not suggest danger. . . . Servius tells us [11] that when Rome was being besieged by Tarquin, a truce was arranged between Porsenna and the Romans while the games of the Circus Maximus were being held in the city, and that the leaders of the enemy came in and took part in the chariot race and were crowned as victors.

7. TO retire with one's army farther inland, as we read in Livy [12] that Philip did, is not a violation of a truce. Nor is it to refortify one's walls or to levy troops, unless some special agreement has been made to the contrary.

8. TO bribe enemy garrisons and then to seize the posts they were holding is indubitably an infraction of a truce. For such a mode of acquisition cannot be legitimate, except under the law of war. The same view must be maintained if any subjects wish to desert and join the enemy. . . . In the fourth book of Thucydides [13] we find that Brasidas in time of truce did receive the city of Mende, which was deserting the Athenians for the Spartans,

but the excuse is given that he on his part was bringing charges against the Athenians.

It is certainly lawful to take over abandoned property, provided it has been really abandoned, that is, with the intention that it shall no longer belong to those whose property it once was; but not if it is merely left unguarded, whether the guard was removed before the truce or after the truce was signed. For as long as ownership lasts, it makes it unlawful for another person to take possession. . . .

9. THE question is asked whether a person who has been prevented by *force majeure* from returning to his own side and is arrested within the enemy's borders after the truce expires still keeps his right to return. If we consider the external law of nations, I think that this person's case is the same as that of the man who comes in peacetime to the enemy's country, and by mishap is caught there in a sudden outbreak of war. We have observed already [14] that he has to remain there as a prisoner until the conclusion of peace. There is some inner justice here, in as far as the property and rights of enemies are held liable for the debts of their state and are taken as payment. Nor has this person more to complain of than have the numberless other innocent people on whom fall the calamities of war. . . . In his case, properly speaking, it is no question of a penalty, but of a right which has been merely suspended for a certain time. Undoubtedly, however, to release him would be a benevolent and noble act.

10. THERE are acts made unlawful in a time of truce by the special nature of its terms. When a truce is granted only in order to bury the dead, nothing else must be changed. So too if a truce is granted to a besieged populace, providing simply that they will not be attacked, it will not be lawful for them to take in auxiliaries and supplies, for, since such a truce is to the advantage of the besieged, it ought not, meanwhile, to make the situation harder for the party who granted it.

Sometimes the terms do not permit any passing back and forth.

Sometimes they protect persons and not things. In which case, if persons are injured while defending their property, it will be no violation of the truce. For although it is lawful to defend one's property, the safety of the persons concerned must be based on the chief provision of the agreement, not on something which follows as a consequence of something else.

11. IF the promise in the truce is broken by one party, the injured party is undeniably free to take up arms, even without a declaration of war. For the terms of the agreement are present in the agreement in the form of a condition, as we said a little earlier. You may indeed find in the histories instances of persons who bore with infractions of a truce up to the end, but you may also read of wars made on the Etruscans and on others, because they had broken a truce. This difference is a proof that the law is as we say it is, but that it rests with the injured party to enforce the law or not.

12. IT is plain that if a demand is made for a penalty agreed on, and it is paid by the one at fault, it is no longer right to make war on him. For the penalty is paid for the purpose of preserving the other portions of the truce intact. On the other hand, if war is resumed, we must suppose that no payment will be made, since a choice was allowed between the two.

13. THE deeds of private individuals do not break a truce, unless some public action supports them, that is, an order or a ratification. It is also to be taken as support when the offenders are neither punished nor surrendered, or when property is not returned.

14. THE right of safe transit, outside of truce time, is a kind of privilege; so in interpreting it the rules laid down for privileges should be followed. It is a privilege neither prejudicial to a third party nor very burdensome to the one who grants it. Hence, within the proper meaning of the words, a broad rather than a strict interpretation should be permitted,[15] the more so when the privilege was not granted as a favor to one asking for it but was offered voluntarily; much more so, when, besides the advantage to private persons, a public advantage of some kind is secured by the arrange-

ment. A strict interpretation then, even when the words would bear it, should be rejected, unless otherwise the result would be something absurd, or unless the most likely conjectures as to the intention of the grantor point in the strict direction. On the other hand, a broader interpretation, even beyond the proper meaning of the words, is justified for the purpose of preventing a similar absurdity, or when strongly supported by inference.

15. HENCE we conclude that a right of free passage granted to soldiers extends not only to officers of middle rank but to supreme commanders as well, since a proper meaning of the word 'soldiers' admits of this interpretation, although there is another interpretation that is narrower. In the same way, a bishop comes under the name of clergy. Even sailors in ships are included in 'soldiers,' as are all without exception who have taken the military oath.

16. A permit to go out is construed to cover also a return, not through any sense of the word, but in order to prevent an absurdity, because a beneficial act ought not to be futile. And a safe conduct to go should be understood as good until the receiver has reached a place where he is safe. Therefore, Alexander was accused of bad faith,[16] because he ordered killed on their journey men to whom he had granted a right to depart. But a man given a right to depart is not also given the right to return, nor is one who is permitted to come himself empowered to send someone else. Nor is the opposite true. These are various cases in which reason does not compel us to stretch the meaning of the words, and where an error, though it bestows no right, yet is not penalized, if any penalty is attached. Again, a man who has a permit to come may come once, but not a second time, unless the length of time allowed him furnishes ground for supposing he may.

17. A son does not accompany his father nor a wife her husband, except as permitted by his right of residence. For we are used to living with our family, but to traveling without it. However, it is understood, even though not expressly stipulated, that one or two servants are included in the permit of a person for whom it would

be undignified to travel without such attendants. For he who grants a thing, grants what necessarily follows it, and the necessity in this instance should be understood as practical.

18. IN the same way, not every kind of property is included in a man's permit but only such as he is accustomed to take on a journey.

19. UNDER the title of escorts should not be included persons whose position is more invidious than that of the one for whom the permit is intended. Such persons are pirates, brigands, fugitives, and deserters. The fact that the nationality of the escorts is stated is proof enough that the permit does not extend to others.

20. THE right of safe passage, since it comes from the power of authority, is not, in cases of doubt, canceled by the death of the person who granted it. This is in accord with what we said earlier [17] with regard to favors granted by kings and other rulers. . . .

22. SAFE passage must be afforded to a person to whom it has been promised, even outside the territory of the grantor, since it was promised as protection against the law of war, which in itself is not limited to a territory, as we said before.

23. THE ransoming of captives is considered an act of great benevolence, especially among Christians, to whom the divine law particularly recommends this type of mercy. . . . Ambrose calls [18] the ransom of captives, especially from a barbarian enemy, the greatest and loftiest beneficence. He defends too his own action and that of the Church in breaking up church vessels, even some which had been consecrated, in order to buy release for the captives. . . .

24. THESE instances have such weight with me that I do not dare to approve wholesale the laws which prohibit the ransoming of prisoners, such as those that, we read, existed among the Romans. . . . That state, Livy says,[19] showed small consideration for prisoners, even in ancient times. . . . What Aristotle criticized in the institutions of the Spartans,[20] is generally considered also a fault in the institutions of the Romans, namely, the concentration of all

effort on matters of war, as if the state's welfare depended on them alone. But if we give only a thought to the cause of humanity, we see that it would often be better that a right for which we make war should be lost than that many men, our relatives or fellow countrymen, should be abandoned to most bitter tribulation.

That kind of law then does not seem to me right, unless there is plainly a need of such severity in order to avert graver evils or a greater number of them, which otherwise would be morally sure to occur. In case of such a necessity, the prisoners themselves by the law of love have to bear their lot with patience. They may be enjoined, as others may be commanded, to offer no resistance, in accord with what we said earlier regarding the surrender of a citizen for the public good.[21]

25. PRISONERS of war are not by our custom slaves. But I do not doubt that the right to exact from a prisoner a price for his ransom may be transferred by the person who holds him prisoner to someone else, for nature allows a transfer of immaterial rights.

26. THE same man may owe a ransom to more than one person, if he was released by one before paying the price, and then taken prisoner by another, for they are different debts, due for different reasons.

27. AN agreement as to the price of ransom, once made, cannot be revoked on the ground that the prisoner is found to be wealthier than he was supposed to be, because, by the external law of nations, which we are discussing, no one is compelled to add more to what by contract he has promised to pay, even though it was less than a fair price, so long as there has been no deceit. This rule may be inferred from our earlier discussion of contracts.[22]

28. FROM what we have just said—that prisoners with us are not slaves—it follows that there is not that complete acquisition of their property, which, as we said above, goes with ownership of persons.[23] Nothing more is acquired by the captor than what he actually lays hands on. So if a prisoner keeps something concealed

about him, the captor will not acquire it, since he has not had it in his possession. . . . Consequently, property concealed in that way may be used to help pay the cost of ransom, on the ground that the prisoner has retained his ownership of it.

29. THE question too is often asked whether a ransom, agreed upon but not paid before the prisoner's death, must be paid by his heir. The answer seems to me simple. If the man died while still in prison, it need not be paid. For the promise to pay contained a condition, that he should be set free, and the dead man was not freed. On the other hand, if he died in a state of liberty, the ransom is due, for he had already gained the prize for which the payment was promised.

I admit that obviously the agreement may be worded differently, so that the ransom becomes due unconditionally from the very moment of the drawing up of the contract, and the prisoner is detained not any longer as a captive by law of war, but as a security deposited by himself. On the other hand, a contract may be drawn to the effect that the payment will be made if on a specified day the prisoner is alive and free. But such terms are less natural, and not to be assumed without unmistakable proofs.

30. IT is also a question whether a man who was released on the understanding that he would procure the freeing of another man, must return to his prison if the other has died first. We have said elsewhere [24] that an act of a third party, promised in a spirit of generosity, is sufficiently performed if the promiser leaves nothing on his side undone, and that in promises for value received a promiser is bound to fulfill no more than the equivalent of his promise. In the case stated, then, the man released is not bound to give himself up again to custody, for that was not the agreement, and our prejudice in favor of liberty does not allow us to suppose a different tacit agreement. However, he should not get his liberty gratis, but should pay the estimated value of the thing he could not perform. . . .

XXII

Good Faith of Subordinate Officers in War.

1. . . . WE said that after discussing promises made by the highest authorities, we should take up those made by their subordinates to one another or to other persons. These subordinate officers are either next to the chief authority, the men who are well called commanders, as to whom note Livy's remark: [1] "We recognize as a commander the man under whose direction a war is carried on." Or else they are lower in rank. Caesar draws the following distinction between them: [2] "The duties of a lieutenant are one thing and those of a general another. The former must act by order, the latter take measures freely for the whole conduct of the war."

2. THERE are two things to be considered in speaking of promises made by subordinates, for two questions arise, whether they are binding on the highest authority, or only on themselves. The first question may be answered by what we said earlier,[3] that we are bound by a person whom we have chosen as the agent of our will, whether that will has been precisely stated to him, or whether he infers it from the nature of his appointment. For one who grants a power grants, as far as in him lies, what is necessary for the exercise of that power, which, in a practical case, should be understood in a practical way. By two methods, then, subordinate officers bind their chiefs by their acts; when they do what may reasonably be considered to be a part of their duty, or do something outside it by

special appointment known to the public, or to those whose interests are concerned.

3. THERE are other ways too through which a supreme authority
is bound by a previous act of his agents. Not that the act is the
cause, strictly speaking, of the obligation, but the occasion. It may
come about in two ways, either by consent of the chief authority or
as a result of the act itself. The consent of the authority is shown
by his ratification of the act, not only when expressed but when
tacit, that is, when the authority knows what was done and allows
other things to be done which can reasonably be attributed to no
other cause. What proceedings follow in that case and how they
follow we have explained elsewhere.[4]

By the act itself, superiors are bound to the extent that they must
not be made richer by another's loss, that is, they must either carry
out the subordinate's promise, by which they expect to obtain some
advantage, or else give up the advantage. On this principle of
equity we have also spoken elsewhere.[5] Thus far and no farther can
we accept the view that a subordinate's promise is valid, provided
it achieves something profitable to high authority. On their part,
the authorities cannot be acquitted of lawlessness who disapprove
of their agent's compact and yet keep what they would not have
had without it; as when the Roman Senate, according to Valerius,[6]
could not approve the act of Gnaeus Domitius, but was unwilling
to rescind it. Many such instances occur in the histories.

4. WE must repeat also what we said above [7] that a man who ap-
points an agent is bound, even if his agent has acted contrary to
his secret instructions, as long as he has kept within the limits of his
public appointment. In a suit with regard to agents, the Roman
praetor observed rightly the following rules of equity. Not everything that is done by an agent is binding on the one who appointed
him, but only such contracts as he makes to carry out the business
for which he was appointed. As soon as it is publicly announced
that no more contracts are to be made with him, he will no longer
be treated as an agent. If, however, the announcement is made

but people do not hear of it, the man who appointed him will still be bound for his acts. The conditions also of his appointment as agent should be observed. If the employer wants a contract made by a certain rule, or introducing someone else, it still is fairest to observe the conditions under which the agent was appointed.

Therefore, some kings or peoples may be bound more clearly by the agreements of their commanders, and some less, as we see, if we note carefully their laws and institutions. If those are not clear, we should follow the course indicated by inference, and take as granted concessions of authority without which official duties cannot be satisfactorily performed.

If a subordinate official has exceeded the limits of his instructions, and is unable to perform what he promised, he himself will be liable for an equivalent, unless some well-known law prevents it. And if he was deceitful too, that is, if he pretended to more authority than he had, he will then be liable both for the damage caused by his wrongdoing and also—since it was a crime—to punishment corresponding to his crime. On the first count, he is liable to forfeit his property, and if that is not sufficient, then his labor or his personal liberty. On the latter count, he is liable in his person or in his property or in both, in proportion to the magnitude of his offense. And what we have just said with regard to deceit will hold, even if he made a statement beforehand to the effect that he assumed no liability, because his liability both for any damage inflicted and for lawful punishment belongs to his offense, not as a matter of his own choice but by a natural connection.

5. SINCE either the sovereign authority or its agent is always bound, certainly therefore the other party is bound, and the agreement cannot be called one-sided. We have finished now an account of the relations of subordinate officers to their superiors.

6. LET us see then what powers the subordinates have over their inferiors. Unquestionably, in my opinion, a commander may oblige his soldiers, or a magistrate his fellow townsmen, to perform any of the acts which habitually come under his authority. In other

cases, he must have their consent. On the other hand, an agreement made by a commander or a magistrate will be unconditionally valid for his inferiors, in matters purely for their welfare; the right to make such agreements is definitely included in his authority. As for making agreements which have burdens attached to them, he has the same right within the limit of matters he is accustomed to control; but outside that limit, only if he has the inferior's consent. . . .

7. IT is not the office of a military commander to settle questions of the causes and consequences of a war, nor is it a part of waging the war to conclude it. Even if he was appointed with absolute power, that power must be understood to take in only the conduct of the war. The answer of Agesilaus to the Persians [8] was: "The right of making peace belongs to the state." Sallust says: [9] "The peace which Aulus Albinus made with King Jugurtha without an order from the Senate the Senate rescinded." And in Livy [10] we find: "How will that peace be valid which we make without the authority of the Senate or the mandate of the Roman people?" . . .

8. IT is in the power of commanders, and officers as well, to make a truce with those against whom they are fighting or whom they are holding besieged, as far as they themselves and their troops are concerned. But they cannot bind other officers of equal rank. The story of Fabius and Marcellus in Livy [11] shows this.

9. IT is not within the power of commanders to give away men, domains, or lands acquired in war. In accordance with this law Syria was taken away from Tigranes, although Lucullus had given it to him.[12] . . . Over other objects captured as booty some right, we see, is granted to generals, not so much on the strength of their authority as a matter of popular custom. But on this we have said enough already.[13]

It is, however, entirely within the commander's power to give away some things which have not yet been won, since often in a war cities and men surrender on condition that their lives or their liberty or their goods be spared. In such cases, circumstances frequently do not permit consulting the wishes of the sovereign authority. For the same reason, this right should be given even to subordinate commanders, within the limit of the things they are commissioned to deal with.

Once, when Hannibal was a long way off, Maharbal promised some Romans, who had escaped from the battle of Trasimenus, not only their lives . . . but, if they gave up their arms, permission to leave with one set of clothing apiece. But Hannibal detained them, giving as his reason that "it was not in Maharbal's power, without consulting him, to promise those who surrendered that he would protect them from injury or punishment." Livy's judgment on this act is: [14] "Hannibal kept the promise with Punic faith." . . .

10. BUT with regard to these agreements made by military commanders, inasmuch as they deal with matters outside their province as far as the nature of the agreement requires, they should be interpreted strictly, so that the supreme authority should not be bound more than it wishes to be by a subordinate's act, or the subordinates themselves suffer damage in the performance of a duty.

11. CONSEQUENTLY, a man received by a commander in simple surrender is presumably received on the understanding that the final decision with respect to him belongs to the people or to the king of his conqueror. . . .

12. HENCE the added proviso, "this to be valid, if the Roman people so approves," which you find often in the treaties, and which means that if their ratification does not follow, the commander himself is bound to nothing, unless he has in some way been enriched by the agreement.

13. THOSE who have promised to give up a town may let the garrison go, as we read the Locrians did.[15]

XXIII

Good Faith of Private Individuals in War.

1. FAMILIAR are the words of Cicero: [1] "If, under the pressure of circumstances, individuals promise something, even to an enemy, their promise should be kept exactly." Whether the individuals are soldiers or civilians, it makes no difference as regards keeping the promise. Strange to say, doctors of law have been found who taught that public agreements with an enemy bound one to keep faith, but that private agreements did not. But since private persons have private rights which they can pledge, and an enemy is capable of acquiring rights, what can stand in the way of a binding pledge? Furthermore, if such a rule is not established, an occasion is created for massacres and liberation is jeopardized, because, if there is no good faith among private persons, captives will often be unable to escape death or obtain freedom.

2. INDEED, both the promises given by a private person to an enemy who is recognized as such by the law of nations, and those given to brigands or pirates are binding, as we said above when speaking of public promises.[2] There is this difference, that if an unlawful fear, inspired by the other party, induced the individual to make the promise, he may demand restitution, or, if the other party refuses, he may obtain it for himself. But in a case of fear created by public war, the law of nations admits no such right. And if the promise was sealed by an oath, then certainly what was promised must be performed by the one who promised it, if he wishes

to avoid the crime of perjury. If such perjury is committed against a public enemy, men usually punish it; if against brigands or pirates, they are apt to overlook it because of the hatred they feel for the men whose interests are in question.

3. IN considering this matter of private good faith, we shall make no exception for minors who have reached the stage where they understand what is being done. For favorable provisions for minors are matters of civil law, and we are investigating the law of nations.

4. AND as for an error, we have said elsewhere [3] that it gives a right to withdraw from an agreement if what the party mistakenly believed had for him the force of a condition.

5. HOW far the power of private individuals to make an agreement extends is a difficult problem. Everyone knows that a private person cannot alienate public property, for if not even military commanders are allowed to do that, as we have just shown, much less can private persons do it. But the question can be raised as to their own actions and property, because these things too, it seems, cannot be put at the enemy's disposal without some damage to their side. Hence such agreements on the part of citizens may be regarded as unlawful because of the state's right of eminent domain, and on the part of enlisted soldiers because of the pledge they made in their oaths.

But we must realize that agreements which prevent the occurrence of a greater or more certain evil should be considered useful rather than hurtful to a state, since the lesser evil takes on the character of something good. . . . And neither a later promise alone—so long as it is not a renunciation of all power over oneself and one's possessions—nor considerations of the public welfare, unauthorized by law, can make void an agreement already made and deprive it of legal effect, even if it was admittedly an infraction of one's duty.

A law may indeed deprive subjects, whether permanent or temporary, of their power. But the law does not always do this, for it is considerate of citizens; nor can it always do it, since human laws, as we have said elsewhere,[4] have binding force only if they are framed in a humane way, not if they impose a burden obviously irreconcilable with reason and nature. Hence special laws and orders which palpably wear such a character should not be regarded as laws; and general laws should receive a benevolent interpretation and allow exceptions for cases of extreme necessity. If, however, it is possible that some individual's act which was forbidden by a law or an order and prevented from taking effect was rightfully forbidden, the act will at once be invalid. And the individual who performed it will be liable to punishment, because he promised what he had no right to promise, especially if he promised on oath.

6. A promise by a prisoner to return to his prison is rightfully allowable, since it does not make the position of the prisoner worse. Therefore the act of Marcus Atilius Regulus was not, as some think, merely glorious; it was also an act of duty. It was Regulus' duty, says Cicero,[5] "not to violate by perjury his terms and war agreements with the enemy." Nor did he hesitate because

> "He knew what fate for him the barbarian
> Torturer was preparing," [6]

for he had known when he made his promise that that might happen. . . .

7. PRISONERS often promise that they will not go back to a certain locality, or will not fight against the person who has them in his power. An instance of the first promise is given by Thucydides,[7] when the people of Ithome promised the Spartans that they would leave the Peloponnesus and never return. . . .

Instances of the second promise are common now. . . . Some writers call such a promise void, because it is contrary to the duty one owes one's own country. But not everything contrary to duty is immediately void, as we have said above and elsewhere. Then too it is not contrary to duty to obtain one's freedom by promising something which at the moment lies in the enemy's hands. And the cause of the prisoner's country is in no way injured, since if he were not set free, it would have to consider him dead.

8. SOME prisoners promise also not to try to escape. This promise is binding on them, even though they were in fetters when they made it. Some writers, however, think the opposite. But by this means captives often save their lives or buy a milder form of imprisonment. If, however, the promiser is later put in chains, he will then be released from his promise, if he made it on the understanding that he would not be chained.

9. THE question whether a man who has been taken captive can later surrender to another is very foolish. Quite certainly no one by an arrangement of his own can deprive another of a right he has won. His captor had won the right to him, either by the law of war alone, or else partly by the law of war and partly by the consent of the person who was conducting the war, as we explained above.[8]

10. AS regards the effects of agreements, it is an important question whether private individuals who have been negligent in carrying out their promises should be compelled by their superiors to fulfill them. It is correct to say that in a time of formal war they should be so compelled, because the law of nations, by which the belligerents are bound, requires each side to render justice to the other, even in cases of acts by private citizens, as when, for example, they attack the enemy's ambassadors. . . .

11. AS for the interpretation of private promises, the rules we have already mentioned several times should be observed. There should be no departure from the proper meaning of the words, except to avoid an absurdity, or because of some different but quite positive conviction as to the meaning. In a case of doubt we should incline to interpret the words adversely to the person who laid down the terms.

12. A man who has received a promise of life has not also thereby a right to liberty. Arms do not come under the name of clothing,

for they are different things. It is right to say that aid has arrived, if it is in sight, even though it is accomplishing nothing, for the very presence of it is invigorating.

13. A man is not said to have returned to the enemy, if he went back stealthily and left at once, because returning should be understood as meaning being once more in the enemy's power. . . .

14. IN case of an agreement to surrender which is not to be carried out if lawful assistance arrives first, the assistance, it should be understood, must be sufficient to put an end to the danger.

15. WE must note too that in case there has been an agreement as to the mode of performance of a promise, that does not inject a condition into the promise; as when they say a payment is to be made at a certain spot and the spot afterward changes owners, the payment is to be made nevertheless. . . .

XXIV

Tacit Pledges.

1. JAVOLENUS has well said [1] that some agreements are reached in silence. This happens often in public and in private and in mixed agreements. The reason is that consent, however indicated and accepted, has power to transfer a right, and there are other signs of consent besides spoken and written words, as we have already remarked more than once. Some signs are contained by nature in an act.

2. LET us take as an instance a man who comes from the enemy or from a foreign country and commits himself to the good faith of another people or king. There should be no doubt but that he tacitly puts himself under obligation to do nothing to harm the state in which he seeks protection. . . .

3. so too the person who asks for or consents to a conference promises tacitly that it will be safe for those who come to it. Livy says [2] that to stage an attack on an enemy under guise of a conference is to violate the law of nations. He adds that the good faith of a conference was violated . . . when Gnaeus Domitius invited Bituitus, king of the Arvenians, to a pretended conference and, after receiving him as a guest, threw him into chains. . . .

4. HOWEVER, tacit consent must not be stretched to signify more than I said. For as long as the persons at a conference suffer no hurt, it is not perfidious, under guise of the conference, to divert the enemy from his plans for war and meanwhile forward one's own interests. That is counted honest guile. . . . The trick by which Hasdrubal saved his army from the Ausetanian passes was one of that kind, as was that by which Scipio Africanus the Elder discovered the location of the camp of Syphax. Livy describes them both.[3] . . .

5. THERE are also mute signals which have a meaning given them by custom. Such were, once, the wearing of fillets and the waving of olive branches. Among the Macedonians, the raising of their spears, among the Romans the setting of their shields on their heads, were signs of humble surrender, which bound them thereafter to lay down their arms. Whether the person who signifies that he accepts such surrender is bound to anything, and how far, may be gathered from what we said above.[4] Today white flags are a tacit sign of a request for a conference. Accordingly, they impose an obligation no less than if the request had been made by word of mouth.

6. HOW far a treaty made by a military commander should be considered tacitly confirmed by his people or his king we have said

already above.[5] It should be so considered when the action is known and some other step has been taken or not taken, the only assignable reason for which is a purpose to confirm the treaty.

7. THAT a penalty is remitted cannot be inferred from the mere fact that it has not been inflicted. There must besides be an act of a kind that in itself shows friendliness, such as a treaty of friendship, or else so good an opinion of the offender's virtues that his deeds deserve to be forgiven, an opinion expressed either in words or in acts which by custom have been given that significance.

XXV

Conclusion, with Admonitions to Good Faith and Peace.

1. AND here I think I may conclude, not because I have said all that could be said, but because what I have said is enough to lay foundations. Whoever may wish to erect on them a handsomer structure will not find me jealous but will instead receive my gratitude.

Yet, as when I was discussing the starting of wars, I inserted some advice with regard to the averting of war, as far as that was possible, so now too, before I dismiss the reader, I shall add a few admonitions for care in the keeping of faith and of peace, which may be helpful during and after a war. For faith should be kept, both on other grounds, and in order that the hope of peace may not

be destroyed. For not only does every state rest on good faith, as
Cicero says,[1] but so does the greater society of nations. Destroy
good faith, as Aristotle truly remarks,[2] and "intercourse between
men comes to an end." . . .

The supreme rulers of mankind should uphold this good faith
the more scrupulously as they can with more impunity than other
men sin against it. Once good faith disappears, they will be like
wild beasts, of whose strength all men stand in dread. About justice
in its various departments there is often something obscure. But
the bond of good faith in itself is clear; indeed it is used for the
purpose of removing all obscurity from negotiations. All the more
then is it incumbent on kings to maintain it religiously, first, for
their own conscience' sake, and then for the sake of their reputation, on which rests their royal authority. Let them not doubt that
those who preach to them the arts of falsehood are practicing the
very thing they teach. A teaching which makes a man a bad member
of the society of men, and also hateful to God, cannot benefit him
long.

2. FURTHER, through all the conduct of a war the soul cannot
be kept untroubled and trusting in God, unless it looks forward
always to peace. Sallust most truly said:[3] "Wise men wage war
for the sake of peace." . . . Aristotle himself[4] more than once
censured nations who looked on warmaking as though it were their
ultimate goal. Violence, which plays a most conspicuous part in
war, is a thing which belongs to wild beasts; wherefore we should
take most diligent pains to temper it with humanity, lest by too
much imitation of the beasts we forget how to be human.

3. IF, then, it is possible for us to have a peace reasonably secure,
it may well be grounded on a pardon for offenses, injuries, and
debts. Especially is this true for Christians, to whom the Lord bequeathed his peace. His best interpreter desires us[5] as far as possible, as far as in us lies, to seek peace with all men. A good man,
we read in Sallust,[6] is unwilling to begin a war and reluctant to
follow it to the very end.

4. THIS one argument should be sufficient, but frequently, too, considerations of human advantage draw men towards a peace. They draw, first, the weaker party, because a long struggle with a superior force is full of danger. As on a ship, a major catastrophe must be avoided even at some cost, and resentment and hope, the deceitful councilors, as Livy rightly called them,[7] must be put aside. . . .

5. BUT they may draw also the stronger party, because, as the same Livy no less truly said,[8] peace is generous and handsome to those who grant it when things are going well with them, and better and safer than a hoped-for victory. One should remember that Mars is the god of both sides. "In wartime," says Aristotle,[9] "we should keep in mind how many and how unexpected vicissitudes are likely to occur." . . . Especially should we fear the recklessness of men driven to desperation, as we do the savage bite of a dying wild beast.

6. AND if both parties regard themselves as equals, then indeed, in Caesar's opinion,[10] is the time most favorable to treat for a peace, while they both have confidence in themselves.

7. PEACE once made on whatever terms should be absolutely kept, because good faith is sacred, as we have said. Not merely perfidy but anything irritating should be carefully avoided. For what Cicero said of private friendships [11] you may apply no less correctly to friendships between states. While they all should be guarded with the utmost scrupulousness and good faith, those should be guarded most carefully of all which are returns from enmity to good will.

8. MAY God, who alone can do it, inscribe these principles on the hearts of those in whose hands lies the government of the Christian world, and implant in them a mind which understands divine and human law, and which always remembers that it was chosen as a servant to rule man, the creature best loved by God.

NOTES

PREFACE

1 Thucydides, *Peloponnesian War,* VI, lxxxv. Thucydides repeats the words of a delegation from Athens, then at the height of its power, to the conquered inhabitants of the small island of Melos: "You know as well as we do that, as the world goes, . . . the strong do all they can and the weak put up with it." Ibid., V, lxxxix.

2 The Stoics, followed by many writers on philosophy and politics down to Grotius' day, had taught the existence of a universal, unchangeable, moral law, implanted by nature in every human being, which showed him the difference between acts inherently good and those inherently base, between justice and injustice. The Skeptics, on the contrary, declared that by nature men were unmoral, knowing no distinction between good and evil. Grotius makes the law of nature the basis for all law among men. He must, therefore, prove the existence of that law as a first step to proving the existence of law between nations.

3 Horace, *Satires,* I, iii, 113.

4 Plutarch, *Consolation,* 608D.

5 *Digest,* I, i, 3.

6 Horace, *Satires,* I, iii, 98.

7 Ibid., I, 3, 111.

8 Plato, *Republic,* II, ii, 359–360. *Gorgias,* XXXVIII.

9 Plutarch, *Solon,* XV.

10 Plato, *Republic,* IX, 578–580. *Gorgias,* LXXX.

11 Stobaeus, *Anthology,* X, 50.

12 Demosthenes, *On the Chersonese,* VIII, 29.

13 *Orations,* 76.

14 Erasmus' tract, *The Complaint of Peace,* was an eloquent plea for Christian pacifism.

15 Grotius wrote this book while living in exile in France. See Introduction, p. xv.

16 At the end of the 13th century, Roger Bacon wished that all the books of Aristotle might be burned, such a hindrance had they become to the discovery of new truth. In Grotius' time, Lord Francis Bacon was still complaining of the dictatorial power of Aristotle over the schools, and Galileo was finding it almost impossible to convince his colleagues in the Italian universities by experiment that Aristotle was mistaken in his astronomy and in his physics.

BOOK ONE

CHAP. I

1 *On Duty*, I, xi, 34.
2 Ibid., III, v, 21.
3 *On Anger*, II, xxxi, 7.
4 A reference to Aristotle's *Metaphysics*, IX, 6–8, where he defines the difference between what is actual and what is potential in the natural world.
5 Xenophon, *Cyropaedia*, I, iii, 17.
6 The law, by its silence, permits those acts which it does not prohibit. Of this kind may be the export of gold, or the import of articles of trade, or the practice of certain professions without proper qualifications. Such acts, before they are prohibited by law, belong in the class of what Grotius calls 'permissions.'
7 *Nicomachean Ethics*, V, x.
8 Ibid., II, vi.
9 *On Abstaining from Eating Animals*, IV, xxi.
10 *On Aristotle's Nicomachean Ethics*, V, x.
11 *Orations*, 76.
12 Cited in Plutarch, *Alexander*, lii.

CHAP. II

1 *On Ends*, III, v, 17.
2 *On Duty*, III, v, 22.
3 *In Defense of Milo*, IV, 10.
4 Ibid., XI, 30.
5 *Digest*, IX, ii, 4.
6 Ibid., I, i, 5.
7 Acts x, 44–48.
8 Matthew v, 38–39.
9 Ibid., v, 41.

10 Matthew v, 43–44.
11 II Samuel ii–iv.
12 Seneca, *On Clemency*, I, ii.
13 Matthew xxvi, 52.
14 *Antiquities*, XIV, x, 12.
15 *Apology for the Christians*, I.
16 *On the Government of God*, III, vi, 22.
17 *Divine Institutes*, V, xvii, 12.
18 Chap. XLII.
19 Chap. XXXVII.
20 Chap. V.
21 In the *Acts of the Martyrs* is told the story of the so-called Theban Legion, which was converted as a body to Christianity during the reign of the Emperor Diocletian. Later the Emperor Maximian ordered the legion, along with the rest of the army, to offer the customary sacrifices to the gods. To a man they submitted to execution by the sword rather than obey him.

CHAP. III

1 *Peloponnesian War*, V, xviii.
2 *Politics*, IV, xiv.
3 *Geography*, IX, iii, 7; XIV, iii, 2.
4 *Politics*, II, ii; III, ix.
5 Exodus xxi, 2–6; *Institutes*, I, iii, 2.
6 Terence, *The Self-Tormentor*, II, iii, 84.
7 *Germania*, XXV.
8 *History*, XLII, v, 3.
9 *Geography*, IV, i, 9; V, iv, 9.
10 *Histories*, I, lxxviii.
11 *Comparison of Philopoemen and Titus*, III.
12 *History*, III, lxxx.
13 *Institutes*, I, ii, 6.

14 Xiphilinus, *Life of Marcus Antoninus*, LXXI, iii.
15 *History*, VI, iii; *Life of Cleo-
menes*, III; *Agesilaus*, I.
16 *Description of Greece*, II, xix.
17 *Politics*, III, xvi.
18 *History*, II, xviii, 8.
19 *Philippics*, I, i, 3.
20 Sozomen, *Ecclesiastical History*,
VI, vi.
21 *On Duty*, II, xii, 41. *History*, I,
xcvi, ff. *Theogony*, 83 ff.
22 *History of the Franks*, V, 19.
23 *Ligurinus*, VIII, 577.
24 *History*, I, xvii, 3.
25 Ibid., II, xv, 3.
26 Ibid., XLV, xviii.
27 *Indica*, XI, 9.
28 *Digest*, XLIX, xv, 19.
29 *Geography*, VIII, v, 1.
30 I Kings IX, 11.
31 *On Monarchy. Life of Themistocles*, XXVII.
32 *Cyropaedia*, VIII, v, 27. The
source of the reference to
Diodorus is not known.
33 Daniel VI, 8, 12, 15. *Themistocles*,
XXVII.
34 *Historical Library*, III, v.
35 Ibid., I, lxx.
36 *History*, VI, ix, ff.
37 *Politics*, III, xv.
38 I Samuel VIII, 11–20.
39 *Roman Antiquities*, IV, xx.
40 *History*, VI, xxxvii, 4.
41 *Peloponnesian War*, I, xxv;
xxxviii.
42 *Digest*, XLIX, xv, 7, 1.
43 Ibid., XLIX, xv, 7, 2.
44 Book II, viii, 27.
45 *Digest*, XLIX, xv, 7, 2.
46 Book II, Chap. XVI, 4.
47 Valerius Maximus, *Memorable
Deeds*, IV, i.
48 *Politics*, III, ix.
49 *On Peace*, XXXVI.

CHAP. IV

1 *Apology*, XVII.
2 *Confessions*, III, viii.
3 Deuteronomy XVII, 12; Joshua I,
18; I Samuel VIII, 11.
4 Matthew XXII, 21.
5 Romans XIII, 2–5.
6 *Histories*, IV, lxxiv.
7 *Peloponnesian War*, II, lx.
8 *Against Auxentius*, V, ii.
9 Averroes, *On the Metaphysics*, V,
vi.
10 *Sermons on the Scriptures*, LXII,
13. *Decretum*, II, xi, 3, 97.
11 Mark II, 23–27; III, 1–5. Luke
VI, 1–10.
12 I Peter II, 13.
13 *Against Opponents of Monarchy*,
III, viii; VI, xxiii; xxiv.
14 I Samuel XXVI, 9.
15 Aristotle, *Problems*, XXIX, 14.
16 I Samuel XXIV, 6.
17 *Histories*, IV, lxvii.
18 *Letters to Atticus*, IX, iv.
19 Lucan, *Pharsalia*, I, 351.
20 Cicero, *Familiar Letters*, I, ix, 18.
21 Matthew XXII, 20.

CHAP. V

1 The efficient cause of a thing or
an act is the maker of the thing
or the doer of the act, as distinguished, for instance, from
the final cause, which is what
furnishes the motive for the
making or the doing. Grotius
expects his readers to be familiar
with Aristotle's famous theory
of the four causes, stated in his
Metaphysics, V, 2.
2 Plutarch, *Solon*, XVIII.
3 Stobaeus, *Anthology*, XLVI, 43.
4 *Divine Institutes*, VI, x, 3.

BOOK TWO

CHAP. I

1 *Roman Antiquities*, VIII, viii.
2 *Olynthiacs*, II, x.
3 *Letters*, XCV, 30.
4 *Histories*, VII, viii, 19.
5 *City of God*, IV, iv.
6 *On Laws*, IX, vi.
7 *On Duty*, I, vii, 24.
8 *Anabasis*, II, v, 5.
9 Aulus Gellius, *Attic Nights*, VI, iii, 26 and 31.
10 Quintilian, *Institutes of Oratory*, V, xiii, 21.
11 *Pharsalia*, V, 685–687.
12 Book I, Chap. II, 8.

CHAP. II

1 *Histories*, XLIII, i, 3.
2 *On Ends*, III, xx, 67.
3 Justin, *Histories*, II, ii, 15.
4 Vergil, *Georgics*, I, 126.
5 Grotius, *Freedom of the Sea*, XV.
6 On Grotius' contribution to the theory of the freedom of the seas, see Introduction, pp. xii–xiii.
7 *Controversies*, IX, iv, 5.
8 *On Duty*, III, vi, 29.
9 Xenophon, *Anabasis*, V, i, 11 ff.
10 *On Duty*, I, xvi, 51.
11 *On Benefits*, IV, xxix.
12 *Symposiacs*, VII.
13 Plutarch, *Agesilaus*, XVI.
14 Tacitus, *Histories*, IV, lxv.
15 *On the Steadfastness of Wise Men*, xiv.
16 *Geography*, XVI, i, 27.
17 Ibid., XVII, i, 19.
18 *On Duty*, III, vii, 45.
19 *History*, I, ix, 4.
20 *Judges* xx.

CHAP. III

1 *Digest*, XLI, ii, 3, 21.
2 *On Benefits*, VII, iv, 2.
3 *Digest*, VIII, iv, 13.
4 Ibid., XLIII, viii, 3.
5 *Institutes*, II, i, 1.
6 *Digest*, XLI, i, 14.
7 Ibid., XLIII, viii, 3.
8 Thucydides, *Peloponnesian War*, V, lvi.
9 *Digest*, VIII, iv, 13.
10 Ibid., XLI, i, 16.

CHAP. IV

1 Grotius uses here the word 'usucaption,' which is the term employed in Roman law for 'the acquisition of ownership by long use or enjoyment.' A somewhat similar idea lies behind the modern phrase, 'squatters' rights.'
2 *Controversies*, II, li, 28.
3 *Judges* xi, 26.
4 *Archidamus*, IX.
5 *On Duty*, II, xxii, 79.
6 *Digest*, XLI, i, 44.
7 Ibid., XXXIX, ii, 15, 21.
8 Livy, *History*, XXXIV, lviii, 10.
9 Cicero, *On Duty*, II, xxiii, 81.
10 Macrobius, *Saturnalia*, II, iv, 18.
11 *Peloponnesian War*, VI, lxxxix.
12 Livy, *History*, XXXV, xvi, 8 and 9.
13 Book I, Chap. III, 6.
14 Book I, Chap. III, 11.

CHAP. V

1 *Germania*, XXIV.
2 I *Corinthians* vii, 20–21; *Ephesians* vi, 5; *Colossians* iii, 22; *Titus* ii, 9.

CHAP. VI

1 Book I, Chap. III, 12.
2 *City of God*, XVIII, ii.

CHAP. VII

1 Book I, Chap. III, 2.
2 Valerius Maximus, *Memorable Deeds*, II, ix, 1.
3 *Code*, V, xiii, i, 5.
4 *Odyssey*, I, 216.
5 *Laws*, XI, vi, 923.
6 *Laws*, XI, vii, 923.
7 Book I, Chap. III, 12–13.
8 *Agricola*, XVI, 1.
9 *Cyropaedia*, VIII, v, 19.

CHAP. VIII

1 Book II, Chap. III.
2 *Digest*, XLI, ii, 3, 14.

CHAP. IX

1 *The Begetting of the Soul*, XXV.
2 *Digest*, VI, i, 23, 5.
3 *On Clemency*, I, iv.
4 *Politics*, III, iii.
5 *Critias*, III.
6 *On the Pallium*, II.
7 *History*, XXVI, xvi, 9–10.
8 Ibid., I, xiii, 5 ff.; xxviii, 7; xxx, 1.
9 *Peloponnesian War*, I, xxxiv.

CHAP. X

1 *On Duty*, III, v, 21.
2 Ibid., III, v, 22.

CHAP. XI

1 *On Duty*, I, vii, 23.
2 *Odes*, I, xxiv, 6.
3 Plato, *Republic*, I, v, 331.
4 Stobaeus, *Anthology*, XLIV, 22.
5 *Nicomachean Ethics*, III, i.
6 Book II, Chap. XVII, 19; Book III, Chap. XIX, 11.
7 Book II, Chap. XII, 9–11.

CHAP. XII

1 *On Duty*, III, x, 66.
2 *On Duty*, III, xii, 52.
3 *Homilies on John*, LX, vi.
4 *On the Nicomachean Ethics*, V, viii.
5 *Natural History*, IX, xxxv, 124.
6 *Against Verres*, II, IV, vii, 14.
7 *Geography*, XVII, i, 13.
8 *On Duty*, III, vi.
9 *Digest*, XIX, ii, 2.
10 Luke x, 29–37.
11 *Epitome of the Divine Institutes*, II, lix.
12 Plautus, *Comedy of Asses*, 172.
13 *Digest*, IV, iv, 16, 4; XIX, ii, 22, 3.
14 I Corinthians xi, 14.

CHAP. XIII

1 *On Duty*, III, xxix, 104.
2 Ibid., III, xxix, 108.
3 *Letters*, CXXV, 4.
4 Hebrews vi, 17.
5 Judges xxi, 16–25.
6 *On Special Laws*, II, iv.
7 *Roman Questions*, XLIV.
8 Matthew v, 34–37.
9 Sermon CLXXX, *On the Words of the Apostle James*, 13.
10 Hebrews vi, 16.
11 *On Duty*, III, xxix, 107.

12 Book III, Chap. III, 1.
13 *On Duty*, III, xxviii, 102.
14 Silius Italicus, *Punica*, VI, 63–64.
15 Matthew v, 33, 34, 37; James v, 12.
16 *On the Decalogue*, XVII.
17 *Politics*, III, xiv.

CHAP. XIV

1 *Civil Law*, Code II, iv, 12.

CHAP. XV

1 *Digest*, II, xiv, 5.
2 Livy, *History*, IX, 5.
3 *Jugurtha*, XXXIX, 3.
4 Aulus Gellius, *Attic Nights*, XIII, xvi, 1.
5 *History*, XXXIV, lvii, 6, 7.
6 *Against Heresy*, Preface, and I.
7 *Odyssey*, III, 71.
8 *Politics*, I, viii.
9 *Peloponnesian War*, III, lxxv.
10 Genesis xxxi, 44.
11 Deuteronomy, xxiii, 7.
12 II Samuel v, 11.
13 *Histories*, V, 5.
14 *Life of Apollonius of Tyana*, V, 33.
15 John iv, 7.
16 Genesis xiv, 8–16.
17 Matthew v, 45.
18 After the Roman army had passed under the humiliating yoke at Caudium, and the fact was reported to the Senate at home, it was said that as the terms of surrender were arranged without the consent of the Senate or the people, the Roman people were not bound by them. Accordingly, a proposal was made that those who had signed the treaty should be given up to the enemy, that thus the people might be released from the engagement. This proposal was agreed to, and a decree to that purpose passed.
19 Livy, *History*, IX, ix, 4.

CHAP. XVI

1 *On Duty*, I, xiii, 40.
2 *Histories*, XI, vi; VII, xxxiv.
3 *On Duty*, III, xxxii, 113.
4 *Paradoxes*, VI, 45.
5 *Histories*, III, lxxii, 11.
6 Thucydides, *Peloponnesian War*, IV, xcviii.
7 *Iliad*, III, 92, 281, 309.
8 Livy, *History*, XXI, xix, 4.
9 Book II, Chap. IX, 8.
10 *Digest*, II, xiv, 7, 8.
11 *On the State*, V, last chapter.
12 *Declamations*, CCCL.
13 Aulus Gellius, *Attic Nights*, I, xiii.
14 *On Duty*, I, x, 32.
15 *On Benefits*, V, xxxv, 2.
16 Livy, *History*, XXXIV, xxxv, 3.

CHAP. XVII

1 *Controversies*, V, v.
2 *On Duty*, III, xxix, 108.

CHAP. XVIII

1 Demosthenes, *Letter of Philip*, XII, 4.
2 *History*, I, xxxii, 6.
3 *Annals*, III, 73.
4 Caesar, *Civil War*, III, xix, 2.
5 II Kings xviii, 36.
6 *History*, II, iv, 7.
7 *Jugurtha*, XXXV, 7.

8 *Philippics*, VIII, viii, 23.

9 Grotius was mistaken in ascribing this statement to Polybius. In doing so he was following Alberico Gentile, an older contemporary, who wrote on various aspects of international law. *On Embassies*, II, xxi.

10 *Digest*, L, vii, 18.

11 Appian, *Punic Wars*, VI, 35.

12 *Digest*, XLVIII, vi, 7.

13 I Chronicles xix.

CHAP. XIX

1 *Controversies*, I, i, 14.

2 *Letters*, last edition, 491.

3 *War with Gildo*, 397 ff.

4 *Novels*, LIII.

5 *Antigone*, 450 ff.

6 Stobaeus, *Eclogues*, I, viii, 38.

7 Ecclesiastes xii, 7.

8 *Suppliants*, 531–536.

9 *Natural History*, VII, lv.

10 *Declamations*, VI, 3.

11 *Divine Institutes*, VI, xii, 30.

12 *The Schism of the Donatists*, VI, vii.

13 *Digest*, XLVIII, xxiv, 1.

14 *Jewish War*, III, viii, 5.

15 *Nicomachean Ethics*, V, xv.

16 Plutarch, *Brutus*, XL.

CHAP. XX

1 *Retractations*, I, ix, 5.

2 See above, Book I, Chap. I, 8.

3 *Digest*, XLIX, xiv, 34.

4 *Chance Remedies*, VII, 1.

5 *Laws*, IX, ii, 854, and XI, xii, 934.

6 *On Anger*, I, xix; II, xxxi.

7 *Gorgias*, XXIII.

8 Publilius Syrus, *Sentences*, 294.

9 *In Defense of Caecina*, XII, 35.

10 *On the Nicomachean Ethics*, VI, 1.

11 *Dissertations*, XVIII, 9.

12 Stobaeus, *Anthology*, XIX, 16.

13 *Delayed Vengeance of the Deity*, IV, xvi.

14 Plautus, *The Threepenny Day*, 23–24.

15 Mark xiv, 21.

16 *On Anger*, I, vi.

17 *Platonic*, II.

18 *Roman Histories*, II, cxviii.

19 *Questions on the Heptateuch*, VI, x.

20 *Orations*, LIX, 77.

21 *Political Precepts*, XXIII.

22 Stobaeus, *Anthology*, XLIV, 17.

23 Matthew v, 38–39.

24 Matthew v, 40.

25 *Apology*, I, vii.

26 *On Anger*, I, xvi.

27 *Historical Library*, I, lxv.

28 *On Photius' Nomocanon*, XVI, 5.

29 *Code*, III, xxvii, 1.

30 *On Anger*, II, xxxi.

31 *On Benefits*, III, vi and vii.

32 *On Clemency*, II, vii, 3.

33 *Against Stephanus*, XLV, 67.

34 Exodus xxii, 1.

35 Marcus Justin, *Histories*, II, ii, 6.

36 Marcus Antoninus the Philosopher, XXIV.

37 Stobaeus, *Anthology*, XLVIII, 25.

38 *Guide for the Perplexed*, III, xli.

39 *Controversies, Excerpts*, IV, vii.

40 Innocent IV, *Commentaries on the Decretals*, III, xxxiv, 8.

41 *Pompey*, LXX, 656.

42 *Cyropaedia*, VIII, i, 28.

43 *The Nature of the Gods*, I, ii, 4.

44 *Civil Law, Code*, I, v, 4.

45 Hebrews xi, 6.

46 *Various Histories*, II, xxxi.

47 *Subjects of Common Knowledge*, XXXII.

48 Dio Chrysostom, *Orations*, XII, 201.
49 *Letters*, X, xcvi.
50 *Republic*, I, xi.

CHAP. XXI

1 *Questions on the Heptateuch*, III, xxvi.
2 Livy, *History*, XLV, xxiii, 8.
3 *Against Piso*, V, 10.
4 Cited in *Decretum*, II, xxiii, 3.
5 *Orations*, XXXVIII, 480.
6 *On Special Laws*, III, xv.
7 *Panathenaic*, 187.
8 *Against Leocrates*, XCIII.
9 *Annals*, III, lx.
10 *Questions on the Heptateuch*, III, xxvi.
11 Book II, Chap. IX, 4.
12 *Anabasis of Alexander*, II, xiv.
13 Plutarch, *Apothegms*, 176.
14 *Digest*, XXXIX, ii, 24, 12.
15 *Letters*, III, *On the Death of Nepotianus*, lx, 8.
16 *Letters*, CXCIV.
17 *On Special Laws*, III, xxx.
18 *Roman Antiquities*, VIII, lxxx.
19 Deuteronomy xxiv, 16.

CHAP. XXII

1 *Peloponnesian War*, I, xxiii, ff.; lvi, ff.
2 *Histories*, III, xli; V, xix.
3 *Rhetoric*, I, iii.
4 Livy, *History*, V, xxxvi, 5.
5 *City of God*, IV, vi.
6 *History*, XXI, vi, 2.
7 *Pyrrhus*, XII, 389.
8 Book I, Chap. II; Book II, Chap. I.
9 Book II, Chap. I, 17.
10 *Germania*, XXXV.

11 *Histories*, IV, lxxiii.
12 Seneca, *Controversies*, VII, vi, 18.
13 *Politics*, I, iii.
14 *On Monarchy*, II.
15 *On the Acts of the Apostles*, Homily III, iv.
16 *On First Thessalonians*, Homily II, ii.
17 *Letter of Mithridates*, V.
18 *Against Faustus*, XXII, lxxiv.

CHAP. XXIII

1 *Nicomachean Ethics*, I, 1.
2 Ibid., III, i.
3 *On Duty*, I, ix, 30.
4 Terence, *The Brothers*, 174.
5 *Orations*, XIV.
6 *On Duty*, I, xi, 34.
7 *History*, VIII, xxiii.
8 Livy, *History*, XXXII, x, 5.
9 Plutarch, *Pompey*, XXXIII.
10 *History*, I, xxiii, 9.

CHAP. XXIV

1 *On Clemency*, I, xx.
2 *Numa*, XII, 68.
3 *Suppliants*, 481 ff.
4 *History*, XXX, xxx, 20.
5 *On Peace*, I, 63.
6 *Histories*, IV, lxvii.
7 *Otho*, XIII, 1072.
8 *Platonic*, II, 283.
9 *Epitome*, IV, xii.
10 *Annals*, III, xliv.
11 *Histories*, IV, xxxii.
12 Suetonius, *Augustus*, XXV.
13 Aulus Gellius, *Attic Nights*, XIII, iii. Valerius Maximus, *Memorable Deeds*, VII, ii, 2.
14 *Camillus*, X, 134.
15 *Dissertations*, XXX, i.

CHAP. XXV

1 *Illustrious Controversies*, I, xiii.
2 *On Anger*, I, v.
3 *Laws*, IX, xvii.
4 *Letter to Mithridates*, I.
5 *Peloponnesian War*, V, xviii.
6 *On Duty*, I, xiii.
7 Sylvester Mazzolini Prirerias, *Summary*, on the word 'bellum,' I, 10.

CHAP. XXVI

1 *Phoenician Maidens*, 1648, 1649.
2 *Against Verres*, II, I, xlii, 108.
3 *Annals*, VI, xiv.
4 *Against Faustus*, XXII, lxxv.
5 Adrian VI, *Twelve Questions*, II.
6 *Apology*, IV; *Against the Heathen*, I, vi.
7 Nazarius, *Panegyric of Constantine*, VII.

BOOK THREE

CHAP. I

1 Book II, Chap. I, 3.
2 Book II, Chap. II, 10.
3 Book II, Chap. I, 4.
4 Procopius, *Gothic War*, I, iii.
5 Plutarch, *Demetrius*, XXXIII, 904.
6 Ibid., *Apothegms*, 209.
7 *Histories*, IX, xii.
8 *Questions on the Heptateuch*, VI, *Joshua*, x.
9 *Digest*, IV, iii, 1, 2.
10 *On Duty*, III, xv, 61.
11 *Digest*, XLIV, vii, 38.
12 *On Interpretation*, IV.
13 *Luke* xxiv, 28.

14 *Iliad*, IX, 312.
15 *Nicomachean Ethics*, II, vii; IV, xiii.
16 *On the Nicomachean Ethics*, V, viii.
17 *Oratorical Institutes*, XII, i, 36.
18 Aulus Gellius, *Attic Nights*, XI, xi.
19 *Republic*, I, v, end.
20 *Enchiridium*, XXII.
21 *On Duty*, I, x, 31.
22 Lucretius, *On the Nature of Things*, I, 939.
23 *Letters*, III, xvi.
24 *On Plato's Republic*.
25 *Oratorical Institutes*, II, xvii, 36.
26 *Various History*, XII, lix.
27 *On the Education of Children*, ii.
28 Plutarch, *Alexander*, XXXI, 683.
29 *Various History*, XII, xxxiii.
30 Livy, *History*, XLII, xlvii, 4–8.
31 *Digest*, XLI, i, 51.

CHAP. II

1 *Digest*, III, iv, 7, 1.
2 *On Benefits*, VI, xx.
3 *Institutes*, I, ii, 2.
4 Livy, *History*, I, xxxii, 13.
5 Plutarch, *Agesilaus*, XII, 602.
6 Demosthenes, *Against Aristocrates*, XXIII, 82.
7 Livy, *History*, XXXIV, lxi, 13.
8 *Digest*, XII, vi, 60.
9 Book II, Chap. XXI, 11.

CHAP. III

1 *Digest*, L, xvi, 118.
2 Ibid., XLIX, xv, 24.
3 *Philippics*, IV, vi, 14.
4 *On Ends*, V, xxx, 92.
5 Cited in Augustine's *City of God*, II, xxi.

6 *City of God*, XIX, xxiv.
7 *Borysthenitica, Orations*, XXXVI; *On the Law, Orations*, LXXV, end.
8 *On Concord, To the Rhodians*, 385.
9 *Gallic War*, VI, xxiii.
10 A Roman triumph could legally be celebrated only over a defeated foreign king or nation, not over suppressed domestic disturbers, rebels, or marauders.
11 *City of God*, IV, iv.
12 Deuteronomy xx, 10.
13 *Cyropaedia*, II, iv, 32.
14 *History*, VIII, xxiii, 7.
15 *Annals*, I, xlviii.
16 Livy, *History*, I, xxxii, 10.
17 *Against the Heathen*, II, lxvii.
18 Varro, *On the Latin Language*, IV.

CHAP. IV

1 *Aeneid*, X, 14.
2 *On the Aeneid*, X, 14.
3 I Corinthians VI, 12.
4 *Institutes*, III, vi, 84.
5 *In Defense of Rabirius Posthumus*, V, 11.
6 Stobaeus, *Anthology*, XLVIII, 14.
7 *In Defense of Balbus*, III, 8.
8 *In Defense of Milo*, XVI, 43.
9 Caesar, *Civil War*, I, xxxv.
10 *In Defense of Marcellus*, IV, 12.
11 *Gallic War*, VII, xli.
12 *Letters*, XCV, 31.
13 *Letters*, I, 6.
14 Thucydides, *Peloponnesian War*, I, xxvi.
15 Fragment, 1076.
16 *History*, XXVIII, xvii, 12.
17 Deuteronomy II, 34.
18 *Peloponnesian War*, VII, xxix.

19 *Annals*, I, 51.
20 Vergil, *Aeneid*, II, 550 ff.
21 *Trojan Women*, 333.
22 *Epistles*, I, xvi, 69.
23 *Iliad*, XX, 463; XXI, 74.
24 *City of God*, I, i.
25 *Histories*, I, xxxvii.
26 *History*, XXIV, xxxvii, 9.
27 Plutarch, *On the Virtues of Women*, 244.
28 *Memorable Deeds*, VI, v, 1.
29 *Annals*, II, lxxxviii.
30 *Counsels*, II, 188.
31 *Policraticus*, VIII, 20.
32 *Epitome*, II, xx.
33 Strabo, *Geography*, X, i, 12.
34 Pausanias, *Description of Greece*, X, xxxvii; Frontinus, *Stratagems*, III, vii, 6.
35 Justin, *Histories*, II, xi, 15.
36 *Punic Wars*, xxxix.
37 Plautus, *Threepenny Day*, 1037.
38 Livy, *History*, XLII, xviii, 1.
39 Justin, *Histories*, XIV, i, 12.
40 *Annals*, XI, xix.
41 Augustine, *City of God*, I, vi.
42 Livy, *History*, XXVI, xlix, 14.
43 Deuteronomy xxi, 10–14.
44 *Expedition of Alexander*, IV, xix, 9. Roxana was the daughter of Oxyartes the Bactrian, whom Alexander conquered. Shortly after Alexander's death, Roxana gave birth to his son.

CHAP. V

1 *On Duty*, III, vi, 32.
2 *Histories*, V, xi.
3 *Digest*, XI, vii, 36.
4 Ibid., I, i, 1, 2.
5 *Annals*, III, lxxi.
6 The speech was made by Caesar. Sallust, *Catiline*, LI, 9.

⁷ *Histories*, V, iv.
⁸ Ibid., V, viii, ix.
⁹ *Jewish War*, VI, iv, 3, and v, 2.
¹⁰ *Digest*, XLVII, xii, 4.

CHAP. VI

¹ Hebrews VII, 1, 2.
² Deuteronomy xx, 14.
³ *On Benefits*, III, xxxiii.
⁴ *On Curses*, I.
⁵ *Cyropaedia*, VII, v, 73.
⁶ *Laws*, I, ii.
⁷ *Politics*, I, vi.
⁸ Livy, *History*, XXXIX, xxix, 2.
⁹ *Digest*, XLI, i, 5, 7.
¹⁰ *Institutes*, II, i, 17.
¹¹ *Politics*, I, viii.
¹² Postliminy, a word taken from Roman law, means the restoration to their former status of persons or things taken in war, when they come again into the possession of the nation to which they belonged.
¹³ *Digest*, XLIX, xv, 5, 1.
¹⁴ Ibid., XLIX, xv, 5, 1.
¹⁵ Ibid., XLI, i, 5, 7.
¹⁶ Livy, *History*, XXVI, xi, 6.
¹⁷ I Samuel xxx, 20.
¹⁸ *Mithridatic Wars*, XV, 106.
¹⁹ *Histories*, XL, ii, 4.
²⁰ *Digest*, XLI, ii, i, 20.
²¹ Book I, Chap. V, 3.
²² *History*, XXX, xi, 9–10.
²³ *Digest*, XLIX, xv, 20.
²⁴ Ibid., XLIX, xv, 12.
²⁵ *Iliad*, I, 125.
²⁶ *History of the Franks*, II, xxvii.
²⁷ *Roman Antiquities*, VII, lxiii.
²⁸ *History*, XXXVII, xxxii, 12.
²⁹ *Roman History*, II, xxxvii.
³⁰ *Letters*, II, xvii, 4.
³¹ *Histories*, X, xvi.

³² *Histories*, IX, lxxxi.
³³ *Selections on Embassies*, 18.
³⁴ Plutarch, *Marcus Cato the Elder*, X, 342.
³⁵ *Pharsalia*, X, 197 f.
³⁶ *Roman Antiquities*, VII, lxiv.
³⁷ *History*, V, xx, 6.
³⁸ *Cyropaedia*, VII, ii, 11.
³⁹ *History*, VI, iv, 11.
⁴⁰ *Memorable Deeds*, V, iii.
⁴¹ *Attic Nights*, XI, xviii.
⁴² *Histories*, X, xvi.
⁴³ *Attic Nights*, XVI, iv.
⁴⁴ *Annals*, XI, vii.
⁴⁵ Livy, *History*, II, xxxiii.
⁴⁶ Quintus Curtius, *Histories of Alexander the Great*, III, xi, 23.
⁴⁷ *Annals*, XIV, xxxvi.
⁴⁸ *Attic Nights*, XVI, iv.

CHAP. VII

¹ Book II, Chap. XXII, 11.
² Book II, Chap. V, 27.
³ *Digest*, XLIX, xv, 5, 1.
⁴ *Orations*, XV, 242.
⁵ *Digest*, I, v, 5, 1.
⁶ *Annals*, I, lix.
⁷ *Controversies*, X, v.
⁸ *Digest*, I, vi, 1, 1.
⁹ *Institutes*, II, ix, 3.
¹⁰ *Digest*, I, v, 24.
¹¹ For explanation of this, see below, Chap. IX, 5.
¹² *Digest*, XLIX, xv, 26.
¹³ Ibid., XLIX, xv, 19.
¹⁴ Nicephorus Gregoras, *Byzantine History*, IV, ix.

CHAP. VIII

¹ *Apology*, XXV.
² *Institutes of Oratory*, V, x, 113.

3 *Histories*, I, i, 7.
4 Book I, Chap. III, 11.
5 *Annals*, XII, xi.
6 *Agesilaus*, I, 22.
7 *History*, XXXIV, lvii, 7.
8 Ibid., XXI, xliii, 6.
9 *Institutes of Oratory*, V, x, 116.

CHAP. IX

1 *Digest*, XLIX, xv, 5, 1.
2 Ibid., XLIX, xv, 19, 3.
3 Ibid., XLIX, xv, 12.
4 Ibid., XLIX, xv, 28.
5 Ibid., XLIX, xv, 12.
6 *History*, XXII, lix, 1.
7 *Digest*, XLIX, xv, 12, 9, and 5, 3.
8 *Digest*, XLIX, xv, 12, 6.
9 Ibid., XLIX, xv, 17.
10 *Attic Nights*, VI, xviii.
11 *Digest*, XLIX, xv, 12, 9.
12 Ibid., XLIX, xv, 19, 5.
13 *Code*, VIII, 1, 12.
14 *Military Laws*, edition of 1607.
15 *Digest*, XLIX, xv, 20, 1.
16 Ibid., VIII, iv, 26.
17 Book II, Chap. X, 9.
18 Book II, Chap. XV, 5.
19 *Digest*, XLIX, xv, 5, 2.

CHAP. X

1 *Trojan Women*, 333 ff.
2 *Protagoras*, XII.
3 *To an Unlettered Prince*, IV.
4 *On Anger*, II, xxviii.
5 *On Clemency*, I, xviii.
6 *Politics*, I, vi.
7 *Divine Institutes*, VI, vi.
8 Isaiah LVIII, 5–7.
9 Jonah III, 8.
10 *History*, IX, i, 5.
11 *Memorable Deeds*, VI, v.

12 Livy, *History*, XLIII, iv, 13.
13 Book II, Chap. X, 9.

CHAP. XI

1 Lucan, *Pharsalia*, I, 349.
2 *On Duty*, I, xi, 33.
3 *On Leuctra*, I, 94.
4 *Plataic Oration*, VIII, 298.
5 Book II, Chap. XXI, 5.
6 *Roman Histories*, II, xxiii.
7 *On the Peloponnesian War*, I, lv.
8 *Expedition of Alexander*, I, xvii.
9 *On the Nicomachean Ethics*, VII, ii.
10 *Rhetoric*, I, xiii.
11 *On Duty*, I, viii, 27.
12 *Against Aristocrates*, xxiii, 148.
13 *Peloponnesian War*, IV, xcviii.
14 This should be Porphyry, *On Abstaining*, III, xviii.
15 *Orations*, VII, 93.
16 *History*, VIII, xx, 11.
17 *Peloponnesian War*, III, xxxvi.
18 *To Herennius*, II, xvii, 25; a treatise on rhetoric ascribed to Cicero.
19 *On Clemency*, II, vii.
20 *Peloponnesian War*, I, xxxii.
21 *On the State*, I, ii, 4.
22 Cicero, *Letters to Brutus*, I, ii.
23 *Speech of Philip*, VI.
24 *On Clemency*, I, v.
25 *To Herennius*, IV, xvi, 23.
26 Eumenius, *Panegyric*, VI, 10.
27 *Jewish War*, VII, v, 6.
28 *Against Verres*, II, V, xxvi, 66.
29 Quotation in *Selections on Embassies*, XXXI, 2.
30 *Histories*, V, xi.
31 *On Anger*, III, xxiv.
32 Ibid., II, x.
33 *History*, V, xxvii, 7.
34 *Camillus*, X.
35 *Histories*, IV, xi, 17.

[36] *Histories*, XXXIX, ii, 7.
[37] This should be Statius, *Thebaid*, V, 258–259.
[38] *History*, XXVIII, xxiii, 1.
[39] *Antiquities of the Jews*, XII, iii, 1.
[40] *Geography*, VIII, iii, 33.
[41] *Historical Library*, II, xxxvi.
[42] *Lexicon*, on the word 'Belisarius.'
[43] *Letters*, CLXXXIX, To Boniface, 6.
[44] XCI, 6–7.
[45] *Expedition of Alexander*, I, ix, 10.
[46] *Gallic War*, II, xxxii.
[47] *Annals*, XII, xvii.
[48] Plutarch, *Brutus*, XXVI, 996.
[49] Book II, Chap. XXI, 18.
[50] *On Peace*, II, 75.
[51] *Expedition of Alexander*, I, xix, 8.
[52] *Iliad*, XXIII, 176.
[53] *On Anger*, II, x.
[54] *In Defense of Cluentius*, XLVI, 128.
[55] *Histories*, I, xii.
[56] *Jugurtha*, XCII, 4.

CHAP. XII

[1] Book II, Chap. II, 9.
[2] *Strategicus*, VI.
[3] *On Plato's Republic*, III, iii.
[4] Deuteronomy xx, 19–20.
[5] *On the Constitution*, XIII.
[6] *Life of Pythagoras*, XXI, 99.
[7] *On Stratagems*, III, x, 5.
[8] *Republic*, V, xvii.
[9] *On Duty*, I, xi, 35. *On his House*, xxiii, 60.
[10] *Histories*, XI, vi, 1.
[11] *History*, XXXII, xxxiii, 11–13.
[12] *Peloponnesian War*, I, lxxx; lxxxi.
[13] *Historical Library*, II, xxxvi.
[14] *Attic Nights*, XV, xxxi.
[15] *Histories*, V, xi.
[16] *History*, XLII, iii, 9.
[17] *Histories*, II, i.

[18] *City of God*, I, i.
[19] *The Woods*, IV, vi, 82.
[20] *Roman History*, XLII, xlviii.
[21] *Epitome of Roman History*, II, vii.
[22] *Peloponnesian War*, I, lxxxii.
[23] *Roman History*, XLIX, xxxvii.
[24] *Flaminius*, V, 371.
[25] *History*, XXVI, xxxviii, 3–4.

CHAP. XIII

[1] Book II, Chap. II, 6–10.
[2] *History*, XXXVII, xxxv, 7.
[3] *Peloponnesian War*, I, cxvii.

CHAP. XIV

[1] *Letters*, III, 12.
[2] Seneca, *On Benefits*, III, xxii.
[3] *On Clemency*, I, xviii.
[4] *Letters*, xlvii, 1.
[5] *The Teacher*, III, xii, 92.
[6] *Letters*, XLVII, 14.
[7] *Letters*, VIII, xvi.
[8] *Cato the Elder*, XXI, 349.
[9] *On Special Laws*, III, xxxv.
[10] *On Clemency*, I, xvi, 4.
[11] *Letters*, XLVII, 14.
[12] *Germania*, XXV.
[13] *Letters*, III.
[14] *On Duty*, I, xiii, 41.
[15] *On Benefits*, III, xxi, 2.
[16] *On the Phormio of Terence*, I, i, 43.
[17] *On Benefits*, III, xix.
[18] *Phormio*, I, i, 44.
[19] *Digest*, XV, i, 5, 7.
[20] *Letters*, VIII, xvi.
[21] *Against Avarice*, III, vii.
[22] Deuteronomy xv, 12, 13.
[23] *Cato the Elder*, V, 338.
[24] *Greek Questions*, XVII, 295.

CHAP. XV

1 *Letters*, II, iv, 409.
2 *Catiline*, XII, 4.
3 *Politics*, VII, xiv, and xv; *Nicoma-chean Ethics*, X, vii.
4 *On Duty*, I, xxiii, 80.
5 *City of God*, IV, xv.
6 *On Anger*, II, xxxiv, 4.
7 Tacitus, *Annals*, XI, xxiv.
8 *History*, VIII, xiii, 16.
9 *Histories*, IV, lxxiv.
10 *Digest*, I, v, 17.
11 Ibid., L, i, 33.
12 *On the Consulship of Stilicho*, III, 154, 159.
13 *Histories*, V, ix.
14 *Letters to Quintus*, I, i, 11, 34.
15 *Histories*, IV, lxxiv.
16 Book II, Chap. XV, 7.
17 *Epitome*, IV, xii.
18 *Apothegms*, 207.
19 Plutarch, *Alexander*, LXV, 701.
20 Aristides, *In Praise of Rome*, 353.
21 Valerius Maximus, *Memorable Deeds*, IV, i, 10.
22 *Annals*, VI, xlii.
23 *Agricola*, XIV.
24 Book I, Chap. III, 17; Book III, Chap. VIII, 3.
25 *Letters*, X, xlvii, lxxix, cxii, cxiv.
26 Philo, *Embassy to Gaius*, XXXVI.
27 *Jewish War*, V, ix, 4; VI, ii, 1.
28 Xenophon, *Cyropaedia*, IV, iv, 10.
29 *Jugurtha*, CII, 6.
30 Livy, *History*, VIII, xxi, 4.
31 Ibid., VIII, xiii, 16.
32 Cicero, *Letters to Atticus*, IX, vii.

CHAP. XVI

1 On Postliminy, see above, Book III, Chap. IX.

2 *On Benefits*, V, xii.
3 *Canonical Letter*, X.
4 *History*, III, x, 1.
5 Ibid., XXXV, i, 12.
6 *Histories*, II, xxxi.
7 *Apothegms*, 200; *Punic Wars*, XX, 133.
8 Genesis xiv, 16.
9 Livy, *History*, XXXIV, lviii, 13.
10 Book II, Chap. IV.

CHAP. XVII

1 Numbers xx, 17–19.
2 *Anabasis*, II, iii, 23 ff.
3 *Agis*, XIV, 801.
4 *Stratagems*, II, xi, 7.
5 Latinus Pacatus, *Panegyric*, XXXII.
6 Ammianus Marcellinus, *History*, XVIII, ii, 7.
7 *Aurelian*, VII.
8 *Various Letters*, VII, iv.
9 Luke III, 14.
10 *Stratagems*, IV, iii, 13.
11 *History*, XL, xxii, 10–11.
12 *Histories*, III, ii.
13 Book III, Chap. I.
14 *Peloponnesian War*, I, xxxv.
15 Livy, *History*, XXXVII, xxviii, 2.
16 Plutarch, *Brutus*, V, 1011.
17 *History*, XXXV, xlviii, 9.

CHAP. XVIII

1 *On Duty*, I, xi, 36.
2 *Digest*, XLIX, xvi, 3, 15.
3 Livy, *History*, VIII, vii, 22.
4 *Catiline*, IX, 4.
5 *Roman Questions*, XXXIX, 273.
6 Servius, *On the Aeneid*, VIII, line 1.
7 Book III, Chap. VI, 24.

8 Book II, Chap. I, 3.
9 Book III, Chap. II, 2.

CHAP. XIX

1 Agesilaus, III, 5.
2 Declamations, CCLXVII;
   CCCXLIII.
3 On Duty, I, xxix, 140.
4 Letters, CLXXXIX, To Boniface,
   6.
5 Description of Greece, VIII, vii, 5.
6 Iliad, VII, 351–352.
7 Book II, Chap. XIII, 15.
8 On Duty, III, vi, 32; xxix, 107.
9 On the Nicomachean Ethics, V,
   x.
10 Civil War, III, xix, 2.
11 Diodorus Siculus, Historical Li-
    brary, XXXVI, i.
12 Book II, Chap. XX, 8.
13 On Duty, III, vi, 32.
14 History, XXXIV, xxxi, 12.
15 Book II, Chap. XI, 7.
16 Book I, Chap. IV.
17 Historical Library, XI, lxxxix.
18 Memorable Deeds, V, iii.
19 Livy, History, XXXIX, xxiii, 6.
20 Book I, Chap. III, 17 ff.
21 On Duty, III, xxix, 107.
22 Against Verres, II, IV, lv, 122.
23 Book II, Chap. XIII, 16.
24 On Duty, I, xxix.
25 Spanish Wars, X, 60.
26 Digest, XVII, ii, 14.
27 Book II, Chap. VII, 2.
28 On Benefits, VI, v, 6.
29 Ibid., VI, iv.
30 Ibid., VI, vi.
31 Ibid., VI, v.
32 Ibid., VII, xvi, 2.
33 Philostratus, Life of Apollonius of
    Tyana, III, xx.
34 Book II, Chap. XI.

CHAP. XX

1 Cicero, On Duty, III, xxvii, 100.
2 Book II, Chap. V, 17.
3 History, XXXII, xx, 6.
4 Book II, Chap. XIV, 10 ff.
5 Famous Controversies, I, iv, end.
6 Book III, Chap. VI, 2; Chap. X,
   5.
7 Book II, Chap. XVI, 12.
8 Digest, XLIX, xv, 12.
9 On the Crown, XVIII, 26.
10 Thucydides, Peloponnesian War,
    V, xvii.
11 Punic Wars, I, v.
12 Roman Antiquities, III, viii, 4.
13 Plataic Oration, XIV, 299.
14 Roman Antiquities, III, ix, 3.
15 Peloponnesian War, I, cxxiii.
16 Book II, Chap. XXI, 2 ff.
17 Plautus, Truculentus, 567.
18 Histories, XVII, iv, 5.
19 Digest, XLIII, xvi, 1, 17.
20 Book II, Chap. V, 24.
21 History, XLII, xli, 7.
22 Book II, Chap. V, 24.
23 Book II, Chap. XXI, 3 ff.
24 Book II, Chap. XIX, 5; XXI, 11.
25 Book II, Chap. XXIII, 10.
26 History, III, ii, 3.
27 Ibid., XXIX; XL.
28 Digest, XVII, ii, 76.
29 Book II, Chap. XXIII, 8.
30 Rhetoric, I, xiii, 19.
31 Punic Wars, XIV, ix, 64.
32 Book III, Chap. VIII, 4.
33 Historical Library, XIII, xxi, 6.
34 Civil Wars, V, v, 45.
35 Selections on Embassies, XX, ix.
36 History, XXXVI, xxviii, 1.
37 Book I, Chap. III, 17.
38 Digest, XLIX, xiv, 31.
39 See Book III, Chap. II, 3.
40 Syrian Wars, VIII, 47.
41 Book II, Chap. XVI, 16.

CHAP. XXI

1 *Attic Nights*, I, xxv, 4.
2 *Panegyric*, IX.
3 I, xl.
4 *Attic Nights*, I, xxv, 1.
5 Ibid., I, xxv.
6 Book II, Chap. XVI, 20.
7 *Metaphysics*, IV, xvii.
8 *Digest*, L, xvi, 133.
9 *History*, XL, xxvii, 9.
10 *Digest*, XLIX, xv, 19, 1.
11 *On the Aeneid*, XI, 134.
12 *History*, XXXI, xxxviii, 10.
13 *Peloponnesian War*, IV, cxxiii.
14 Book III, Chap. IX, 4.
15 Book II, Chap. XVI, 12.
16 Plutarch, *Alexander*, LIX, 698.
17 Book II, Chap. XIV, 11, 12.
18 *On Duty*, II, xv, 71; II, xxviii.
19 *History*, XXII, lxi, 1.
20 *Politics*, II, ix; VII, xiv.
21 Book II, Chap. XXV, 3.
22 Book II, Chap. XII, 26.
23 Book III, Chap. VII, 4.
24 Book II, Chap. XI, 22.

CHAP. XXII

1 *History*, IV, xx, 6.
2 *Civil War*, III, li, 4.
3 Book II, Chap. XI, 12.
4 Book II, Chap. IV, 5; Chap. XV, 17.
5 Book II, Chap. X, 2.
6 Valerius Maximus, *Memorable Deeds*, IX, vi, 3.
7 Book II, Chap. XI, 12, 13.
8 Plutarch, *Agesilaus*, X, 601.
9 *Jugurtha*, XXXIX, 3.
10 *History*, XXXVII, xix, 2.
11 Ibid., XXIV, xix.
12 Justin, *Histories*, XL, ii, 3.
13 Book III, Chap. VI, 15.
14 *History*, XXII, vi, 12.
15 Livy, *History*, XXIV, iv, 1.

CHAP. XXIII

1 *On Duty*, I, xiii, 39.
2 Book II, Chap. XI, 7; Book III, Chap. XIX, 5.
3 Book II, Chap. XI, 6.
4 Book I, Chap. IV, 7; Book II, Chap. XIV, 12.
5 *On Duty*, III, xxix, 108.
6 Horace, *Odes*, III, v, 49–50.
7 *Peloponnesian War*, I, ciii.
8 Book III, Chap. VI, 23 ff.

CHAP. XXIV

1 *Digest*, XIX, ii, 51.
2 *History*, XXXVIII, xxv, 8.
3 Ibid., XXVI, xvii; XXX, iv.
4 Book III, Chap. IV, 12; Chap. XI, 15.
5 Book II, Chap. XV, 17; Book III, Chap. XXII, 3.

CHAP. XXV

1 *On Duty*, II, xxiv, 84.
2 *Rhetoric*, I, xv, 22.
3 *On Public Administration*, I, vi, 2.
4 *Politics*, VII, ii, 9; xiv, 11.
5 *Romans* XII, 18.
6 Cicero, *Letters to his Friends*, IV, vii, 2.
7 *History*, VII, xl, 19.
8 Ibid., XXX, xxx, 18.
9 *Rhetoric to Alexander*, ii.
10 *Civil War*, III, x.
11 Quoted by Jerome, *Defense against Rufinus*, I, i.

List of Writers Cited by Grotius
In This Abridged Text

(*Not Including Biblical Writers*)

ADRIAN, VI, POPE (1459-1523), Dutch scholar and theologian.

AELIAN, CLAUDIUS (2nd century), author of a collection of historical anecdotes, known as *Various History*.

AESCHYLUS (525-456 B.C.), first great Greek tragic dramatist.

ALFENUS VARUS (1st century), Roman jurist, mentioned by Horace.

AMBROSE, ST. (c. 340-397), bishop of Milan, writer on religious and ecclesiastical subjects; one of the fathers of the Western church.

AMMIANUS MARCELLINUS (c. 330-c. 395), Greek historian of the later Roman empire.

ANDRONICUS OF RHODES (1st century B.C.), Peripatetic philosopher, head of the Aristotelian school at Rome.

ANTIPHON (480-411 B.C.), famous Athenian orator, leader of the aristocratic party, executed after the failure of the revolution of the Four Hundred.

APOLLONIUS OF TYANA (1st century), neo-Pythagorean philosopher, head of a school at Ephesus.

APPIAN, LUCIUS, of Alexandria (2nd century), author of a Greek history of Rome, compiled from earlier writers.

ARISTIDES, AELIUS (117-c. 180), Greek rhetorician and priest of Aesculapius, friend and adviser of Marcus Aurelius.

ARISTOTLE (384-322 B.C.), celebrated Greek philosopher and scientist, founder of the Peripatetic school at Athens.

ARNOBIUS (3rd century), rhetorician of Numidia, apologist for Christianity, author of *Against the Heathen*.

ARRIAN, FLAVIUS (2nd century), Greek historian, geographer, and Stoic philosopher, author of works on India and on Alexander's Asiatic expedition.

ATHANASIUS, ST., of Alexandria (c. 296-373), Greek father of the church, defender of orthodoxy, influential in framing the Nicene Creed.

ATHENAGORAS (2nd century), Greek Christian Platonic philosopher, author of a defense of Christianity.

AUGUSTINE, AURELIUS, ST. (354-430), most famous father of the Western church, bishop of Hippo in Numidia, author of *Confessions, City of God*, and many other works on religious subjects.

AURELIUS ANTONINUS, MARCUS (121-180), Roman emperor and Stoic philosopher, author of the famous *Meditations*.

AYALA, BALTHAZAR DE (c. 1545-1584), Spanish jurist, writer on military law.

AZOR, JUAN (1533-1603), Spanish Jesuit theologian, author of *Moral Institutions*.

BALSAMON, THEODORE (late 12th century), Byzantine writer on Greek canon law.

BARCLAY, WILLIAM (c. 1546-1608), Scottish jurist and writer on political and ecclesiastical institutions.

BARTOLUS OF SASSOFERRATO (1313-1357), Italian jurist, founder of a new school of commentators on Roman law, defender of imperial power.

BODIN, JEAN (1530-1596), distinguished French writer on politics, economics, and historical method.

CARNEADES (c. 213-129 B.C.), Greek Skeptic philosopher, one of the founders of the New Academy.

CATO, MARCUS (234-149 B.C.), called the Elder or the Censor, Roman statesman, general, and writer, defender of old Roman customs and morals.

CELSUS, PUBLIUS JUVENTIUS (2nd century), Roman jurist, cited in Justinian's *Digest*.

CHRYSIPPUS (280-207 B.C.), one of the founders of the Stoic school of philosophy at Athens.

CHRYSOSTOM, ST. JOHN (344-407), patriarch of Constantinople, father of the Greek church, celebrated for his preaching and religious writings.

CICERO, MARCUS TULLIUS (106-43 B.C.), famous Roman orator, statesman, and philosopher, defender of republican institutions.

CLAUDIAN, CLAUDIUS (c. 370-c. 404), Latin author of political panegyrics in verse.

CLEMENT, TITUS FLAVIUS (c. 150-c. 220), head of the religious school at Alexandria, a father of the Greek church.

CONNAN, FRANÇOIS DE (1508-1551), French writer on Roman civil law.

CONON (3rd century B.C.), Greek astronomer and mathematician.

CURTIUS RUFUS, QUINTUS (1st century), author of a history of Alexander the Great.

CYPRIAN, THASCIUS CAECILIUS, ST. (c. 200-258), bishop of Carthage, martyred under Valerian, author of influential works on church unity and discipline.

DEMOCRITUS (c. 460-c. 360 B.C.), Greek philosopher, one of the founders of the atomistic school.

DEMOSTHENES (c. 383-322 B.C.), renowned Attic orator, leader of the Athenians against the rising power of Macedonia.

DIO CASSIUS (c. 155-c. 230), Greek author of a massive history of Rome.

DIO CHRYSOSTOM OF PRUSA (c. 50-117), popular Greek rhetorician and philosopher, eighty of whose orations are still extant.

DIODORUS SICULUS (1st century B.C.), Greek author of a *Historical Library*, a general history from mythical times down to the invasion of Britain by Julius Caesar.

DIONYSIUS OF HALICARNASSUS (1st century B.C.), Greek essayist and historian of Roman institutions.

ERASMUS, DESIDERIUS (1465-1536), famous Dutch humanist, social and religious reformer, author of the *Praise of Folly*, and many other works.

EURIPIDES (480-406 B.C.), celebrated Athenian tragic dramatist.

FLORENTINUS (3rd century), Roman jurist, frequently cited in Justinian's *Digest*.

FLORUS, LUCIUS ANNAEUS (2nd century), Roman author of an abridgment of the history of Rome to the time of Augustus.

FRONTINUS, SEXTUS JULIUS (1st century), Roman governor of Britain and engineer; author of treatises on the art of war and the building of aqueducts.

GAIUS (2nd century), influential teacher and writer on Roman law, quoted in Justinian's *Digest*.

GALEN, CLAUDIUS (2nd century), Greek physician to Marcus Aurelius, philosopher and author of works on medicine long considered authoritative.

GELLIUS, AULUS (2nd century), Latin grammarian, author of *Attic Nights*, an anthology of extracts from Greek and Roman writers on literature, law, philosophy, and science.

GENTILI, ALBERICO (1552-1608), north Italian Protestant jurist who taught at Oxford, author of important works on the law of war and of embassies; Grotius' immediate predecessor in the field of international law.

GREGORAS, NICEPHORUS (c. 1295-c. 1359), Byzantine scholar, author of a Byzantine history from the beginning of the 13th century, and of works on philosophy and theology.

GREGORY OF TOURS (544-594), Frankish bishop, author of a history of Merovingian Gaul.

HERMOGENIANUS (4th century), Roman jurist, cited in Justinian's *Digest*.

HERODOTUS (c. 484-c. 424 B.C.), called the Father of History, author of the earliest extant history of Greece down through the age of the Persian wars.

HESIOD (c. 8th century B.C.), Greek author of two famous poems on the origins of the gods, and on rustic life.

HOMER (c. 9th century B.C.), traditional Greek author of the two great epic poems, the *Iliad* and the *Odyssey*.

IAMBLICHUS (d. c. 330), Syrian neo-Platonic philosopher, mathematician and prolific writer on such subjects as the *Egyptian Mysteries*, an *Exhortation to Philosophy*, etc.

INNOCENT IV, POPE (d. 1254), Italian author of a much-quoted commentary on canon law.

ISAEUS (4th century B.C.), jurist and head of the Attic school of oratory; many of his orations and works on the law of inheritance have survived.

ISIDORE OF PELUSIUM, ST. (c. 370-c. 440), Alexandrian theologian and moralist.

ISIDORE OF SEVILLE, ST. (c. 560-636), Spanish encyclopedist, theologian, and historian of the Gothic kings.

ISOCRATES (436-338 B.C.), an admired Attic orator and teacher of eloquence.

JARCHI, SOLOMON BEN ISAAC, RABBI (c. 1040-1105), eminent French Jewish scholar and commentator on the Talmud and Old Testament.

JAVOLENUS, PRISCUS (early 2nd century), Roman jurist, cited in Justinian's *Digest*.

JEROME, EUSEBIUS, ST. (c. 340-420), scholar and father of the Western church, author of Biblical commentaries and preparer of the Latin version of the Bible, known as the Vulgate, which became the authoritative text of the Roman church.

JOHN OF SALISBURY (c. 1115-1180), bishop of Chartres, English man of letters and ecclesiastical statesman, writer on government and education.

JOSEPHUS, FLAVIUS (37-c. 100), Jewish historian, author of the famous history of the Jews from earliest times, and of an account of their conquest by Rome.

JUSTIN, MARCUS (2nd century), Roman historian and compiler of an historical *Epitome*. See under Trogus.

JUSTIN MARTYR (c. 103-c. 165), Greek convert from pagan philosophy and defender of Christianity, martyred under Marcus Aurelius.

JUSTINIAN, FLAVIUS ANICIUS (483-565), Byzantine emperor at whose command was prepared the monumental compilation of Roman law known as the *Corpus Juris Civilis*, which included the *Code*, the *Digest*, the *Institutes*, and the *Novels*.

LACTANTIUS, LUCIUS CAECILIUS (early 4th century), Latin writer in defense of Christian doctrine against paganism.

LIVY, TITUS (59 B.C.-17 A.D.), author of the most famous history of Rome, from the founding of the city to the age of Augustus.

LUCRETIUS CARUS, TITUS (c. 96-55 B.C.), Roman philosophical poet, who in his great work, *On the Nature of Things*, described the universe from the Epicurean viewpoint.

LYCURGUS (c. 396-323 B.C.), Athenian aristocrat and orator, manager of the public revenues.

MAIMONIDES, MOSES (1135-1204), celebrated Spanish Jewish philosopher, theologian, and physician.

MAXIMUS OF TYRE (2nd century), Greek Platonic philosopher and essayist.

MENIPPUS (3rd century B.C.), Greek Cynic and satirical wit whose works are now lost.

MICHAEL OF EPHESUS (11th century), Byzantine monk and commentator on Aristotle.

MOLINA, LUIS DE (1535-1600), Spanish Jesuit theologian and jurist, noted for his writings on freedom of the will, and on law and justice.

MOSCHION (date uncertain), Greek tragic poet, known through fragments preserved in Stobaeus' *Anthology*.

MUSONIUS, RUFUS GAIUS (1st century), Roman Stoic philosopher, some of whose sayings are preserved in Stobaeus' *Anthology*.

ONESANDER (1st century), Greek writer on philosophy and military subjects.

OPTATUS OF MILEVIS, ST. (c. 315-c. 386), Christian bishop, defender of orthodoxy against Donatist heresy.

PACATUS, LATINUS, the Panegyrist (late 4th century), Latin rhetorician and author of a political panegyric on the emperor Theodosius I.

PATERCULUS, GAIUS VELLEIUS (c. 19 B.C.-c. 35 A.D.), Roman soldier and author of a concise history of Rome to the reign of Tiberius.

PAULUS, JULIUS (early 3rd century), Roman jurist, often cited in Justinian's *Code*.

PAUSANIAS (2nd century), Greek geographer and student of antiquities and art, author of a detailed *Description of Greece*, a guide for sightseers.

PHILO JUDAEUS (C. 20 B.C.-c. 45 A.D.), learned Hellenistic Jew of Alexandria, author of influential works which aimed at reconciling Judaism and Greek philosophy.

PLATO (c. 428-347 B.C.), illustrious Athenian philosopher, pupil of Socrates, founder of the Academy at Athens.

PLINY SECUNDUS, GAIUS, THE ELDER (23-79), Roman official and naturalist, author of an encyclopedic *Natural History*.

PLINY SECUNDUS, GAIUS, THE YOUNGER (62-c. 114), nephew of the above, Roman provincial governor and letter writer.

PLUTARCH (c. 50-c. 120), Greek platonic philosopher, essayist and historian, author of many works, the most famous being the *Parallel Lives* of noble Greeks and Romans.

POLYBIUS (c. 205-c. 125 B.C.), Greek historian and commentator on Rome and Roman institutions.

POMPONIUS, SEXTUS (2nd century), Roman jurist, cited in the *Digest*.

PROCLUS (412-485), neo-Platonic philosopher of Byzantium, commentator on Hesiod and Plato.

PROCOPIUS (c. 495-c. 565), Byzantine historian of the age of Justinian, and of his wars with the Goths and Vandals.

PROCULUS, SEMPRONIUS (1st century), Roman jurist, cited in Justinian's *Institutes*.

QUINTILIAN, MARCUS FABIUS (c. 35-c. 100), Roman rhetorician, author of a much-used manual of rules of oratory.

RUFUS (date and country unknown), author of a Latin treatise on military law, published at Antwerp in 1607.

SABINUS, MASURIUS (1st century), Roman jurist, cited in the *Digest*.

SALLUST CRISPUS, GAIUS (c. 86-c. 34 B.C.), Roman historian of events of his own and immediately preceding times, such as the war with Jugurtha, the conspiracy of Catiline, etc.

SALVIAN (5th century), Christian priest at Marseilles, author of a popular treatise on *God's Government*.

SENECA, MARCUS ANNAEUS, THE ELDER (c. 60 B.C.-c. 35 A.D.), Roman rhetorician and special pleader in the courts.

SENECA, LUCIUS ANNAEUS, THE YOUNGER (c. 19 B.C.-c. 65 A.D.), son of the preceding, Roman Stoic philosopher, councilor to Nero, author of many plays and essays on morals.

SERVIUS, MARCUS HONORATUS (4th century), Roman grammarian and commentator on Vergil.

SOLON (c. 639-c. 559 B.C.), Athenian sage, lawgiver, and poet; as archon, he laid the foundation of the later constitution of Athens.

STATIUS, PUBLIUS PAPINIUS (c. 55-c. 96), Roman composer of epics on traditional Greek themes.

STOBAEUS, JOANNES (c. 5th century), Macedonian Greek author of a valuable anthology of extracts from earlier writers.

STRABO (c. 60 B.C.-c. 24 A.D.), Greek traveler and geographer, author of a description of the world from Britain to Ceylon.

SUIDAS (10th century), Greek lexicographer, author of a vast lexicon of Greek literature, Christian and pagan.

TACITUS, PUBLIUS CORNELIUS (c. 55-c. 118), eminent Roman historian of events under the emperors who followed Augustus, and author of a famous treatise on the Germans of his day.

TERTULLIAN, QUINTUS SEPTIMIUS (c. 160-c. 230), Carthaginian jurist and champion of the Christian faith against pagans and heretics, a father of the Latin church.

THEMISTIUS (4th century), Aristotelian philosopher and rhetorician of Byzantium and Rome.

THEODOSIUS II (401-450), emperor of the East, famous for the so-called *Theodosian Code*, a collection of Roman laws from Constantine to 439, which later formed part of Justinian's *Code*.

THEOPHILUS (6th century), Roman jurist, one of the compilers of Justinian's *Institutes* and *Digest*.

THEOPOMPUS OF CHIOS (4th century B.C.), Greek historian and rhetorician, leader of the pro-Macedonian party in Chios.

THUCYDIDES (c. 471-c. 401 B.C.), Athenian statesman, naval commander, and author of the celebrated history of the Peloponnesian War.

TROGUS, POMPEIUS (1st century B.C.), Roman author of a general history, abridged by Justin for his *Epitome*.

TRYPHONIUS, CLAUDIUS (3rd century), Roman jurist, cited in the *Digest*.

ULPIAN, DOMITIUS (c. 170-228), Roman prefect and jurist whose quoted opinions make up about one third of the *Digest*.

VALENS (c. 328-378), Roman emperor of the East, mistakenly named by Grotius (Bk. II, Ch. V, 21) as co-author with Theodosius II of an edict contained in Justinian's *Code*. For actual co-author, see Valentinian III.

VALENTINIAN III (419-455), Western colleague of the emperor of the East, Theodosius II, and with him author of a collection of imperial laws, later inserted in Justinian's *Code*.

VALERIUS MAXIMUS (1st century), Roman rhetorician, author of a popular collection of historical anecdotes.

VARRO, MARCUS TERENTIUS (116-c. 28 B.C.), Roman encyclopedic writer, much quoted by later authors; naval commander under Pompey.

VASQUEZ, FERNANDO (early 16th century), Spanish jurist and author of a book on *Famous Disputes*.

VERGIL, PUBLIUS MARO (70-19 B.C.), renowned Roman poet of the greatness of Rome; author of the *Aeneid*.

VICTORIA, FRANCISCUS DE (c. 1480-1546), Spanish Dominican theologian and jurist, author of treatises on the law of war, and on the authority of state and church.